How to
Master Skills for the

Second Edition

TOEFL® iBT

LISTENING · Intermediate

 DARAKWON

How to
Master Skills for the
Second Edition
TOEFL® iBT
LISTENING Intermediate

Publisher Kyudo Chung
Editor Sangik Cho
Authors Will Link, Monika N. Kushwaha, Michael Kato, E2K
Proofreaders Michael A. Putlack, Brian Stuart
Designers Minji Kim, Kyuok Jeong

First Published in February 2007 By Darakwon, Inc.
Second edition first published in November 2024 by Darakwon, Inc.
Darakwon Bldg., 211, Munbal-ro, Paju-si, Gyeonggi-do 10881
Republic of Korea
Tel: 02-736-2031 (Ext. 250)
Fax: 02-732-2037

ISBN 978-89-277-8090-8 14740
        978-89-277-8084-7 14740 (set)

www.darakwon.co.kr

Photo Credits
Shutterstock.com

Components Main Book / Answer Key / Free MP3 Downloads
7 6 5 4 3 2 1   24 25 26 27 28

Table of
Contents

INTRODUCTION

1 Information on the TOEFL® iBT

A The Format of the TOEFL® iBT

Section	Number of Questions or Tasks	Timing	Score
Reading	**20 Questions** • **2 reading passages** – with 10 questions per passage – approximately 700 words long each	35 Minutes	30 Points
Listening	**28 Questions** • **2 conversations** – 5 questions per conversation – 3 minutes each • **3 lectures** – 6 questions per lecture – 3-5 minutes each	36 Minutes	30 Points

Speaking	**4 Tasks**
	
	• **1 independent speaking task**
	– 1 personal choice/opinion/experience
	– preparation: 15 sec. / response: 45 sec.
	
	• **2 integrated speaking tasks: Read-Listen-Speak**
	– 1 campus situation topic
	  reading: 75-100 words (45 sec.)
	  conversation: 150-180 words (60-80 sec.)
	– 1 academic course topic
	  reading: 75-100 words (50 sec.)
	  lecture: 150-220 words (60-120 sec.)
	– preparation: 30 sec. / response: 60 sec.
	
	• **1 integrated speaking task: Listen-Speak**
	– 1 academic course topic
	  lecture: 230-280 words (90-120 sec.)
	– preparation: 20 sec. / response: 60 sec.
		17 Minutes	30 Points

Writing	**2 Tasks** • **1 integrated writing task: Read-Listen-Write** – reading: 230-300 words (3 min.) – lecture: 230-300 words (2 min.) – a summary of 150-225 words (20 min.) • **1 academic discussion task** – a minimum 100-word essay (10 min.)	30 Minutes	30 Points

B What Is New about the TOEFL® iBT?

- The TOEFL® iBT is delivered through the Internet in secure test centers around the world at the same time.

- It tests all four language skills and is taken in the order of Reading, Listening, Speaking, and Writing.

- The test is about 2 hours long, and all of the four test sections will be completed in one day.

- Note taking is allowed throughout the entire test, including the Reading section. At the end of the test, all notes are collected and destroyed at the test center.

- In the Listening section, one lecture may be spoken with a British or Australian accent.

- There are integrated tasks requiring test takers to combine more than one language skill in the Speaking and Writing sections.

- In the Speaking section, test takers wear headphones and speak into a microphone when they respond. The responses are recorded and transmitted to ETS's Online Scoring Network.

- In the Writing section, test takers must type their responses. Handwriting is not possible.

- Test scores will be reported online. Test takers can see their scores online 4-8 business days after the test and can also receive a copy of their score report by mail.

2 Information on the Listening Section

The Listening section of the TOEFL® iBT measures test takers' ability to understand spoken English in English-speaking colleges and universities. This section has 2 conversations that are 12-25 exchanges (about 3 minutes) long and 3 lectures that are 500-800 words (3-5 minutes) long. Each conversation is followed by 5 questions and each lecture by 6 questions. Therefore, test takers have to answer 28 questions in total. The time allotted to the Listening section is 36 minutes, including the time spent listening to the conversations and lectures and answering the questions.

A Types of Listening Conversations and Lectures

- Conversations
  - Between a student and a professor or a teaching assistant during office hours
  - Between a student with a person related to school services such as a librarian, a housing director, or a bookstore employee

- Lectures
  - Monologue lectures delivered by a professor unilaterally
  - Interactive lectures with one or two students asking questions or making comments
    cf. One lecture may be spoken with a British or Australian accent.

B Types of Listening Questions

- Basic Comprehension Questions
  - Listening for Main Ideas Question: This type of question asks you to identify the overall topic or main

idea of a lecture or conversation.

   – Listening for Main Purpose Question: This type of question asks you why the speakers are having a conversation or why a lecture is given.

   – Listening for Major Details Question: This type of question asks you to understand specific details or facts from a conversation or lecture.

- Pragmatic Understanding Questions

   – Understanding the Function of What Is Said Question: This type of question asks you why a speaker mentions some point in the conversation or lecture. It may involve replaying part of the listening passage.

   – Understanding the Speaker's Attitude Question: This type of question asks you what a speaker's feelings, opinions, or degree of certainty is about some issue, idea, or person. It may involve replaying part of the listening passage.

- Connecting Information Questions

   – Understanding Organization Question: This type of question asks you how the listening passage is organized or how two portions of the listening passage are related to each other.

   – Connecting Content Question: This type of question asks you to classify or sequence information in a different way from the way it was presented in the listening passage.

   – Making Inferences Question: This type of question asks you to draw a conclusion based on information given in the listening passage.

C Question Formats

- There are four question formats in the Listening section: traditional multiple-choice questions with four answer choices and one correct answer, multiple-choice questions with more than one answer, questions that ask test takers to make the order of events or steps in a process, and questions that ask test takers to match objects or text to categories in a chart.

HOW TO USE THIS BOOK

How to Master Skills for the TOEFL® iBT Listening Intermediate is designed to be used either as a textbook for a TOEFL® iBT listening preparation course or as a tool for individual learners who are preparing for the TOEFL® test on their own. With a total of eight units, this book is organized to prepare you for the test with a comprehensive understanding of the test and thorough analysis of every question type. Each unit consists of seven parts and provides a step-by-step program that provides question-solving strategies and the development of test-taking abilities. At the back of the book is one actual test of the Listening section of the TOEFL® iBT.

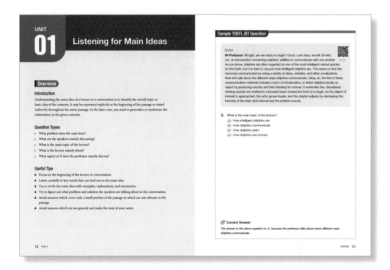

❶ Overview

This part is designed to prepare you for the type of question the unit covers. You will be given a full description of the question type and its application in the passage. You will also be given some useful tips as well as an illustrated introduction and a sample.

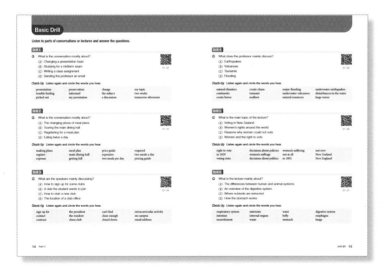

❷ Basic Drill

The purpose of this section is to ensure that you understand the new types of questions that were described in the overview. You will be given a chance to confirm your understanding in brief scripts before starting on the practice exercises. You will listen to some simple conversations or lectures and answer questions of a particular type. This part will help you learn how to deal with each type of question on the Listening section of the TOEFL® iBT.

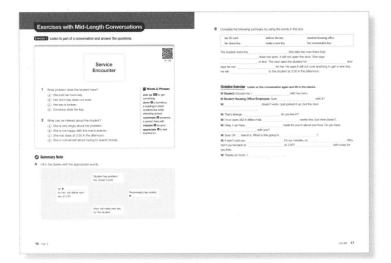

❸ Exercises with Mid-Length Conversations

This part is one of the two practical exercise sections where you can actually practice and improve your ability to solve questions. With a total of four conversations, you will be able to confirm your understanding of the question types and master skills presented in each unit. Glossed vocabulary and well-organized notes will be given to help you understand the material and answer the questions.

❹ Exercises with Mid-Length Lectures

This part is the other practical exercise section where you can actually practice and improve your ability to solve questions. With a total of four lectures, you will be able to confirm your understanding of the question types and master skills presented in each unit. Glossed vocabulary and well-organized notes will be given to help you understand the material and answer the questions.

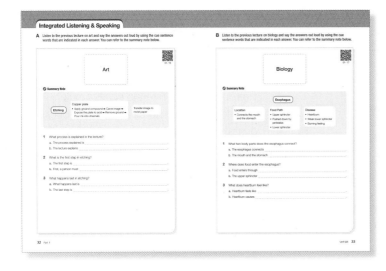

❺ Integrated Listening & Speaking

The TOEFL® iBT is different from previous tests in that it is more integrated than ever. So in this part, you are given the chance to experience the iBT style study by linking your listening skills with your speaking skills. Listen to the different versions of the previous lectures and answer the questions. But remember that this time, you have to say the answers. There is no writing.

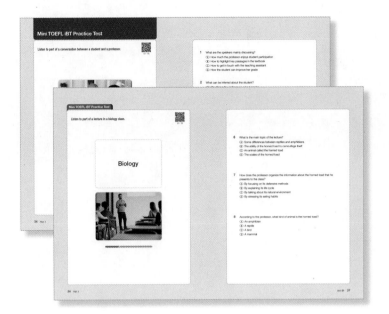

❻ Mini TOEFL iBT Practice Test

This part will give you a chance to experience an actual TOEFL® iBT test. You will be given a conversation with five questions and a lecture with six questions. The topics are similar to those on the actual test, as are the questions.

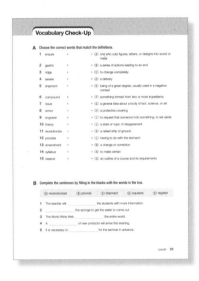

❼ Vocabulary Check-Up

This part offers you a chance to review some of the words you need to remember after finishing each unit. Vocabulary words for each unit are also provided at the back of the book to help you prepare for each unit.

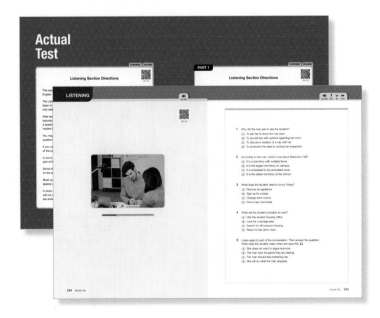

❽ Actual Test

This part offers one full practice test that is modeled on the Listening section of the TOEFL® iBT. This will familiarize you with the actual test format of the TOEFL® iBT.

PART I

Basic Comprehension

Basic comprehension of the listening passage is tested in three ways: listening for the main ideas, listening for the main purpose, and listening for the major details. Listening for the main idea is to identify the overall topic of the contents. Listening for the main purpose is to search for the reason behind the contents. For questions about the major details, you must understand and remember explicit details and facts from a lecture or conversation.

Listening for Main Ideas

Overview

Introduction

Understanding the main idea of a lecture or a conversation is to identify the overall topic or basic idea of the contents. It may be expressed explicitly at the beginning of the passage or stated indirectly throughout the entire passage. In the latter case, you need to generalize or synthesize the information in the given contents.

Question Types

▶ What problem does the man have?

▶ What are the speakers mainly discussing?

▶ What is the main topic of the lecture?

▶ What is the lecture mainly about?

▶ What aspect of X does the professor mainly discuss?

Useful Tips

■ Focus on the beginning of the lecture or conversation.

■ Listen carefully to key words that can lead you to the main idea.

■ Try to verify the main idea with examples, explanations, and summaries.

■ Try to figure out what problem and solution the speakers are talking about in the conversation.

■ Avoid answers which cover only a small portion of the passage or which are not relevant to the passage.

■ Avoid answers which are too general and make the most of your notes.

Script

W Professor: All right, are we ready to begin? Good. Last class, we left off with, um, an introduction concerning dolphins' abilities to communicate with one another. As you know, dolphins are often regarded as one of the most intelligent animal species on the Earth, but it is hard to say just how intelligent dolphins are. The reason is that this mammal communicates by using a variety of clicks, whistles, and other vocalizations. Now let's talk about the different ways dolphins communicate. Okay, uh, the first of these communication methods includes a form of echolocation, in which dolphins locate an object by producing sounds and then listening for echoes. It works like this. Broadband clicking sounds are emitted in a focused beam toward the front of a target. As the object of interest is approached, the echo grows louder, and the dolphin adjusts by decreasing the intensity of the inter-click interval and the emitted sounds.

01-01

Q What is the main topic of the lecture?

Ⓐ How intelligent dolphins are

Ⓑ How dolphins communicate

Ⓒ How dolphins swim

Ⓓ How dolphins use echoes

✅ Correct Answer

The answer to the above question is Ⓑ because the professor talks about some different ways dolphins communicate.

Basic Drill

Listen to parts of conversations or lectures and answer the questions.

Drill 1

Q What is the conversation mostly about?

   Ⓐ Changing a presentation topic

   Ⓑ Studying for a midterm exam

   Ⓒ Writing a class assignment

   Ⓓ Sending the professor an email

01-02

Check-Up Listen again and circle the words you hear.

presentation	preservation	change	my topic
trouble finding	informed	the subject	two weeks
picked out	my permission	a discussion	tomorrow afternoon

Drill 2

Q What is the conversation mostly about?

   Ⓐ The changing prices of meal plans

   Ⓑ Touring the main dining hall

   Ⓒ Registering for a meal plan

   Ⓓ Eating twice a day

01-03

Check-Up Listen again and circle the words you hear.

making plans	meal plan	price guide	required
register	main dining hall	expensive	two meals a day
expense	getting full	two meals per day	pricing guide

Drill 3

Q What are the speakers mainly discussing?

   Ⓐ How to sign up for some clubs

   Ⓑ A club the student wants to join

   Ⓒ How to start a new club

   Ⓓ The location of a club office

01-04

Check-Up Listen again and circle the words you hear.

sign up for	the president	can't find	extracurricular activity
contact	the resident	close enough	on campus
contract	chess club	closed down	email address

Drill 4

Q What does the professor mainly discuss?

   Ⓐ Earthquakes

   Ⓑ Volcanoes

   Ⓒ Tsunamis

   Ⓓ Flooding

01-05

Check-Up Listen again and circle the words you hear.

natural disasters	create chaos	major flooding	underwater earthquakes
continents	tsunami	underwater volcanoes	disturbances in the water
create havoc	seafloor	natural resources	large waves

Drill 5

Q What is the main topic of the lecture?

   Ⓐ Voting in New Zealand

   Ⓑ Women's rights around the world

   Ⓒ Reasons why women could not vote

   Ⓓ Women and the right to vote

01-06

Check-Up Listen again and circle the words you hear.

right to vote	decisions about policies	women's suffering	not over
in 1829	women's suffrage	not at all	New Zealand
voting riots	decisions about politics	in 1892	New England

Drill 6

Q What is the lecture mainly about?

   Ⓐ The differences between human and animal systems

   Ⓑ An overview of the digestive system

   Ⓒ Where nutrients are extracted

   Ⓓ How the stomach works

01-07

Check-Up Listen again and circle the words you hear.

respiratory system	nutrients	waist	digestive system
intestine	internal organs	belly	esophagus
nourishment	waste	stomach	lungs

Exercises with Mid-Length Conversations

Exercise 1 Listen to part of a conversation and answer the questions.

01 - 08

Service Encounter

1 What problem does the student have?

- Ⓐ She lost her room key.
- Ⓑ Her dorm key does not work.
- Ⓒ Her key is broken.
- Ⓓ Someone stole her key.

2 What can be inferred about the student?

- Ⓐ She is very angry about her problem.
- Ⓑ She is not happy with the man's actions.
- Ⓒ She has class at 3:30 in the afternoon.
- Ⓓ She is concerned about having to spend money.

📖 Words & Phrases

pick up phr to get something

dorm n a dormitory; a building in which students live while attending school

roommate n someone a person lives with

mistake n an error

appreciate v to feel thankful for

✏️ Summary Note

A Fill in the blanks with the appropriate words.

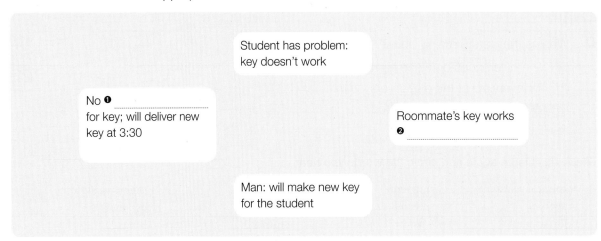

Student has problem: key doesn't work

No ❶ _____ for key; will deliver new key at 3:30

Roommate's key works ❷ _____

Man: will make new key for the student

B Complete the following summary by using the words in the box.

her ID card	deliver the key	student housing office
her dorm key	make a new key	her roommate's key

The student visits the _____. She tells the man there that _____ does not work. It will not open the door. She says _____ is fine. The man asks the student for _____ and says he can _____ for her. He says it will not cost anything to get a new key. He will _____ to the student at 3:30 in the afternoon.

Dictation Exercise Listen to the conversation again and fill in the blanks.

W Student: Excuse me. I _____ with my room.

M Student Housing Office Employee: Sure. _____ with it?

W: _____ doesn't work. I just picked it up, but the door _____.

M: That's strange. _____ do you live in?

W: I'm in room 342 in Milton Hall. _____ works fine, but mine doesn't.

M: Okay. I can have _____ made for you in about one hour. Do you have _____ with you?

W: Sure. Uh . . . here it is. What is this going to _____?

M: It won't cost you _____. It's our mistake, so _____. Why don't you be back at _____ at 3:30? _____ with a key for you then.

W: Thanks so much. I _____.

01 - 09

Service Encounter

1 What are the speakers mainly discussing?
- Ⓐ A textbook the student needs
- Ⓑ The student's newest class
- Ⓒ How to borrow books
- Ⓓ The location of the library

2 What does the woman tell the student to do?
- Ⓐ Borrow a classmate's book
- Ⓑ Visit another store
- Ⓒ Make an online purchase
- Ⓓ Find some material in the library

📖 **Words & Phrases**

brand-new adj never used before
horrible adj very bad
in stock phr available
research n an inquiry into something new
reserve v to request that someone hold something; to set aside

✏️ **Summary Note**

A Fill in the blanks with the appropriate words.

The student
❶ _____

The employee provides a solution

Reserve a copy of the book

Use ❷ _____

B Complete the following summary by using the words in the box.

| out of stock | getting behind | assigned two chapters |
| shipment will arrive | looking for a book | makes a suggestion |

A student is _____ at the campus bookstore. The woman informs him that the textbook is _____. She says a new _____ in a week. The student panics because his professor has already _____ to read. The woman _____. She thinks the student should see if the book is on reserve at the library. That way, the student can do his reading without _____ while he waits for the new shipment of textbooks.

Dictation Exercise Listen to the conversation again and fill in the blanks.

W Bookstore Employee: How's _____? Can I help you with anything?

M Student: Yeah, I hope so. I _____ this book that I need for my, um, my research methods class. The professor wants us to start _____ now and going over the material, but _____ to find it on the shelves.

W: All right, let me see if I _____ with that. _____ of the book? Oh, and if you _____, that would be really helpful, too.

M: Okay, hold on. I have to find where I _____. Hmm . . . The title of the book is *Methods of Educational Research*. And the author is, um, Wiersma.

W: All right, let me _____ into the computer to see if we have _____. Um, Wiersma, did you say? And *Methods of Educational Research*?

M: Yeah, that's it.

W: Wow, those _____. We had a brand-new shipment come in yesterday—fifty books—and they were gone _____.

M: Oh, no! I knew I _____ by yesterday. I just got so carried away with _____. Are you expecting to get more in?

W: Hmm . . . Yes, I think we're going to _____ in about a week. But it's going to _____. I think just twenty books or so.

M: Oh, man! I need to have _____ by next week. I don't know what I'm going to do. What _____ to start the semester!

W: I _____. You could _____ to reserve one of the copies that'll be in, and in the meantime, maybe you could check the library to see if _____ on reserve. But if you're going to do that, you should probably do it quickly because I'm sure _____ are going to be in your position.

M: Yeah, I guess I'll try that. Um, okay, so _____ a copy of the textbook?

W: We can do that _____. But remember that you have to pick up the book within _____, or you'll lose your reservation, and it'll go to _____.

M: All right. Thanks for _____.

01-10

Service Encounter

1 What are the speakers mainly discussing?

- (A) How to start borrowing books
- (B) Where the circulation desk is
- (C) Where the student's ID card is
- (D) What an ID card can be used for

2 Why is the student worried about losing his ID card?

- (A) He thinks someone will steal his money.
- (B) He will not be able to check out library books.
- (C) There are a lot of accounts on his card.
- (D) It will be very difficult to replace.

📕 Words & Phrases

affiliated adj connected or joined to

assign v to appoint to something or someone

attach v to affix to

ensure v to make certain

✏️ Summary Note

A Fill in the blanks with the appropriate words.

How to start borrowing books	The student is worried about losing his card
• Go to the circulation desk	• A library account will be added to his card
• A barcode will be put on ❶ _____	• Are ❷ _____ on his card already

B Complete the following summary by using the words in the box.

account attached to	get a barcode	affiliated with
his money accounts	reassures him	informing the student

A librarian is _____ about the book borrowing process. She tells him the first step is to _____ attached to his student identification card. She says it is important to have photo identification when borrowing books because only people _____ the university are allowed to borrow books. The student worries about having another _____ his ID card because it already holds _____ and meal plan. He's afraid he will lose it. The librarian _____ that he will be fine.

Dictation Exercise Listen to the conversation again and fill in the blanks.

W Librarian: All first-year students _____ to do a one-on-one orientation with a librarian or a librarian's aide their _____.

M Student: Thank you.

W: _____ I'm going to do is walk you through how to borrow books from the library. What you need to do first is make sure your _____ is registered at the front desk. The circulation desk employee will, um, _____ and then assign you a barcode that will be swiped every time you _____.

M: But why is that _____ my student ID card? I mean, couldn't I get a _____? That's how things were at _____ back home.

W: It's really important for your library card to _____ of you on it for, um, for identification purposes. Only students, professors, and people affiliated with the university _____ borrow books from this library. So by attaching a barcode to your student ID, we're pretty much ensuring that you _____ this university. Plus, since your ID already has your picture on it, we don't have to _____ anyone else using your ID and taking out books.

M: I guess I understand that. It's _____ to me to have one card for everything here. I mean, it already has _____ and a cash account on it, and it lets me back into my dorm.

W: Well, that's kind of _____. You _____ carrying around a lot of cards.

M: It's kind of bad, too. If I lose it, _____. I guess I have to be really careful.

W: I guess you do. _____. Don't worry.

M: Thanks. Okay, so the first thing I have to do before I _____ is, um, take my student ID to the circulation desk for a barcode?

W: That's right. Once you do that, you can _____.

01 - 11

Office Hours

1 What problem does the student have?

Ⓐ School is too expensive for her.

Ⓑ She is about to lose her scholarship.

Ⓒ She was rejected for a scholarship.

Ⓓ The price of tuition is rising.

2 Why does the professor mention the financial assistance office?

Ⓐ To suggest going there

Ⓑ To say he knows a worker there

Ⓒ To recommend avoiding it

Ⓓ To tell the student to ask questions there

📖 Words & Phrases

aggravated adj frustrated

eligible adj qualified to be chosen

financial adj having to do with money

interface n a place where independent entities can communicate with each other

📝 Summary Note

A Fill in the blanks with the appropriate words.

Apply for loans and ❷ _____

Financial aid   Professor's suggestion   Fill out ❶ _____

Complete on paper or online

B Complete the following summary by using the words in the box.

urges her	get a loan	departmental scholarships
receiving financial aid	fill out	grateful for

The student asks the professor for advice about _____. Her professor tells her that to _____ or a scholarship, she must _____ the financial aid form. The form can be found at the financial assistance office or online. The professor _____ to fill out the form as soon as possible. He says this because there are _____ available for the following semester. The student is very _____ her professor's help and advice.

Dictation Exercise Listen to the conversation again and fill in the blanks.

W Student: Hi, Professor Carlos. I was wondering if I could ask you _____.

M Professor: Of course. What can I do for you?

W: Well, I was going over _____, and I'm really aggravated about it because I just don't think I'm going to be able to _____ for more than a year. And I really would prefer _____. I mean, I love it here.

M: Okay, well, I'm sure we can _____. Um, have you filled out _____ yet?

W: No, I don't think so.

M: All right. Then that's _____. That form will help determine _____ for loans and, um, need-based scholarships. Actually, I'm certain you have to complete that form even if you're going for a _____.

W: Where can I get it? And who do I _____? And what _____ does it ask for?

M: I'm pretty sure you can pick it up at the _____. That is where you should return it as well. Actually, I think the financial assistance office has _____ so that you can complete the form via the Internet.

W: Really? Wow, that's _____!

M: Yes, it really is. Um, _____ for the university's financial assistance office, and you can probably hyperlink to the form from there.

W: I think _____ right now. Wait. Do you know what kind of information I'll need to _____?

M: Um, I think it would be _____ to fill out the form with a copy of last year's tax returns. That should have _____ you'll need.

W: Okay. I _____ of that in my room.

M: And if you _____ within the next couple of days, you might be eligible for some of the departmental scholarships we're awarding _____. We have both need- and merit-based scholarships available.

W: _____! Thank you so much.

Exercise 1 Listen to part of a lecture and answer the questions.

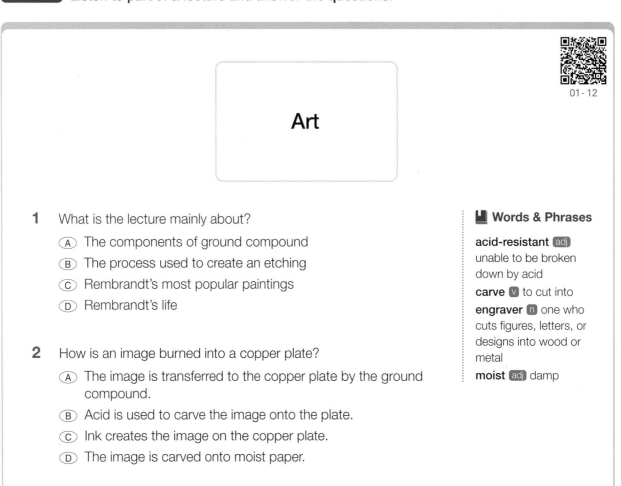

01-12

Art

1 What is the lecture mainly about?
- Ⓐ The components of ground compound
- Ⓑ The process used to create an etching
- Ⓒ Rembrandt's most popular paintings
- Ⓓ Rembrandt's life

2 How is an image burned into a copper plate?
- Ⓐ The image is transferred to the copper plate by the ground compound.
- Ⓑ Acid is used to carve the image onto the plate.
- Ⓒ Ink creates the image on the copper plate.
- Ⓓ The image is carved onto moist paper.

📕 Words & Phrases

acid-resistant adj unable to be broken down by acid

carve v to cut into

engraver n one who cuts figures, letters, or designs into wood or metal

moist adj damp

✏ Summary Note

A Fill in the blanks with the appropriate words.

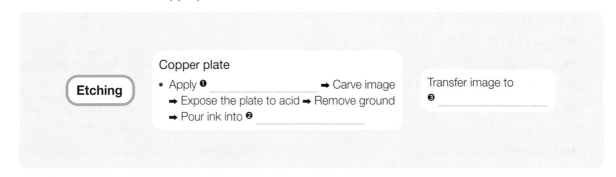

Etching

Copper plate
- Apply ❶ _____ ➡ Carve image
➡ Expose the plate to acid ➡ Remove ground
➡ Pour ink into ❷ _____

Transfer image to
❸ _____

B Complete the following summary by using the words in the box.

remain untouched	ground compound	onto moist paper
get eaten away	pours acid	cuts an image

Etchings are created by covering a copper plate with a _____. Then, the artist _____ into the compound until the copper plate is exposed underneath. Next, the artist _____ over the compound. The parts of the copper plate that are covered with the compound _____. The other parts _____ by the acid. This creates channels. The artist removes the compound and pours ink into the channels. Finally, the plate is pressed _____. This creates a print.

Dictation Exercise Listen to the lecture again and fill in the blanks.

M1 Professor: So we've talked about Rembrandt _____ and a bit about his work. He was a _____ and engraver. _____ his talents in those activities aren't what made him so famous. Rembrandt _____ the art of etching. We talked a bit about _____ before. Remember? Who can tell me what etching is?

W Student: Doesn't it involve _____ onto a metal plate?

M1: That's right. The artist usually has _____ that he coats or covers with an acid-resistant substance. Um, this stuff _____ beeswax and resin, and this substance is called bitumen. Altogether, it's called _____. What the artist does is cover _____ with the ground compound—all that stuff I just mentioned—and he carves a design through it with _____. You have to _____ because you want to get through the ground to uncover the copper underneath. Then, the artist _____ to acid, the parts that are uncovered by the ground get eaten away, and the metal is recessed into those areas, _____. Who knows what's done with the metal plates afterward?

M2 Student: They're used to _____, right?

M1: Great job. Yes, after the ground compound is removed, _____ into the parts that have been eaten away. These channels _____ really well. Then, the plate is pressed onto _____, and you get a print. Rembrandt was a genius _____ etchings. I think that after a while, etchings were _____. Um, let me see. Does anyone recognize this etching?

M2: I know that one. It's in a museum in Washington, D.C. Um, I think it's called *Woman and Arrow*.

M1: _____. It's called *The Woman with the Arrow*. Rembrandt _____ in 1661.

Exercise 2 Listen to part of a lecture and answer the questions.

01-13

Biology

1 What is the main topic of the lecture?
- Ⓐ The reason people get heartburn
- Ⓑ An overview of the esophagus
- Ⓒ The location of the esophagus
- Ⓓ The process of peristalsis

2 Why do people experience heartburn?
- Ⓐ Because the esophagus gets blocked during peristalsis
- Ⓑ Because the heart is located near the esophagus
- Ⓒ Because the lower sphincter gets weak
- Ⓓ Because they have a burning feeling

📖 Words & Phrases

armor ⓝ a protective covering
digestive adj having to do with the processing of food in the body
esophagus ⓝ a body organ necessary to digestion that is located between the mouth and the stomach
gastric adj having to do with the stomach

🖉 Summary Note

A Fill in the blanks with the appropriate words.

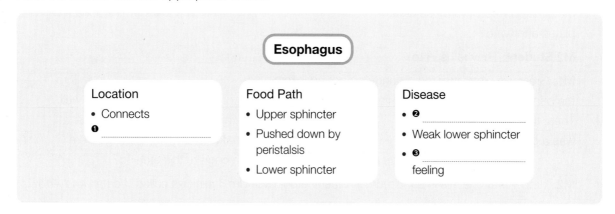

Esophagus

Location
- Connects
- ❶ ....

Food Path
- Upper sphincter
- Pushed down by peristalsis
- Lower sphincter

Disease
- ❷ ....
- Weak lower sphincter
- ❸ .... feeling

B Complete the following summary by using the words in the box.

enters the esophagus	muscles squeeze	pushed through
leaves the esophagus	leaves the mouth	connects

After food _____, digestion goes on in the esophagus. The esophagus is a long tube that _____ the mouth and the stomach. Food _____ through the upper sphincter. Then, the food is _____ the esophagus by a process called peristalsis. Peristalsis happens when the _____ food down the tube. Food _____ through the lower sphincter. If the lower sphincter is weak, a person can get heartburn.

Dictation Exercise Listen to the lecture again and fill in the blanks.

W Professor: After _____, the digestive process keeps going in the esophagus. The esophagus is basically _____. It pretty much goes straight up and down from _____ to your stomach. At the top of the esophagus is the upper sphincter, which is a _____. It stays closed most of the time and for _____. After you swallow, the upper sphincter opens to _____. Then, it _____ so that the food doesn't come back out.

  Um, so once food is let into the esophagus, _____ that's called peristalsis. This is the _____ of the muscles. During peristalsis, the muscles in the esophagus push the food _____. Picture a toothpaste tube. To get toothpaste _____, you have to squeeze from one end to the other. That's what peristalsis is like _____ there's a wave-like motion from the top of the tube to the bottom. _____ in front of the wave till it reaches the bottom of the esophagus. At the bottom of the, um, the esophagus, is the lower sphincter. When food _____, the lower sphincter opens up to let food pass into the stomach. Then, it _____ so that the acids from the stomach can't get into the esophagus.

  And _____ getting into the esophagus, those acids are what cause the feeling called heartburn. Heartburn doesn't actually have _____ the heart. Actually, um, heartburn _____ in the esophagus. It's what happens when the lower sphincter gets weak. Gastric acids _____ enter the esophagus. They cause _____. These acids don't cause problems in the stomach because the stomach has, um, well, it has a lining, _____, that keeps it from getting hurt. The esophagus doesn't have that kind of _____, so gastric acids can really harm it.

Exercise 3 Listen to part of a lecture and answer the questions.

01-14

Geology

1 What is the lecture mainly about?

- Ⓐ Earthquakes that do not occur on fault lines
- Ⓑ The severity of earthquakes
- Ⓒ Plate tectonic theory
- Ⓓ The causes of earthquakes

2 Why do the most severe earthquakes occur?

- Ⓐ Because one plate gets pushed under another
- Ⓑ Because one plate rubs against another
- Ⓒ Because a fault line gets agitated
- Ⓓ Because three plates collide with one another

📖 Words & Phrases

disconnected adj not joined

earthquake n the shaking of the ground

ridge n a raised strip of ground

seismic zone n an area where earthquakes tend to occur

severe adj being of a great degree, usually used in a negative context

✏ Summary Note

A Fill in the blanks with the appropriate words.

Earthquakes

Plate tectonic theory
- Earth's plates continue to move
- Plates meet each other at
  ❶ ....

Severity of quakes
- Most severe: one plate pushed underneath another
- Less severe: plates
  ❷ ....
  each other

Quakes not on fault lines
- Scientists don't know why
  ❸ ....

B Complete the following summary by using the words in the box.

rub against	plate tectonic theory	major earthquake zones
pushed underneath	made up of plates	ground stress

One theory about why earthquakes happen is called _____. The Earth's surface is _____ that move against one another. The most severe quakes happen when one plate gets _____ another one. Less severe quakes happen when plates _____ each other. Scientists do not really know what causes them. There are three _____ on the Earth. But sometimes earthquakes happen away from seismic zones due to _____.

Dictation Exercise Listen to the lecture again and fill in the blanks.

M1 Professor: The next chapter in our book discusses earthquakes. Um, well, I hope you've all read this chapter because I will _____ from the chapter for participation points today. Okay, to begin, the authors talk about plate tectonic theory as a _____ explanation for earthquakes. Who can tell me what this theory states? Yes, go ahead . . .

W Student: I think the authors wrote that plate tectonic theory is the idea that the Earth's surface is made up of _____ that are kind of disconnected. I think they move _____.

M1: Very good. Yes, the Earth's surface is not _____ of land. Um, it's made up of these plates that move against each other. _____ tend to happen where one plate is kind of pushed under another. These quakes start _____ in the ground. Other quakes, um, less severe quakes, happen where the plates _____. How many major earthquake zones are there?

M2 Student: Three.

M1: And what are they?

M2: Um, _____ around the Pacific Ocean. Another is called the, um, the trans-Asiatic belt. _____ across the Mediterranean countries and then across Asia. And the third, the third one is in the Atlantic Ocean and is called the mid-ocean ridges.

M1: Excellent. Does anyone have questions about plate tectonic theory?

W: What about earthquakes _____ in these zones? I mean, aren't there ever earthquakes that, um, that _____ a seismic zone?

M1: Great question. Yes, I think that sometimes earthquakes _____ from, um, seismic zones. These ones are _____ though. Quakes that don't occur _____ are called, um, intraplate earthquakes. I don't think scientists have figured out the _____ yet, but I think they do agree that, um, there's a lot of ground stress where _____.

Exercise 4 Listen to part of a lecture and answer the questions.

01-15

History

1 What is the main topic of the lecture?
- Ⓐ A constitutional amendment giving women the right to vote
- Ⓑ The history of the American women's suffrage movement
- Ⓒ The National Woman Suffrage Association
- Ⓓ The anti-slavery movement

2 Why was the National Woman's Suffrage Association created?
- Ⓐ To get women the right to vote
- Ⓑ To educate more women
- Ⓒ To help fight slavery
- Ⓓ To help women get more jobs

📖 **Words & Phrases**

affect Ⓥ to influence
amendment Ⓝ a change or correction
constitution Ⓝ established law or custom; the highest law
federal ⓐⓓⒿ having to do with national government
issue Ⓝ a state of disagreement

✏️ **Summary Note**

A Fill in the blanks with the appropriate words.

Women's Suffrage Movement

1776-1922
- Women didn't
  ❶ ....

1850s
- Meetings held; women realized there was no way to unify suffrage
  ❷ ....

1869
- The National Woman's Suffrage Association was created to get an amendment that would
  ❸ ....

B Complete the following summary by using the words in the box.

push for an amendment	started meeting about	of voting rights
anti-slavery movement	fighting for	many rights

There is a long history of a lack _____ for women. In the mid-1800s, American women started _____ their right to vote. This started during the _____. While women were fighting for rights for others, they realized that they did not have _____ themselves. American women _____ what to do. They realized that the only way that all American women would get the right to vote would be to _____ to the Constitution. So they created the Natioual Woman's Suffrage Association for that purpose.

Dictation Exercise Listen to the lecture again and fill in the blanks.

W Professor: A thing to note about the women's suffrage movement in this country is that _____, um, I guess you could say it was a tough battle. Oh, by the way, suffrage means _____. There had been _____ of women not having the right to vote. Even in _____, in ancient Greece and Rome, women couldn't vote. And experts say that these times gave us the best _____ of all time.

Anyway, let's just say that women had a lot of history to break down before _____. So women in Great Britain and the United States _____ the right to vote during the 1800s and the 1900s. Women in Great Britain struggled _____ American women did for this right. However, we're just going to look at American women and _____. So the women's suffrage movement started in the U.S. around the same time as _____. Um, that would have been during the, um, the mid-1800s. So this is what happened. A group of _____ started pushing for anti-slavery laws. And while they were doing this, they found that _____ in America also needed to be looked at.

These women realized that _____ about how women were treated. So this is what they did. They held a couple of meetings in different parts of the country to _____ in those regions into the cause. Now, the problem was that _____ to give women the right to vote nationally. A state could give this right to women. But that would only affect women _____. Because of this, these women believed that _____ to get an amendment, or change, to the Constitution to give women the right to vote. This would give women the right to vote _____. So what they did was _____ called the National Woman's Suffrage Association. _____ the, um, the NWSA was to get an amendment to the Constitution.

Integrated Listening & Speaking

A Listen to the previous lecture on art and say the answers out loud by using the cue sentence words that are indicated in each answer. You can refer to the summary note below.

Art

01-16

✎ **Summary Note**

Etching

Copper plate
- Apply ground compound ➡ Carve image ➡ Expose the plate to acid ➡ Remove ground ➡ Pour ink into channels

Transfer image to moist paper

1 What process is explained in the lecture?

   a. The process explained is _____ .

   b. The lecture explains _____ .

2 What is the first step in etching?

   a. The first step is _____ .

   b. First, a person must _____ .

3 What happens last in etching?

   a. What happens last is _____ .

   b. The last step is _____ .

B Listen to the previous lecture on biology and say the answers out loud by using the cue sentence words that are indicated in each answer. You can refer to the summary note below.

01-17

Biology

Summary Note

Esophagus

Location	Food Path	Disease
• Connects the mouth and the stomach	• Upper sphincter • Pushed down by peristalsis • Lower sphincter	• Heartburn • Weak lower sphincter • Burning feeling

1 What two body parts does the esophagus connect?

a. The esophagus connects _____ .

b. The mouth and the stomach _____ .

2 Where does food enter the esophagus?

a. Food enters through _____ .

b. The upper sphincter _____ .

3 What does heartburn feel like?

a. Heartburn feels like _____ .

b. Heartburn causes _____ .

Listen to part of a conversation between a student and a professor.

01-18

1 What are the speakers mainly discussing?

    (A) How much the professor enjoys student participation

    (B) How to highlight key passages in the textbook

    (C) How to get in touch with the teaching assistant

    (D) How the student can improve her grade

2 What can be inferred about the student?

    (A) She thinks the professor is a hard grader.

    (B) She is concerned about her class grade.

    (C) She does not have enough time to study.

    (D) She is likely going to drop the class.

3 Why does the student mention Piaget's stages of development?

    (A) To state she disagrees with them

    (B) To express her confusion about them

    (C) To note that she learned them

    (D) To ask the professor about them

4 What does the professor tell the student to do?

    (A) Attend the review sessions

    (B) Ask the teaching assistant for old exams

    (C) Memorize Piaget's stages of development

    (D) Study with some other students

5 What is the professor's attitude toward the student?

    (A) He criticizes her for her poor study habits.

    (B) He feels that she should change her major.

    (C) He believes she is doing very well in his class.

    (D) He attempts to help her with her questions.

Listen to part of a lecture in a biology class.

01 - 19

Biology

6 What is the main topic of the lecture?

    Ⓐ Some differences between reptiles and amphibians

    Ⓑ The ability of the horned toad to camouflage itself

    Ⓒ An animal called the horned toad

    Ⓓ The scales of the horned toad

7 How does the professor organize the information about the horned toad that he presents to the class?

    Ⓐ By focusing on its defensive methods

    Ⓑ By explaining its life cycle

    Ⓒ By talking about its natural environment

    Ⓓ By stressing its eating habits

8 According to the professor, what kind of animal is the horned toad?

    Ⓐ An amphibian

    Ⓑ A reptile

    Ⓒ A bird

    Ⓓ A mammal

9 What does the professor imply about the horned toad?

    (A) Its most important defense is its poison.

    (B) It lives in many places around the world.

    (C) Cold temperatures are able to harm it.

    (D) Many animals are unable to kill and eat it.

10 Why does the professor discuss camouflage?

    (A) To state it is used by the horned toad

    (B) To claim that most reptiles use it

    (C) To argue that it is not very effective

    (D) To compare its uses by two different animals

11 What is one type of protection the horned toad has?

    (A) It can create a bad smell that bothers attackers.

    (B) It uses great speed to escape from predators.

    (C) It can lose a limb when a predator bites it.

    (D) It can shoot a substance from its eyes.

Vocabulary Check-Up

A Choose the correct words that match the definitions.

1 ensure •   • Ⓐ one who cuts figures, letters, or designs into wood or metal

2 gastric •   • Ⓑ a series of actions leading to an end

3 ridge •   • Ⓒ to change completely

4 severe •   • Ⓓ a delivery

5 shipment •   • Ⓔ being of a great degree, usually used in a negative context

6 compound •   • Ⓕ something formed from two or more ingredients

7 issue •   • Ⓖ a general idea about a body of fact, science, or art

8 armor •   • Ⓗ a protective covering

9 engraver •   • Ⓘ to request that someone hold something; to set aside

10 theory •   • Ⓙ a state or topic of disagreement

11 revolutionize •   • Ⓚ a raised strip of ground

12 process •   • Ⓛ having to do with the stomach

13 amendment •   • Ⓜ a change or correction

14 syllabus •   • Ⓝ to make certain

15 reserve •   • Ⓞ an outline of a course and its requirements

B Complete the sentences by filling in the blanks with the words in the box.

Ⓐ revolutionized	Ⓑ provide	Ⓒ shipment	Ⓓ squeeze	Ⓔ register

1 The teacher will _____ the students with more information.

2 _____ the sponge to get the water to come out.

3 The World Wide Web _____ the entire world.

4 A _____ of new products will arrive this evening.

5 It is necessary to _____ for the seminar in advance.

UNIT 02

Listening for Main Purpose

Overview

Introduction

Understanding the purpose of a lecture or a conversation is being able to identify the reason behind the contents. This type of question often occurs after conversations rather than lectures. As in the main idea, the purpose may be expressed explicitly in the beginning of the contents or stated indirectly and spread throughout the passage. In the latter case, you need to generalize or synthesize information in the given contents.

Question Types

▶ Why does the student visit the professor?

▶ Why does the student visit the Registrar's office?

▶ Why did the professor ask to see the student?

▶ Why does the professor explain X?

Useful Tips

■ Focus on the reason behind the lecture or conversation.

■ Listen carefully to the ends of casual talks.

■ Try to verify the purpose with the following solution.

■ Avoid answers that cover only a small portion of the listening or which are not relevant to the listening.

■ Avoid answers that are too general and make the most of your notes.

02-01

Script

W Student: Hello, Mr. Shanks. I'm Marcy Walker from room 322. My phone line is dead, so I can't call anyone or access the Internet. Can you help me get the phone turned back on?

M Housing Office Employee: Marcy, I know why your telephone line was shut off. You haven't paid your bill for the last two months. It's not up to me whether your phone gets shut off or not. It's up to the phone company.

W: Yeah, I didn't pay my bill on time because I spent the money reserved for the phone bill in my budget on shopping.

M: Now you have to pay your bill as well as a late fee of two percent. Then, you'll have to fill out a reconnection form and wait for a service technician to schedule an appointment to reconnect your line.

Q Why did the student visit the man?
- Ⓐ To pay her phone bill
- Ⓑ To complain about her phone service
- Ⓒ To have a phone connected in her room
- Ⓓ To get her phone turned back on

✅ Correct Answer

The answer to the above question is Ⓓ. The reason that the student is visiting the man is that she wants her phone turned back on. Then, she can use the Internet and make phone calls.

Basic Drill

Listen to parts of conversations or lectures and answer the questions.

Drill 1

Q Why does the student visit the professor?

ⓐ To inquire about tuition
ⓑ To complain about his grade
ⓒ To ask about scholarships
ⓓ To discuss quitting school

02-02

Check-Up Listen again and circle the words you hear.

withdraw	can't afford	apply for	situation
draw	pay off	scholarly	fill in
price of tuition	outstanding	describe	recommendation

Drill 2

Q Why did the student visit the professor?

ⓐ To ask for a letter of recommendation
ⓑ To negotiate the cost of extra tutoring sessions
ⓒ To get help with learning difficult material
ⓓ To figure out how to get to the learning center

02-03

Check-Up Listen again and circle the words you hear.

advice	test book	material	tactics
suggestion	difficult	key words	methods
learning center	complicated	ideas	cost

Drill 3

Q Why does the student visit the study abroad office?

ⓐ To ask about credit while studying abroad
ⓑ To get suggestions on good programs
ⓒ To find out which programs have classes in English
ⓓ To inquire about the cost of studying abroad

02-04

Check-Up Listen again and circle the words you hear.

studying abroad	considering	the best thing	automatically
this semester	getting credit	at ten	have a partner
concerned about	giving credit	partnership	very helpful

Drill 4

Q Why does the professor explain the effects of pollution?

  (A) To say that pollution has been increasing recently

  (B) To claim that pollution kills many people and animals

  (C) To focus on how humans can reduce pollution in places

  (D) To show how technology is harming the environment

02-05

Check-Up Listen again and circle the words you hear.

pollution	environment	computers	humans
harmful	smoke	recycle	garbage heaps
landfall	smog	not recyclable	waste

Drill 5

Q Why does the professor explain the trickle-down effect in economics?

  (A) To argue that all countries should practice it

  (B) To state how people for and against it feel

  (C) To name the person who came up with it

  (D) To express her support for this theory

02-06

Check-Up Listen again and circle the words you hear.

big businesses	professors	definitely	financial
sub-par	trickle-down	regulation	regulate
government	taxes	economic theorists	allowable

Drill 6

Q Why does the professor explain a change in the film industry?

  (A) To give an overview of Charlie Chaplin's career

  (B) To describe how movies changed when they used sound

  (C) To compare silent movies with talkies

  (D) To discuss the effect of talkies on Charlie Chaplin

02-07

Check-Up Listen again and circle the words you hear.

silent comedy	popularity	speaking parts	talkies
industry	fame	silent films	acting
character roles	famous	comedic	actors

Exercises with Mid-Length Conversations

Exercise 1 Listen to part of a conversation and answer the questions.

02-08

Office Hours

1 Why did the professor ask to see the student?

Ⓐ To tell him to pay attention in class

Ⓑ To discuss his performance on a test

Ⓒ To inform him about a work opportunity

Ⓓ To advise him to take an easier class

2 Why does the student mention his part-time job?

Ⓐ To say he will quit his job soon

Ⓑ To tell the professor why he leaves class early

Ⓒ To discuss his need for money

Ⓓ To explain why he performed poorly

📖 Words & Phrases

concerned adj worried

midnight n twelve o'clock at night

substitute v to work in another person's place

shift n the time when a person works at a job

favor n an act of kindness for another person

pull out phr to accomplish; to achieve

✏️ Summary Note

A Fill in the blanks with the appropriate words.

> Did poorly on midterm exam

> Professor was expecting more from the student

> Had to work late at
> ❶ _____
> the night before the exam

> Will not work late again before test; will do his best on
> ❷ _____

B Complete the following summary by using the words in the box.

delivers food	is concerned about	improve his grade
until after midnight	he had to substitute	an excellent student

The professor tells the student she _____ his test performance. She was told

he is _____, but he got a B on the midterm exam. The student says that he

had to work _____ the night before the exam, so he could not study for it

much. He explains that he _____ for a restaurant. _____

for the other driver the night before the test. He promises to do well on the final exam and the paper

and to _____.

Dictation Exercise Listen to the conversation again and fill in the blanks.

W Professor: Ivan, thanks for coming here. I need to speak with you about _____.

I'm _____ about your class performance.

M Student: What do you mean? I got a B on _____.

W: Yes, but I was expecting _____. Your advisor told me that you're an excellent

student, so I was expecting _____ a B from you.

M: Ah, I see. Well . . .

W: Yes?

M: _____, I didn't study much for the exam. I had to work at

_____ until after midnight the night before the test, so . . .

W: What kind of job do you have that makes you _____?

M: I work at Nate's Pizza as _____. I had to substitute for

_____ that night, and Nate's doesn't close until two in the morning.

W: I see. Do you finish late _____?

M: Yes, but I normally _____ on Friday and Saturday nights. I only

_____ on a Tuesday night because the other driver was sick. I was

_____.

W: Okay. I guess that explains _____.

M: I will do my best on _____ and the paper. I will try to get

_____ up.

W: I'm glad to hear you say that. You can _____ an A in this class if you ace both

of them.

M: That's _____. Thank you for saying that.

Exercise 2 Listen to part of a conversation and answer the questions.

02-09

Office Hours

1 Why does the student visit the professor?
- Ⓐ To ask about getting his grade early
- Ⓑ To inquire about a new finance class
- Ⓒ To find out about a program in Rome
- Ⓓ To discuss his minor in classics

2 Why does the student want to study abroad?
- Ⓐ To spend time with foreign relatives
- Ⓑ To visit museums in Europe
- Ⓒ To complete his minor
- Ⓓ To learn a foreign language

📖 **Words & Phrases**

abroad adv beyond the boundaries of one's country
perspective n a point of view
precise adj exact

📝 Summary Note

A Fill in the blanks with the appropriate words.

Student to professor

Student needs
❶ _____
early

Why: Study abroad
application deadline

Complete classics minor

Gain ❷ _____

B Complete the following summary by using the words in the box.

to turn in his grade	for a favor	a study abroad program
learning new things	her teaching assistant	taking an opportunity

The student asks his professor _____ . He is applying for
_____ in Rome. He needs his professor _____
early to meet the application deadline. The professor is pleased that her student is
_____ to go abroad. The student is excited about _____
and gaining a new perspective. The professor says she will make a note and inform
_____ to get the student's grade to the Registrar's office.

Dictation Exercise   Listen to the conversation again and fill in the blanks.

W Professor: Hi. Can I help you?

M Student: Hi, Professor Madison. My name is John Smith. I wonder if _____
something.

W: Of course, John.

M: I know _____ is in a week. And I know generally professors don't have
to _____ in for two weeks afterward. But the thing is that I've applied for
a _____ that starts in four weeks, and I need to have all my grades in
_____ to be accepted to the program. So I wonder if you can grade my exam early
so that I can complete _____ on time.

W: Hmm . . . When is _____ ?

M: A week and a half from today. Three days after the final exam _____ .

W: And which _____ is this?

M: I'm doing a program in Rome. If I'm there _____ , it'll take care of my classics
minor.

W: Wow, that sounds so exciting. So you're _____ your minor first? And then
_____ your major?

M: Yes. I'm already _____ on my finance major, so I can afford to take
a semester just _____ . Plus, it's a great way to travel and to get a little
_____ .

W: I _____ . I think _____ should do a study abroad
program. Anyway, back to your question. I'll make a note of your situation and copy that to
_____ . One of us will make sure to _____ first and get your
grade to the Registrar's office.

M: Thank you so much. I really appreciate it.

W: No problem. _____ . Good luck on the exam and in Rome.

M: Thanks!

Exercise 3 Listen to part of a conversation and answer the questions.

02-10

Service Encounter

1 Why does the student visit the dining hall?
- Ⓐ To ask to fill out a student survey there
- Ⓑ To go to her new on-campus workplace
- Ⓒ To sign up for a new meal plan
- Ⓓ To find out about getting a job there

2 What will the student probably do next?
- Ⓐ Make a payment
- Ⓑ Fill out a form
- Ⓒ Begin working her shift
- Ⓓ Sit down for an interview

📖 Words & Phrases

availability [n] the state of being present or ready
dibs [n] a claim or right
eligible [adj] qualified to participate or to be chosen
flexible [adj] yielding
preference [n] a more favorable option

📝 Summary Note

A Fill in the blanks with the appropriate words.

| How to get a dining hall job | Fill out ❶ _____ | Indicate job preference |
| | | Indicate ❷ _____ |

B Complete the following summary by using the words in the box.

she has a job	fill out an application	hours of availability
is still hiring	she is eligible	inquiring about

A student is _____ positions at the dining hall. The man tells her that the dining hall _____ and asks if she is eligible for work-study. He says that work-study students are hired first. The student confirms that _____ . The employee tells the student that she needs to _____ and indicate her position preferences and _____ . Then, the dining hall staff will match their needs with the student's preferences and availability. The student will find out if _____ by tomorrow.

Dictation Exercise Listen to the conversation again and fill in the blanks.

M Dining Services Office Employee: Can I help you?

W Student: Yes, I heard that there are _____ here at the dining hall. Do you still have openings?

M: Yes, we do. Are you _____ ?

W: Yes, I am.

M: Okay, the way _____ here is that students who are eligible for work-study usually have first dibs at the jobs. After that, we _____ who aren't eligible for work-study. _____ for work-study?

W: Yes, I am. The financial aid office actually _____ . The person there said you might be hiring dining hall staff and that this would probably be the _____ place to work around my classes.

M: Well, we _____ students' schedules here. So I'm going to give you _____ to fill out. Just let me know what you want to do in terms of whether you want to cook, serve, clean, _____ , or whatever. You rank _____ in your order of preference. Oh, you also need to let us know what _____ . You know, what _____ you can work. Then, we'll match your preferences and availability with _____ .

W: Okay.

M: So if you want, you can just take a seat at _____ and fill out the application right away.

W: Great. Oh, how long after I turn in the application will I _____ if I'm going to be hired?

M: You'll surely be hired if _____ matches what we need. You'll probably _____ by tomorrow.

W: Wonderful. Thanks. All right, I'll turn this in _____ I'm done.

Exercise 4 Listen to part of a conversation and answer the questions.

02-11

Office Hours

1 Why did the professor ask to see the student?

Ⓐ To talk about her score on the most recent exam
Ⓑ To return a paper of hers that he graded
Ⓒ To encourage her to participate more in class
Ⓓ To advise her to study hard for the next test

📙 **Words & Phrases**

comfortable adj at ease
nervous adj uneasy
shame n something to be regretted
semester n a term into which an academic year is divided

2 In the conversation, the student makes a number of statements about herself. Indicate whether each of the following statements is true or not.
Click in the correct box for each sentence.

	True	False
① The student gets nervous talking in front of others.		
② The student appreciates the advice she received in the past.		
③ The student needs help for an upcoming class presentation.		
④ The student does not want the professor to call on her in class.		

✏ Summary Note

A Fill in the blanks with the appropriate words.

Student is nervous about
❶ _____

Class participation = 10% of grade

Student can get A if she participates

Professor has a suggestion

Professor will
❷ _____

Student will eventually raise her hand

B   Complete the following summary by using the words in the box.

get an A	have improved a lot	on her own
a couple of times	in front of the class	participate more

The professor tells the student to _____ in class. He says that she is doing
really well and that her test scores _____. The only thing she has not improved
in is class participation. The student feels nervous about speaking _____. The
professor suggests calling on her _____. Then, when she is more comfortable
talking in front of the class, she can volunteer answers _____. The professor
finally tells the student that she can probably _____ in the class.

Dictation Exercise   Listen to the conversation again and fill in the blanks.

W Student: Hi, Professor Denver. You want to see me?

M Professor: Yes, I do. Remember how you asked for advice on _____ in my
class up a couple of months ago?

W: Yes, I do. And I want to thank you again _____.

M: Not a problem. You've done _____ so far. _____
have improved a lot. The only thing that hasn't really gotten better is _____. I'm
_____ about that. It's a _____ to get an extra ten percent on
your grade.

W: I've tried, Professor. I just _____ talking in front of the class.

M: Why is that?

W: I just don't want to _____ in front of everyone.

M: Don't worry about that. You really _____, you know. It shows from
_____. You're doing well in the class otherwise. Besides, we've got
_____.

W: I know. I just can't seem to bring myself to _____.

M: This isn't _____, but if you'd like, I can _____
at first a couple of times. Then, maybe after you answer a couple of questions, you'll be
_____ raising your hand.

W: Well, I guess. I mean, we could try.

M: That's really all I ask. If _____, you might be able to bring your grade up to an A
by the time the semester's over.

W: Oh, wow. I didn't know I _____.

M: You are. It would _____ if this was what was holding you back.

W: Okay, uh, _____ to do my best.

Exercises with Mid-Length Lectures

Exercise 1 Listen to part of a lecture and answer the questions.

02-12

Geology

1 Why does the professor explain the rock cycle?

Ⓐ To prove that volcanoes can form rocks
Ⓑ To explain why rocks form so slowly
Ⓒ To show how rocks can change types
Ⓓ To note some different kinds of rocks

2 Why does the professor mention granite?

Ⓐ To call it an igneous rock
Ⓑ To explain how it is form
Ⓒ To state how people use it
Ⓓ To say it is formed with sediment

Words & Phrases

lava n hot, melted rock that comes from a volcano
transform v to change
intense adj very strong; powerful
erode v to break down over time

Summary Note

A Fill in the blanks with the appropriate words.

Types of Rocks

Sedimentary
- Forms from sediment
- Includes limestone and shale

Igneous
- Forms from ❶ ______________
- Includes granite and pumice

Metamorphic
- Forms from other rocks due to intense ❷ ______________
- Includes soapstone and slate

The rock cycle
- ❸ ______________ hardens ➡ metamorphic rock
- erosion breaks down the rock ➡ sedimentary rock
- Heat and pressure ➡ metamorphic rock
- The volcano erupts ➡ the metamorphic rock becomes lava

B Complete the following summary by using the words in the box.

three types of rocks	forms sedimentary rock	heat and pressure
a volcano erupts	becomes lava	the rock cycle

The professor says that there are ＿＿＿＿＿＿＿＿＿＿＿. Sedimentary rocks are formed from sediment while igneous rocks are volcanic. Metamorphic rocks form when ＿＿＿＿＿＿＿＿＿＿＿ change other types of rocks. Then, the professor talks about ＿＿＿＿＿＿＿＿＿. ＿＿＿＿＿＿＿＿＿＿＿, and lava comes out and then hardens. Over time, the rock is eroded and breaks down into sediment. The sediment combines and ＿＿＿＿＿＿＿＿＿＿＿. It is then pushed down into the ground, where it becomes metamorphic rock. Then, the volcano erupts, and the metamorphic rock melts and ＿＿＿＿＿＿＿＿＿＿＿.

Dictation Exercise Listen to the lecture again and fill in the blanks.

W Professor: We all know that there are ＿＿＿＿＿＿＿＿＿＿＿ rocks. They are sedimentary rocks, igneous rocks, and metamorphic rocks. Sedimentary rocks are formed when sediment ＿＿＿＿＿＿＿＿＿＿＿ over the course of many years and forms rocks. Limestone and shale are ＿＿＿＿＿＿＿＿＿＿＿ of sedimentary rocks. Igneous rocks are ＿＿＿＿＿＿＿＿＿＿＿. You know, uh, they form when ＿＿＿＿＿＿＿＿＿＿＿. Volcanoes eject lava, which ＿＿＿＿＿＿＿＿＿＿＿ over time. Granite and pumice are both volcanic rocks. Metamorphic rocks form when other types of rocks are transformed through intense ＿＿＿＿＿＿＿＿＿＿＿. Marble is a kind of metamorphic rock, and so are soapstone and slate.

Now, uh, ＿＿＿＿＿＿＿＿＿＿＿ is that there is something called the rock cycle. You see, rocks ＿＿＿＿＿＿＿＿＿＿＿ change. These changes may occur over the course of millions of years, but ＿＿＿＿＿＿＿＿＿＿＿. Here, uh, let me give you an example of how ＿＿＿＿＿＿＿＿＿＿＿.

A volcano erupts, and ＿＿＿＿＿＿＿＿＿＿＿ onto the ground. ＿＿＿＿＿＿＿＿＿＿＿, the hot lava cools off and hardens, becoming igneous rock. Well, as time passes, the igneous rocks are ＿＿＿＿＿＿＿＿＿＿＿ by the weather. The wind and the rain both combine to break down the rock into ＿＿＿＿＿＿＿＿＿＿＿ sediment. This sediment ＿＿＿＿＿＿＿＿＿＿＿ and is buried by other rocks and soil. Over time, the sediment ＿＿＿＿＿＿＿＿＿＿＿, becoming rock. This is sedimentary rock. Millions of more years may pass, and the sedimentary rock ＿＿＿＿＿＿＿＿＿＿＿ more layers of rock and soil. It ＿＿＿＿＿＿＿＿＿＿＿ farther into the ground. The pressure and the heat increase, ＿＿＿＿＿＿＿＿＿＿＿ the sedimentary rock into metamorphic rock. Later, when the volcano erupts again, the metamorphic rock melts and ＿＿＿＿＿＿＿＿＿＿＿, which goes back up to the surface, and the cycle starts ＿＿＿＿＿＿＿＿＿＿＿.

02-13

Economics

1 Why does the professor explain how a publishing company can profit?

   Ⓐ To claim that most publishers prefer bestsellers

   Ⓑ To give an example of the trickle-down effect

   Ⓒ To say that it will make more than its writers

   Ⓓ To argue that most publishers are not profitable

2 What does the professor imply about the trickle-down effect?

   Ⓐ It is extremely prominent in the publishing industry.

   Ⓑ It is not accepted by the majority of economists.

   Ⓒ It has become a popular theory in recent times.

   Ⓓ It can help many people and companies make money.

📖 Words & Phrases

abstract adj difficult to understand

economy n the overall interaction of financial information and exchange

mark-up n an increase in price over what was paid for a product

premise n a basis

✏ Summary Note

A Fill in the blanks with the appropriate words.

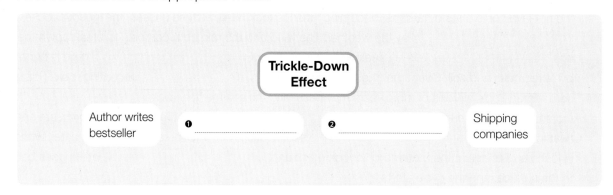

Trickle-Down Effect

Author writes bestseller

❶ _____

❷ _____

Shipping companies

B Complete the following summary by using the words in the box.

profit from the book	the book	of one business
bestselling novel	debated economic theory	

The trickle-down effect is a _____. It concerns how the actions _____ can affect many others in a country's economy. An example of how this theory works can be an author who writes a _____. The author will make money off _____. Other companies that will _____ are the publisher, the booksellers, and the shippers.

Dictation Exercise   Listen to the lecture again and fill in the blanks.

M1 Professor: The next topic we have to discuss is the trickle-down effect. Now this is a theory that has been _____ in economic circles. It's _____, but maybe we can figure it out together. Now, _____ the trickle-down effect? Yes?

W Student: Okay, I'm not sure about this, but I think the _____ is that by large businesses doing well and making profits, everybody else does well, too. I mean, because the businesses _____ throughout the economy.

M1: Absolutely right. Now, it is still quite _____. So we're going to use an example that isn't quite the same, but it'll help us _____ the trickle-down effect. Okay. So _____ we have an author. This author writes _____. Of course, the author will _____. But who else makes money? Any ideas?

M2 Student: Um . . . the publishing company?

M1: Definitely. The publishing company will also make a lot of money because it will be _____ of the book. All right, who else will make money?

W: The booksellers will definitely make money off a bestseller. They charge a _____, right?

M1: Right again. If a book is in _____, and most bestsellers are, the booksellers can make a profit because of the mark-up price. They pay a certain amount of money to _____ for the books. Then, they _____ more. That way, they're making a profit. Let me see . . . Another industry that _____ from an author writing a bestseller is _____. The books have to get from the publishing house _____. So shipping companies would _____ from that and profit. Anyway, are there any questions about this?

02-14

Film

1 Why does the professor explain how the crank camera worked?

Ⓐ To compare it with the motorized camera

Ⓑ To describe why films in the past were so long

Ⓒ To discuss filmmaking techniques in the past

Ⓓ To point out why it often broke down

2 How were special effects created before the 1930s?

Ⓐ The cameraman would change the pace he was advancing the film.

Ⓑ The cameraman would change the height of the tripod the camera was on.

Ⓒ The cameraman would add another reel onto the camera.

Ⓓ The cameraman would add a motor to the camera.

📖 Words & Phrases

crank Ⓥ to move by winding

motorize Ⓥ to equip with a motor

pace Ⓝ a rate of movement

popular ⓐⓓⓙ commonly liked or approved

reel Ⓝ a revolving device around which something is wound

📝 Summary Note

A Fill in the blanks with the appropriate words.

> **Filmmaking Pre-1930s**

> **Camera**
> - Crank camera: not motorized camera

> **Technique**
> - Camera on tripod
> - Crank handle to
>   ❶ _____
> - Change crank pace for
>   ❷ _____

> **Reel**
> - Single reel till before World War I
> - Double-reel around 1914: cinema icon

B Complete the following summary by using the words in the box.

advance the film	on a single reel	two types of cameras
easier to carry	alter the pace	before the 1930s

Filmmaking _____ used _____ : motorized
cameras and crank cameras. Filmmakers generally used crank cameras because they
were _____ . The cameramen would turn the handle on them to
_____ . This was difficult and took a lot of practice. When a cameraman
mastered this skill, he could _____ to make special effects. During most of this
era, films were shot _____ . Then, just before 1914, the double-reel process
was introduced. This is where the double-reel film icon comes from.

Dictation Exercise Listen to the lecture again and fill in the blanks.

M Professor: Today, we're going to talk about how _____ before the
1930s. Before the 1930s, most filmmaking was done using what were called crank cameras.
There were _____ cameras back then. There were motorized cameras and
_____ . When using crank cameras, a person had to crank the film forward
_____ . Motorized cameras would _____ automatically. But
the motors on these cameras were so _____ that they were really hard to carry
around. Instead, filmmakers used _____ .

   How these crank cameras worked was the cameraman would either _____
or have the camera on a tripod. Just so you know, women didn't make films during this era,
so we can call the person _____ a cameraman. The cameraman
would _____ at the scene he was trying to record. Then, he would
_____ on the camera to advance the film. Now, this process could be
_____ . The cameraman had to crank the handle _____ so
that the movie didn't seem rushed or delayed, which took _____ . But once the
cameraman had mastered this skill, he could _____ to make special effects. For
example, _____ could decrease the number of cranks for a scene. This would
make the actions on film look rushed and _____ .

   In addition, _____ of this time, films were shot on a single reel. This meant
most films were pretty short—fifteen to twenty minutes usually. Then, right before the First World
War, which started in 1914, _____ the double-reel process. This allowed
for _____ . This was also where the icon of the double-reel camera that
_____ comes from.

02-15

Music

1 Why does the professor explain Duke Ellington's contributions?

ⓐ To state why jazz music is popular in many countries

ⓑ To claim that he was not as important as people think

ⓒ To compare them with those of other jazz musicians

ⓓ To show how much he influenced jazz music

2 What does the professor say about "Take the 'A' Train"?

ⓐ Few people know it today.

ⓑ It is a famous song.

ⓒ It is about life in Los Angeles.

ⓓ It is a rock song.

📙 **Words & Phrases**

gig ⓝ an entertainer's engagement

hotspot ⓝ a place that is popular for entertainment or vacations

✏️ Summary Note

A Fill in the blanks with the appropriate words.

Duke Ellington

Birth
• Born in North Carolina

❶ _____ , Harlem
• First major gig, weekly radio show

Contributions
• Took jazz ❷ _____
• Wrote and recorded many songs ("Take the 'A' Train")

B Complete the following summary by using the words in the box.

famous	jazz musician	the Cotton Club
all around the world	his first big gig	most famous jazz club

Duke Ellington was a famous _____ from the early twentieth century.
He was born in North Carolina and got _____ in New York City at
_____. This gig made him _____. It also made
the Cotton Club the _____ in Harlem. Ellington and his band traveled
_____. His most famous song is called "Take the 'A' Train."

Dictation Exercise Listen to the lecture again and fill in the blanks.

W1 Professor: Now that we know a bit about jazz music, I'm going to talk about
_____. Personally, I think there's _____ to start than with one
of my favorites, Duke Ellington. He was born in North Carolina, but he didn't _____
till he moved to . . . Does anyone know?

M Student: New York City! He played in Harlem, right?

W1: That's right. Duke Ellington got his first New York City gig at the Cotton Club in Harlem. Harlem
was _____ for up-and-coming music and musicians back then. That's where
Duke Ellington started to _____. So _____ at the Cotton
Club, Duke Ellington got a weekly radio show. And that _____ everywhere.
Then, _____ famous individuals started to go to the Cotton Club as well. This
made the Cotton Club the most famous _____ in Harlem. The Duke made
_____ to jazz. First of all, he brought jazz music to _____
the world. His band _____ around the world. Secondly, he wrote and recorded
_____. Can anyone name any famous Duke Ellington songs?

W2 Student: Um . . . "Take the 'A' Train."

W1: Yes. "Take the 'A' Train" is probably his _____. It's about
_____ you take in New York City to get up to Harlem and the Cotton Club. Some
of the Duke's other famous songs are "Rockin' in Rhythm," "Satin Doll," "New Orleans," and "Crescendo
in Blue."

Integrated Listening & Speaking

A Listen to the previous lecture on geology and say the answers out loud by using the cue sentence words that are indicated in each answer. You can refer to the summary note below.

02 - 16

Geology

✎ **Summary Note**

Sedimentary
- Forms from sediment
- Includes limestone and shale

Types of Rocks

Igneous
- Forms from volcanic eruptions
- Includes granite and pumice

Metamorphic
- Forms from other rocks due to intense heat and pressure
- Includes soapstone and slate

The rock cycle
- Lava hardens ➡ metamorphic rock
- Erosion breaks down the rock ➡ sedimentary rock
- Heat and pressure ➡ metamorphic rock
- The volcano erupts ➡ the metamorphic rock becomes lava

1 What is this lecture about?

   a. The purpose of this lecture is _____.

   b. The topic of this lecture is _____.

2 What is the rock cycle?

   a. The rock cycle shows how _____.

   b. It is the way that _____.

3 When does rock become metamorphic rock?

   a. It becomes metamorphic rock when it is _____.

   b. That happens when it is underground and is _____.

B Listen to the previous lecture on film and say the answers out loud by using the cue sentence words that are indicated in each answer. You can refer to the summary note below.

Film

🖉 **Summary Note**

Filmmaking Pre-1930s

Camera
- Crank camera: not motorized camera

Technique
- Camera on tripod
- Crank handle to advance film Change crank pace for special effects

Reel
- Single reel till before World War I
- Double-reel around 1914: cinema icon

1 What does the professor discuss in the lecture?

    a. The professor explains _____ .

    b. The lecture is about _____ .

2 Why didn't early filmmakers use motorized cameras?

    a. Filmmakers didn't use _____ .

    b. Filmmakers preferred _____ .

3 How did cameramen create special effects?

    a. Cameramen created special effects by _____ .

    b. Special effects were created by _____ .

Listen to part of a conversation between a student and a librarian.

02-18

1 Why does the student visit the librarian?

    Ⓐ To renew some books that he has

    Ⓑ To turn in a book that is overdue

    Ⓒ To learn how to recall a book

    Ⓓ To ask about checking out books

2 According to the woman, how long can students check out books for?

    Ⓐ One week

    Ⓑ Two weeks

    Ⓒ Four weeks

    Ⓓ Two months

3 Why does the woman explain the library's renewal policy?

    Ⓐ To explain how to renew books online

    Ⓑ To tell the student about library fines

    Ⓒ To emphasize how difficult the process is

    Ⓓ To remind the student to renew his books soon

4 What is the woman's attitude toward the student?

    Ⓐ She speaks somewhat impolitely to him.

    Ⓑ She is friendly and helpful to him.

    Ⓒ She is unwilling to answer his questions.

    Ⓓ She believes the student is a hard worker.

5 What will the student probably do next?

    Ⓐ Make some photocopies

    Ⓑ Check out some books

    Ⓒ Recall a book from another user

    Ⓓ Search for a book he needs

Listen to part of a lecture in a biology class.

02- 19

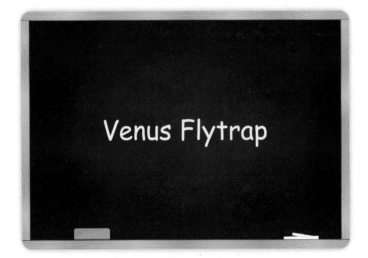

6 What aspect of the Venus flytrap does the professor mainly discuss?

(A) How it grows

(B) How it gets nutrients

(C) Where it lives

(D) How it reproduces

7 According to the professor, what does the Venus flytrap usually eat?
Click on 2 answers.

(A) Lizards

(B) Spiders

(C) Birds

(D) Insects

8 What purpose do the hairs on the Venus flytrap serve?

(A) They catch animals on the plant.

(B) They help the plant grow larger.

(C) They tell the trap when to shut.

(D) They keep rain out of the trap.

9 What can be inferred about the Venus flytrap?

    (A) It evolved over a period of millions of years.

    (B) It consumes other plants on some occasions.

    (C) It takes a long time to develop seeds.

    (D) It does not need to eat many animals to survive.

10 Why does the professor explain where the Venus flytrap grows?

    (A) To answer a question by one of the students

    (B) To say why it cannot rely on the soil for nutrients

    (C) To point out that many animals live in that place

    (D) To show how it can grow to such a large size

11 What is the professor's opinion of the Venus flytrap?

    (A) It is not a very attractive plant.

    (B) It has a unique way of getting nutrients.

    (C) It is the most successful plant he knows.

    (D) It is an ideal houseplant for people.

Vocabulary Check-Up

A Choose the correct words that match the definitions.

1 eligible	•	• Ⓐ	a three-legged stand
2 abroad	•	• Ⓑ	very strong; powerful
3 dibs	•	• Ⓒ	net gains minus expenses
4 transform	•	• Ⓓ	as if done by a machine; mostly involuntary
5 automatically	•	• Ⓔ	a more favorable option
6 profit	•	• Ⓕ	based on general ideas rather than specific examples
7 intense	•	• Ⓖ	beyond the boundaries of one's country
8 financial	•	• Ⓗ	relating to money
9 preference	•	• Ⓘ	a term into which an academic year is divided
10 abstract	•	• Ⓙ	a claim or right
11 semester	•	• Ⓚ	exact
12 precise	•	• Ⓛ	to change
13 shift	•	• Ⓜ	the time when a person works at a job
14 shame	•	• Ⓝ	a strong feeling of regret
15 tripod	•	• Ⓞ	qualified to participate or be chosen

B Complete the sentences by filling in the blanks with the words in the box.

Ⓐ lava   Ⓑ scholarship   Ⓒ application   Ⓓ erode   Ⓔ abroad

1 He hopes to win a(n) _____ to pay his tuition next year.

2 The wind can _____ even large rocks over time.

3 Fill out this _____ in order to become a member.

4 She hopes to study _____ in Europe next year.

5 The volcano erupted, so _____ came down its sides.

Listening for Major Details

Overview

Introduction

In detail questions, you must understand and remember explicit details or facts from a lecture or conversation. These details are typically related to the main idea of the text by giving examples and by elaborating on a topic or many other supporting statements. Questions are mostly asked about major details in the conversation or lecture, not minor ones.

Question Types

▶ According to the professor, what is one way that X can affect Y?

▶ What are X?

▶ What resulted from the invention of the X?

▶ According to the professor, what is the main problem with the X theory?

Useful Tips

■ No question type needs note taking more than detail questions. Make most of your notes about details.

■ Listen carefully to the major details of the conversation or lecture, not the minor ones.

■ The answer to a detail question is mostly written in paraphrased sentence form from the text.

■ If you are not sure of the correct response, decide which one of the choices is the most consistent with the main idea of the conversation or lecture.

Script

03-01

M1 Professor: Boiling water on a portable stove or fire will kill most bacteria and viruses. Another option is to be sure you carry a portable pump filter. But in this case, you have to disinfect the water with a third method. Who can tell me what a third might be?

M2 Student: How about electricity?

M1: No, actually, I was thinking of a couple of chemicals. One is iodine, which kills many, but not all, of the most common, uh, pathogens in natural fresh water sources. Second, used only in emergency situations, is chlorine-based bleach. Just add two drops of five-percent bleach per quart of clear water and let it stand, uh, covered, for about an hour. All right, that is three so far. Would anyone like to take a stab at the last option?

W Student: Uh, sunshine?

M1: Bonus points for whoever said that in the back row. Yes, sunlight is another valid option. We call it solar purification. Water is placed in a transparent plastic bottle, which is oxygenated by shaking. It is placed in full sun for six hours, which raises the temperature and gives an extended dose of solar radiation, killing any microbes that may be present.

Q According to the professor, what can sunlight do to water?

- Ⓐ It can oxygenate water.
- Ⓑ It can kill small living things.
- Ⓒ It can boil water.
- Ⓓ It can disinfect water.

 **Correct Answer**

The correct answer to the above question is Ⓑ. The word microbe means a very small living thing.

Basic Drill

Listen to parts of conversations or lectures and answer the questions.

Drill 1

Q What happened to the student's purse?

    Ⓐ Someone stole it.

    Ⓑ She left it in her room.

    Ⓒ She lost it.

    Ⓓ She let a friend borrow it.

03- 02

Check-Up Listen again and circle the words you hear.

problem	kidding	door	entrance
passport	building	follow	roommate
forgot	locked	credit cards	excuse me

Drill 2

Q What is the topic of the student's paper?

    Ⓐ American economics

    Ⓑ American history

    Ⓒ American federalism

    Ⓓ American archaeology

03- 03

Check-Up Listen again and circle the words you hear.

good points	newspaper	paper	advanced degree
published	exam	federalism	grade
graduate	editor	homework	scholarship

Drill 3

Q Why does the student say he will miss orientation?

    Ⓐ He has to do his part-time job.

    Ⓑ He needs to fix his schedule.

    Ⓒ He will be with his family.

    Ⓓ He is planning to take a trip.

03- 04

Check-Up Listen again and circle the words you hear.

roommate	nine o'clock	teachers	mandatory
schedule	clubs	cancel	room assignment
professors	business trip	library	orientation

Q According to the lecture, what did Kennedy agree to in secret?

- (A) Avoid invading Cuba
- (B) Cease plans to attack the Soviet Union
- (C) Decrease the number of American missiles
- (D) Remove American missiles from Turkey

03- 05

Check-Up Listen again and circle the words you hear.

Cold War	nuclear	disadvantage	tension
tank	promise	promote	Russia
Caribbean	bomb	Turkey	blockade

Q According to the professor, what was the top of the Empire State Building originally planned to be?

- (A) A five-star restaurant
- (B) An observation tower
- (C) A dock for airships
- (D) A radio station

03- 06

Check-Up Listen again and circle the words you hear.

wonder	taller	transition	market
skyscraper	shadows	Boston	airplane
building	collapse	business	design

Q Where did the original settlers in America come from?
Click on 2 answers.

- (A) Italy
- (B) Germany
- (C) France
- (D) Ireland

03- 07

Check-Up Listen again and circle the words you hear.

border patrol	foreign	Mexican	St. Patrick's Day
immigration	security	pubs	movies
immigrants	melting pot	culture	German

Exercises with Mid-Length Conversations

Exercise 1 Listen to part of a conversation and answer the questions.

03-08

Office Hours

1   Why does the student need an extension on her paper?
   Ⓐ Her other classes are keeping her busy.
   Ⓑ She has not started writing it yet.
   Ⓒ The paper is too hard to write.
   Ⓓ Her sister is getting married.

2   What problem does the student mention?
   Ⓐ Her outline was never approved by her professor.
   Ⓑ Two sources she requested have not arrived yet.
   Ⓒ The topic she selected is not interesting to her.
   Ⓓ She has not had time to start writing the paper.

📖 Words & Phrases

extension ⓝ an increase in an amount of time
incomplete ⓐⓓⱼ not finished
majority ⓝ most
source ⓝ a supplier of information
grant ⓥ to allow or give, especially a favor

📝 Summary Note

A   Fill in the blanks with the appropriate words.

The student needs an extension on her term paper
- Her sister is ❶ ....
- She is still ❷ ....

The professor will give a one-week extension
- The student must email her paper and outline by tomorrow

B   Complete the following summary by using the words in the box.

finish the paper	mostly written	her outline
her term paper	getting married	two more books

The student asks for an extension on _____ . Her sister is
_____ , and she does not have time to _____ before the
deadline. The professor wonders how much work the student has done so far. The professor says
that the paper is _____ , but she is waiting for _____
from the library to finish. The professor tells her to email what she has written and
_____ by tomorrow, and she will get a one-week extension.

Dictation Exercise   Listen to the conversation again and fill in the blanks.

M Professor: Hi, Susan. You wanted to speak to me about something?

W Student: Yes, I was wondering if I could talk to you about _____ in two weeks.

M: Sure. _____ ?

W: My sister is _____ next weekend, and I'm the maid of honor, so this week is
_____ . I was wondering if I could _____ on the term paper.

M: How much do you _____ ? With a paper this size, I would expect that you
would have _____ taken care of by now.

W: I have taken care of _____ . The delay has been in _____ .
I needed to request them from a library _____ , and it is taking a really
long time for them to get here. I requested the books _____ . And they're
_____ to my paper. I just feel that it _____ without those
sources.

M: So when do you expect _____ ?

W: According to the library, they should be here tomorrow. But I _____ to go
through them until next week.

M: Well, if you turn in your outline and your paper as it is tomorrow in class, I can grant you a
_____ .

W: Thanks so much! But _____ .

M: What problem?

W: Well, tomorrow I have to meet my sister _____ . I am going to leave at 6:00 AM,
so _____ all my classes tomorrow. What can I do?

M: In that case, why don't you _____ the paper and the outline? You should have
_____ because I put it on the class syllabus.

W: Ah, okay. I can do that. Thanks.

03-09

Service Encounter

1 What does the student want to do in his room?
- (A) He wants to hang up some paintings.
- (B) He wants to put a new lock on the door.
- (C) He wants to paint it a different color.
- (D) He wants to change some of the furniture.

2 What does the employee think the student should do?
- (A) Put up posters and wall hangings
- (B) Speak with her supervisor
- (C) Move to a different dormitory
- (D) Pay a fee to have the room painted

📖 **Words & Phrases**

approve (v) to accept
effort (n) hard work
process (n) a series of actions to an end
protocol (n) a standard procedure; predetermined actions to perform after an event

✏️ Summary Note

A Fill in the blanks with the appropriate words.

Approval can take a long time

The student wants to paint his room

The student decides
❷ ....

Most students
❶ ....

B Complete the following summary by using the words in the box.

approved	up to a month	his dorm room
wall hangings	might be easier	to paint it

The student does not like the color of _____. He wants

_____ a different color. The housing office employee says he must get the

paint choice _____ by the Housing Department. This process can take

_____. According to the woman, most students just put up posters and

_____ instead. The student thinks that that _____ to

do.

Dictation Exercise Listen to the conversation again and fill in the blanks.

M Student: Excuse me. May I ask you a question?

W Housing Office Employee: Sure. How can I help you?

M: I was just wondering _____ this dorm is.

W: _____. It was built the same year that _____.

M: Well, I was wondering what the protocol for _____ is. Right now, it's a gross

pale green color, and I just want to _____.

W: I _____ your wanting to repaint your room. But you have to

_____ by the Housing Department. And you also have to repaint it

_____ at the end of the year.

M: Really? That's _____. Why do I need to _____?

W: We just need to make sure you're using paint _____. You know, it should be

_____.

M: Oh, well _____. How long does that process _____?

W: Depending on _____, it can take up to a month.

M: Really? That's _____ for an eight-month stay.

W: Yeah, it is. Most students _____ putting up wall hangings and posters. It saves

a lot of _____. And there isn't nearly as much _____ around

that.

M: Yeah, I can understand that. I _____ doing the same thing.

W: It's certainly a _____.

M: Yeah, I guess I'll try that. Can I _____ with the Housing Department and

then cancel later if the posters look okay? If they don't look good, then I will have already started

_____.

W: I don't _____ with that. It's a good idea. _____.

M: Okay. Thanks for your help.

03-10

Office Hours

1 What would the student like to do after graduating?

    Ⓐ Attend graduate school

    Ⓑ Do some volunteer work

    Ⓒ Find employment

    Ⓓ Travel to another country

2 What does the professor suggest that the student do?
Click on 2 answers.

    Ⓐ Keep his current major

    Ⓑ Speak with another professor

    Ⓒ Try to get a double major

    Ⓓ Attend summer school

📖 Words & Phrases

option 🄝 a choice

requirement 🄝 something that is necessary or must be done

seminar 🄝 an advanced class that usually involves discussion and independent research

advisor 🄝 a teacher or professor who advises students on academic matters

---

✏️ Summary Note

A Fill in the blanks with the appropriate words.

The student is thinking about his future

Wants to ❶ _____ after he graduates

No longer interested in majoring in ❷ _____

Can change his history minor to a major ➡ needs to talk to a professor in the History Department

B   Complete the following summary by using the words in the box.

minor in history	attend graduate school	summer school classes
stop doing economics	change majors	in the future

The student is not sure what he wants to do _____. He does not want to _____, but he would prefer to find a job. However, he does not like his major anymore, so he wants to _____. The professor thinks it may be too late to _____ since the student will be a senior next semester. However, the student can change his _____ to a major by taking five more classes. The professor suggests taking _____ and talking to a professor in the History Department.

Dictation Exercise   Listen to the conversation again and fill in the blanks.

M Student: Professor Waddle, do you _____ to speak to me?

W Professor: Of course, Pierre. I _____ for one of my best students. What's up?

M: As you know, I'm going to be _____ next semester. I've been thinking about my future, but I'm not really sure _____.

W: Have you thought about _____?

M: I'm _____ in that. I'd prefer to _____.

W: Okay. Your major in Economics, so you have _____. You could work at a bank or _____ financial institution.

M: Yeah, but that's the problem. I don't actually _____ anymore, and I don't think I want to do anything related to economics in the future.

W: I see . . . Well, it's _____ to change majors unless you want to stay here for a fifth year.

M: That's a good point. But I'm also _____ in history. I checked the requirements, and I might be able to change the major into a minor.

W: How _____ would you have to take?

M: Five more, _____.

W: That's possible, but you should _____ this summer and take a history class or two then.

M: That's a good idea. Should I talk to someone in the History Department as well?

W: Definitely. You'll _____ there if you're going to change your major.

Listen to part of a conversation and answer the questions.

03- 11

Office Hours

1 How does the professor suggest the student improve his writing? Click on 2 answers.

Ⓐ He needs to use more description.

Ⓑ He needs to make the main character talk more.

Ⓒ He should have more characters.

Ⓓ He should include more action scenes.

2 What does the professor say about *The Lord of the Rings*?

Ⓐ It was written by a great author.

Ⓑ It is a series about good and evil.

Ⓒ It is her favorite series.

Ⓓ It has many unique characters.

📖 **Words & Phrases**

balanced adj even; not relying on one thing

unique adj different

📝 **Summary Note**

A Fill in the blanks with the appropriate words.

The professor comments on the student's writing assignment	The main character ❶ _____
	The other characters ❷ _____
	The story needs more characters

B Complete the following summary by using the words in the box.

talk more	main character	like in a play
more characters	come to life	creative writing assignment

The professor tells the student why his _____ is not good. She says that
the _____ talks so much that the story is _____ .
He needs to have more description. In addition, he must make the other characters
_____ . They do not talk enough. She uses the example of *The Lord of the
Rings* to tell him he needs _____ and, through their words, make them
_____ .

Dictation Exercise Listen to the conversation again and fill in the blanks.

W Professor: Tim, may I _____ of your time, please?

M Student: Of course. What can I do for you?

W: I want to talk about _____ .

M: Really? Did you like it?

W: Well, the story was okay, and our class is a _____ , but there is a lot of
_____ .

M: Oh . . . Okay. What did _____ ?

W: First of all, your story was _____ . Your main character talks
_____ . At times, I thought I was reading a play. Do you know why?

M: No.

W: Because in a play, the writer only writes what people say and _____ about their
actions, and then the actors do the rest. Are you _____ ?

M: No, I wasn't. I just . . .

W: Remember that you need to _____ . Tell me what is going on. For example,
_____ says, "What a wonderful tree." I know it was a wonderful tree because he
says so, but tell me why it was a wonderful tree. _____ to me.

M: Ah, okay. Is there anything else?

W: Yes, there is. I believe that only _____ talks. The others don't
_____ . Let everyone else _____ . You might want to add
some more characters, too.

M: Yes, ma'am, I understand. _____ by the main character.

W: Your _____ is *The Lord of the Rings*, right? Do you know one reason why
_____ by people? One reason is that the author made _____ .
They all participate in the action, and they all make their own _____ . That is what
you _____ .

Exercises with Mid-Length Lectures

Exercise 1 Listen to part of a lecture and answer the questions.

03-12

History

1   When did Abraham Lincoln deliver the Gettysburg Address?
   - Ⓐ Immediately after the Battle of Gettysburg
   - Ⓑ Six months after the Battle of Gettysburg
   - Ⓒ Six months before the Civil War began
   - Ⓓ Long after the Civil War ended

2   What was the Gettysburg Address about?
   - Ⓐ The differences between the Union states and the Confederate states
   - Ⓑ The war between the Union States and the Confederate States
   - Ⓒ The events of the Battle of Gettysburg
   - Ⓓ The importance of freedom in the nation

📕 Words & Phrases

shift 🅥 to change
nation 🅝 a country
union 🅝 something that is made by combining parts
content 🅝 the topic of a written work
Confederate States 🅝 the government of the rebelling forces during the American Civil War

✏️ Summary Note

A Fill in the blanks with the appropriate words.

The Gettysburg Address

What
- Speech given by
  ❶ ....

When/Where
- Six months after the Battle of Gettysburg during the Civil War
- At the ❷ .... at Gettysburg

Content
- Importance of
  ❸ ....
  in the nation

B Complete the following summary by using the words in the box.

that battle was fought	famous speech	on the battleground
either side	in the nation	very important

The Gettysburg Address was a _____ given by President Abraham Lincoln. He gave this speech _____ at Gettysburg half a year after _____. The Gettysburg Address is famous mostly because of its content. In this address, Lincoln talked about the importance of freedom _____. The language he used was _____. The reason is that he did not exclude soldiers from _____ of the war.

Dictation Exercise Listen to the lecture again and fill in the blanks.

M1 Professor: Since we've been talking about the Civil War _____, it's about time for us to talk about another important thing related to it. We're going to _____ a bit and talk about the Gettysburg Address. Who can tell me _____ the Gettysburg Address?

W Student: That's easy. Everyone knows it was Abraham Lincoln.

M1: That's right. President Lincoln gave the Gettysburg Address. Now who can tell me when he _____ ?

M2 Student: Didn't he _____ after the Battle of Gettysburg? I think the week _____, right?

M1: No, not quite. I know _____ that he would give the Gettysburg Address soon after the Battle of Gettysburg, but actually, he gave it _____ after the Battle of Gettysburg was fought. Lincoln made the speech _____ at Gettysburg. That's why it's called the Gettysburg Address. Now there are _____ why this speech is famous. Probably the most important reason is _____. Lincoln spoke about the _____ in the nation. One thing that _____ is that whenever he talked about the United States, he called it a "nation," not a "union." Can anyone tell me why _____ is important?

M2: Well, probably because he wanted to make it a point _____ the Confederate States. By saying "nation," he was _____ that the Union states and the Confederate states were both part of _____. That country was formed by _____, and they're all basically the same people.

M1: Excellent. That's exactly right. By talking about everyone as a nation, he made sure to include everyone who was _____. This helped motivate the North as well as welcome back the South after the war.

Exercise 2 Listen to part of a lecture and answer the questions.

03-13

Architecture

1 What does the professor say about the Roman Empire?

Ⓐ It was larger than the Ottoman Empire.

Ⓑ It had an effect on the founding of the Ottoman Empire.

Ⓒ It covered the same territory as the Ottoman Empire.

Ⓓ It was defeated by the Ottoman Empire.

2 Which structures did Ottoman architecture popularize?
Click on 2 answers.

Ⓐ Arches

Ⓑ Domes

Ⓒ Vaults

Ⓓ Columns

📖 Words & Phrases

empire Ⓝ a political unit that encompasses many different peoples

mosque Ⓝ a place of worship for Muslims

splendid adj grand

vault Ⓝ an arched structure that forms a ceiling or roof

✏️ Summary Note

A Fill in the blanks with the appropriate words.

**Turkish Architecture
(Ottoman Architecture)**

General
- Ottoman Empire: 1300 to 1920
- Architecture: fourteenth and fifteenth centuries

Structures
- ❶ _____, vaults, semi-domes, and columns

Mosques
- Before Ottomans: big, open, dull spaces
- After Ottomans: ❷ _____

B Complete the following summary by using the words in the box.

architecture	plain and boring	use of
lasted from	to create	very lovely

Turkish architecture usually means Ottoman architecture. The Ottoman Empire
_____ 1300 to 1920, and its _____ flourished during
the fourteenth and fifteenth centuries. The Ottomans popularized the _____
domes, vaults, and semi-domes. What the Ottomans mostly used these structures for was
_____ beautiful mosques. Before the Ottomans, mosques were really
_____. Afterward, they were _____ in appearance.

Dictation Exercise Listen to the lecture again and fill in the blanks.

W1 Professor: _____ in our discussion on architecture and cover Turkey.
Now, Turkey was _____ of the Ottoman Empire, so when we talk about Turkish
architecture from a long time ago, we are _____ Ottoman architecture. Who can
tell me _____ the Ottoman Empire lasted from?

W2 Student: I am not sure, but didn't it start about 500 B.C. and fall about 500 A.D.?

W1: You're thinking of the Roman Empire, which did play a huge role in _____ the
Ottoman Empire, but that is not correct. Anyone else?

M Student: It lasted _____, didn't it? From about 1300 to 1920, didn't it?

W1: Yes, _____. But the architecture of the Ottoman Empire flourished during the
fourteenth and fifteenth centuries. Who can tell me some of _____ of Ottoman
architecture?

W2: It _____ domes, didn't it?

W1: Yes, it did. The Ottomans actually made the dome a _____ architectural
structure. Okay, anyone else?

M: Um . . . I think I read something about vaults.

W1: Great. Vaults are very much Ottoman _____. In addition to domes and
vaults, the Ottomans also used a lot of _____. Now, if you'll remember, the
Greeks _____ the column. But it's such a _____ that
many groups of people have used it throughout history. What the Ottomans did with these structures is
that they used them to make mosques _____. Before the Ottomans, mosques
were usually big, open, and _____. But the Ottomans designed mosques
_____ in appearance. You _____ of their mosques all
around Turkey.

M: I heard that their houses _____ on the roof. Is that correct?

W1: It is correct, but we will talk about that next week.

Exercise 3 **Listen to part of a lecture and answer the questions.**

03-14

Sociology

1   According to the professor, when did Spain control New Orleans?

   ⓐ Starting in the 1600s

   ⓑ After the French and Indian War

   ⓒ At the time when President Jefferson bought it

   ⓓ After the English influence on it ended

2   Why is the United States a melting pot?

   ⓐ All the different immigrants mix together to create something new.

   ⓑ It was colonized by England and Spain.

   ⓒ The different immigrants retain their identities but help create a new flavor.

   ⓓ It has different jargon from England.

📖 Words & Phrases

immigrant ⓝ a person that permanently moves to a different country to make a new home

jargon ⓝ special words and expressions that are used by particular groups of people

influx ⓝ an addition

✏️ Summary Note

A   Fill in the blanks with the appropriate words.

French settlement   Unique ❶ _____   Garden salad

New Orleans

Controlled by Spain   Purchased by United States   Immigrants from ❷ _____

B Complete the following summary by using the words in the box.

different from	garden salad	culture of the city
a melting pot	heavily influenced	French influence

Most of the United States is considered _____ because the different immigrants mix together. In the Mississippi River Valley, New Orleans is _____ the rest of the United States. It is a _____. Its different pieces have retained their identities. New Orleans was _____ from its French beginnings. Later, Spanish, American, English, and Latin immigrants all added to the _____. One example of this difference is the jargon. The local jargon has a heavy _____.

Dictation Exercise Listen to the lecture again and fill in the blanks.

W Professor: Last week, we talked about the United States being _____, where all the different immigrants mix together to create something new. Well, everything _____, including our melting pot, right? In the Mississippi River Valley, there is _____ that is part melting pot and part garden salad. In Louisiana, or _____, New Orleans, there have been a few major cultural influences that _____ the rest of the United States. Unlike the rest of the United States, _____ by England and Spain, New Orleans was predominantly a French settlement. It was also a unique _____.

While the rest of the U.S. was a melting pot, mixing all its parts to _____, New Orleans became a garden salad. Right now, you are _____ what I mean by garden salad, aren't you? A garden salad has many parts that are combined to make _____. Each piece retains its _____, but combined, they make something new and hopefully better. This contrasts with the melting pot because in a melting pot, all of the pieces _____ to form something new.

So in New Orleans, there was a _____ with French culture, food, language, and lifestyle. Added in over the centuries was a bit of a Spanish influence, when Spain _____ for about fifty years after the French and Indian War. After that was the American and English influence after President Jefferson _____ from France. And last _____ of Latino culture from Mexico and the Caribbean.

The result now is that New Orleans has a _____ apart from the United States. Because of _____, people from New Orleans have different jargon, such as they say, "I'm making groceries," instead of, "I am grocery shopping." Again, this is due to the French influence. In French, _____ is "to make groceries," not "to buy or go shopping."

Exercise 4 Listen to part of a lecture and answer the questions.

03-15

Communication

1 Why have cellphones made phone conversations faster?

- (A) People do not like using phones in restaurants or other public places.
- (B) Cellphone conversations are considered private, so they are short in public.
- (C) Shorter conversations cost less money.
- (D) People are usually in a hurry when they use their cellphones.

2 What is the lecture mainly about?

- (A) Changes in cellphone technology
- (B) Reasons why people like cellphones
- (C) Where people speak on cellphones
- (D) How technology has affected language

Words & Phrases

evolving adj slowly changing, usually to become better

dominate v to control; to have the most influence

infuse v to add to

chat v to talk about something that is not important

Summary Note

A Fill in the blanks with the appropriate words.

Use them in public

We hurry to
_____

Language Evolving by Cellphones

Changes in privacy

Conversations become
_____

B Complete the following summary by using the words in the box.

how we speak	consider private	evolving language
shortened conversations	without saying bye	once considered private

English is an _____. One way a language can evolve is through technology. Cellphones have changed _____. Cellphones allow us to speak in public places. This has changed what we _____. Many things we discuss in public were _____ and should not be spoken in public. People also talk quickly on cellphones to save money. This has _____. We often do not greet people the same as we did, and we end conversations _____.

Dictation Exercise Listen to the lecture again and fill in the blanks.

M Professor: Let's keep talking about the idea of _____. I talked about how war changes a language because one culture _____ another and infuse aspects of its language into a new language. Now, I will talk about another way a language can change. It is . . . can anyone guess . . .? Technology.

One example is, hmm, a cellphone. Cellphones have changed and _____ the way we communicate with each other. Only fifty years ago, phone conversations were considered _____. For example, if I was at your house, and your phone rang, I would leave the room so that you could have _____. With cellphones, people _____ everywhere. I mean, uh, at restaurants, on dates, umm, and even on public transportation, you can see people _____.

Now people are talking about what _____ in public. We talk about work, people we dislike, our relationships, and our plans in front of _____. The things we now talk about on the phone would have been considered _____ to say in public fifty years ago. Back then, you would be chastised by someone for talking about your _____ or a party you went to the night before.

Um, what else? We are changing _____ as well. We all get _____, so talking on the phone means you are using money. So the faster you talk, the less money you use. This means we often _____ our phone conversations quickly. Before, we would take our time on the phone, ask someone how _____, chit chat for a bit, and then get to the point. We _____ the conversation and often say bye two or three times. Now, we _____ and then maybe say goodbye, and the conversation is over. That would have been _____ only twenty years ago.

Integrated Listening & Speaking

A Listen to the previous lecture on architecture and say the answers out loud by using the cue sentence words that are indicated in each answer. You can refer to the summary note below.

03-16

Architecture

🖊 **Summary Note**

> **Turkish Architecture (Ottoman Architecture)**

General	Structures	Mosques
• Ottoman Empire: 1300 to 1920	• Domes, vaults, semi-domes, and columns	• Before Ottomans: big, open, dull spaces
• Architecture: fourteenth and fifteenth centuries		• After Ottomans: splendid structures

1 What was the biggest influence on Turkish architecture?

 a. The biggest influence on Turkish architecture ....

 b. The Ottoman Empire was ....

2 When was the peak of Ottoman architecture?

 a. The peak of Ottoman architecture was ....

 b. The height of architecture in the Ottoman Empire ....

3 What are some common characteristics of Turkish architecture?

 a. Some common characteristics of Turkish architecture ....

 b. Domes, semi-domes, vaults, and columns ....

B Listen to the previous lecture on sociology and say the answers out loud by using the cue sentence words that are indicated in each answer. You can refer to the summary note below.

03-17

Sociology

✏ **Summary Note**

| French settlement | Unique slave culture | Garden salad |

New Orleans

| Controlled by Spain | Purchased by United States | Immigrants from Latin countries |

1 Why is New Orleans considered a garden salad?

   a. The city has its own culture, and _____ .

   b. The city's culture is made of many pieces _____ .

2 What is meant by the United States being a melting pot?

   a. All of the pieces become _____ .

   b. The pieces no longer have _____ .

3 Why do the people of New Orleans say "making groceries?"

   a. The people of New Orleans say _____ .

   b. Due to their French origins, people in New Orleans say _____ .

Listen to a part of a conversation between a student and a student services center employee.

03- 18

1 What are the speakers mainly discussing?

    Ⓐ Where to get a new car

    Ⓑ Rules for parking on campus

    Ⓒ Life in Minnesota

    Ⓓ Parking lots on campus

2 What can be inferred about the student?

    Ⓐ She is a fourth-year student.

    Ⓑ She just got her driver's license.

    Ⓒ She is from a different state.

    Ⓓ She enjoys driving on campus.

3 Why does the man mention Minnesota?

    Ⓐ To note how much it snows there

    Ⓑ To describe where in the country it is

    Ⓒ To explain a parking regulation

    Ⓓ To point out how many people drive there

4 What kind of parking pass does the man suggest buying?
Click on 2 answers.

    Ⓐ A one-day pass

    Ⓑ A one-month pass

    Ⓒ A one-semester pass

    Ⓓ A one-year pass

5 Listen again to part of the conversation. Then answer the question.
What does the student mean when she says this: 🎧

    Ⓐ She will take the bus to school for a few days.

    Ⓑ She will not drive her car on campus.

    Ⓒ She wants to buy a parking pass now.

    Ⓓ She will not buy a parking pass for a while.

Listen to part of a lecture in a history class.

03-19

6 What is the lecture mainly about?

    (A) Why Europeans liked feudalism

    (B) The collapse of feudalism

    (C) The advantages of feudalism

    (D) An overview of feudalism

7 What did feudalism originate from?
Click on 2 answers.

    (A) Roman law

    (B) English tradition

    (C) Roman fiefs

    (D) Germanic tradition

8 What can be inferred about a feudal lord?

    (A) He was more powerful than a vassal.

    (B) He could only be a king.

    (C) He ruled a small amount of land.

    (D) He paid for fiefs with lots of gold.

9 Why does the professor mention fiefs?

    Ⓐ To explain how much they cost to buy

    Ⓑ To describe what they typically looked like

    Ⓒ To say how many most lords usually owned

    Ⓓ To provide the name of the land vassals got

10 According to the professor, how did lords get soldiers for their armies?

    Ⓐ They had standing armies.

    Ⓑ They made farmers become soldiers.

    Ⓒ They got soldiers from their vassals.

    Ⓓ They hired mercenaries.

11 What is the professor's opinion of feudalism?

    Ⓐ It was a good way to rule.

    Ⓑ It oppressed many people.

    Ⓒ It was fair to lords and vassals.

    Ⓓ It was inefficient.

Vocabulary Check-Up

A Choose the correct words that match the definitions.

1 source • • Ⓐ slowly changing, usually to become better

2 immigrant • • Ⓑ a person that permanently moves to a different country to make a new home

3 extension • • Ⓒ an advanced class that usually involves discussion and independent research

4 jargon • • Ⓓ special words and expressions that are used by particular groups of people

5 splendid • • Ⓔ a supplier of information

6 dominate • • Ⓕ something that is necessary or must be done

7 evolving • • Ⓖ grand

8 chat • • Ⓗ a teacher or professor who advises students on academic matters

9 predominantly • • Ⓘ an increase in a length of time

10 point • • Ⓙ to control or have the most influence

11 balanced • • Ⓚ the main reason or purpose

12 advisor • • Ⓛ mostly

13 seminar • • Ⓜ to talk about something that is not important

14 tiny • • Ⓝ very small

15 requirement • • Ⓞ even; not relying on one thing

B Complete the sentences by filling in the blanks with the words in the box.

Ⓐ published	Ⓑ characteristics	Ⓒ annoying	Ⓓ option	Ⓔ crisis

1 There is an economic _____ going on in that country right now.

2 One of her _____ is that she is incredibly honest.

3 The book will be _____ sometime this spring.

4 It can be _____ when there are loud noises during a test.

5 He chose the first _____ out of the three he was given.

PART II

Pragmatic Understanding

Pragmatic Understanding questions test understanding of certain features that go beyond basic comprehension. Generally, two question types test pragmatic understanding: Function of What Is Said and Speaker's Attitude. Function of What Is Said questions test whether you can understand the underlying intentions of what is said. Speaker's Attitude questions test whether you can understand a speaker's attitude or opinion that has not been directly expressed. Pragmatic Understanding questions typically involve a replay of a small portion of the listening passage.

Understanding the Function of What Is Said

Overview

Introduction

Function of What Is Said questions test whether you can understand the underlying intentions of what is said. The underlying intentions are typically hidden in the context surrounding the text of the question. Frequently, the intentions are acquired by synthesizing the entire text. This question type often involves replaying a portion of the listening passage.

Question Types

▶ What does the professor imply when he says this: (replay)

▶ What can be inferred from the professor's response to the student? (replay)

▶ What is the purpose of the woman's response? (replay)

▶ Why does the student say this: (replay)

Useful Tips

■ Practice reading between the lines.

■ Try to take notes on the context of the lecture or conversation.

■ Refer to the tones the speakers are using in the conversation or lecture.

Script

04-01

M Student: What do you think of the story I just submitted for our creative writing class, Professor Kepler?

W Professor: I only took a quick glance at it since I've been busy. However, it looks like you chose an interesting topic to write about. How did you get interested in time travel?

M: I read a lot of science fiction.

W: Ah, that explains it. Well, I'm looking forward to reading it. I'll return it and the other stories the students turned in sometime next week.

Q Listen again to part of the conversation. Then answer the question.
What can be inferred from the student's response to the professor?

Ⓐ The student wrote a book of science fiction.

Ⓑ Science fiction is popular with university students.

Ⓒ The student dislikes science-fiction movies.

Ⓓ Science fiction features stories on time travel.

✅ Correct Answer

The answer to the above question is Ⓓ. The professor asks how the student came to know about time travel, and he says that he reads a lot of science fiction. It can therefore be inferred that science fiction features stories on time travel.

Basic Drill

Listen to parts of conversations or lectures and answer the questions.

Drill 1

Q Listen again to part of the conversation, Then answer the question.
Why does the employee say this: 🎧

04-02

Ⓐ To explain why the student has a different roommate

Ⓑ To tell the student she must change roommates

Ⓒ To explain that the student used the wrong form

Ⓓ To tell the student how to fill out the form

Check-Up Listen again and circle the words you hear.

roommate	Emerson	room number	loan
class schedule	tuition	professor	class president
registration	extension	tomorrow	wrong with it

Drill 2

Q Listen again to part of the conversation. Then answer the question.
What can be inferred about the professor's response to the student?

04-03

Ⓐ She is not interested in speaking with the student.

Ⓑ The student needs to give her a good excuse.

Ⓒ She allows late work on some occasions.

Ⓓ Students must turn their work in on time.

Check-Up Listen again and circle the words you hear.

extension	part-time job	report	tomorrow
suggestion	midterm exam	policy	test material
tuition	scholarship	homework	cost

Drill 3

Q Listen again to part of the conversation. Then answer the question.
What is the purpose of the student's response?

04-04

Ⓐ To claim that he will fix a problem

Ⓑ To disagree with the professor

Ⓒ To ask the professor to reconsider his opinion

Ⓓ To show his awareness of a problem

Check-Up Listen again and circle the words you hear.

important	wrong with them	word processor	editorial
action verb	understand	grammar	proofread
common problems	study habits	librarian	printing error

Drill 4

Q Listen again to part of the lecture. Then answer the question.
What does the professor imply when he says this: 🎧

04-05

Ⓐ Fruits taste better than vegetables.

Ⓑ Vegetables are not sweet.

Ⓒ Vegetables are plants that have no seeds.

Ⓓ Most people think tomatoes taste good.

Check-Up Listen again and circle the words you hear.

banana	plant	seeds	medicine
juice	sweet	digest	farm
pickle	herb	eaten	root

Drill 5

Q Listen again to part of the lecture. Then answer the question.
What does the professor imply when she says this: 🎧

04-06

Ⓐ Deep water can cause waves to form.

Ⓑ Weather has no effect on deep water.

Ⓒ The surface layer is larger than deep water.

Ⓓ Dense water can be hard to swim in.

Check-Up Listen again and circle the words you hear.

pycnocline	fishing	surface	snow
salt water	deep water	marine	constantly
weather	shallow water	gradual	clouds

Drill 6

Q Listen again to part of the lecture. Then answer the question.
What does the professor imply when he says this: 🎧

04-07

Ⓐ A large number of butterflies look similar to one another.

Ⓑ It is possible for some butterflies to scare away various predators.

Ⓒ Animals do not eat butterflies that resemble the monarch butterfly.

Ⓓ The monarch butterfly has many other butterflies that look like it.

Check-Up Listen again and circle the words you hear.

monarch butterfly	consumes	right	resemble
easy	poison	coloring	another
recognizable	predators	very similar	mistaken

Exercises with Mid-Length Conversations

Exercise 1 Listen to part of a conversation and answer the questions.

04-08

Service Encounter

1 Listen again to part of the conversation. Then answer the question. What can be inferred from the student's response to the man?

- Ⓐ She does not have the addresses with her.
- Ⓑ She needs to borrow the man's pen.
- Ⓒ She forgot to bring her credit card.
- Ⓓ She needs to go back to her dormitory now.

2 Why did the student visit the Registrar's office?

- Ⓐ To confirm that she made a payment
- Ⓑ To ask about changing a class
- Ⓒ To pay her tuition
- Ⓓ To request copies of her transcript

📕 Words & Phrases

transcript ⓝ a record of classes taken and grades
prepare ⓥ to get ready
fill out phr to complete something, such as a form
accept ⓥ to take

✏️ Summary Note

A Fill in the blanks with the appropriate words.

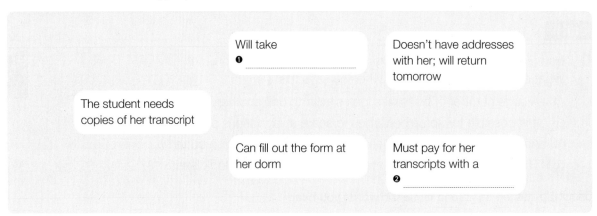

Will take
❶ _____

Doesn't have addresses with her; will return tomorrow

The student needs copies of her transcript

Can fill out the form at her dorm

Must pay for her transcripts with a
❷ _____

B   Complete the following summary by using the words in the box.

paying with cash	the addresses	accepts credit cards
of her transcript	back to her dorm	did not realize

The student needs some copies _____, and the man says that it will take twenty-four hours to prepare them. He adds that she can write _____ of the places where they should send the transcript to on the form. The student says she _____ the Registrar's office would do that. The man says to take the form _____, fill out it, and return later. The student asks about _____, but the man says that the office only _____.

Dictation Exercise   Listen to the conversation again and fill in the blanks.

W Student: Hello. I need to get some copies of _____, but I'm not sure what to do.

M Registrar's Office Employee: It's simple. Just fill out this form here, and we'll _____.

W: Great. So _____ in a few minutes?

M: Sorry. It takes us around twenty-four hours _____. We're pretty busy these days and have lots of _____ to deal with.

W: Okay. I understand. _____ does it cost?

M: _____ of your transcript costs six dollars. That fee includes the cost of _____ to whichever school or organization you're planning on sending it to.

W: Oh, _____ you would mail them for me. That's great.

M: Sure. You just need to write _____ the places you want us to send them to on that form.

W: Um . . . I guess I'll have to _____.

M: That's all right. Just take the form back to your dorm, _____, and bring it here when you can.

W: That's fine. I'm not really _____. Oh, do you _____?

M: Not anymore. We only accept _____.

W: Okay. Thanks for letting me know. I'll make sure I _____ when I come tomorrow. Thanks a lot.

M: You're welcome. Have a nice day.

04-09

Office Hours

1 Listen again to part of the conversation. Then answer the question. What does the professor imply when she says this: 🎧

  Ⓐ The student's paper was not long enough.

  Ⓑ The student had many mistakes in his work.

  Ⓒ The student's report did not have enough sources.

  Ⓓ The student did not do the assignment properly.

2 What problem does the student have?

  Ⓐ He failed to study for the midterm exam.

  Ⓑ He could not finish a report on time.

  Ⓒ He made too many grammar mistakes.

  Ⓓ He is unhappy with a grade he received.

📖 Words & Phrases

evidence n facts to support an idea or opinion

knock down phr to lower a grade

primary source n a person's account of an event, such as a journal or letter

✏️ Summary Note

A Fill in the blanks with the appropriate words.

Strengths of paper	Weaknesses of paper
• Few ❶ _____	• Writing not clear
• Clear thesis	• Not many ❷ _____
• Lots of evidence	• ❸ _____
• Proper page requirements	

B Complete the following summary by using the words in the box.

deserved an A	few grammatical errors	discuss the people
cited his work	details of his paper	grade on a paper

A student talks to a professor about his ＿＿＿＿＿＿＿＿＿＿. He believes his paper was good, and he ＿＿＿＿＿＿＿＿＿＿ on it. He tells the professor why his paper was good. He had ＿＿＿＿＿＿＿＿＿＿, a clear thesis, and lots of evidence, he ＿＿＿＿＿＿＿＿＿＿, and he wrote the appropriate length. The professor asks him the ＿＿＿＿＿＿＿＿＿＿, which was about the War of 1812. The student did not do the assignment properly because he did not ＿＿＿＿＿＿＿＿＿＿ affected by the war.

Dictation Exercise Listen to the conversation again and fill in the blanks.

M Student: Hello, Professor Winthrop. May I talk to you?

W Professor: ＿＿＿＿＿＿＿＿＿＿.

M: I'm curious about the grade on the report ＿＿＿＿＿＿＿＿＿＿.

W: Is there a problem?

M: You gave me a B, but I think I deserved ＿＿＿＿＿＿＿＿＿＿. I thought I was going to get an A.

W: Why don't you tell me why you think you ＿＿＿＿＿＿＿＿＿＿?

M: First, there were only two ＿＿＿＿＿＿＿＿＿＿ in the report, so you shouldn't have ＿＿＿＿＿＿＿＿＿＿ for that. My thesis was very clear. My thesis was that England actually won the War of 1812. I supported it with ＿＿＿＿＿＿＿＿＿＿, I cited all my work, and I fulfilled your ＿＿＿＿＿＿＿＿＿＿, so I don't understand how you gave me a B.

W: Okay, how about telling me what ＿＿＿＿＿＿＿＿＿＿ in that paper?

M: Yes, sometimes my writing is not clear. I know that's not one of ＿＿＿＿＿＿＿＿＿＿. I didn't use very ＿＿＿＿＿＿＿＿＿＿. I know you wanted us to use that, but I couldn't ＿＿＿＿＿＿＿＿＿＿.

W: First, ＿＿＿＿＿＿＿＿＿＿ that England won the War of 1812. You ＿＿＿＿＿＿＿＿＿＿ all the military and political victories England had as well as the treaty that ended the war, right?

M: Yes.

W: Well, the assignment was to describe how a war ＿＿＿＿＿＿＿＿＿＿ of the countries fighting it. Did you talk about ＿＿＿＿＿＿＿＿＿＿ Canada, America, or England?

M: No, I didn't.

W: That is why you got a B. Understand?

M: Ah, yes. I ＿＿＿＿＿＿＿＿＿＿.

Exercise 3 Listen to part of a conversation and answer the questions.

04-10

Office Hours

1 Listen again to part of the conversation. Then answer the question. What does the student imply when she says this: 🎧

(A) She would like to change majors.

(B) She dislikes one of her current professors.

(C) She prefers to study history by herself.

(D) She does not have any job offers yet.

2 What is the student thinking of doing in the future?

(A) Traveling to another country

(B) Becoming a chemistry teacher

(C) Working as a professor

(D) Attending medical school

📖 Words & Phrases

major 🅝 a field of study in college or university

freshman 🅝 a first-year student

minor 🅝 a secondary field of study

degree 🅝 a title given to students by a school after completing a program of study

✏️ Summary Note

A Fill in the blanks with the appropriate words.

Student wants to change majors	Wants to be a doctor
	Become ❶ _____
	Has done well in ❷ _____

B Complete the following summary by using the words in the box.

some basic questions	change her major	making the right decision
made an appointment	grants her permission	help her future

A student _____ to talk to her advisor. She is currently a history major, but she wants to change to become a chemistry major. She needs permission to _____. The advisor asks her _____ to make sure she is _____. The advisor determines the student has thought about it long enough, the change will _____, and the student has performed well. The advisor decides the change in majors is good for the student and _____.

Dictation Exercise Listen to the conversation again and fill in the blanks.

W Student: Hello, Professor Gray. I _____ with you.

M Professor: Sure. Your name is Heather, right?

W: Yes, I want to _____, but I was told I must get permission from you.

M: _____ in history, right?

W: Yes, but I want to change _____. What do I need to do?

M: First, tell me why you want to change.

W: When I was a freshman, I _____, so I decided to study it. In fact, I still like it a lot. I am sure I will keep _____. But I have been thinking about _____ a lot lately. Honestly, history doesn't seem like _____.

M: Keep going.

W: I've recently _____ being a doctor, so I have decided I go to _____. History won't help me get into medical school, but _____.

M: How long _____ about this?

W: Hmm, about six weeks. My cousin is in _____, and we talked about what it would take to get in and _____.

M: Okay, that is good, but what will you do _____ if you don't get into medical school?

W: I have thought about that, too. There is _____ for nurses. I also am getting a minor in education, so I could _____. Or I could be _____ until I get into medical school.

M: Have you taken _____?

W: Yes, I have. I got an A in _____ and a B+ in chemical analysis. I actually _____ from a chemistry professor supporting me.

M: Sounds good. Let's _____.

04-11

Office Hours

1 Listen again to part of the conversation. Then answer the question. Why does the student say this: 🎧

    (A) To say that she will come up with a new topic

    (B) To ask about the quality of her paper topic

    (C) To agree to write about the uses of Roman roads

    (D) To state that she needs more information about the Roman Empire

2 What is the professor's attitude toward the student?

    (A) He thinks she needs to work harder.

    (B) He is very eager to assist her.

    (C) He is concerned about her grade.

    (D) He believes she is an outstanding student.

📖 Words & Phrases

sophisticated adj
advanced

step n a stage

legion n a Roman army

merchant n a person
who buys and sells
goods

📝 Summary Note

A Fill in the blanks with the appropriate words.

Student
- Doesn't believe ❶ _____
  are still in existence today

Professor
- the Romans were great builders;
  many of their buildings are still
  standing
- Romans had ❷ _____
  way of making roads

Student wants to write about Roman roads ➡
Professor agrees with her project and tells her
to focus on how the Romans used the roads

B Complete the following summary by using the words in the box.

were master builders	Roman roads	her term paper
agrees with her suggestion	used sophisticated methods	built 2,000 years ago

The student asks the professor how it is possible that _____ are still in existence since they were _____. The professor says that the Romans _____ as some of the old buildings are still standing. He notes that the Romans _____ to build roads. They used several steps to make the roads. The student asks if she can write _____ about Roman roads, and the professor _____.

Dictation Exercise Listen to the conversation again and fill in the blanks.

W Student: Professor Lawson, I have a question about _____.

M Professor: Sure, Lily. What is it?

W: I'm _____ about something you said about Roman roads. You mentioned that some of the roads they built _____. But, uh, but that's _____, is it? I mean, they _____ around 2,000 years ago.

M: It actually is possible. The Romans, you see, were _____. Just look at how many of _____ are still standing.

W: Oh . . . That's _____.

M: To get back to the roads, the Romans had a _____ way of making them.

W: How so?

M: Well, they didn't just _____ and then put stones on the ground. Instead, there were several steps Roman builders took to make them. The result was _____ that were used by Roman legions, merchants, and travelers all throughout _____.

W: It _____. Would you mind if I wrote _____ about the roads?

M: Not at all. I think it's _____. In fact, you're _____ in nine or ten years to choose that topic.

W: Thanks. I'm looking forward to _____ on how they made the roads.

M: You should also focus on how the Romans _____. You see, _____ of the roads was one reason that the empire was able to stay together for so long.

W: _____ to do that. Thanks, sir.

Exercises with Mid-Length Lectures

Exercise 1 Listen to part of a lecture and answer the questions.

04-12

Mechanics

1 Listen again to part of the lecture. Then answer the question. What does the professor imply when she says this:

- Ⓐ There are many ways to get an airplane to fly.
- Ⓑ Planes became popular after the Wright brothers' first flight.
- Ⓒ It is not difficult to design and build an airplane.
- Ⓓ The Wright brothers did a lot of original work.

2 What does a turn on the vertical axis make the airplane do?

- Ⓐ Spin
- Ⓑ Go up and down
- Ⓒ Roll
- Ⓓ Go left or right

📖 Words & Phrases

manipulate 🆅 to change or control

axis 🅽 a straight line in which an object can be rotated

clockwise 🆊🆍 in the same direction that a clock's hands move

lateral 🆊🆍🆍 related to the side

longitudinal 🆊🆍🆍 related to the lengthwise part of an object

✏️ Summary Note

A Fill in the blanks with the appropriate words.

Controls of an Airplane

Vertical axis	Longitudinal axis	Lateral axis
• Fins turn ❶ _____	• One fin turns up, the other left	• Fins turn up or down
• Plane turns left or right	• Plane ❷ _____	• Plane ❸ _____

B Complete the following summary by using the words in the box.

air stream	three basic turns	three axes
desired turn	set of fins	the longitudinal axis

Airplanes have _____. Each axis has its own _____
built into the aircraft's wings. The fins turn and react with the _____ to enable
the airplane to turn. _____ are capable. The airplane can turn up or down on the
lateral axis, it can turn left or right on the vertical axis, and it can spin on _____.
For the first two types of turns, the fins turn in the direction of the _____. For a
spin, the fins turn in opposite directions.

Dictation Exercise Listen to the lecture again and fill in the blanks.

W Professor: Today, we are going to talk about _____ an airplane. Umm, but
as you know, I like to talk a bit about the _____.
the Wright brothers for having accomplished the first manned flight of an airplane. Their work
_____ when you consider they had to do all their own research and there were
_____ for them to look at. Even something _____ controlling
the airplane had to be imagined, tested, developed, and perfected.

Over the past 100 years, the technology of airplanes has changed, but the controls
_____. Today, airplanes have _____: turning up and down,
turning left and right, and spinning. Airplanes turn by _____ that are designed in
their wings. When a pilot moves the fins in the air stream, they react with _____ to
turn the aircraft.

You see, an airplane has _____. A turn in the lateral axis can make
the plane move _____. A turn in the longitudinal axis can make the
plane _____. The third axis is the vertical axis. This turns the plane
_____.

Each axis has its own _____ on the aircraft. To make a turn on the lateral or
vertical axis, a pilot only needs to turn the fins _____ the desired turn. For example,
if the pilot _____, he would turn the vertical axis left. _____
that flows around the aircraft would change, and the aircraft would turn right.

In order to turn on the longitudinal axis, the pilot must do something _____. For
this axis, a turn is achieved by _____ in the same direction. To achieve a spin, the
fins go _____. For example, to spin clockwise, the right fin would turn down, so the
right side of the aircraft _____. The left fin would turn right, so the left side of the
aircraft _____. With one side rising and one side dropping, the aircraft then would
perform _____.

Exercise 2 Listen to part of a lecture and answer the questions.

04-13

Geology

1 Listen again to part of the lecture. Then answer the question. What is the purpose of the professor's response?

Ⓒ To encourage the student to pay closer attention in class

Ⓓ To tell the class to listen carefully to the student

Ⓔ To ask the student to provide a different answer

Ⓕ To say that the student's answer is not completely wrong

2 According to the professor, what effect can a volcanic eruption have?
Click on 2 answers.

Ⓒ It can increase the albedo.

Ⓓ It can change the Earth's appearance.

Ⓔ It can make the Earth warmer.

Ⓕ It can emit various gases.

📕 Words & Phrases

ozone layer 🅝 a part of the atmosphere that reflects the sun's heat and radiation

albedo 🅝 a part of the ozone layer

geyser 🅝 a part of the ground that releases hot water and water vapor at different times

fumarole 🅝 a hole near a volcano that emits gas and water vapor

✏️ Summary Note

A Fill in the blanks with the appropriate words.

How Volcanoes Affect the Earth

Lava	Gases	Earthquakes
• ❶ _____ for plants	• Cool down the Earth	• Hot springs, ❸ _____, and fumaroles
• Destroy the environment	• Toxic gases destroy ❷ _____	

B Complete the following summary by using the words in the box.

lies in its path	good fertilizer	damage the ozone layer
three basic types	other side effects	several gases

Volcanoes have _____ of effects on the Earth. First, volcanoes produce lava. Lava can destroy or severely damage anything that _____. Later, lava works as a _____. Second, volcanoes emit _____ into the atmosphere. Some of the gases are beneficial. They can help increase the albedo. Other gases can _____ or create acid rain. Last, there are several _____, such as geysers and earthquakes.

Dictation Exercise Listen to the lecture again and fill in the blanks.

M1 Professor: We have studied the _____. Now, I want to _____ volcanoes have on the Earth. We can classify the effects into _____. Can anyone _____ what they are?

W1 Student: Well, I am sure one of them is lava or is _____ lava.

M1: Yes, you are right. There are a few different kinds of _____. All of them can _____ the immediate environment, but later they are very beneficial to plant life. Lava, when it is not hot, is _____ for plants. Volcanoes also emit _____. But we will get into that tomorrow. What other categories are there besides lava and _____?

M2 Student: What about _____ emissions, like gases? Volcanoes emit _____, right?

M1: Yes, volcanoes emit many _____ gases, such as sulfur dioxide. Of course, not all the gases released _____, like water vapor, but others wreak havoc on _____. When sulfur dioxide _____ and reacts to change into sulfuric acid, it increases the Earth's albedo. What is the albedo?

W1: The albedo reflects _____. That reaction increases the Earth's albedo.

M1: Yes, why?

W1: Doesn't that mean volcanoes can _____ the effects of global warming and cool the Earth down?

M1: Very good. The eruptions of the past half century _____ the albedo enough to cool the surface of the Earth by half a degree Fahrenheit. But many of the gases emitted also destroy parts of _____ and can create acid rain. What other effects are there?

M2: In the movies, _____ run away before a volcano.

M1: You _____. There are volcanic _____. There are events that occur _____ but are not emitted from volcanoes. Any guesses?

W2 Student: Earthquakes. Earthquakes and volcanoes occur _____ and often accompany each other. Sometimes volcanoes cause _____.

M1: Yes, there are also _____, geysers, fumaroles, and mud pots.

Listen to part of a lecture and answer the questions.

04-14

Zoology

1 Listen again to part of the lecture. Then answer the question. What does the professor imply when she says this: 🎧
- (A) Few people have ever seen a Bobak marmot.
- (B) The Olympic marmot is faster than the Bobak marmot.
- (C) There are more Olympic marmots than Bobak marmots.
- (D) The Olympic marmot is not hunted by people.

2 Why does the professor mention defense calls?
- (A) To claim that they are not very effective
- (B) To show how marmots protect themselves
- (C) To demonstrate how they sound to the students
- (D) To compare those of the marmot with those of other animals

📖 **Words & Phrases**

genus n a category of animal that is more general than species

descending adj getting lower

trill n a sound made by alternating between a high and low sound

terrain n a category of land, such as desert or mountain

✏️ **Summary Note**

A Fill in the blanks with the appropriate words.

Two Types of Marmots

Olympic Marmot
- Location: Olympic Peninsula in northwest U.S.
- Geography of home: alpine meadows near mountains
- Defense calls: ❶ _____
  – Identifies kinds of predators
- Contact with humans: humans have little contact

Bobak Marmot
- Location: Central Asia and Russia
- Geography of home:
  ❷ _____ and cultivated land
- Defense calls: simple
  – One call for all predators
- Contact with humans: humans have eaten and used to make
  ❸ _____

B Complete the following summary by using the words in the box.

the state of Washington	open grasslands	warn other marmots
during famine	different kinds of predators	a source of fur

Two different species of marmots are the Olympic marmot and the Bobak marmot. The Olympic marmot lives near the Olympic Mountains in the Olympic Peninsula in _____. The Bobak marmot lives in _____ in Central Asia and Russia. Both animals have calls to _____ of a predator, but the Olympic marmot's calls are more advanced and recognize _____. The Bobak marmot has been eaten by Russian people _____, and it has also been used as _____ for clothes.

Dictation Exercise Listen to the lecture again and fill in the blanks.

W Professor: Today, we are going to compare _____ that are the same genus. The two animals _____ are the Olympic marmot and the Bobak marmot. First, they live a world apart. The Olympic marmot lives in _____ in North America. It lives on the Olympic Peninsula in _____ Washington. Excluding Alaska, it is the northwesternmost part of the United States. Oh, yeah, and Hawaii is _____. The Bobak marmot's home is on _____ of the world in the steppes of Russia and Central Asia. Even though they are both marmots, they _____ to live. The Olympic lives in _____ near the Olympic Mountains. The Bobak marmot is not like most marmots and lives in _____ and has also been known to live near cultivated fields.

Let's go on to _____. All species of marmots have _____ to alert others of predators. The Olympic marmot has _____ calls though. Most research shows that the Bobak marmot only _____. This call communicates any and all forms of predators. Some studies have hinted that its call _____ depending on the terrain. In flat areas, the call is slow. In rugged terrain, the calls _____.

Umm, okay, the Olympic marmot's calls are _____. Its calls _____ as ascending, descending, flat, and trills. The different calls are used to designate _____ predator, for example, a bird of prey or a bear. The trills are believed to be used for _____.

The Olympic marmot's _____ are mainly the coyote and the puma and, to a lesser extent, _____ and bobcats. The Bobak marmot's natural enemies are similar animals: _____ and packs of hunting canines. This may sound strange, but the Bobak marmot has been a source of _____ for many Russian people. In times of extreme hardship and famine, the Bobak marmot has been used by people to provide both _____. Due to this, you can guess that the Olympic marmot is _____ around people.

Exercise 4 Listen to part of a lecture and answer the questions.

04-15

Physical Education

1 Listen again to part of the lecture. Then answer the question. Why does the professor say this: 🎧

    Ⓐ To say that American football is more popular in China than in the United States

    Ⓑ To claim that American football is very popular in Canada

    Ⓒ To imply that not everyone considers football the most popular sport

    Ⓓ To point out that many people are not interested in sports at all

2 What school played a Canadian university and changed the style of American football?

    Ⓐ Harvard University

    Ⓑ Yale University

    Ⓒ McGill University

    Ⓓ Oxford College

📖 Words & Phrases

unorganized adj lacking order; badly planned

line of scrimmage n the imaginary line between two teams in football

thwart v successfully to oppose or stop

✏️ Summary Note

A Fill in the blanks with the appropriate words.

American Football

| Rugby-style football: Harvard adopted Canadian rules | Early football: ❶ _____ changed the rules | Modern football: ❷ _____ caused the rules to change |

B Complete the following summary by using the words in the box.

similar to soccer	large number of deaths	Canadian style
European soccer	passed on	American universities

American football is derived from _____. In the 1820s, _____ made the sport popular, but they played a game _____. Harvard played a game more like rugby. Harvard then played a Canadian football team and adopted the _____ of football. Harvard _____ this style to other American universities. Walter Camp changed the game even further by adding downs and the line of scrimmage and by reducing the number of players. The _____ resulted in more changes, like the forward pass and a fourth down.

Dictation Exercise   Listen to the lecture again and fill in the blanks.

M1 Professor: Let's talk about what some people consider the _____ in the United States. Football was _____. _____ were played all over the world. The Chinese played a game called *cuju* over 2,200 years ago. Native Americans were playing a game like soccer before _____ in the Americas.

W Student: _____ did the Native Americans have on football? Did settlers play with them?

M1: I am sure settlers and Native Americans played, but that had _____ on the development of football. Football became popular due to _____ playing the game around the 1820s. It was mainly _____ of mob-style soccer. Harvard played a game _____. In 1874, McGill University of Montreal played Harvard. Harvard adopted the Canadian version of football, which was _____ to today's football. Harvard spread _____ football to other schools, who were playing a soccer-style game.

M2 Student: Do you mean Canadians were playing American-style football before Americans?

M1: _____. They were playing a game similar to rugby, but they did influence _____ football. By 1883, a coach named Walter Camp made _____ to the game, such as reducing the number of players from fifteen to eleven, adding the line of scrimmage, and adding a rule that if the ball is not moved five yards after three downs, the other team would _____ the ball. This rule was created to thwart Yale's strategy of controlling the ball without _____.

W: Didn't Harvard and Yale _____?

M1: Football was very dangerous. Harvard invented the flying wedge, which _____ seven Yale players in one game. Eighteen players were killed in 1905. This led to _____, such as the forward pass and adding a fourth down. After this, the game _____ to the football that is played today.

A Listen to the previous lecture on geology and say the answers out loud by using the cue sentence words that are indicated in each answer. You can refer to the summary note below.

04-16

Geology

✎ **Summary Note**

┌─────────────────────────────────────┐
│ **How Volcanoes Affect the Earth** │
└─────────────────────────────────────┘

Lava	Gases	Earthquakes
• Fertilizer for plants	• Cool down the Earth	• Hot springs, geysers, and fumaroles
• Destroy the environment	• Toxic gases destroy ozone	

1 What do the gas emissions from volcanoes do to the albedo?

a. The gas emissions from volcanoes ....

b. The albedo is increased ....

2 First, lava can destroy the surrounding environment. What does lava do next?

a. Lava destroys ....

b. At first, lava can destroy ....

3 What is one of the gases emitted from a volcano?

a. One of the gases emitted ....

b. During an eruption, volcanoes will emit ....

B Listen to the previous lecture on zoology and say the answers out loud by using the cue sentence words that are indicated in each answer. You can refer to the summary note below.

04-17

Zoology

🖉 **Summary Note**

> **Two Types of Marmots**

Olympic Marmot
- Location: Olympic Peninsula in northwest USA
- Geography of home: alpine meadows near mountains
- Defense calls: complex
  – Identifies kinds of predators
- Contact with humans: humans have little contact

Bobak Marmot
- Location: Central Asia and Russia
- Geography of home: rolling grasslands and cultivated land
- Defense calls: simple
  – One call for all predators
- Contact with humans: humans have eaten and used as clothes

1 Where does the Olympic marmot live?

a. The Olympic marmot lives _____.

b. The Olympic marmot's home is _____.

2 What is the purpose of the marmot's calls?

a. The purpose of the marmot's calls is _____.

b. The marmot will call other marmots _____.

3 How has the Bobak marmot served people?

a. The Bobak marmot has served people as _____.

b. People have used the Bobak marmot to _____.

04-18

Listen to part of a conversation between a student and a professor.

1 What is the student's problem?

    Ⓐ No companies have offered him an internship.

    Ⓑ He is not ready to make a decision yet.

    Ⓒ His grades are not very good this semester.

    Ⓓ There are few jobs available for recent graduates.

2 Why does the student want to wait for the other companies?

    Ⓐ Because they are in his hometown

    Ⓑ Because they are paid positions

    Ⓒ Because they are near the school

    Ⓓ Because they are related to his major

3 What does the professor imply about the student?

    Ⓐ He is doing very well in her class.

    Ⓑ He will be offered positions by all three companies.

    Ⓒ He should take a class during summer.

    Ⓓ He should turn down the Landis position.

4 What will the professor probably do next?

    Ⓐ Ask the student a question

    Ⓑ Discuss a new issue with the student

    Ⓒ Attend her next class

    Ⓓ Go to a faculty meeting

5 Listen again to part of the conversation. Then answer the question.
What does the student imply when he says this: 🎧

    Ⓐ He is happy with the results of his recent test.

    Ⓑ Nobody knows when positions will be offered.

    Ⓒ One company will likely offer him an internship.

    Ⓓ Everyone must wait until Monday for the results.

Listen to part of a lecture in an architecture class.

04-19

Architecture

6 What is the lecture mainly about?

    Ⓐ Styles of American houses 100 years ago

    Ⓑ Why rural houses are better than city houses

    Ⓒ The advantages of living in the country

    Ⓓ Reasons American houses are different from the past

7 What trend does the professor discuss?

    Ⓐ Builders making unique-looking houses

    Ⓑ Families turning to farming lifestyles

    Ⓒ Homeowners paying for houses with cash

    Ⓓ People moving out of big cities

8 According to the professor, what is one advantage of living in the suburbs?

    Ⓐ Land prices are low.

    Ⓑ Schools are high in quality.

    Ⓒ There is little pollution.

    Ⓓ Traffic is not a problem.

9 Why does the professor mention fireplaces?

    Ⓐ To describe their functions in the past

    Ⓑ To explain why many new homes lack them

    Ⓒ To note that she likes how they look

    Ⓓ To ask the student to describe how they appear

10 What can be inferred about the average modern-day American family?

    Ⓐ It is more commonly found in large cities than in suburbs.

    Ⓑ It is popular for them to send their children to private schools.

    Ⓒ It is easy for them to move from one city to another.

    Ⓓ It is smaller than families that lived on farms in the past.

11 Listen again to part of the lecture. Then answer the question.
What does the professor imply when she says this: 🎧

    Ⓐ Houses in the suburbs are not expensive.

    Ⓑ It is easy to build houses that look the same.

    Ⓒ There is a lot of variety of houses in the suburbs.

    Ⓓ Most suburban homes are small in size.

Vocabulary Check-Up

A Choose the correct words that match the definitions.

1 descending •   • Ⓐ to get ready

2 manipulate •   • Ⓑ to change or control

3 evidence •   • Ⓒ a first-year student

4 terrain •   • Ⓓ an animal that hunts, kills, and eats other animals

5 predator •   • Ⓔ a classification of land, such as forest, desert, or mountain

6 degree •   • Ⓕ a straight line in which an object can be rotated

7 prepare •   • Ⓖ facts to support an idea or opinion

8 toxic •   • Ⓗ to eat

9 freshman •   • Ⓘ a title given to students by a school after completing a program of study

10 unorganized •   • Ⓙ poisonous

11 genus •   • Ⓚ a record of classes taken and grades

12 topic •   • Ⓛ a subject

13 axis •   • Ⓜ lacking order; badly planned

14 consume •   • Ⓝ a category of animal that is more general than species

15 transcript •   • Ⓞ getting lower

B Complete the sentences by filling in the blanks with the words in the box.

Ⓐ science fiction	Ⓑ decision	Ⓒ internship	Ⓓ mimicry	Ⓔ realize

1 She does not _____ the importance of this class.

2 You need to make a(n) _____ before the end of the day.

3 _____ is the act of looking like a different animal or plant.

4 He has a summer _____ working at a bank.

5 Many people enjoy reading _____ and watching movies about it.

Understanding the Speaker's Attitude

Introduction

Speaker's Attitude questions test whether you can understand a speaker's attitude or opinion. This question asks you about the speaker's feelings, likes and dislikes, or reason behind various emotions. You are also often asked about a speaker's degree of certainty. This question type often involves replaying a portion of the listening passage.

Question Types

▶ What can be inferred about the student?

▶ What is the professor's attitude toward X?

▶ What is the professor's opinion of X?

▶ What can be inferred about the student when she says this: (replay)

▶ What does the woman mean when she says this: (replay)

Useful Tips

■ Focus on the tone of voice, the intonation, and the sentence stress the speakers use in the lecture or conversation.

■ Practice distinguishing between referencing and giving personal opinions.

■ Avoid answers that are too far from the general tone of the lecture or conversation.

■ Try to take notes on the context of the lecture or conversation.

■ Pay attention to adjectives and verbs of feeling.

Sample TOEFL iBT Question

Script

05-01

M Student: Professor Roosevelt, one of my friends told me that you handed out some review sheets for the final exam in yesterday's class. I wonder if you have any copies of them.

W Professor: Weren't you in class yesterday, Alexander?

M: Sorry, ma'am. I had an interview for an internship, so I couldn't make it. I actually emailed you about it two days ago.

W: Ah, I see. I haven't checked my email in a while. I've been too busy. Anyway, here are the papers. I don't think you'll need them though. You're already doing very well in my class.

M: Thanks for saying that, but I'd like to get the highest grade possible.

W: That's a great way to look at things, Alexander. Good luck on the test.

Q What is the professor's opinion of the student?

    Ⓐ He is the best student she has ever had.

    Ⓑ He needs to work harder in her class.

    Ⓒ He is a very good student in her class.

    Ⓓ He will make a great intern this summer.

✔ Correct Answer

The correct answer to the above question is Ⓒ. The professor states that the student is doing well in her class, so she thinks he is a very good student.

Basic Drill

Listen to parts of conversations or lectures and answer the questions.

Drill 1

Q Listen again to part of the conversation. Then answer the question. What does the man mean when he says this: 🎧

05-02

    Ⓐ He cannot comply with the student's request.

    Ⓑ The student's problem is not very important.

    Ⓒ He will not finish his shift for a couple of hours.

    Ⓓ The student should return to her room and try again.

Check-Up Listen again and circle the words you hear.

help through	key car	does appear	properly
hope so	problem	damages	permission
gain access	card	worked fine	my replacement

Drill 2

Q What is the professor's attitude toward the student?

05-03

    Ⓐ She is not sympathetic.

    Ⓑ She is very helpful to him.

    Ⓒ She is unconcerned.

    Ⓓ She is pleased with his actions.

Check-Up Listen again and circle the words you hear.

speak about you	enter a view	out of town	this assignment
interview project	the mayor	terrific	a couple of dolls
scheduled	can cells	especially	arrange for you

Drill 3

Q What can be inferred about the student?

05-04

    Ⓐ She usually gets good grades in her classes.

    Ⓑ She is pleased with the results of her project.

    Ⓒ She thinks her professor is being unfair to her.

    Ⓓ She believes it will be easy to make the corrections.

Check-Up Listen again and circle the words you hear.

for a moment	in that case	handed in	be the case
cite your sources	in a moment	take a book	handy things
recite your courses	between the lines	line up between	take a look

Drill 4

Q What is the professor's opinion of Avram Noam Chomsky?

Ⓐ She thinks Chomsky does poor work.

Ⓑ She believes Chomsky is better known for his politics.

Ⓒ She dislikes many of the activities Chomsky does.

Ⓓ She considers Chomsky an outstanding scholar.

05-05

Check-Up Listen again and circle the words you hear.

living scholar	keynote speaker	significant	contributions
left-wing politics	lively collar	signature copy	key intellectual figure
strong coffee	strongly criticized	right-wing radical	most notably

Drill 5

Q What is the professor's opinion of the buildings affected by the earthquake?

Ⓐ He is happy that they were only slightly damaged.

Ⓑ He is disappointed that many collapsed.

Ⓒ He is upset about the extreme destruction.

Ⓓ He is impressed by their engineering.

05-06

Check-Up Listen again and circle the words you hear.

big earthquake	very few	models	sway
that's it	collapsed	essentially	able to retwist
really impressed	skyscraper	earthquake proven	very flexible

Drill 6

Q What is the professor's opinion of the autocratic management style?

Ⓐ He thinks it has good and bad points.

Ⓑ He thinks it is the best way to manage.

Ⓒ He thinks it is a terrible way to manage.

Ⓓ He thinks the laissez-faire style is a better way to manage.

05-07

Check-Up Listen again and circle the words you hear.

spend some time	high standards	accomplish his goals	overly dependent
under confident	hot chocolate	highly creative	not deliberate
all the time	score a goal	very determining	send a typewriter

Exercises with Mid-Length Conversations

Exercise 1 Listen to part of a conversation and answer the questions.

05-08

Office Hours

1 What can be inferred about the student?
- Ⓐ She believes the professor will not help her.
- Ⓑ She thinks her project needs some supplements.
- Ⓒ She hopes to visit Guatemala in the future.
- Ⓓ She has visited the Guatemalan Consulate before.

2 What can be inferred about the professor's friend?
- Ⓐ She has not helped students before.
- Ⓑ She is a student at the university.
- Ⓒ She lives in Guatemala now.
- Ⓓ She enjoys helping the professor.

📖 **Words & Phrases**

spruce v to enliven
spearhead n the sharp metal end of a spear
antique n something that is old and of value
laminated adj coated in a molded plastic covering

✏️ Summary Note

A Fill in the blanks with the appropriate words.

Student	Professor
• Asks for help for ❶ _____	• Gives the telephone number for the Guatemalan Consulate
• Needs big laminated posters, enlarged photographs, or information about the tourism industry	• Says that the consulate hands out ❷ _____ the student needs

B Complete the following summary by using the words in the box.

final project	campaign to increase	supplements
archaeological antiques	Guatemalan Consulate	about the time

The student tells the professor that she is working on her _____ for her international business development class. She needs to make a _____ tourism to Guatemala. She asks her professor if he has any _____ she could use in the presentation. He offers her some _____, but those are not what she is looking for. Then, he offers to connect her with the _____. He says that it will probably have some materials for her to use. Finally, he tells her a story _____ when his friend at the Guatemalan Consulate helped him.

Dictation Exercise Listen to the conversation again and fill in the blanks.

W Student: Hi, Professor Caruso. May I _____ of your time?

M Professor: Hello, Mary. What's up?

W: I'm working on _____ for my international business development class. I have to _____ as if it were a campaign to increase tourism for Guatemala. Since you're a professor of Latin American studies, I was hoping you might _____ that I could add to my presentation to spruce it up. You know, like _____ or brochures.

M: Hmm, let me think for a second. Well, I have an ancient Mayan spearhead and _____ of Stone Age pottery. Would those _____ be of any use if I loaned them to you?

W: Uh, those sound interesting. But I was hoping for something _____. I was thinking you might have some big laminated posters, some enlarged photographs, or maybe some information about _____.

M: Aha, I see. You're doing a booth to _____ about visiting Guatemala. Okay, I can help. But I don't _____ here. Let me give you _____ for the Guatemalan Consulate downtown. I know the deputy ambassador there. I'm sure she would be happy to furnish you with some _____. I know the consulate has packets of _____ that it hands out for free.

W: Thank you so much. That sounds like just what I need. I'll _____ right away.

M: Sure, let me just check my rolodex here for Marta's phone number. I'll call her and put in _____ for you. She's _____ when I refer students. Let me tell you about one time. Last year, we took a study trip there, and two of my students _____. There was a mix-up _____, and I called her. She got it all sorted out for us.

W: Wow, it's good to _____.

M: You bet it is.

05-09

Service Encounter

1 What is the man's attitude toward the student?

(A) He does not believe her.

(B) He is very apologetic to her.

(C) He is not particularly helpful.

(D) He is willing to accept her apology.

2 Listen again to part of the conversation. Then answer the question. What does the man mean when he says this: 🎧

(A) The student is free to leave now.

(B) His boss is gone but will return to the office soon.

(C) The student does not have to pay any money.

(D) He can take the chair to the student's room now.

📙 **Words & Phrases**

fine (n) money that must be paid for breaking the law or a rule

inspection (n) a checkup

replacement (n) something that takes the place of another thing

completely (adv) totally

✏️ **Summary Note**

A Fill in the blanks with the appropriate words.

Student
- Has to pay a ❶ _____
- Doesn't know what the fine is for
- Says that there was ❷ _____ when she got the room

Employee
- Says the fine is for a missing chair
- Was found during an inspection
- Checks the computer and sees that the student already noted the missing chair
- ❸ _____

B Complete the following summary by using the words in the box.

she does not know	the student is right	was no chair
was found missing	deliver her a chair	got a notice

The student visits the student housing office because she _____ indicating she must pay a fine of fifty dollars. However, _____ what the fine is for. The man checks and says that the fine is for a chair that _____ during an inspection. The student says that there _____ when she moved in and that she already asked about it. The man confirms _____. He promises to _____ and removes the fine.

Dictation Exercise **Listen to the conversation again and fill in the blanks.**

W Student: _____, but I think I need to speak with someone in this office.

M Housing Office Employee: Sure. You can talk to me.

W: Great. Thanks. I just _____ in my mailbox. Could you take a look at it, please?

M: Okay . . . Hmm . . . According to this, you need to _____ of fifty dollars.

W: Yeah, but, uh . . . why do I have to pay a fine? The notice _____ what this is for.

M: It doesn't . . . ? Oh, yeah. You're right. Just a moment while I type _____ into the computer.

W: Sure.

M: Okay. Apparently, there was _____ your room three days ago. Do you remember that?

W: Yes, the RA told me about it, but _____ when it happened.

M: Okay. Anyway, during the inspection, the person from the housing office noticed that _____ from your room. So the fine is to pay for _____.

W: Um . . . There wasn't a chair in the room when _____ after the semester started a month ago. I actually came here and _____, but nobody ever brought me a new chair.

M: _____. Let me check on that . . . Okay, uh, I just typed your name into the computer, and what you said is _____. This is _____. I'm going to personally _____ to your room right after lunch ends.

W: And the fine?

M: _____. I'm very sorry for _____. I'll make sure something like this _____.

Listen to part of a conversation and answer the questions.

05-10

Office Hours

1 What can be inferred about the student?

Ⓐ He does not really enjoy teaching.

Ⓑ He is taking a class with the professor this semester.

Ⓒ He is nervous about his class being observed.

Ⓓ He is worried about the professor's health.

2 Why is the student showing Hollywood adaptations in his class?

Ⓐ To prove that movies are better than books

Ⓑ To make the students in his class happy

Ⓒ To show students movies from the past

Ⓓ To have students contrast movies with novels

📖 **Words & Phrases**

appendectomy n
surgery to remove an
appendix from a human

shipshape adj in top
condition

contrast v to cite
differences between two
or more things

overambitious adj trying
to accomplish more than
one is capable of

✎ Summary Note

A Fill in the blanks with the appropriate words.

Professor

• Had an appendectomy last summer

• Is observing the student's class next week on Tuesday

Student

• Is a student-teacher

• Teaches ❶ _____

• Reads a novel and then watches ❷ _____ and discusses the differences

B Complete the following summary by using the words in the box.

fully recovered	a student-teacher	university administration
compares and contrasts	Hollywood adaptations	overambitious

The professor tells the student that he was in the hospital for an appendectomy. He says his body is
_____ now. The student says he enjoys being _____.
The professor says that the _____ is sending him to observe the student's
class. The professor asks the student what he is teaching. The student responds that he is taking
a unit that _____ novels and their _____. The student
wonders if the professor thinks this syllabus is _____. The professor says it
may be.

Dictation Exercise Listen to the conversation again and fill in the blanks.

M Student: Professor Simmons, how are you doing? I _____ since last year.

W Professor: Hey, Fred. Long time, no see. I had an appendectomy last summer. I was
_____ for two weeks. But I'm _____ now and feeling great.
My body is one-hundred-percent shipshape. So how are you? I hear you're _____
these days.

M: That's right. I'm teaching the freshmen introduction to _____.

W: That's what I heard. As a matter of fact, that's why I called and asked you to
_____ today. The university has assigned me to _____ next
week on Tuesday, and I wanted to tell you _____.

M: Oh, really? Did I do something wrong? Was there _____?

W: No, nothing of the sort. It's just a _____ that the university does on all new
student-teachers.

M: Hmm, okay. _____ because I would think someone would have told me about it
earlier.

W: Well, you know, the university administration likes to use _____ sometimes.
They want me to observe your _____. Speaking of which, what are you teaching
this semester?

M: I'll email you my syllabus and _____ before you come. But in brief, I'm doing a
compare-and-contrast unit, during which we _____ and then watch the Hollywood
adaptation and discuss the difference.

W: That sounds really interesting. Which _____ are you doing?

M: First, we're reading and watching William Golding's *Lord of the Flies*. Then, we're going
to do Shakespeare's *Hamlet* with the Kenneth Brannaugh film adaptation. After that, if we
_____, we'll take a look at Joseph Conrad's *Heart of Darkness* with Francis Ford
Coppola's *Apocalypse Now* for _____.

W: Wow! That's _____.

M: Do you think _____?

W: Maybe a little.

Exercise 4 Listen to part of a conversation and answer the questions.

05-11

Service Encounter

1 What can be inferred about the student?

- Ⓐ She is interested in helping others.
- Ⓑ She is currently a first-year student.
- Ⓒ She lives in a room by herself.
- Ⓓ She has helped prospective students in the past.

2 Listen again to part of the conversation. Then answer the question. What does the man mean when he says this: 🎧

- Ⓐ The student can have a part-time job.
- Ⓑ He is ready to go on his lunch break.
- Ⓒ His office needs more volunteers.
- Ⓓ He has time to talk to the student now.

📖 **Words & Phrases**

host n a person who is responsible for a guest
prospective adj potential
unpleasant adj negative
impression n a thought or opinion about something

✏️ **Summary Note**

A Fill in the blanks with the appropriate words.

Man is happy the student showed up

Student wants to host a
❶ _____
in high school

Student needs to sign her
❷ _____

Can read a pamphlet explaining the school's expectations

Needs students who like the school to host visitors

B Complete the following summary by using the words in the box.

who like the school	high school student	name and phone number
gives her a pamphlet	her roommate	is happy

The student tells the man that one of her friends will be hosting a visiting _____,
and she wants to do the same thing. The man _____ the student showed
up. He says that around 200 prospective students in high school will be visiting. The school needs
students _____ to act as hosts. The student says that she likes the school
and that _____ is fine with someone staying with them. The man asks the
student to sign her _____ and states that she will be contacted later. He
_____ containing the school's expectations and asks her to read it.

Dictation Exercise Listen to the conversation again and fill in the blanks.

M Student Activities Office Employee: Good morning. How are you doing today?

W Student: I'm great. Thanks. How are you?

M: I'm _____. So . . . what brings you to the office today?

W: One of my friends told me _____ as a host for a high school student who's
going to be visiting in a couple of weeks. That sounds _____, so I thought I would
ask if you need any volunteers.

M: I'm so glad _____ just now.

W: Oh . . . Okay. So what can I do?

M: On the weekend of October 15 and 16, we're going to have around 200 _____
in high school visiting us. We try to put them up in dorms so that they can _____.

W: Ah, okay. I've got a roommate, but she's fine with _____ with us for the
weekend.

M: Great. First . . . do you _____?

W: Sure. I love it here.

M: That's good. We don't want any students staying with people who are having
_____ at school. They might get _____ of the school.

W: That _____. So what do I need to do?

M: Just sign your name here and provide _____. We'll find someone to
_____ and call you in a couple of days. Why don't you _____,
which explains what we hope you can do while the student is here?

W: _____ to me.

Exercises with Mid-Length Lectures

Exercise 1 Listen to part of a lecture and answer the questions.

05-12

Architecture

1   Listen again to part of the conversation. Then answer the question. What does the professor mean when she says this: 🎧
   - (A) Many people think the Eiffel Tower is unattractive.
   - (B) The Eiffel Tower can be seen from anywhere in Paris.
   - (C) Nothing in Paris is taller than the Eiffel Tower.
   - (D) It was not very difficult to construct the Eiffel Tower.

2   What aspect of the Eiffel Tower does the professor mainly discuss?
   - (A) Its popularity
   - (B) Its appearance
   - (C) Its cost
   - (D) Its construction

📖 Words & Phrases

puddle iron (n) wrought iron made by expelling carbon

rivet (n) a bolt for holding together metal plates

shaft (n) a long, narrow, vertical passage

✏️ Summary Note

A   Fill in the blanks with the appropriate words.

Tallest structure in Paris

Workers:
❶ ....

Eiffel Tower

Iron: 18,038 pieces
Rivets:
❷ ....

Deaths: 1

B Complete the following summary by using the words in the box.

the tallest structure	puddle iron	erect
held the record	expired	firmly entrenched

The Eiffel Tower was designed by Gustave Eiffel. It is still _____ in Paris. The iron structure of the tower weighs 7,300 tons. It required 300 workers to join 18,038 pieces of _____ and three and a half million rivets to _____ the tower. It _____ for tallest building in the world for over forty years. The Eiffel Tower was the entrance arch for the 1898 World's Fair. Only one worker died during its construction. By the time the tower's permit _____, it was so _____ in French culture that the government could not tear it down.

Dictation Exercise   Listen to the lecture again and fill in the blanks.

W1 Professor: Today, we are going to discuss the construction of one of the world's most famous _____. It's located _____ Paris, France.

W2 Student: You're talking about the Eiffel Tower, _____ Gustave Eiffel and built between 1887 and 1889.

W1: That's _____. The Eiffel Tower today remains _____ in Paris, standing 300 meters high. _____ of the tower weighs a total of 7,300 tons. It required 300 workers to _____ 18,038 pieces of puddle iron with three and a half million rivets to _____.

M Student: That doesn't sound like _____.

W1: In a way, you're right. By _____, building that kind of structure would be quite easy. But at the time, it was _____ in the world. It _____ for over forty years. The tower was erected to be the _____ for the 1898 World's Fair in Paris. Did you know that _____ died during construction? He was killed when he _____ the elevator shaft.

W2: Well, as famous as it is, I still think it looks like _____ a building.

W1: You wouldn't be _____ who has thought the tower was an eyesore. Many members of the French public did not _____ the tower. _____ even ate his lunch at a restaurant near the tower because he felt it was the only place in Paris where he could eat without _____.

   Furthermore, the city government of Paris _____ with Gustave Eiffel that after twenty years, rights to the tower would be theirs, at which time they would _____. But since it proved to be _____ for radio communications, the city allowed Eiffel's permit to expire. By that time, the tower was _____ in French culture that they could not tear it down.

05-13

Marketing

1 What is the professor's opinion of online marketing?

    Ⓐ It can have negative results if done improperly.

    Ⓑ It is too expensive for most companies to use.

    Ⓒ It is inferior to traditional marketing.

    Ⓓ It has advantages that can help companies.

2 Listen again to part of the lecture. Then answer the question.
What can be inferred about the professor when he says this: 🎧

    Ⓐ He is a strong supporter of influencer marketing.

    Ⓑ He considers influencer marketing a waste of time and money.

    Ⓒ He has not thought much about influencer marketing.

    Ⓓ He employed influencer marketing at his own business.

📖 **Words & Phrases**

typically `adv` normally; usually

primary `adj` main

influential `adj` having a big effect on others

✏ Summary Note

A Fill in the blanks with the appropriate words.

Two Categories of Marketing

Traditional Marketing
- Word of mouth
- Print based: newspapers, magazines, and journals
- ❶ _____
- Radio and television

Online Marketing
- Uses the Internet
- Content marketing: videos, blogs, and e-guides
- ❷ _____
  – Very effective
- ❸ _____
  – Hire influencers to promote products
- Email marketing

B Complete the following summary by using the words in the box.

with large audiences	radio and television	get word out
social media marketing	thanks to the Internet	content marketing

The professor states that businesses use marketing to ＿＿＿＿＿＿＿＿＿＿ about their products. In the past, word of mouth, print-based marketing, and marketing on ＿＿＿＿＿＿＿＿＿＿ were used. Today, there are many more types of marketing ＿＿＿＿＿＿＿＿＿＿. ＿＿＿＿＿＿＿＿＿＿ uses videos, blogs, and e-guides to provide information about products. ＿＿＿＿＿＿＿＿＿＿ can be effective since hundreds of millions of people use social media. Influencer marketing uses influencers ＿＿＿＿＿＿＿＿＿＿ to promote products. A fourth one is email marketing.

Dictation Exercise   Listen to the lecture again and fill in the blanks.

M Professor: Companies that want to sell more ＿＿＿＿＿＿＿＿＿＿ typically invest in marketing. This enables them to ＿＿＿＿＿＿＿＿＿＿ their products out both to existing and potential customers. In the past, most marketing was either ＿＿＿＿＿＿＿＿＿＿, as people told others about a business and its products, or print based. In other words, marketing appeared in various newspapers, magazines, and journals or as ＿＿＿＿＿＿＿＿＿＿. Of course, once radio and television were developed, marketing was done ＿＿＿＿＿＿＿＿＿＿, too.

Nowadays, thanks to ＿＿＿＿＿＿＿＿＿＿, there are many more types of marketing that companies can engage in. One ＿＿＿＿＿＿＿＿＿＿ of using the Internet is that a business can market its products literally to anyone with an Internet connection. So rather than merely focusing on ＿＿＿＿＿＿＿＿＿＿ customers, businesses can market their products to people all around the world. This can help businesses ＿＿＿＿＿＿＿＿＿＿ if they take advantage of this opportunity.

What are ＿＿＿＿＿＿＿＿＿＿ of online marketing? Well, let's think for a moment . . . Content marketing is one. This may utilize videos, blogs, and e-guides as businesses ＿＿＿＿＿＿＿＿＿＿ with information about their products, which may convince people to purchase these goods or services. Another type is ＿＿＿＿＿＿＿＿＿＿. There are many popular ＿＿＿＿＿＿＿＿＿＿ used by hundreds of millions of people around the world. This type of marketing can be ＿＿＿＿＿＿＿＿＿＿ at times.

＿＿＿＿＿＿＿＿＿＿ is yet another type of Internet-based marketing method. You all know what influencers are, right? Well, many businesses ＿＿＿＿＿＿＿＿＿＿ to promote their products. Some influencers may have hundreds of thousands—or even millions—of followers, and the most, uh, influential ones can be ＿＿＿＿＿＿＿＿＿＿ at marketing products. Some companies should ＿＿＿＿＿＿＿＿＿＿ employing them. In just a moment, I'm going to give you a couple of examples of these. But first, I ＿＿＿＿＿＿＿＿＿＿ talking about different online marketing methods. A fourth one I'd like to discuss now is ＿＿＿＿＿＿＿＿＿＿. Can anyone tell me what that is?

Listen to part of a lecture and answer the questions.

05-14

Climatology

1 What is the professor's opinion of El Nino?

   Ⓐ It is not harmful at all.

   Ⓑ It is a complex subject to discuss.

   Ⓒ It barely changes local weather.

   Ⓓ It helps farmers in many places.

2 What signifies a period of El Nino or La Nina?

   Ⓐ Thunderstorms lasting many months

   Ⓑ An extended change in the temperature

   Ⓒ Hurricanes that are stronger than normal

   Ⓓ Times of drought in Africa

📙 **Words & Phrases**

phenomenon n an event

oscillation n the act of moving to and from certain points

fluctuation n the act of varying irregularly

sustain v to maintain something over a period of time of food or natural resources

🖉 Summary Note

A Fill in the blanks with the appropriate words.

El Nino: - 0.5℃ Celsius up

El Nino & La Nina

La Nina: - 0.5℃ Celsius down

Effects

- Affect ❶ _____ on the continents of South America and Africa ➡ can have a great socio-economic impact
- Cause abnormal climate
- Damage to ❷ _____

B Complete the following summary by using the words in the box.

temperature change	most affected	occur irregularly
upswelling	fish population	nutrient-rich

El Nino and La Nina signify a _____ of 0.5° Celsius higher or lower than normal for more than five months. Countries on the continents of South America and Africa are the _____ by El Nino. These episodes _____ every two to seven years. They reverse normal climates. An example of El Nino in action is when warm water flows toward the South American coast. The absence of cold water _____ sends the _____ out to sea. This is due to the fact that fish follow the cool _____ water. The causes of El Nino are still not fully understood by scientists.

Dictation Exercise Listen to the lecture again and fill in the blanks.

M Professor: I'd like to provide you with _____ the El Nino and La Nina weather phenomena. These patterns are not easy to understand, so _____.

The El Nino Southern Oscillation, or just El Nino _____, is a global coupled ocean-atmosphere phenomenon. Pacific Ocean signatures such as El Nino and La Nina are major _____ in surface waters of the tropical eastern part of the Pacific Ocean. El Nino signifies a rise of 0.5° Celsius or more and La Nina a drop of the same that is sustained for a period _____.

Many of the countries most affected by El Nino are _____ on the continents of South America and Africa. Their economies are _____ on the agricultural and fishing sectors as major sources of food, employment, and foreign exchange. New capabilities for _____ can have a great socio-economic impact.

_____ usually occur irregularly every two to seven years. They usually last for one or two years. The effects of El Nino are _____. Many places experience weather that is the reverse of _____. Some areas even experience _____ due to excess rainfall or forest fires because of heavy drought. _____ the drastic weather changes around the Southern Hemisphere, the fishing and manure industries in South America are _____.

In the normal Pacific pattern, equatorial winds gather. Then, warm water pools _____. Cold water upswells along the South American coast. Since fish follow the _____ water, this brings them up the coast, where they support the local fishing industry. When El Nino _____, the warm water flows toward the South American coast. The absence of cold upswelling increases warming and sends _____ out to sea instead of along the coast. These conditions are severely damaging to _____.

The causes of El Nino and La Nina temperature changes are _____. But many scientists are dedicating their careers to better understanding this _____.

Exercise 4 Listen to part of a lecture and answer the questions.

05-15

Philosophy

1 Listen again to part of the lecture. Then answer the question. What can be inferred about the student when he says this: 🎧
- Ⓐ He agrees with the doctrine of Solipsism.
- Ⓑ He thinks Descartes was the first existentialist.
- Ⓒ He thinks the professor agrees with Kierkegaard.
- Ⓓ He thinks math can prove truth about the universe.

2 According to the professor, who said, "I think; therefore, I am"?
- Ⓐ Soren Kierkegaard
- Ⓑ Socrates
- Ⓒ Rene Descartes
- Ⓓ Jean Paul Sartre

📖 **Words & Phrases**

existentialist n a proponent of the existential view of philosophy
intersected adj crossed at a point; overlapped
drastic adj intense or strong

📝 Summary Note

A Fill in the blanks with the appropriate words.

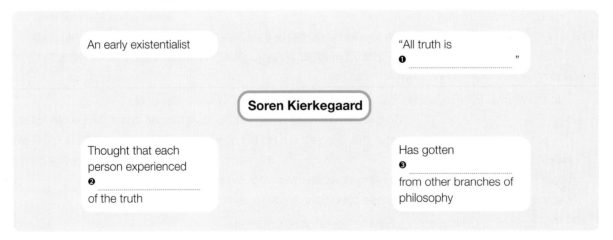

An early existentialist

"All truth is
❶ _____ "

Soren Kierkegaard

Thought that each person experienced
❷ _____
of the truth

Has gotten
❸ _____
from other branches of philosophy

B Complete the following summary by using the words in the box.

natural philosopher	prove truth	early existentialist
statement on truth	doctrine of Solipsism	branches of philosophy

The professor begins the lecture with the quote, "I think; therefore, I am." It is from Rene Descartes. Descartes was a _____. He was also a mathematician who believed math could be used to _____ about the universe. Soren Kierkegaard was an _____. He said, "All truth is subjective." The professor and the students then discuss the meaning of truth to individual people. Kierkegaard's _____ led to the _____, that all individuals are alone with the rest of the universe. Solipsism has suffered much criticism from other _____ for being selfish and egotistical.

Dictation Exercise   Listen to the lecture again and fill in the blanks.

M1 Professor: I'd like to start this class with a question. Who here can tell me which great philosopher said, "I think; therefore, I am"?

W Student: I've heard that before. Was it . . . Jean Paul Sartre?

M1: That's _____, but no. This philosopher lived almost three hundred years before Jean Paul Sartre. His name is Rene Descartes. He is considered _____ modern philosophy.

M2 Student: Was he an existentialist?

M1: No, he wasn't. Descartes was a _____. He was also a mathematician. His love for _____ intersected. He felt math could be used to _____ about the universe. But it's interesting that you brought up the existentialists. That's _____ from modern Western philosophy. Let's talk about an early existentialist named Soren Kierkegaard.

Soren Kierkegaard was a _____ who lived in the 1800s. He made a very _____ on truth. He said, "All truth _____."

W: Does that mean that up is down, black is white, and two plus two equals five?

M1: No, his viewpoint was _____. Kierkegaard just thought that each person experienced _____ of the truth based on the perspective from where they were standing. For example, two men are looking at _____. One man says the glass of water is _____. The other man says the glass is _____. _____ seem to be conflicting. Are they? No, they are both right. Each man possesses _____. _____ is more right or more wrong. Their truths are _____. This was a precursor to the existentialist view that each person is alone in their relationship with the _____. This viewpoint, called the doctrine of Solipsism, has gotten _____ from other branches of philosophy. _____ of being selfish and egotistical.

M2: But _____ to me.

M1: Sure. Existentialism and teen angst have always gone _____.

Integrated Listening & Speaking

A Listen to the previous lecture on marketing and say the answers out loud by using the cue sentence words that are indicated in each answer. You can refer to the summary note below.

05-16

Marketing

✏ Summary Note

Two Categories of Marketing

Traditional Marketing
- Word of mouth
- Print based: newspapers, magazines, and journals
- Printed advertisements
- Radio and television

Online Marketing
- Uses the Internet
- Content marketing: videos, blogs, and e-guides
- Social media marketing
  – Very effective
- Influencer marketing
  – Hire influencers to promote products
- Email marketing

1 Why do businesses use marketing?

a. Businesses use marketing because they want to _____.

b. In order to _____, businesses use marketing.

2 What is content marketing?

a. _____ to provide information about products.

b. _____ to provide information about products in content marketing.

3 How is influencer marketing as a technique?

a. _____ since some influencers have large audiences.

b. Due to _____, it can be very effective.

B Listen to the previous lecture on philosophy and say the answers out loud by using the cue sentence words that are indicated in each answer. You can refer to the summary note below.

05-17

Philosophy

✏️ **Summary Note**

An early existentialist

"All truth is subjective"

Soren Kierkegaard

Thought that each person experienced a different version of the truth

Has gotten criticism from other branches of philosophy

1 What famous statement does the professor begin the lecture with?

a. The professor begins the lecture _____.

b. "I think; therefore, I am" is _____.

2 What did Descartes believe about math?

a. He believed that _____.

b. The truth about the universe _____.

3 What famous statement did Kierkegaard make?

a. All truth _____.

b. Every truth _____.

Listen to part of a conversation between a student and a Biology Department office employee.

05-18

1 Why does the student visit the Biology Department office?

    (A) To ask about a professor's location

    (B) To submit a class assignment

    (C) To find out where a classroom is

    (D) To apply for a part-time position

2 What is the man's attitude toward the student?

    (A) He is eager to assist her.

    (B) He is businesslike in his approach.

    (C) He has little time to chat with her.

    (D) He is very inquisitive about her.

3 According to the man, what is Professor Pokorny doing now?

    (A) Attending a staff meeting

    (B) Conducting office hours

    (C) Teaching a class

    (D) Grading homework assignments

4 What can be inferred about the student?

    (A) She is going to change her major to biology.

    (B) She is attending the school on an academic scholarship.

    (C) She has taken a class with Professor Paulson before.

    (D) She will visit Professor Pokorny tomorrow morning.

5 Listen again to part of the conversation. Then answer the question.
What can be inferred about the man when he says this: 🎧

    (A) He does not personally know Professor Paulson.

    (B) He thinks the student made a mistake.

    (C) He has not done much research himself.

    (D) He believes the student should call the professor.

05-19

Listen to part of a lecture in an art class.

Art

6 What is the lecture mainly about?
Click on 2 answers.
Ⓐ Cubist painters
Ⓑ Realist painters
Ⓒ Impressionist painters
Ⓓ Surrealist painters

7 What prevailing European style of painting did Caravaggio go against?
Ⓐ Impressionism
Ⓑ Realism
Ⓒ Cubism
Ⓓ Mannerism

8 Why does the professor mention *Impression, Sunrise*?
Ⓐ To talk about a painting by Caravaggio
Ⓑ To name her favorite painting
Ⓒ To describe what it looks like
Ⓓ To say how Impressionism got its name

9   What does the professor imply about Jean Francois Millet?

    Ⓐ He was taught by some famous artists.

    Ⓑ He painted pictures in the Realist style.

    Ⓒ He sold his works for large amounts of money.

    Ⓓ He preferred to paint landscapes.

10   What is the professor's opinion of *Sunday Afternoon on the Island of La Grande Jatte*?

    Ⓐ It was not the artist's best painting.

    Ⓑ It uses bright colors very well.

    Ⓒ It should have taken a short time to finish.

    Ⓓ It is an impressive work of art.

11   What will the professor probably do next?

    Ⓐ Collect the students' homework

    Ⓑ Take a short break

    Ⓒ Discuss another painting

    Ⓓ Show the students a short video

Vocabulary Check-Up

A Choose the correct words that match the definitions.

1 appendectomy •   • Ⓐ especially or particularly

2 cite •   • Ⓑ to fall down

3 fine •   • Ⓒ trying to accomplish more than one is capable of

4 replacement •   • Ⓓ something that takes the place of another thing

5 collapse •   • Ⓔ ruling absolutely

6 rivet •   • Ⓕ an enriching additive

7 supplement •   • Ⓖ an officially appointed assistant to one holding an official office

8 host •   • Ⓗ a person who is responsible for a guest

9 sustain •   • Ⓘ to maintain over a period of time

10 deputy •   • Ⓙ likely

11 probably •   • Ⓚ a bolt for holding together metal plates

12 overambitious •   • Ⓛ having a big effect on others

13 notably •   • Ⓜ surgery to remove an appendix from a human

14 influential •   • Ⓝ money that must be paid for breaking the law or a rule

15 autocratic •   • Ⓞ to list or make mention of something

B Complete the sentences by filling in the blanks with the words in the box.

Ⓐ prospective   Ⓑ impression   Ⓒ inspection   Ⓓ completely   Ⓔ unpleasant

1 The _____ of the facility will take several hours.

2 She is a(n) _____ employee at the company.

3 We were _____ surprised when he arrived early.

4 He made a good _____ on everyone during the interview.

5 The weather is so _____ because it is cold and cloudy.

PART III

Connecting Information

Connecting Information questions test your ability to integrate information from different parts of the listening passage to make inferences, to draw conclusions, to form generalizations, and to make predictions. To choose the right answer, these question types require you to make connections between or among pieces of information in the text and to identify the relationships between the ideas and the details.

UNIT

06

Understanding Organization

Overview

Introduction

Organization questions require you to identify the overall organization of the listening passage or the relationship between different portions of the listening passage. In organization questions, you are also asked to recognize the role of specific information such as topic changes, exemplifying, digressing, and inducing introductory and concluding remarks. This is to see whether you know how the specific part of the sentence is related to the entire content. This question type usually appears after lectures rather than conversations and sometimes requires you to choose more than one answer.

Question Types

▶ How does the professor organize the information about X that he presents to the class?

▶ How is the discussion organized?

▶ Why does the professor discuss X?

▶ Why does the professor mention X?

Useful Tips

■ Typical types of organizations include the following patterns:
  – giving examples
  – contrasting
  – comparing
  – classifying or categorizing
  – describing causes and effects
  – explaining in chronological order

■ Listen carefully for the transitions that indicate the sequence.

■ Focus on the relationship between the contents led by the transitional words.

Script

W Professor: Asteroids are basically rocky bodies which orbit the sun. Some are tiny while others are several hundred kilometers in diameter. A large number of asteroids orbit the sun between Mars and Jupiter. This is known as the asteroid belt. Ceres, which is considered a dwarf planet now, is the largest asteroid in the asteroid belt. There are many other fairly large asteroids found there. Now, uh, if you watch movies, you might think that the asteroids are very close to one another. But that's not actually the case. Sure, sometimes an asteroid may collide with another one. But most of them are quite far from one another.

One question many people ask is why the asteroid belt actually exists. I mean, um, what caused so many asteroids to appear where they are. The most reasonable explanation is that these asteroids were once part of a planet. However, this planet was basically ripped apart because of its close proximity to Jupiter. Essentially, Jupiter's gravitational pull, which is quite powerful, either kept the planet from forming or simply broke it up. So all those pieces of rock very possibly were once part of a planet.

06-01

Q Why does the professor mention Jupiter?
- Ⓐ To compare its gravity with that of the sun
- Ⓑ To say it is the largest planet in the solar system
- Ⓒ To explain its role in creating the asteroid belt
- Ⓓ To point out how much bigger than Ceres it is

✅ Correct Answer

The correct answer to the above question is Ⓒ. The professor talks about how Jupiter's gravity possibly pulled apart a planet and created the asteroid belt.

Basic Drill

Listen to parts of conversations or lectures and answer the questions.

Drill 1

Q Why does the professor mention criminology and forensic science?

06-02

- Ⓐ He would like the student to major in them.
- Ⓑ He believes that they are important to study.
- Ⓒ They are two subjects that go well together.
- Ⓓ He thinks society needs more forensic detectives.

Check-Up Listen again and circle the words you hear.

fine art	complement each other	doubled over	declaration
declaring	sculpted	social science	artistically finite
double major	completed	sculpture	scientific society

Drill 2

Q Why does the librarian mention the reservations desk?

06-03

- Ⓐ To tell the student to check out books there
- Ⓑ To say that a librarian is not there now
- Ⓒ To claim that the book he needs is there
- Ⓓ To show the student where to arrange to get a book

Check-Up Listen again and circle the words you hear.

carded results	due in two days	wandering	water fountain
copied reservations	wondering	clerk	two weeks of duty
reservation card	waterfall	reserved a copy	cluck

Drill 3

Q Why does the worker mention the student center?

06-04

- Ⓐ To suggest looking for jobs there
- Ⓑ To say that it is hiring employees now
- Ⓒ To state that the dining hall is next to it
- Ⓓ To explain where his manager is

Check-Up Listen again and circle the words you hear.

position is filled	I don't blame you	my cup of tea	have a tale
want a cup of tea	turning around	might be hiring	keep looking around
what does that entail	I blame you	what position is it	we're not hiring

Drill 4

Q Why does the professor explain the nucleus of a comet?

   Ⓐ To say how large it can get

   Ⓑ To explain why it orbits the sun

   Ⓒ To describe what it is made of

   Ⓓ To compare it with the tail

06-05

Check-Up Listen again and circle the words you hear.

solar system	troposphere	heavily affected	Heaven's gate
constantly changing	solar power	atmosphere	horribly afflicted
heavenly body	changeable constant	throwing up	thrown out of

Drill 5

Q Why does the professor mention bacteria?

   Ⓐ To compare them with fungi

   Ⓑ To describe how they decompose matter

   Ⓒ To show where most of them live

   Ⓓ To explain how they can harm people

06-06

Check-Up Listen again and circle the words you hear.

externally	eternally	nutrient molecules	semantic relation
primary decomposers	erotic	used extensively	neutral molecule
eukaryotic	primitive composer	extra use	symbiotic relationships

Drill 6

Q Why does the professor mention encoding, storage, and recall?

   Ⓐ Because they are his favorite aspects of memory

   Ⓑ To explain the three main stages in the retrieval of memory

   Ⓒ Because he wants the students to describe each of them

   Ⓓ Because cognitive neuroscience of psychology is important

06-07

Check-Up Listen again and circle the words you hear.

traditional studies	cogent psychoanalyst	marriage between	marinated beef
listen carefully	loosen carelessly	trade students	realm of philosophy
regional philosopher	cognitive psychology	recent decades	recently decadent

Exercise 1 **Listen to part of a conversation and answer the questions.**

06-08

Service Encounter

1 Why does the student mention the recreational hockey league?

- Ⓐ To say why his weekends are always busy
- Ⓑ To give the reason why he does not work part time
- Ⓒ To tell the woman about the team he is on
- Ⓓ To explain why he wants to change his schedule

2 What is the student's problem?

- Ⓐ He is doing poorly in his classes.
- Ⓑ He needs to change his class schedule.
- Ⓒ He cannot afford the fee to play hockey.
- Ⓓ He needs to practice hockey every day.

📕 Words & Phrases

recreational adj for fun; not serious or professional

shift v to change in some manner

calculus n a particular method of calculation or reasoning

rearrange v to change the order of something

📝 Summary Note

A Fill in the blanks with the appropriate words.

Student

- Wants to change class schedule to play in ❶ _____
- 3 changes
  - Change intro to modern literature class to night class
  - Join Tuesday morning calculus class
  - Drop Chemistry 101

Employee

- Counsels student
- 3 reasons not to change schedule
  - Intro to modern literature night class is full
  - Tuesday morning calculus class is ❷ _____
  - Chemistry 101 is a ❸ _____ ; cannot drop

Student decides not to play in hockey recreational league

B Complete the following summary by using the words in the box.

shift	changes his mind	too advanced
recreational hockey league	might not be able	drop

A student wants to change his schedule so that he can join a _____ .
He wants to _____ his classes to different times. He also wants to
_____ his Chemistry 101 class. The assistant tells him that the classes he
wants to change into are either full or _____ for him. She also tells him that
he _____ to graduate in four years if he drops Chemistry 101. The student
_____ and decides not to play hockey.

Dictation Exercise Listen to the conversation again and fill in the blanks.

M Student: Hi. Who should I talk to about changing _____ for this semester?

W Registrar's Office Employee: You can talk to me about it. I'm the Registrar's assistant.

M: Great. You're _____ I need to talk to. I want to join the
_____ . So I'm going to have to shift my calculus class to Tuesday mornings, my
intro to modern literature course to _____ , and maybe drop Chemistry 101.

W: Hmm, that sounds like _____ . Are you sure you want to do that
_____ the hockey league?

M: Oh, totally, for sure. Hockey versus Chemistry 101 . . . Which one would you choose?

W: Do you want to graduate with _____ in four years?

M: Yeah, but that's not for years. I need to _____ this winter. That seems
_____ right now.

W: Okay, I'm looking at your schedule here, and I _____ . First of all, the night class
for intro to modern literature is full. _____ you can get in there.

M: Oh, that stinks.

W: Secondly, you _____ to the Tuesday morning calculus class. But
_____ you that it's an accelerated class. That means that the professor will
move through the book _____ than the low-level class you're currently in.
Are you prepared to _____ the increased course speed? Is calculus one of
_____ ?

M: Well, no, but maybe I could . . .

W: Finally, about dropping Chemistry 101. Your major is Microbiology. You have to have Chemistry 101
_____ to take most of the other classes in your major. If you drop it this semester,
it'll _____ from taking any other courses in your major next semester. You could set
_____ back a year just to play recreational hockey. Do you really want to do that?

M: Hmm, I guess _____ . Thanks anyway.

W: No problem. Have a nice day!

06-09

Office Hours

1 Why does the student mention Professor Monroe?
   - (A) To point out he is in the History Department
   - (B) To state that she dislikes his class
   - (C) To note that he is her academic advisor
   - (D) To say she is taking a class with him

2 What will the student probably do next?
   - (A) Fill out a form
   - (B) Visit her freshman advisor
   - (C) Attend her next class
   - (D) Go to the library

📖 Words & Phrases

recall Ⓥ to remember
declare Ⓥ to state officially or out loud
lecturer Ⓝ a teacher
signature Ⓝ a person's signed name

✏️ Summary Note

A Fill in the blanks with the appropriate words.

| The student wants to declare economics as ❶ _____ and have the professor be her advisor | The professor agrees to help her | The student has ❷ _____ for the professor to sign | The student needs to get her freshman advisor to sign the form, too |

B   Complete the following summary by using the words in the box.

sign a form	her academic advisor	major in economics
declare economics	the professor's class	two economics classes

The student says that she took _____ last year and enjoyed it. Now, she wants

to _____ her major and have the professor be _____.

The professor asks her if she is sure she wants to _____, and she says

yes. So he agrees to be her advisor. The student is also taking _____ this

semester. The professor needs to _____ the student has already filled out.

Then, she will get her freshman advisor's signature.

Dictation Exercise   Listen to the conversation again and fill in the blanks.

W Student: Good morning, Professor Johanssen. May I _____ with you, please?

M Professor: Hello. Oh . . . I remember you. You _____ in microeconomics

last semester. I seem to recall that you _____ in it. But . . . I'm afraid I don't

_____.

W: I'm Amy Riley, sir.

M: Ah, that's right. I _____ that. So what can I do for you today, Amy?

W: Well, uh, this is the start of _____, so I need to declare a major. I really

_____ that I took with you, and I thought you were a great professor.

M: Thank you for saying that.

W: I'd therefore _____ economics my major and ask you to be

_____. Would that be possible?

M: Of course, it's possible. But I need to ask you . . . Are you sure that you want to

_____?

W: Yes, sir. I am. I am actually taking _____ this semester. The first is with Professor

Monroe while the second one is with, um, Professor Parkins.

M: Ah, those should be _____. Both of them are _____.

W: Yes, I'm learning a lot in each class. So, uh, I need to fill out a form and _____,

right?

M: _____, but I'm afraid that I don't have this form in my office.

W: Don't worry. I brought it with me. I just need to _____ and the signature of my

freshman advisor. I plan to do that right after I _____.

M: I'm glad to see that you've already got the form. Let me _____ somewhere.

Exercise 3 Listen to part of a conversation and answer the questions.

Service Encounter

06-10

1 Why does the woman discuss the proofreading job?

- (A) To describe its benefits
- (B) To recommend avoiding it
- (C) To say how much it pays
- (D) To compare it with her job

2 What does the student give the woman?

- (A) A writing sample
- (B) A copy of his transcript
- (C) A letter of recommendation
- (D) An application form

📕 **Words & Phrases**

tutor (n) a private teacher
hold on (phr) to wait
proficient (adj) skilled; able; talented
proofread (v) to check writing for mistakes

✏️ **Summary Note**

A Fill in the blanks with the appropriate words.

Student
- Wants a position as ❶ _____
- Has a ❷ _____ from a professor
- Is a good writer
- Does not make grammar mistakes

Employee
- Reads the student's letter
- Tells the student about the ❸ _____ position and the proofreading position
- Recommends that the student take the proofreading position

The student decides to be a proofreader

B Complete the following summary by using the words in the box.

the writing center	grammar mistakes	a proofreading job
explains its benefits	writing tutor	letter of recommendation

The student visits _____ to talk about a job as a writing tutor. He has a _____ from a professor. The professor writes that the student never makes _____ and is a technically proficient writer. The woman describes the job of _____ and then says that _____ is available as well. She recommends the proofreading job and then _____. The student decides to become a proofreader.

Dictation Exercise Listen to the conversation again and fill in the blanks.

M Student: Good afternoon. I'm _____ Juliet Harrison. Do you know where I can find her?

W Writing Center Employee: Hello. I'm Juliet. Is there something I can help you with?

M: I sure hope so. My name is Samuel Wallace. I spoke _____ with you earlier this morning.

W: Ah, right. You are here about a job as _____, right?

M: That's correct. I, uh, I have a _____ from Professor McMurray in the English Department. Here you are.

W: Thank you. _____ and let me look at it really quickly, please . . .

M: Sure. _____.

W: Hmm . . . It looks like the professor thinks _____ your writing skills. He also notes that you never make _____ on your papers and that your writing is technically proficient.

M: He's very kind.

W: Well, we have a couple of jobs that _____ for students like you. The first is to be _____ Basically, you would work one on one with various students to help them _____.

M: What's _____?

W: The other position is proofreader. You'd be responsible for proofreading students' _____. You would need to catch mistakes and also _____ on how to improve their papers. Personally, I think you'd _____ taking this job.

M: Why is that?

W: You can work from home since papers _____ to you. The pay is really good, and you'll _____ to make a lot of money if you do a good job.

M: I guess _____ that position then. Thanks.

Exercise 4 Listen to part of a conversation and answer the questions.

06-11

Office Hours

1 Why does the professor mention Hungarian exchange students?
- Ⓐ To encourage the student to meet them
- Ⓑ To say what their majors are
- Ⓒ To praise them for their high grades
- Ⓓ To point out that they speak English well

2 Why does the student visit the professor?
- Ⓐ To request help on his homework
- Ⓑ To inquire about scholarships
- Ⓒ To ask for help with a class
- Ⓓ To talk about studying abroad

📙 **Words & Phrases**

exchange Ⓥ to change two or more things for each other
abroad adv outside one's homeland
determine Ⓥ to finally decide

✏ Summary Note

A Fill in the blanks with the appropriate words.

Two countries where the student would like to study

❶ _____
- First choice
- Civil War ➡ not a good choice

Hungary
- Second choice
- ❷ _____ in Budapest; the student speaks Hungarian fluently ➡ a good choice

166 Part **III**

B Complete the following summary by using the words in the box.

an unrealistic idea	studying abroad	speaks Hungarian fluently
exchange students	second choice	student exchange program

The student is interested in _____. He talks to the professor, who
is in charge of the _____. The professor asks the student where he
would like to study. The student says he would like to study in the Sudan. The professor says
it is _____ because the country is in civil war. The student says his
_____ is Budapest because he _____.
The professor thinks it is a good idea. He offers to introduce the student to some Hungarian
_____ at the school.

Dictation Exercise   Listen to the conversation again and fill in the blanks.

M Student: Hi, Professor Jones. May I _____ for a few moments?

W Professor: Sure, Mark. How can I _____ to you today?

M: I heard you are _____ the student exchange program for the International
Studies Department.

W: That's right. Are you interested in _____?

M: Well, _____ about it before. But I've been reading my course book, and it
recommends _____ abroad for students like me majoring in international law.

W: That's absolutely correct. For students in your major, _____ you spend six
months to a year abroad. It will prepare you for the type of work you'll be doing, and it will help you
determine _____ of focus. So where do you think you'd like to study?

M: Well, I've been thinking about _____. I've always wanted to go to Sudan.

W: The Sudan? Isn't it in the middle of _____? Do you really want to go there?

M: I've been reading about it, and I think I could help _____ or something.

W: Hmm, I don't think that's a _____ for you to get much studying done. Do you
have a _____ choice?

M: Yeah, you're probably right. My parents are Hungarian. So I _____. It
_____ for me to study in Budapest since I speak the language.

W: Now that is a _____ idea. I actually know of a _____
located in Budapest. We have _____ studying here now. Maybe I could introduce
you to them, and you could _____.

M: That would be great. I'd love to _____ if I went there. It would be nice to know
some people right away.

Exercises with Mid-Length Lectures

Exercise 1 Listen to part of a lecture and answer the questions.

Botany

06-12

1   How does the professor organize the information about the pollination process that she presents to the class?
   Ⓐ By speaking chronologically
   Ⓑ By going from the most important to the least important
   Ⓒ By putting it into different categories
   Ⓓ By narrating as she shows the class a video

2   What is the female gamete?
   Ⓐ The anther
   Ⓑ The stigma
   Ⓒ The ovule
   Ⓓ The carpel

📖 Words & Phrases

gamete ⓝ a mature germ cell able to unite with another in sexual reproduction
angiosperm ⓝ any plant reproducing flowers by seeds enclosed within a carpel
gymnosperm ⓝ any of various plants having seeds unprotected by an ovary
horticulture ⓝ the art of garden cultivation

✏️ Summary Note

A   Fill in the blanks with the appropriate words.

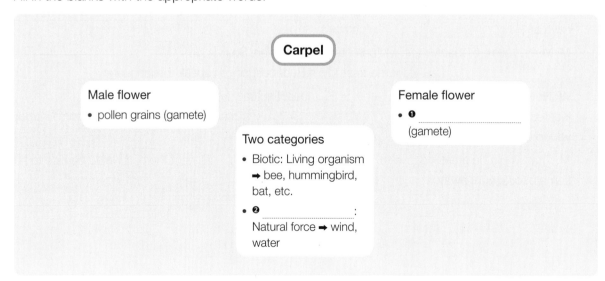

Carpel

Male flower
• pollen grains (gamete)

Two categories
• Biotic: Living organism
   ➡ bee, hummingbird, bat, etc.
• ❷ _____ :
   Natural force ➡ wind, water

Female flower
• ❶ _____
   (gamete)

B Complete the following summary by using the words in the box.

refers to	process of pollination	act as agents
carried out	living organisms	reproduction

Pollination is important for the _____ of seed plants. Many plants will not develop if their ovules are not fertilized. The _____ requires pollinators to _____ and to carry pollen grains from the anther to the carpel. Pollination can either be _____ by biotic or abiotic means. Biotic refers to pollination by other _____. This often includes hummingbirds, bees, and bats. Abiotic _____ pollination by natural means, such as wind and water. Most pollination is biotic.

Dictation Exercise Listen to the lecture again and fill in the blanks.

W Professor: Class, today I want to tell you about the _____. Pollination is an important step in _____ seed plants. This is the name for the transfer of _____ to the plant carpel. The carpel is the structure that _____. The pollen grains are the male gamete, and the ovule is _____. _____ of the carpel is called a stigma in the flowers of angiosperms and a micropyle in gymnosperms.

The study of pollination brings together _____, such as botany, horticulture, entomology, and ecology. Pollination is important in horticulture because _____ will not develop if the ovules are not fertilized. The pollination process as an interaction between _____ was first addressed in the eighteenth century by Christian Konrad Sprengel.

The process of pollination _____ as agents that carry or move the pollen grains from the anther to the receptive part of the carpel. The various flower traits that _____ are known as pollinator syndromes.

One method of pollination _____ is entomophily, which is pollination by insects. Bees, wasps, butterflies, and flies are just a few of the insects that usually _____ this process. Another method is called zoophily. This denotes pollination by vertebrates, such as _____. The hummingbird and the honeyeater _____ with this process.

Yet _____ of pollination is anemophily, which is by the wind. _____ with many types of grasses and deciduous trees. In the case of _____, pollination by water is called hydrophily. All of these pollination processes are covered by _____, biotic and abiotic pollination. Biotic covers pollination by organisms, including entomophily and zoophily. This includes eighty percent of _____. Abiotic pollination _____ not carried out by other organisms, including anemophily and hydrophily. Of the twenty percent this covers, ninety-eight percent is by wind and just two percent _____.

Exercise 2 Listen to part of a lecture and answer the questions.

06-13

Psychology

1 Why does the professor mention patting the head and rubbing the belly at the same time?

- (A) Because it is a fun activity
- (B) Because he wants to see who can do it
- (C) Because it is an important ability to learn
- (D) Because it is an example of splitting attention

2 What does the professor imply about the female student?

- (A) She can do something not everyone can.
- (B) She needs to read the textbook more closely.
- (C) She should try to answer her own question.
- (D) She was doing the activity improperly.

📖 Words & Phrases

circular adj in a round motion

coordinate v to manage action between two or more people or things

cognitive adj relating to the processes of thinking

🖉 Summary Note

A Fill in the blanks with the appropriate words.

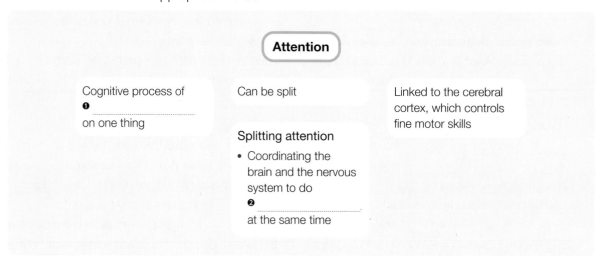

Attention

Cognitive process of
❶ ....
on one thing

Can be split

Splitting attention

- Coordinating the brain and the nervous system to do
❷ ....
at the same time

Linked to the cerebral cortex, which controls fine motor skills

170 Part **III**

B   Complete the following summary by using the words in the box.

cognitive process	simultaneous	trains of thought
at the same time	fine motor skills	major psychologists

Coordinating the brain and the nervous system to do two different actions
_____ is called splitting attention. Attention is the _____
of selectively concentrating on one thing while ignoring other things. William James was one of the
first _____ . He defined attention as "the taking possession by the mind, in
clear and vivid form, of one out of what seem to be several _____ possible
objects or _____ ." The attention of one's mind is linked to the cerebral cortex,
which controls _____ .

Dictation Exercise   Listen to the lecture again and fill in the blanks.

M1 Professor: All right, class. Let's get started. I'd like to begin today's class with
_____ . With your left hand, I want you to _____ on the
head. With your right hand, I want you to _____ with a circular motion. Can you do
it?

M2 Student: Hey, this is really difficult! I can't do it.

W Student: I've got it! It just takes _____ . Check this out!

M1: Okay, everyone _____ . I asked you to do this because I wanted you
to notice _____ it is for your brain and nervous system to coordinate two
different actions _____ . This is called splitting your attention. Attention is the
_____ of selectively concentrating on one thing while ignoring other things.
One example is listening carefully to what someone is saying while _____ in
the room. This is called the _____ . Attention can also be split, such as when
a person _____ and talks on a cellphone. Sometimes our attention shifts to
matters unrelated to _____ . This is referred to as _____ or
spontaneous thought.

W: But I was able to pat my head and rub my belly _____ . What does that mean
about me?

M1: Well, that means that you _____ splitting your attention. That reminds
me of the _____ of attention by one of the first major psychologists, William
James. He said, "Everyone knows what attention is. It is the taking possession by the mind in
_____ form, of one out of what seem to be several simultaneously possible objects
or trains of thought. It _____ from some things in order to deal effectively with
others."

W: Hmm, that sounds interesting. But how is the action of rubbing my belly and patting my head
_____ focusing my mind?

M1: Good question. It is linked because your cerebral cortex controls your _____ ,
which is what those motions require.

Exercise 3 Listen to part of a lecture and answer the questions.

06-14

Education

1 How is the discussion organized?

  Ⓐ Alphabetically

  Ⓑ Chronologically

  Ⓒ From general to specific

  Ⓓ From complex to simple

2 What was the first colony to establish compulsory education?

  Ⓐ The West Virginia Colony

  Ⓑ The Georgia Coastal Colony

  Ⓒ The Massachusetts Bay Colony

  Ⓓ The New York River Colony

📖 **Words & Phrases**

colonial adj of or pertaining to colonists

mandatory adj required by law

scheme n a plan or system

compulsory adj subjected to enforcement by law

✏️ **Summary Note**

A Fill in the blanks with the appropriate words.

Development of the American Educational System

1640s-1750s

- Massachusetts Bay Colony made education ❶ _____
  ➡ all colonies followed Massachusetts
- ❷ _____ established

Public School System

- 1840: reformers such as Horace Mann called for public school system
- 1900: 31 states required children 8 to 14 years of age to attend school
- 1918: every state required students to complete elementary school
- Early 20th century: most states increased compulsory school attendance age to
  ❸ _____

B Complete the following summary by using the words in the box.

school systems	skyrocket	educational reformers
heavier emphasis	secondary education	entitled

The first American schools opened during the Colonial Era. After the revolution, a _____ was placed on education. _____ remained private until the 1840s. Then, _____ began calling for public education systems. They believed everyone was _____ to the same content in education. By 1900, thirty-one states required children eight to fourteen years of age to attend school. _____ progressed more slowly. In the early twentieth century, strict child labor laws and growing acceptance of higher education caused the number of high school graduates to _____ .

Dictation Exercise Listen to the lecture again and fill in the blanks.

M Professor: Right now, I'd like to tell you about the development of the _____ . The first American schools opened during the Colonial Era. As the colonies _____ , many of them instituted mandatory education schemes. In 1642, the Massachusetts Bay Colony made "proper" _____ . Similar statutes _____ in other colonies in the 1640s and 1650s. Virtually _____ that opened as a result of this were private. Most of the universities which appeared between 1640 and 1750 form the contemporary Ivy League. _____ Harvard, Yale, Columbia, Brown, and the University of Pennsylvania. _____ , an even heavier emphasis was put on education. This made the United States have one of the highest _____ of the time.

The school systems remained _____ and unorganized until the 1840s. _____ such as Horace Mann of Massachusetts began calling for public education systems for all. He helped create _____ of common schools, which referred to the belief that everyone was entitled to the same content in education. These early efforts focused primarily on _____ .

The common-school movement began to _____ . By 1900, thirty-one states required children eight to fourteen years of age _____ . In 1918, every state required students to _____ . Lessons consisted of students reading aloud from their texts, such as the *McGuffery Readers*, and _____ on rote memorization. Teachers often used _____ , such as hitting students on the knuckles with birch switches for _____ .

Secondary education progressed _____ , remaining the province of the affluent and the domain of private tutors. In 1870, only two percent of teens fourteen to seventeen years old graduated _____ . The introduction of strict _____ and the growing acceptance of higher education in general in the early twentieth century caused the number of high school graduates to skyrocket. Most states passed laws which increased the age for _____ to sixteen.

06-15

Astronomy

1 How is the discussion organized?

Ⓐ The professor provides the students with lists of statistics.

Ⓑ The professor compares Mars with Venus.

Ⓒ The professor tells several anecdotes about Mars.

Ⓓ The professor answers questions that the students ask.

2 Why does the professor mention the contents of Mars's atmosphere?

Ⓐ To say that humans cannot breathe it

Ⓑ To point out how much oxygen it has

Ⓒ To compare it with Earth's atmosphere

Ⓓ To explain why Mars might have life

📖 **Words & Phrases**

flyby (n) the motion past a place or object made by an airborne vehicle that does not land

canal (n) a large channel made to control the flow of water

axial (adj) forming or belonging to an axis

📝 Summary Note

A Fill in the blanks with the appropriate words.

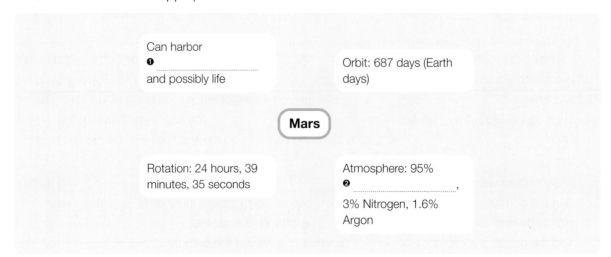

Can harbor
❶ _____
and possibly life

Orbit: 687 days (Earth days)

Mars

Rotation: 24 hours, 39 minutes, 35 seconds

Atmosphere: 95%
❷ _____,
3% Nitrogen, 1.6% Argon

B Complete the following summary by using the words in the box.

traces	most likely place	open question
seasonal periods	once believed	condenses

Mars is the fourth planet from the sun. Canals on the planet's surface that were
_____ to exist do not. But Mars is still the _____
in the solar system, besides Earth, to harbor liquid water and possibly life. Mars has
_____ similar to Earth's. But its year is almost twice as long. The Martian
atmosphere contains only _____ of oxygen. During the winter months, the
atmosphere gets so cold that it _____ into dry ice. Whether living organisms
exist on Mars is still an _____.

Dictation Exercise Listen to the lecture again and fill in the blanks.

W1 Professor: That's enough about Venus. Let's move on to _____ from the sun.
It's named after Mars, the _____. Until the first flyby of Mars by *Mariner 4* in 1965,
it was thought that there were channels of _____ on the planet's surface. People
called these Martian canals. Observations later showed that these channels _____.
Still, of all the planets in our solar system after Earth, Mars is _____ to harbor liquid
water and possibly life.

M Student: What about time on Mars? I heard it takes longer to _____ than Earth
does.

W1: Very good. That's right. Mars has a similar axial tilt to that of Earth, so it has
_____. But it's _____ the sun and takes longer to orbit. So a
Martian year is 687 Earth days long. _____, a solar day on Mars is almost the same
as Earth, being twenty-four hours, thirty-nine minutes, and thirty-five seconds.

W2 Student: What about _____? Is it possible for humans
_____ on Mars?

W1: Well, Mars has an atmosphere. But since it contains only _____, you
wouldn't want to breathe it. The Martian atmosphere is ninety-five percent carbon dioxide, three
percent nitrogen, and 1.6% argon. During the winter months, the atmosphere gets so cold that
_____ thick slabs of dry ice.

M: But you just said that _____ for life to exist there. What kind of life could live in
that kind of atmosphere?

W1: That's an interesting question. Some evidence suggests that the planet was once significantly
_____ than it is today. But whether living organisms ever existed there
is still _____. The *Viking* probes of the mid-1970s carried experiments
designed to _____ in Martian soil and had some positive results. But these
_____ by many scientists.

Integrated Listening & Speaking

A   Listen to the previous lecture on psychology and say the answers out loud by using the cue sentence words that are indicated in each answer. You can refer to the summary note below.

06-16

Psychology

✎ **Summary Note**

(**Attention**)

Cognitive process of selectively concentrating on one thing

Can be split

Splitting attention

- Coordinating the brain and the nervous system to do two different actions at the same time

Linked to the cerebral cortex, which controls fine motor skills

1   How does the professor ask his students to split their attention?

   a. He asks them to ....

   b. He tells them about ....

2   How does the professor explain attention?

   a. He says it is a ....

   b. He explains that it is the ....

3   How is attention linked to physical actions?

   a. It is linked by ....

   b. It is linked to ....

B Listen to the previous lecture on education and say the answers out loud by using the cue sentence words that are indicated in each answer. You can refer to the summary note below.

06-17

Education

📝 **Summary Note**

Development of the American Educational System	**1640s-1750s**	**Public School System**

1640s-1750s
- Massachusetts Bay Colony made education compulsory
  → all colonies followed Massachusetts
- Ivy League established

Public School System
- 1840: reformers such as Horace Mann called for public school system
- 1900: 31 states required children 8 to 14 years of age to attend school
- 1918: every state required students to complete elementary school
- Early 20th century: most states increased compulsory school attendance age to 16 years

1 How does the professor begin the lecture?

a. He begins by _____.

b. He begins with _____.

2 When did the United States put a heavier emphasis on education?

a. A heavier emphasis was put on _____.

b. The United States put a heavier emphasis on _____.

3 What were many of the teaching methods like?

a. Many of the teaching methods were _____.

b. Many teaching methods were _____.

06-18

Listen to part of a conversation between a student and a professor.

1 Why does the student visit the professor?

    Ⓐ To request help on doing some research

    Ⓑ To find out why her grade is not high

    Ⓒ To ask the professor for an extension

    Ⓓ To mention a problem with a class assignment

2 Why does the student mention Karen Rochester?

    Ⓐ To praise the work that she has done

    Ⓑ To say that she is her advisor

    Ⓒ To state the name of her partner

    Ⓓ To complain about the quality of her work

3 According to the student, how has she tried to communicate with her partner?
Click on 2 answers.

    Ⓐ By telephone

    Ⓑ In person

    Ⓒ By text message

    Ⓓ By email

4 What can be inferred about the professor?

    Ⓐ He does not have time to help the student.

    Ⓑ He does not want the student to work with a partner.

    Ⓒ He does not believe the student's story.

    Ⓓ He does not remember the student's partner.

5 What will the professor probably do next?

    Ⓐ Go home for the day

    Ⓑ Call a student on the phone

    Ⓒ Teach another class

    Ⓓ Go to the department office

06- 19

Listen to part of a lecture in a mechanics class.

6 What is the lecture mainly about?

ⓐ The way to operate a bicycle

ⓑ The advantages of bicycles

ⓒ The history of bicycles

ⓓ The most efficient types of bicycles

7 How does the professor organize the information about bicycles that he presents to the class?

ⓐ By talking about them chronologically

ⓑ By telling historical stories about them

ⓒ By asking questions and then having the students answer them

ⓓ By talking about the lives of bicycle inventors

8 What is the professor's opinion of the recumbent bicycle?

ⓐ It is very easy to control.

ⓑ It requires a lot of energy to use.

ⓒ It looks nicer than most bicycles.

ⓓ It should be considered a real bicycle.

9 According to the professor, where were bicycles first introduced?

  Ⓐ In Asia

  Ⓑ In North America

  Ⓒ In Africa

  Ⓓ In Europe

10 Why does the professor mention the velocipede?

  Ⓐ To name the person who invented it

  Ⓑ To call it an ancestor of the modern bike

  Ⓒ To compare it with a recumbent bicycle

  Ⓓ To claim it had more than two wheels

11 According to the professor, what did Kirkpatrick MacMillan do?

  Ⓐ He invented the first real bicycle.

  Ⓑ He put a motor on a bicycle.

  Ⓒ He made a recumbent bicycle.

  Ⓓ He was the inventor of the e-bike.

Vocabulary Check-Up

A Choose the correct words that match the definitions.

1 accelerated •   • Ⓐ to withhold one's attention

2 due •   • Ⓑ required for submittal at a given time

3 declare •   • Ⓒ faster than usual

4 orbit •   • Ⓓ to move around in a curved path

5 mandatory •   • Ⓔ to answer

6 wander •   • Ⓕ skilled; able; talented

7 discipline •   • Ⓖ a specialized area of subject matter and activity

8 private •   • Ⓗ to change in any manner

9 shift •   • Ⓘ a person with whom one works together

10 ignore •   • Ⓙ not public

11 partner •   • Ⓚ to announce officially

12 realm •   • Ⓛ to roam without an intended destination

13 symbiosis •   • Ⓜ required by law

14 proficient •   • Ⓝ a mutually beneficial relationship

15 respond •   • Ⓞ a place or area

B Complete the sentences by filling in the blanks with the words in the box.

Ⓐ tutor   Ⓑ collide   Ⓒ invention   Ⓓ declare   Ⓔ signature

1 The computer is an important _____ from the twentieth century.

2 You must _____ which person you are supporting.

3 The two trains will _____ if they do not stop.

4 She decided to work as a(n) _____ to make some extra money.

5 Please write your _____ at the bottom of this form.

Overview

Introduction

Connecting Content questions require you to identify the relationships among ideas in a lecture or conversation. These relationships may be explicitly stated, or you may have to infer them from the words you hear. For example, you may be asked to classify items in categories, identify a sequence of events or steps in a process, or specify relationships among ideas in a manner different from the way they were presented in the listening passage. In other Connecting Content questions, you may be required to make inferences about things mentioned in the listening passage and to predict an outcome, to draw a logical conclusion, or to extrapolate some additional information.

Question Types

▶ What is the likely outcome of doing procedure X before procedure Y?

▶ What can be inferred about X?

▶ What does the professor imply about X?

▶ Based on the information in the lecture, indicate which . . . the sentences refer to.
Click in the correct box for each sentence.

	X	Y
1 [a sentence or phrase]		
2 [a sentence or phrase]		
3 [a sentence or phrase]		
4 [a sentence or phrase]		

Useful Tips

■ Pay attention to the way you format your notes.

■ Focus on the category words, their characteristics, and examples.

07-01

Script

M1 Professor: Yesterday, we started talking about how geological formations take a long time to be created. One of these formations is called the glacier. Does anyone know what a glacier is?

W Student: It's a lot of ice!

M1: Well, kind of. It's certainly a lot of ice, but it's a little more than just that. A glacier is like a river of ice that moves slowly. The way a glacier moves depends on the slope of the land. A glacier will move with gravity. So I have to talk about how these glaciers are formed. See what happens is that snowfall covers mountainous regions. And this snow never completely melts. But it might thaw a bit and then refreeze. So you have this thawing and refreezing, which changes the snow to granules. Over the course of many years, more and more snow accumulates. Can anyone guess what happens to the snow that's at the bottom of this pile?

M2 Student: Wouldn't it get really firm from all the pressure?

M1: Exactly! So over thousands of years, from lots and lots of pressure, these huge sheets of slow-moving ice form. That's how a glacier is made. The cool thing about these glaciers is that they leave imprints in the ground kind of like fossils. So we can tell what the world was like when it was covered by glaciers back during the last ice age.

Q Based on the information in the lecture, indicate whether each of the following sentences is a fact or not.
Click in the correct box for each sentence.

	Fact	Not a Fact
1 A glacier can sometimes move very fast.		
2 The size of a land determines how a glacier moves.		
3 A glacier flows in response to gravity.		
4 Glaciers leave marks on the land surface.		

✅ Correct Answer

According to the lecture, a glacier moves slowly and the way a glacier moves is dependent upon the slope of the land. Thus choices 1 and 2 are incorrect. Meanwhile, the professor mentions that a glacier moves with gravity and that it leaves imprints in the ground, so choices 3 and 4 are correct.

Basic Drill

Listen to parts of conversations or lectures and answer the questions.

Drill 1

Q What can be inferred about the student's essay?

- (A) It lacks enough details.
- (B) It is too specific.
- (C) It supports the evidence well.
- (D) It contains several charts.

07-02

Check-Up Listen again and circle the words you hear.

describe	essay assignment	not explained	sort of
easy reassignment	can't explain	because of effects	introduction section
kind of	cause and effect	reintroduction	prescribe

Drill 2

Q What is the likely outcome of the student staying at school this summer?

- (A) He will write a good senior honors thesis.
- (B) He will get to graduate one semester early.
- (C) He will receive A's in most of his classes.
- (D) He will have time to apply to graduate schools.

07-03

Check-Up Listen again and circle the words you hear.

your email	school year	would like	your search
your mail	remember	will like	change my plants
senior honors thesis	correction	find a job	spend more time

Drill 3

Q What does the professor imply about overseas graduate programs?

- (A) They are hard for many students to get in to.
- (B) Some of them have high-rated programs.
- (C) Foreign students in them tend to work very hard.
- (D) Professors in them can speak English well.

07-04

Check-Up Listen again and circle the words you hear.

congratulate	practice experiment	more choices	overseas
a word with you	graduate students	awarded you	practical experience
broaden	few chances	overland	broken

Drill 4

Q What does the professor imply about radiocarbon dating?

   Ⓐ It is difficult to do properly.

   Ⓑ It is not very accurate.

   Ⓒ Few people are able to do it.

   Ⓓ It requires sensitive equipment.

07-05

Check-Up Listen again and circle the words you hear.

only basic tools	debris	contained samples	radiocarbon dating
by academics	rocky overhangs	more numerals	buy academies
increasing numbers	paper hangings	contaminated samples	some fools

Drill 5

Q What can be inferred about the relationship between apes and humans?

   Ⓐ Humans and apes are exactly the same.

   Ⓑ Humans and apes should be put into separate categories.

   Ⓒ The term "apes" should be changed in the dictionary.

   Ⓓ Humans and apes are closely related.

07-06

Check-Up Listen again and circle the words you hear.

still don't think	no other grapes	the other apes	not considerate
to be included	more times	still can't drink	quite apparent
quite different	not considered	increasing frequency	to be excluded

Drill 6

Q What is a possible outcome of the dolphin's ability to use echolocation?

   Ⓐ Dolphins can easily locate food.

   Ⓑ Dolphins have many different eating habits.

   Ⓒ Dolphins can become incredible swimmers.

   Ⓓ Dolphins will become even more intelligent.

07-07

Check-Up Listen again and circle the words you hear.

most intelligent	living in groups	to locate	variety of clicks
living in pods	relocated	vocalizations	least diligent
variety of picks	emitting calls	hitting a wall	speaking

Exercises with Mid-Length Conversations

Exercise 1 Listen to part of a conversation and answer the questions.

07-08

Office Hours

1 What is the likely outcome of the student and his partners giving a presentation on Friday?

- Ⓐ The professor will not grade them harshly.
- Ⓑ Allison will help give the presentation.
- Ⓒ They will get the highest grade in the class.
- Ⓓ Other groups will try to imitate them.

2 What does the professor imply about Allison?

- Ⓐ Allison will be offered a job by the company.
- Ⓑ She is displeased with Allison's actions.
- Ⓒ Her grade will be the lowest in the class.
- Ⓓ She will have to give a solo presentation.

📖 Words & Phrases

definitely adv surely; certainly

role n a part played by a person or thing

leeway n tolerance; an amount of freedom

✏️ Summary Note

A Fill in the blanks with the appropriate words.

Group can't give presentation on Friday ➡ group member has a ❶ _____	Professor will ask ❷ _____ to switch ➡ if not, group must speak	Group will get leeway from professor

B Complete the following summary by using the words in the box.

some leeway	change the date	upcoming presentation
give their presentation	to change times	missing student's part

The student says that there is a problem with his group's _____. One of the group members has a job interview on Friday, which is when the presentation is. The company will not _____, so the student cannot attend the presentation. The professor says she will ask if any groups want _____, but she doubts that will happen. She tells the student that his group might have to _____ on Friday, but she will give them _____ since they have to learn the _____.

Dictation Exercise   Listen to the conversation again and fill in the blanks.

W Professor: Good afternoon, Hans. What are you doing here?

M Student: I need to ask you for _____, Professor Voss.

W: Does this _____ your presentation? Is your team _____?

M: Yes, I am here about our presentation, but we _____. We finished _____ a couple of days ago, and we're _____ with the results.

W: Then . . . what's going on?

M: As you know, there are four people in our group: Allison Watts, Martin Peterson, Sally Druthers, and myself. Unfortunately, it looks like Allison _____ on the day we're supposed to give our presentation.

W: Why not?

M: Apparently, she has _____ scheduled for Friday. She _____ it to another day, but the company told her she has to interview then. So she's going to _____.

W: Can't you do the presentation _____?

M: Hmm . . . I guess we could, but she has an _____. One of the other three of us would _____ it quickly. We only _____ to do that.

W: I could ask _____ in class today if they want to speak on Friday. But that's probably not going to happen. Most of the groups _____ to speak yet.

M: Okay. Then what if we have to _____ on Friday?

W: Just learn Allison's role. I'll give you some leeway in case you _____. And I really need to talk to Allison. She's the one who _____ here. It shouldn't have been you.

M: Ah, okay. Thanks, ma'am.

07-09

Service Encounter

1 What can be inferred about the student's artwork?

- Ⓐ It imitates the styles of some modern artists.
- Ⓑ The woman considers it to be of high quality.
- Ⓒ Some of it has already been sold to collectors.
- Ⓓ It has been displayed in public in the past.

2 What is the likely outcome of the woman meeting the professors in the Art Department?

- Ⓐ They will discuss the classes that they are teaching.
- Ⓑ They will observe some artwork on display.
- Ⓒ They will choose which works they want to sell.
- Ⓓ They will agree to display the student's work.

📖 **Words & Phrases**

select Ⓥ to choose
beneficial adj helpful
portfolio ⓝ a collection of one's work, such as art

📝 Summary Note

A Fill in the blanks with the appropriate words.

Woman is ❶ _____ student's artwork

Student wants to display art at exhibition

Is not an art major; is just an amateur painter

Wants to borrow student's portfolio to show it to ❷ _____

B Complete the following summary by using the words in the box.

an art major	borrow his portfolio	an amateur painter
a painting displayed	is impressed with	some pictures

The student asks the woman about getting _____ at an upcoming exhibition. The woman asks if the student is _____. He says that he is _____. The woman responds that most artwork chosen is by students in the Art Department. The student asks the woman if she would look at _____ of his work. She agrees and _____ the work he has done. She wants to _____ to show to some art professors she is meeting soon.

Dictation Exercise Listen to the conversation again and fill in the blanks.

M Student: Hello. I'm here about the _____ the school gallery will be holding.

W Art Gallery Employee: Yes? What would you like to know about it?

M: It's going to _____ in April, right?

W: _____. It will be held during the first two weeks of April like _____.

M: That's great. So, uh . . . how can I get one of my works to _____?

W: Hmm . . . Are you a student in the Art Department? Is that _____?

M: No, it's not. I'm just _____. I like to paint in _____. I'm a chemistry major.

W: Well, the works that are exhibited here _____ by professors in the Art Department. They _____ students majoring in art since having a work displayed here is _____ to the students.

M: I see. Well, uh, would you mind _____ my work really quickly? I have some pictures of _____ with me.

W: I _____ doing that. Let me see them, please.

M: Here you are . . .

W: Well . . . Hmm . . . This is a _____ done in the Realist style . . . And this one is a great work that resembles _____ the Italian Renaissance. Hmm . . . I must say I'm _____. Do you mind if I _____ for a bit? I'm _____ from the Art Department in ten minutes. I'd like to show them your work.

M: That would be wonderful. If it's okay with you, I'll _____ and check out the artwork on display.

W: That's perfectly _____. _____ in around an hour.

07-10

Office Hours

1 What can be inferred about the professor?

- Ⓐ He believes the student may have done the work properly.
- Ⓑ He gives few high grades in his classes.
- Ⓒ He wants the student to do the experiment a second time.
- Ⓓ He believes the student should speak with her classmates.

2 What is the likely outcome of the students in the class submitting their lab reports?

- Ⓐ None of them will have the right answers.
- Ⓑ The majority will be done correctly.
- Ⓒ Most of them will be turned in late.
- Ⓓ Many will have incorrect results.

📖 **Words & Phrases**

lab report Ⓝ a paper describing an experiment
tricky adj difficult
improperly adv incorrectly; wrongly
pay attention phr to concentrate

✏️ **Summary Note**

A Fill in the blanks with the appropriate words.

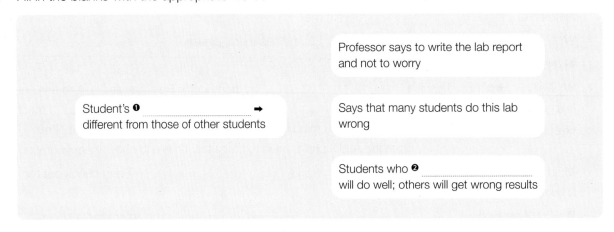

Professor says to write the lab report and not to worry

Student's ❶ _____ ➡ different from those of other students

Says that many students do this lab wrong

Students who ❷ _____ will do well; others will get wrong results

B Complete the following summary by using the words in the box.

her lab report	her lab results	lab is tricky
pay attention	the other students	are different

The student says she has a problem with _____ because they
_____ than those of other students in the class. The professor tells her to
write _____ and to turn it in. He says that _____ may
be wrong while she may be right. He then adds that the _____ and that many
students do it improperly because they do not _____.

Dictation Exercise Listen to the conversation again and fill in the blanks.

W Student: Professor Alvarez, I have something of a problem concerning _____.

M Professor: What happened? Did you _____?

W: Uh, no. I didn't do that. It's just that the results I got are _____ than what
everyone else got.

M: _____ sometimes.

W: Yeah, but . . . what am I supposed to do?

M: Just write _____ with your partner and turn it in.

W: _____ if the results I got were wrong?

M: How do you know that your results are wrong and that _____ are right? Just
because everyone else got different answers _____ make them correct.

W: I, uh . . . I never _____ like that.

M: Let me tell you something. The lab you just did is one of the _____. Every year,
more than eighty percent of the class does this lab improperly and _____.

W: Why do you give such a _____?

M: It's not actually hard. It's basically a test to see if the students can _____
precisely. Most of the students don't _____, so they make a mistake or
two. That leads to _____. So . . . it's entirely possible that you're right while
_____.

W: I see. Okay. Thanks for letting me know, sir.

M: _____. See you in class tomorrow.

Exercise 4 Listen to part of a conversation and answer the questions.

07-11

Service Encounter

1 What can be inferred about the woman?
- (A) She has never visited Stanley Hall before.
- (B) She is currently a senior at the school.
- (C) She is surprised that a single room is available.
- (D) She has helped the student in the past.

2 What is the likely outcome of the student moving to Stanley Hall?
- (A) He will have to pay more for his room.
- (B) He will have a new roommate.
- (C) He will get to his classes faster.
- (D) He will be able to study in quiet.

Words & Phrases

shot [n] an attempt
transfer [v] to move from one place to another
incredibly [adv] very; highly
constant [adj] continual
designate [v] to appoint

Summary Note

A Fill in the blanks with the appropriate words.

| Student wants to transfer ➡ current dorm is ❶ _____ | Woman says that student probably won't get a single room | Student doesn't care ➡ asks about new dorm with ❷ _____ | Woman says that there is one single room available | Student wants it |

B Complete the following summary by using the words in the box.

constant interruptions	is surprised	single room available
his current room	quiet floors	to transfer

The student says that he wants _____ from his single room, and the woman _____ . She says that most available rooms are double or triple rooms. The student says that the students in _____ are very noisy. He needs to study and does not want _____ . He asks about the new dorm with _____ . The woman checks for him and learns that there is a _____ on a quiet floor. The student wants to take it.

Dictation Exercise   Listen to the conversation again and fill in the blanks.

M Student: Hello. I wonder if you can give me _____ .

W Student Housing Office Employee: If it has to do with your dorm room, I'll give it _____ .

M: Thanks a lot. I have a single in Robertson Hall, but I'm thinking of _____ another dorm.

W: Huh? You want to transfer _____ ? You know that most of the rooms _____ are either doubles or triples, right? You _____ a freshman to me.

M: No, I'm a senior.

W: Then why do you want to move?

M: Basically, the students on my floor are _____ and make way too much noise at all hours of the day. I'm taking _____ courses, including two seminars, I have a part-time job, and I'm busy applying to _____ . I can't deal with _____ . I need to _____ there.

W: Ah, sure. I _____ . Where are you thinking of going?

M: I heard that the new dorm _____ has a couple of quiet floors. Is that correct?

W: Yes, it is. The fourth and fifth floors of Stanley Hall are designated as _____ , so students living there have to be quiet _____ a day.

M: It _____ . Are there any rooms open there?

W: Let me check . . . Hmm . . . That's incredible. Do you know what? Today is _____ .

M: How so?

W: A single on the fifth floor of Stanley Hall _____ about thirty minutes ago. Are you interested?

M: _____ , please!

Exercises with Mid-Length Lectures

Exercise 1 Listen to part of a lecture and answer the questions.

07-12

Anthropology

1 What can be implied about the student's reaction to the professor's examples?

    Ⓐ She prefers the example of Koko to the other ones the professor gives.

    Ⓑ She is not particularly interested in the examples that are given.

    Ⓒ She is impressed with the results of the examples he provides.

    Ⓓ She thinks they are not sufficient enough to make valid conclusions.

> **📖 Words & Phrases**
>
> **identical** adj similar or alike in every way
> **isolate** v to set apart; to be alone
> **tool** n something that is used to perform work

2 In the lecture, the professor talks about different primates. Indicate whether each of the following statements describes gorillas or chimpanzees.
Click in the correct box for each statement.

	Gorillas	Chimpanzees
1 Can learn from experience		
2 Use tools when fishing		
3 Have been seen using tree stumps as bridges		
4 Can gauge the depth of water by using tools		

📝 Summary Note

A Fill in the blanks with the appropriate words.

> Chimps learn from experience
>
> 92-98% of Gorillas' DNA identical to humans
>
> **Cognitive Skills of Apes**
>
> A few have been taught a subset of
> ❶ _____
>
> Gorillas use
> ❷ _____

196 Part **III**

B Complete the following summary by using the words in the box.

learning capabilities	set apart	actually learn
conclusive evidence	the DNA content	quite difficult

Not long ago, humans were thought to be distinctly _____ from apes. Recent research has shown that this is not the case. For example, _____ of apes and humans is very similar in addition to the fact that some studies of apes in the wild have shown _____ of apes being capable of learning. It is known that certain species of apes are able to use tools. What is not known is the extent of apes' _____ as well as the limit to what they can _____. Further studies are needed to answer these questions although this could be _____ to do.

Dictation Exercise Listen to the lecture again and fill in the blanks.

M Professor: Let's talk about _____ the cognitive skills between apes and humans. As you all know, humans and apes share many similarities, including the ability to _____ and to imitate others.

W Student: Sir, can you explain how apes _____?

M: Well, various studies have shown that baby chimps _____ while baby humans just imitate what they are shown. These studies have given scientists _____ in understanding the cultural aspects of ape life and the evolutionary similarities between _____.

W: Can you give us _____ showing how, um, humans and apes are so similar?

M: Sure. Let's take the gorilla. With ninety-two to ninety-eight percent of its DNA being identical to that of a human, it is _____ living relative to humans after the chimpanzee. A few individuals _____, such as, ah, Koko, have even been taught a subset of _____.

W: But isn't Koko _____? I mean, I haven't heard of _____ where gorillas have shown any kind of cognitive process.

M: Actually, there's _____ available to support this fact. For example, a team of scientists observed gorillas using tools _____. A female gorilla, um, was recorded using a stick to _____ of water while crossing a swamp. A second female was seen using a tree stump _____ and also as a support while fishing in a swamp. While this was the _____ for a gorilla, um, for over forty years, chimpanzees had been seen using tools in the wild such as when _____.

W: Are you serious? You can _____ on one hand. Surely, more observations are needed to infer that apes and humans have _____.

M: That's true, and I agree that there have not been enough observations to make _____, and that's why several field studies are _____. But _____ about the studies we have discussed here. We should also be realistic, um, with the numbers of _____ since it's not easy to study apes in the wild.

Exercise 2 Listen to part of a lecture and answer the questions.

Biology

1 What does the professor imply about dolphin intelligence?

Ⓐ It is difficult to determine just how intelligent dolphins are.

Ⓑ Since dolphins have no spoken language, they are not smart.

Ⓒ Although they use echolocation, it does not make them smart.

Ⓓ Dolphins are equally as smart as human beings and other animals.

2 What can be inferred about why dolphins whistle?

Ⓐ They use whistles as a language.

Ⓑ Their whistles are like a submarine's sonar.

Ⓒ They have a signature whistle for identifying each other.

Ⓓ They use body movements to communicate their whistles.

📖 Words & Phrases

echolocation 🅝 a sonar-like system used by dolphins

signature 🅐🅳🅹 unique to an individual

sonar 🅝 a method of locating objects submerged in water by echolocation

🖊 Summary Note

A Fill in the blanks with the appropriate words.

| Dolphin Echolocation | Object approached ➡ echo grows ❶ _____ | Decrease intensity and interval of emitted clicks | Extract shape info ➡ form ❷ _____ of target |

B Complete the following summary by using the words in the box.

the most intelligent	effective method	locate a target
a variety of clicks	emit a series of	not fully understood

Dolphins are considered one of _____ animal species on the Earth. This is due to their ability to communicate by using _____, whistles, and other vocalizations. For example, the most _____ of communication they use is a form of echolocation, in which they _____ clicking sounds to _____. This is done much like a submarine's sonar system. They also use whistles, which are unique to each individual. The use of body movements and vocal bursts is still _____.

Dictation Exercise Listen to the lecture again and fill in the blanks.

M Professor: All right, are we ready to begin? Good. In the last class, we left off with, um, an introduction concerning _____ to communicate with others of its species. As you know, dolphins are regarded as one of _____ animal species on the Earth, but it is hard to say just how intelligent they are. The reason is due to this mammal's _____ by using a variety of clicks, whistles, and other vocalizations. Now, let me talk about the different ways _____.

Okay, the first of these _____ includes a form of echolocation, in which dolphins _____ by producing sounds and then listening for the echo. It works like this . . . Broadband clicking sounds _____ in a focused beam toward the front of a target. As the _____ is approached, the echo grows, um, louder; and the dolphins adjust by decreasing the inter-click interval and the intensity of _____. We know dolphins use _____ of click production in a, um, click train, which gives rise to the familiar barks, squeals, and growls they use. _____ with a repetition rate of more than 600 per second is called a burst pulse. Because of this process, it has been accepted by researchers that dolphins are able to form _____ of their targets. I guess you could say it's a lot like a submarine's _____.

Dolphins also communicate with _____ and vocal bursts. These vocal bursts are produced by using six air sacs near their blowhole since dolphins _____. What these vocal bursts represent is _____. Yet each animal does have a characteristic frequency-modulated, narrow-band signature whistle, which is _____. In this mode of communication, um, dolphins do use about thirty _____. However, many researchers scoff at the idea that this is a form of _____.

Exercise 3 Listen to part of a lecture and answer the questions.

American Literature

07-14

1 What can be inferred about Raymond Chandler?

Ⓐ His complex characters are hard for readers to understand.

Ⓑ He was one of the youngest successful writers of his time.

Ⓒ His most famous published works were written later in his life.

Ⓓ He was a personal friend of many writers during his successful years.

📖 Words & Phrases

corrupt adj lacking integrity; crooked

idealism n the pursuit of noble goals

philosophical adj rational, reasonable, and calm

2 In the lecture, the professor describes some American detectives in novels. Indicate which detective each statement refers to.

Click in the correct box for each statement.

	Sam Spade	Philip Marlowe	Mike Hammer
1 Can be violent and is full of rage			
2 Plays chess and is philosophical			
3 Does not care about the law			
4 Appears in the novel *The Maltese Falcon*			

✏️ Summary Note

A Fill in the blanks with the appropriate words.

Great American Detective Novels

The Maltese Falcon
- Sam Spade
  – Has tarnished idealism

❶ _____
- Philip Marlowe
  – Philosophical; enjoys chess

I, the Jury
- Mike Hammer
  – Prototypical,
  ❷ _____

B Complete the following summary by using the words in the box.

detective novels	major characteristic	endeared readers
tough guys	similar attributes	so memorable

Some of the greatest American _____ written were created by three authors: Samuel Dashiell Hammett, Raymond Chandler, and Mickey Spillane. Each of these authors created at least one memorable detective character that has _____ for over fifty years. Characters like Sam Spade, Mike Hammer, and Philip Marlowe have many _____, yet each character has at least one _____ which sets him apart from the others. All three of these detective characters are characterized as _____, which probably makes them _____.

Dictation Exercise Listen to the lecture again and fill in the blanks.

W Professor: I'd like to explore some of the greatest _____ written by three of the best novelists of the twentieth century. My personal favorite is *The Maltese Falcon*, written by American author Samuel Dashiell Hammett. His _____, of course, is Sam Spade, a man who sees the, um, _____ side of life but still retains his tarnished idealism. Even though Spade _____, he is also a sentimentalist at heart, which makes him one of _____ detective characters ever created.

Next is American author Raymond Chandler, who based _____, detective Philip Marlowe, initially on Hammett's Sam Spade. Marlowe _____ in the novel *The Big Sleep*, published in 1939. Underneath the wisecracking tough guy public image, Marlowe is quietly philosophical and enjoys _____. While he is not afraid to _____, he, hmm, never becomes violent merely to settle scores. Chandler's treatment of the detective novel exhibits _____ to develop the art form. His _____, *The Big Sleep*, was published when Chandler was fifty-one years old while his last, *Playback*, came out when he was seventy. Incidentally, all seven of _____ were produced in the last two decades of his life. I can say that all of these novels _____ of Philip Marlowe's character, but each novel has _____ of narrative tone, depth, and focus that set it apart from the others.

Finally, I just love reading the last writer's work. I'm talking about Mickey Spillane, who _____ Mike Hammer in the book *I, the Jury*. Hammer is in many ways the prototypical _____ since he is brutally violent and fueled by a, um, genuine rage that never afflicts Chandler's and Hammett's heroes. While _____ kind of bend the law, Hammer holds it in total contempt, seeing it as nothing more than a means _____. And, well, this is _____ Chandler's and Hammett's characters.

07-15

Archaeology

1 What does the professor imply about cave art found outside of Europe?

    Ⓐ Asian cave art has taught archaeologists a lot about rock art galleries.

    Ⓑ African cave paintings show how early humans looked.

    Ⓒ The work is not as important as the cave art found in the Chauvet Cave.

    Ⓓ Cave art found outside Europe is more important because of its old age.

📖 **Words & Phrases**

previously `adv`
occurring before something else

uncharacteristically `adv`
unusually

unsurpassed `adj`
cannot be improved on

depict `v` to describe

2 In the lecture, the professor discusses cave art. Indicate whether the following statement describe cave art from Europe or from other places.
Click in the correct box for each statement.

	Europe	Other Places
1 Has caves containing galleries of rock paintings		
2 Has the world's oldest known cave art		
3 Has cave art of the highest quality		
4 Features cave art done by the San people		

✏ Summary Note

A Fill in the blanks with the appropriate words.

Prehistoric Cave Art

Europe
- Europeans discovered Magdalenian paintings, 1879, Spain
- Best Example:
  ❶ _____ in France ➡ 32,000 years old; discovered in 1994

❶ _____
- Cave paintings done by San people 8,000 years ago

Asia
- Thailand, Malaysia, and Indonesia: all contain galleries of rock paintings ➡ 6,000 years old

B Complete the following summary by using the words in the box.

communication tool	quality and quantity	first encountered them
complete human figures	uncharacteristically large	are covered with

Cave paintings were an important _____ used by humans' ancestors
for thousands of years. Cave paintings were unknown to modern man until Europeans
_____ in 1879. The best example is the Chauvet Cave, which is
_____ and has the best _____ of cave art discovered
so far. For example, the walls of the Chauvet Cave _____ predatory animals
such as lions, panthers, bears, owls, rhinos, and hyenas. As is typical of most cave art, there are no
paintings of _____ .

Dictation Exercise Listen to the lecture again and fill in the blanks.

M Professor: Why don't we move on to _____ now? As we discussed previously,
cave paintings were an _____ used by our ancestors for thousands of years. Cave
paintings _____ until Europeans first encountered the Magdalenian paintings of the
Altamira Cave, in Spain, um, in 1879.

W Student: Professor, could you tell us which cave has _____ ?

M: The place with the oldest cave art is the Chauvet Cave in southern France. It
_____ through radiocarbon dating back to 32,000 years. The cave
_____ Jean-Marie Chauvet, who discovered it on December 18, 1994.

W: _____ about the Chauvet Cave?

M: Well, it is uncharacteristically large, and the quality and, hmm, _____
found in it, makes it, well, unsurpassed compared to other caves that have been found
with _____ . The walls of the Chauvet Cave are covered with
_____ like lions, panthers, bears, owls, rhinos, and hyenas. Um, as is typical of
most cave art, there are no paintings of _____ . Researchers have found that the
cave _____ for 20,000 to 30,000 years.

W: Are there any other caves that have been discovered with similar paintings in
_____ the world?

M: Oh, sure. _____ , in South Africa, there are caves in which the paintings are
thought to have been done by the San people, _____ in the area 8,000 years ago.
The paintings depict animals and humans and are thought to represent religious beliefs.

W: Are there _____ ?

M: There are also _____ in caves in Malaysia and Indonesia. In Thailand, in the
nineteenth century, some caves were found along the Thai-Burmese border _____
other caves overlooking the Mekong River in Nakhon Sawan Province.
galleries of rock paintings thought to be about 6,000 years old.

Integrated Listening & Speaking

A Listen to the previous lecture on biology and say the answers out loud by using the cue sentence words that are indicated in each answer. You can refer to the summary note below.

07 - 16

Biology

Summary Note

Dolphin Echolocation	Object approached → echo grows louder	Decrease intensity and interval of emitted clicks	Extract shape info → form echo image of target

1 What is the dolphin's most effective method of communication?

    a. The most effective method ⎯⎯⎯⎯⎯⎯⎯⎯⎯⎯⎯⎯⎯⎯⎯ .

    b. An effective method ⎯⎯⎯⎯⎯⎯⎯⎯⎯⎯⎯⎯⎯⎯⎯⎯⎯ .

2 What kind of image can dolphins form?

    a. Dolphins can ⎯⎯⎯⎯⎯⎯⎯⎯⎯⎯⎯⎯⎯⎯⎯⎯⎯⎯⎯ .

    b. Dolphins are able to ⎯⎯⎯⎯⎯⎯⎯⎯⎯⎯⎯⎯⎯⎯⎯⎯ .

3 What factor accounts for dolphins' high intelligence?

    a. Dolphin intelligence can ⎯⎯⎯⎯⎯⎯⎯⎯⎯⎯⎯⎯⎯⎯ .

    b. In a display of high intelligence, dolphins ⎯⎯⎯⎯⎯⎯⎯⎯ .

B Listen to the previous lecture on American literature and say the answers out loud by using the cue sentence words that are indicated in each answer. You can refer to the summary note below.

07-17

American Literature

🖊 **Summary Note**

Great American Detective Novels

The Maltese Falcon
- Sam Spade
  – Has tarnished idealism

The Big Sleep
- Philip Marlowe
  – Philosophical; enjoys chess

I, the Jury
- Mike Hammer
  – Prototypical, brutally violent

1 What did each author create?

   a. Each author created _____.

   b. At least _____.

2 What is similar about each detective?

   a. Each detective's _____.

   b. Similarly, each detective _____.

3 How many authors are mentioned in the passage?

   a. There are _____.

   b. In the passage, _____.

Listen to part of a conversation between a student and a professor.

07-18

1 What are the speakers mainly discussing?

Ⓐ How to apply to be a teaching assistant

Ⓑ The importance of teaching assistants

Ⓒ The duties of a teaching assistant

Ⓓ The school's need for teaching assistants

2 What does the student give the professor?

Ⓐ Her updated résumé

Ⓑ A copy of her transcript

Ⓒ A signed application form

Ⓓ A list of her current courses

3 According to the professor, what duties do TAs have?
Click on 2 answers.

Ⓐ Acting as lecturers

Ⓑ Serving as graders

Ⓒ Leading tutorials

Ⓓ Being academic advisors

4 What will the student probably do next?

Ⓐ Put her name on a list

Ⓑ Speak with her advisor

Ⓒ Conduct some more research

Ⓓ Update her résumé

5 Listen again to part of the conversation. Then answer the question.
What does the professor imply when he says this: 🎧

Ⓐ He thinks that the student is smart.

Ⓑ It is not easy to be a teaching assistant.

Ⓒ He is looking for a teaching assistant for a class.

Ⓓ There are too many grad students in the department.

Listen to part of a lecture in a biology class.

07- 19

Biology

Polar Bears

6 What aspect of polar bears does the professor mainly discuss?

    Ⓐ How it finds shelter

    Ⓑ How it hunts

    Ⓒ How it reproduces

    Ⓓ How it stays warm

7 What is the professor's opinion of the polar bear?

    Ⓐ It must be kept from extinction.

    Ⓑ It is an apex predator.

    Ⓒ It is dangerous to humans.

    Ⓓ It should not be allowed to expand its territory.

8 Why does the professor discuss a polar bear's guard hairs?

    Ⓐ To prove they are longer than any other hairs

    Ⓑ To compare them with hairs of other bears

    Ⓒ To question the uses of these hairs

    Ⓓ To show how they keep the polar bear dry

9   Where on a polar bear's body does it release excess heat?
Click on 2 answers.

    (A) Its muzzle

    (B) Its stomach

    (C) Its back

    (D) Its shoulders

10   According to the professor, why do polar bears hibernate?

    (A) To stay warm

    (B) To digest food

    (C) To give birth

    (D) To avoid storms

11   What will the professor do next?

    (A) Give the students a test

    (B) Reply to some questions

    (C) Show several pictures of polar bears

    (D) Discuss grizzly bears

Vocabulary Check-Up

A Choose the correct words that match the definitions.

1 belief   •   • (A) to set apart; to be alone

2 constant   •   • (B) to describe

3 click   •   • (C) a slight, sharp sound

4 maintain   •   • (D) incorrectly; wrongly

5 improperly   •   • (E) to choose

6 designate   •   • (F) to meet or find something unexpected

7 identical   •   • (G) continual

8 isolate   •   • (H) something that is considered true

9 leeway   •   • (I) tolerance; an amount of freedom

10 encounter   •   • (J) to appoint

11 depict   •   • (K) difficult

12 select   •   • (L) to continue; to preserve

13 transfer   •   • (M) helpful

14 tricky   •   • (N) similar or alike in every way

15 beneficial   •   • (O) to move from one place to another

B Complete the sentences by filling in the blanks with the words in the box.

(A) role   (B) lab report   (C) portfolio   (D) incredibly   (E) definitely

1 They thought the firefighter was _____ brave.

2 The _____ took them several hours to write.

3 She submitted her _____ for the professor to review.

4 The player has an important _____ to play on the team.

5 You should _____ be careful in the jungle.

UNIT

08

Making Inferences

Overview

Introduction

Making Inference questions requires you to reach a conclusion based on facts presented in the listening passage. In other words, you must see beyond the lines in the passage and predict the outcome. The questions may be about different things from a simple process to a cause and effect to a comparison and contrast.

Question Types

▶ What does the professor imply about X?

▶ What will the student probably do next?

▶ What can be inferred about X?

▶ What does the professor imply when he says this: (replay)

Useful Tips

■ While taking notes, try to add up the details from the passage to reach a conclusion.

■ Make an effort to generalize about what you hear in the listening passages.

■ Try to find out the meaning behind the directly stated words.

■ Focus on the answers that use vocabulary not found in the listening passages.

08-01

Script

W Student: Professor Pollio, could you take a look at this homework assignment, please?

M Professor: Sure. What do you have a question about?

W: I wonder why I didn't get full credit for my answer on question number three.

M: Ah, you didn't show your work. Yes, you got the right answer, but I needed to see how you did that.

W: I wasn't aware that I always had to do that.

M: You should have been. I announce in all of my classes each time I assign math homework that you need to show your work. So you really have no excuse for not doing that.

W: Yes, sir. I see your point.

Q   What does the professor imply about the student?

    Ⓐ She is getting a good grade in the class.

    Ⓑ She was not paying attention in class.

    Ⓒ She should redo her homework assignment.

    Ⓓ She should attend a group study session.

✅ Correct Answer

The correct answer is Ⓑ. The professor says that he announces in every class that the students need to show their work on their homework. So he therefore implies that the student was not paying attention in class.

Listen to parts of conversations or lectures and answer the questions.

Drill 1

Q What can be inferred about the student?

08-02

Ⓐ She is exceptional.

Ⓑ She does not work hard.

Ⓒ She is a poor writer.

Ⓓ She is improving.

Check-Up Listen again and circle the words you hear.

by winter	insightful	my seminar	no doubt
four winning	fight into	best writers	sore biting
quite intelligent	professorship	for writing	scholarship

Drill 2

Q What can be inferred about the student?

08-03

Ⓐ He is getting poor grades in his classes.

Ⓑ He has to do a part-time job.

Ⓒ He is going to graduate next semester.

Ⓓ He needs assistance to pay his tuition.

Check-Up Listen again and circle the words you hear.

are uncertain	may I	could have stayed	apprehension
can defer	haven't paid	economically	be canceled
aid check	in the shade	without her	extension

Drill 3

Q What can be inferred about the professor?

08-04

Ⓐ She is complacent.

Ⓑ She is adamant.

Ⓒ She is strict.

Ⓓ She is supportive.

Check-Up Listen again and circle the words you hear.

incident	sent around	talkative	past year
activation code	intimidated	experimental	confidence
so profound	more active	retracted it	last semester

Drill 4

Q What can be inferred about the human brain?

08-05

Ⓐ It is an involuntary organ.

Ⓑ It is a secondary organ.

Ⓒ It is a primary organ.

Ⓓ It is a vulnerable organ.

Check-Up Listen again and circle the words you hear.

peak time	unique result	control center	sensory perception
blood loss	great deal	in the head	primary
massive number	organ of thought	beside the nerve	extremely complex

Drill 5

Q What can be inferred from Chomsky's theory?

08-06

Ⓐ Children are born without language basics.

Ⓑ Children develop language only with formal instruction.

Ⓒ Children have difficulty learning their native language.

Ⓓ Children are born with the fundamental principles of language.

Check-Up Listen again and circle the words you hear.

parameters	explicit subjects	requires formal	paragraphs
inquires from	faintly utter	liability	majority of
deduce	language acquisition	reduce	fully utilize

Drill 6

Q What is implied about the environmental movement's membership?

08-07

Ⓐ It is well organized.

Ⓑ It is falling apart.

Ⓒ It is very diverse.

Ⓓ It is highly profitable.

Check-Up Listen again and circle the words you hear.

human rights	revitalize	is recognized	political movement
long lives	is represented	strong beliefs	grassy lands
public policy	naturalistic	recognition	bright lights

Exercises with Mid-Length Conversations

Exercise 1 Listen to part of a conversation and answer the questions.

Service Encounter

08-08

1 What can be inferred about the student?
- (A) He is not interested in writing for the paper.
- (B) He is getting a major in photography.
- (C) He used to work for his high school newspaper.
- (D) He has had some of his pictures published before.

2 What will the student probably do next?
- (A) Begin his first assignment
- (B) Answer the woman's questions
- (C) Discuss his potential salary
- (D) Show the woman some pictures

📖 Words & Phrases

piece n an article
underclassman n a freshman or sophomore
dedicate v to commit to a goal or objective; to devote

✏️ Summary Note

A Fill in the blanks with the appropriate words.

Student wants to work for the newspaper	Doesn't want to write ➡ wants to be a ❶ _____	Shows the woman some pictures	Has a ❷ _____ that can take good photos	Is asked how much time he can work each week

B   Complete the following summary by using the words in the box.

be a photographer	a nice camera	the student newspaper
write opinion pieces	spend working	some of his pictures

The student responds to an ad about the need for workers at _____. He says that he wants to _____. The woman is surprised because most people want to _____. The newspaper has a photographer, but she is busy, so the student can work at the paper. The student shows the woman _____, and she thinks they are good. The student says that he has _____ that lets him take good pictures. The woman then asks him how much time he can _____ each week.

Dictation Exercise   Listen to the conversation again and fill in the blanks.

M Student: Good afternoon. I _____ that was in the paper about your need for workers here.

W Student Newspaper Employee: That's great. What kind of work _____ in doing at the paper?

M: I'd really love to _____.

W: Huh, most people say that they want to _____. It's nice to hear _____ for a change.

M: Photography is my hobby. I've been doing it _____. I'm, uh, I'm not really _____, so I don't think I could help you out very much there.

W: That's not a problem. We _____ on staff, and most of them are underclassmen, so they'll be here for at least another year or two after _____.

M: That's great to hear. So . . . do you happen to _____?

W: We have one, but she's _____ these days and doesn't always have time to take pictures. So, yes, we could _____.

M: I'm happy to hear that.

W: Do you happen to have _____ your work with you?

M: Yes, I do. _____ a few examples with me. You can _____ at them.

W: Hmm . . . These are _____. It's nice to see that you don't just take _____ like many people do. These pictures of people are well done.

M: Thanks for saying that. I've got a really nice camera that lets me _____.

W: Cool. So _____ do you think you can dedicate to the paper each week, and when are you _____?

Exercise 2 Listen to part of a conversation and answer the questions.

08-09

Office Hours

1   Listen again to part of the conversation. Then answer the question. What does the student imply when he says this: 🎧

   Ⓐ He believes the professor disliked his work.

   Ⓑ He is concerned about his grade on the paper.

   Ⓒ He thinks the professor must have made a mistake.

   Ⓓ He wants the professor to check his work again.

2   What can be inferred about the professor?

   Ⓐ She is a professor in the History Department.

   Ⓑ She will give the student a different assignment.

   Ⓒ She does not like to regrade students' papers.

   Ⓓ She wants to help the student improve his work.

📖 Words & Phrases

proposal Ⓝ something written that is put forward for consideration

general adj not specific

recession Ⓝ a time when an economy does poorly

focus on phr to concentrate on

✏️ Summary Note

A   Fill in the blanks with the appropriate words.

Professor
- Says the paper is too general
- Needs the student to
  ❶ ....

Student
- Should focus on
  ❷ .... in the 1900
- Can compare and contrast them

B Complete the following summary by using the words in the box.

what recessions are	too general	red ink
from the 1900s	compare and contrast	paper proposal

The professor wants to talk to the student about a _____ that he
submitted. The student sees a lot of _____ and thinks the professor
disliked it. The professor says that his proposal is _____. He should not
just describe _____. Instead, she wants him to choose two recessions
_____. Then, he can _____ them in his paper. The
student appreciates the help that the professor gives him.

Dictation Exercise   Listen to the conversation again and fill in the blanks.

W Professor: Russ, I've finished checking out _____. Do you have a couple of
moments to look at it with me now?

M Student: Sure, Professor Bascomb. _____ with my classes for the day.

W: Wonderful. Why don't you _____ there, please?

M: Thanks a lot.

W: Okay, uh, here is the proposal _____.

M: Um . . . There's a lot of _____ on the paper.

W: Yes, I had _____ comments about it.

M: I guess you _____, did you?

W: Well, let's just say that I found some ways to _____. You see, uh,
Russ, the paper that you proposed is _____. You want to write about
_____. That's a fine topic, but you didn't _____.

M: What do you mean?

W: Well, according to your proposal, all you're planning to do is describe _____.
That's too general. You need to _____ in depth.

M: How can I do that?

W: Well, mostly, you need to _____ a couple of recessions that happened in
the past. Research them and write about _____ as well as what their effects
were. You could try choosing _____ and then comparing and contrasting their
_____. If you _____, you'll see that I suggested a couple of
recessions from the 1900s.

M: Wow. Thanks a lot, Professor. I really appreciate your _____ to help me. I think I
understand what you want _____ now.

Exercise 3 Listen to part of a conversation and answer the questions.

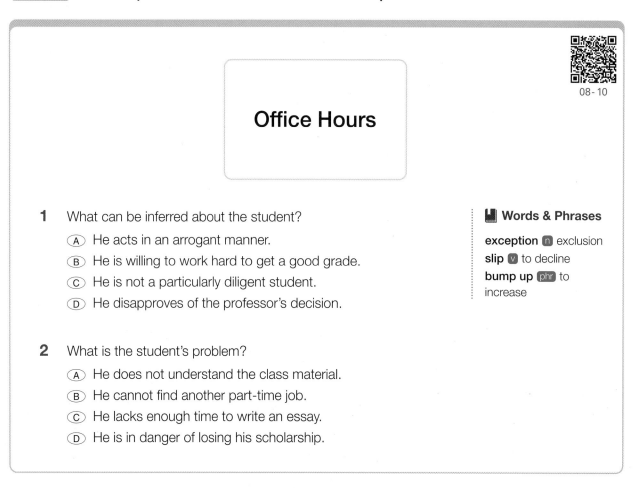

Office Hours

08-10

1 What can be inferred about the student?
- (A) He acts in an arrogant manner.
- (B) He is willing to work hard to get a good grade.
- (C) He is not a particularly diligent student.
- (D) He disapproves of the professor's decision.

2 What is the student's problem?
- (A) He does not understand the class material.
- (B) He cannot find another part-time job.
- (C) He lacks enough time to write an essay.
- (D) He is in danger of losing his scholarship.

📖 Words & Phrases

exception n exclusion
slip v to decline
bump up phr to increase

✏ Summary Note

A Fill in the blanks with the appropriate words.

Student did poorly on exam → could ❶ _____

Asks to redo exam

Can't do exam over

Write ❷ _____, and final average will rise

B Complete the following summary by using the words in the box.

discussing a test	recently quit	lose his scholarship
not satisfied with	extra credit work	retake the exam

A student is _____ he took in the professor's class the previous week. The student is _____ his performance and is afraid he will _____. He asks the professor if he can take it again. The professor asks the student why he believes he did so poorly. The student explains that he was too busy with his part-time job that he _____. Because of his honesty, the professor decides not to allow him to _____ but to do some _____ instead.

Dictation Exercise   Listen to the conversation again and fill in the blanks.

M Student: Excuse me, Professor Adams. Do you have a minute?

W Professor: Sure. What would you like to talk about?

M: It's about the test _____. I didn't do very well, and I was hoping I could _____.

W: A retest? You know, I _____ students to take tests over unless they have a very, very good reason. Explain to me why I should _____ in your case.

M: Well, um, I'm afraid that if I _____ a C in this class, I could _____. My academic scholarship states that _____ an A average in all of my classes, and in your education class, my grade is slipping a bit.

W: Hmm, let me see. Uh, yes, _____ you got a C+ on the test last week, which has brought _____ down to a B right now. Why do you think your grade _____ in my class? Is the workload _____?

M: Honestly, ma'am, I haven't really had enough time to study because of _____. I've been working the night shift as _____ to earn some extra money, but it has really been _____, so I quit yesterday.

W: Well, I _____. I know how hard it can be to _____ while attending school full time. I'm not going to allow you to _____, but I am going to assign you an _____. If you complete the essay to _____, I'll bump your score up on the test to a B+. This way, you'll be able to get an A- or _____ an A in the class, depending on how you do on the final. How _____ to you?

M: That sounds great! Thank you, ma'am, for _____ and for giving me the opportunity to make up _____. I won't _____.

08- 11

Service Encounter

1 What can be inferred about the student?

Ⓐ She hopes to be a professional actress.

Ⓑ She is the director of the performance.

Ⓒ She is a member of the school choir.

Ⓓ She enjoys performing on stage.

2 Listen again to part of the conversation. Then answer the question. What does the man imply when he says this: 🎧

Ⓐ The students only need to practice once a week.

Ⓑ Few groups on campus need to use the theater.

Ⓒ There are no open time slots on Wednesday.

Ⓓ The theater stage needs to be repaired soon.

📖 **Words & Phrases**

ideal adj perfect

book v to reserve

choir n a group of people who sing together

📝 Summary Note

A Fill in the blanks with the appropriate words.

Student
- Needs to reserve times to
  ❶ _____

Employee
- Says she can practice on Mondays
- No time slots available on
  ❷ _____

Student decides to reserve time slot on Friday evening

B Complete the following summary by using the words in the box.

there is time	school drama club	can practice
Monday and Thursday	scheduling a time	no time slots

The student visits the theater manager to discuss _____ to use the theater.
She is the president of the _____, so the members need to practice for their
performance. The student suggests reserving times on _____. The man
says that _____ on Monday but no time on Thursday. Likewise, there are
_____ available on Wednesday. She decides to reserve a time on Friday
evening so that the members _____ twice a week.

Dictation Exercise Listen to the conversation again and fill in the blanks.

W Student: Hello, Mr. Carmichael. My name is Kathy Scriber. I spoke with you _____
yesterday.

M Theater Manager: Hello. Uh, I'm really sorry, but I've had a busy week and don't
_____. Could you let me know _____?

W: Of course. I'm the president of _____, and we're putting on a performance this
spring.

M: Ah, right. I remember now. You need to _____ to use the theater so that you
can rehearse. That's what we talked about, isn't it?

W: That's correct.

M: So when would you like to reserve the theater _____?

W: Well, we'd like to rehearse _____ on Monday and Thursday. We're thinking that
six to seven thirty _____. Does that _____?

M: Let me take a look in _____ here . . . Hmm . . . Monday from six to seven thirty
is _____ at all. However, the Drama Department has booked Thursday evenings
from five to seven.

W: Is anyone _____ after seven?

M: Oh, yeah. It looks like the school choir is going to _____ at that time. I'd say
that Thursday is not _____ for your group.

W: What about Wednesday?

M: Unless you only want to practice _____, you're going to have to reserve a time
on _____.

W: That's not what we were hoping for, but if we _____, then we'll do it. How about
five thirty to seven on Friday? _____?

M: I'll _____ for that time.

Exercises with Mid-Length Lectures

Exercise 1 Listen to part of a lecture and answer the questions.

08-12

Physiology

1 What can be inferred about thermal homeostasis?

   Ⓐ It is not vital for the survival of warm-blooded animals.

   Ⓑ It is an involuntary response by warm-blooded animals to the elements.

   Ⓒ It is a critical defense mechanism in warm-blooded animals.

   Ⓓ It gives warm-blooded animals an advantage over cold-blooded animals.

2 Why does the professor mention going to the beach?

   Ⓐ To warn the students of the dangers of sun exposure

   Ⓑ To provide a practical example for the students

   Ⓒ To scare the students into avoiding the beach

   Ⓓ To add an abstract theory to the lecture

📖 Words & Phrases

thermal (adj) relating to or caused by heat

core (n) a central, essential part

endothermy (n) the ability of some creatures to control their body temperature

constant (adj) uniform; regular

organism (n) a lifeform

✏️ Summary Note

A Fill in the blanks with the appropriate words.

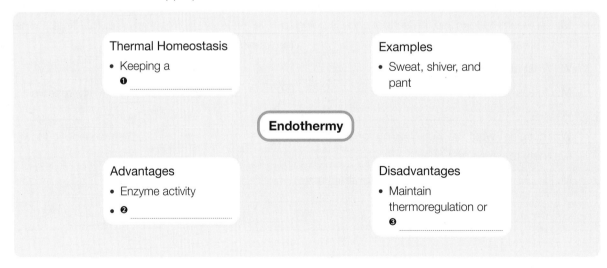

Thermal Homeostasis
- Keeping a
  ❶ _____

Examples
- Sweat, shiver, and pant

Endothermy

Advantages
- Enzyme activity
- ❷ _____

Disadvantages
- Maintain thermoregulation or
  ❸ _____

B Complete the following summary by using the words in the box.

could perish	a constant level	cold-weather situations
temperature control	a great amount of	shivering

Warm-blooded animals are able to keep their body temperatures at _____.
They use means such as _____ and sweating to do this. Another term for this
_____ is endothermy. Endotherms spend _____ energy
to maintain body temperature. If they do not do this, they _____. Advantages
of this regulation are increased enzyme activity and increased activity in _____.

Dictation Exercise Listen to the lecture again and fill in the blanks.

M Professor: _____ maintain thermal homeostasis. What I mean is they keep
their body core temperature at a nearly _____ regardless of the temperature of the
surrounding environment, which is the _____. What we call this is endothermy.

Endothermy is the ability of some creatures to control _____ through internal
means such as shivering, fat burning, panting, and sweating. You all know what I'm talking about, right?
When _____ because it's so cold in the winter or when you are sweating buckets
in the summer, all your body is trying to do is maintain a _____ of 98.6 degrees.

Now, um, there are some advantages and disadvantages to all of these. The advantages are increased
_____ and a constant body temperature, which allows warm-blooded animals
to _____ in cold temperatures. A big disadvantage is the, uh, need to maintain
thermoregulation or, in other words, _____, even during inactivity; otherwise, the
organism will die. That's right. It could mean _____.

Heat regulation is one of the most important _____ in a warm-blooded
organism. For example, in the winter, there may not _____ to enable an endotherm
such as a hungry grizzly bear to keep _____ stable all day. Um, so some
animals, like the grizzly bear, go into _____ of hypothermia called hibernation,
or torpor. This deliberately lowers the body temperature _____. Is everyone
still with me? Good. Now, in hot weather, like when you were at the beach last weekend soaking up
all those dangerous _____ to make yourself look tan and pretty, endotherms
expend _____ to avoid overheating. They may pant, sweat, lick, or seek
_____.

Exercise 2 Listen to part of a lecture and answer the questions.

08-13

Linguistics

1 What can be inferred about Old English?

   Ⓐ It is a diverse language.

   Ⓑ It is the basis for many other languages.

   Ⓒ It is a relatively shallow language.

   Ⓓ It has difficult pronunciation patterns.

2 Listen again to part of the lecture. Then answer the question. What does the professor imply when she says this: 🎧

   Ⓐ Most students are very involved in the lecture.

   Ⓑ Most students are eager to learn about Old English.

   Ⓒ Most students do not speak up in class.

   Ⓓ Most students are not interested in the lecture.

📖 **Words & Phrases**

dialect Ⓝ a distinct variety of a language
invasion Ⓝ an intrusion
layer Ⓝ a level; depth
flexible adj adaptable; elastic

✏️ **Summary Note**

A Fill in the blanks with the appropriate words.

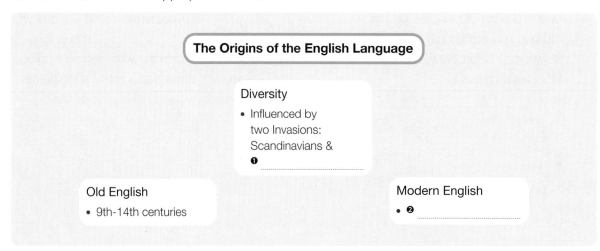

The Origins of the English Language

Diversity
- Influenced by two Invasions: Scandinavians & ❶ _____

Old English
- 9th-14th centuries

Modern English
- ❷ _____

B Complete the following summary by using the words in the box.

two later invasions	standardized	diverse and elaborate
originated in	brought to	stood on its own

English is a West-Germanic language that _____ German and the
Netherlands and was _____ England by settlers. _____
by the Scandinavians and Normans heavily influenced the language by making it more
_____ . Modern English began around the fifteenth century. It was affected by
the _____ dialect of the government. By the time of Shakespeare, modern
English was a clearly recognized language which _____ .

Dictation Exercise Listen to the lecture again and fill in the blanks.

W Professor: Okay, everyone. Calm down. I know you are all _____ being
able to read a bit of Old English. I congratulate you. Job well done, but _____
yet to go. Now, it is time for us to take a look at the _____ . Who can tell me
_____ ?

M Student: That's easy. England, of course. Everyone knows that the language
_____ the country.

W: Uh, that's _____ . English is a West Germanic language.
_____ the Anglo-Frisian dialects brought to Britain by settlers from parts
of what is now northwest Germany and the northern Netherlands. At first, Old English was a
_____ reflecting the different origins of the Anglo-Saxon kingdoms of England.
The original Old English language _____ by two waves of invasion. The first
was by _____ of the Scandinavian branch of the Germanic family. They
_____ parts of Britain in the eighth and ninth centuries. The second was the
Normans in the eleventh century. They spoke _____ French. These two invasions
caused English to become mixed _____ . What kind of effect do you guys think this
mixing _____ ?

M: Wouldn't that have made English _____ ?

W: I see somebody is _____ . Exactly. English became a very rich,
_____ of words. And later, English developed into a borrowing language of
_____ with a huge vocabulary. So what about modern English? Who can give us
an idea of _____ ?

M: I believe it was around the, um, fifteenth century, wasn't it?

W: Yes, it was. Modern English _____ from the Great Vowel Shift, which took place
mainly during the fifteenth century. English _____ by the spread of a standardized
London-based dialect in government and administration and by _____ of printing.
By the time of William Shakespeare, around the, uh, middle to late sixteenth century, the language had
become _____ as modern English.

08-14

Geography

1 What does the professor imply about the Amazon River?

- Ⓐ It is in danger of disappearing.
- Ⓑ It can be very powerful.
- Ⓒ It is important to the environment.
- Ⓓ It is not as large as people think.

2 Why does the professor mention the Mississippi River?

- Ⓐ To explain why it sometimes changes paths
- Ⓑ To claim it is longer than the Amazon
- Ⓒ To show how it pales in comparison to the Amazon
- Ⓓ To describe its importance to the United States

📖 Words & Phrases

pulsate Ⓥ to expand; to contract
main stream Ⓝ the main course of a river
extraordinary adj rare; uncommon
diminish Ⓥ to reduce
runoff Ⓝ excess water

✏️ Summary Note

A Fill in the blanks with the appropriate words.

The Amazon River

Average annual discharge equals ❶ _____ of the total continental runoff of all rivers on the Earth

High level:
❷ _____
above average level

Low level:
❸ _____
lower than average

B Complete the following summary by using the words in the box.

beach-like	all the world's	large surge
reported increases	half of the year	per second

The Amazon River experiences a _____ about once a year. This occurs
between the months of November and May. Some areas _____ in the waterline
by as much as forty to fifty feet in the late 1980s. During the other _____,
the water recedes, exposing sandbars and _____ white sand. The average
discharge of the river is between three and 8.5 million cubic feet _____.
Finally, contrary to some published accounts, the Amazon holds less than one ten-thousandth of
_____ fresh water.

Dictation Exercise Listen to the lecture again and fill in the blanks.

W Professor: The Amazon River pulsates, surging _____. From November
through May, the volume of the, uh, _____. For example, as stated in your
text, on June 1, 1989, the _____ at Manaus, 900 miles from the ocean, was
forty-five feet _____, nearly reaching the 1953 all-time high-water mark on
_____. Now, the Amazon's volume in that month _____
the combined flow of the next eight largest rivers on the Earth, a _____ stat if you
think about it. It does this _____ every May, even in years of normal flow. During
the second half of the year, this, um, _____. All right, uh, yes, here it is in your
text on page 372. In November of 1990, also around Manaus, stretches of white beaches and sandbars
_____ the sun for the first time in living memory. The river had fallen fifty feet to
its lowest level _____ this century. The only _____ of the
main stream flow were done in 1963 and 1964, which, uh, were years estimated as, uh, having less than
_____ by the U.S. Geological Survey. _____ at Obidos,
600 miles inland, where the Amazon _____ a single channel—very narrow in
comparison—a little more than a mile wide. Findings gave the average minimum discharge at three million
cubic feet per second while _____ reached 8.5 million.
_____, our own Mississippi River at Vicksburg averages 620,000 cubic feet per
second. It has been suggested that the Amazon's _____ equals twenty percent of
the total continental runoff of all rivers on the Earth. Note that this does not mean that the Amazon system
holds one-fifth of the entire _____, as some books have interpreted this data. In
fact, all the Amazon's waterways _____ one ten-thousandth of the world's fresh
water, most of which, by the way, is locked up _____.

Exercise 4 Listen to part of a lecture and answer the questions.

08-15

Chemistry

1   What does the professor imply about water purification?
   Ⓐ It is a simple task.
   Ⓑ It can be quite expensive.
   Ⓒ It takes a lot of time and effort.
   Ⓓ It is not always necessary to do.

2   What does the professor imply the most practical method of water purification is?
   Ⓐ Solar purification
   Ⓑ Boiling
   Ⓒ Chemicals
   Ⓓ Pump-filters

📖 **Words & Phrases**

purify Ⓥ to cleanse; to clean
portable adj moveable
disinfect Ⓥ to destroy diseases
emergency Ⓝ a condition of urgent need
stab Ⓥ to try; to take a chance

📝 Summary Note

A   Fill in the blanks with the appropriate words.

❶ _____

A portable pump-filter

Methods of Purifying Dirty Water

Chemicals:
iodine and chlorine

❷ _____

B Complete the following summary by using the words in the box.

filtering	main methods	outdoor activities
time consuming	chemicals	can be harmful

Water purification is important when camping or doing other _____.
If it is not done, dirty or polluted water _____ to human beings. There
are four _____ of purifying water in the outdoors: boiling, filtering, using
_____, and using sunlight. Boiling is the easiest and most complete while
_____ might not kill all of the viruses. Iodine is a chemical used to kill most
pathogens in water, and sunlight, though _____, is another valid option.

Dictation Exercise   Listen to the lecture again and fill in the blanks.

M Professor: Could you close the door, please? Great. Thanks. Today, we're going
to _____. That's right; dirty water, or more importantly, how to
_____ so that you can drink it and not get sick. Sure, you can go out and buy
portable drinking water systems or expensive _____, but there are other methods
you can use if you don't have this stuff available. Who can name one?

W Student: Whenever my dad takes us all camping, he _____, and no one in my
family has ever gotten sick.

M: Sure. Boiling water on a portable stove or fire will kill most _____. At higher
elevations, though, _____ of water drops, so several minutes of continuous
boiling are required. Another option is just to be sure you carry a _____. Some
of these, um, like the charcoal filter ones, don't _____. In this case, you have to
_____ with a third method. Who can tell me what a third might be?

W: How about electricity?

M: _____. No, actually, I was thinking of _____.
One is iodine, which kills many, but not all, of the most common, uh, pathogens in natural
_____. Second, to be used only in _____, is chlorine-
based bleach. Just _____ of five-percent bleach per quart of clear water and
let it stand, uh, covered, for about an hour. All right, now that is three so far. Would anyone like to
_____ at the last option?

W: Uh, sunshine?

M: Very well done. Yes, sunlight is _____. We call it solar purification.
Water is placed in a _____, which is oxygenated by shaking. It is placed
_____ for six hours, which raises the temperature and gives an extended dose of
solar radiation, killing _____ that may be present.

Integrated Listening & Speaking

A Listen to the previous lecture on geography and say the answers out loud by using the cue sentence words that are indicated in each answer. You can refer to the summary note below.

08-16

Geography

📝 **Summary Note**

The Amazon River

Average annual discharge equals 20 percent of the total continental runoff of all rivers on the Earth

High level: 45 feet above average level

Low level: 50 feet lower than average

1 What does this lecture teach about the Amazon River?

   a. The Amazon is _____.

   b. Throughout the year, the Amazon is _____.

2 What water level did the Amazon River reach in 1989?

   a. The water level _____.

   b. The water level _____.

3 How does the Amazon River compare to the Mississippi River?

   a. Compared to the Mississippi, _____.

   b. The Amazon's average discharge is _____.

B Listen to the previous lecture on chemistry and say the answers out loud by using the cue sentence words that are indicated in each answer. You can refer to the summary note below.

Chemistry

08-17

📝 Summary Note

Boiling water	A portable pump-filter

Methods of Purifying Dirty Water

Chemicals: iodine and chlorine	Solar purification

1 What is the best method of water purification?

a. The best method _____.

b. Boiling is _____.

2 What amount of time does solar purification take?

a. Solar purification _____.

b. At six hours, _____.

3 What is the focus of the lecture?

a. The lecture focuses on _____.

b. In the lecture, _____.

Mini TOEFL iBT Practice Test

Listen to part of a conversation between a student and a dining services office employee.

08- 18

1 Why does the student visit the dining hall?

    Ⓐ To apply for a position

    Ⓑ To pay for a meal plan

    Ⓒ To complete a survey

    Ⓓ To have a meal

2 What does the student do in the evening?

    Ⓐ Attends seminars

    Ⓑ Studies in a group

    Ⓒ Practices with her band

    Ⓓ Goes to the library

3 What duties does the man discuss?
Click on 2 answers.

    Ⓐ Delivering food to people

    Ⓑ Using a computerized register

    Ⓒ Running errands

    Ⓓ Handling money

4 What is the man's opinion of the student?

    Ⓐ He feels that she lacks relevant experience.

    Ⓑ He considers her the best employee.

    Ⓒ He believes she will be a good worker.

    Ⓓ He thinks she needs to try a bit harder.

5 Listen again to part of the conversation. Then answer the question.
What does the man imply when he says this: 🎧

    Ⓐ The student is overqualified.

    Ⓑ The student might be too busy.

    Ⓒ The student has a good personality.

    Ⓓ The student takes too many classes.

Listen to part of a lecture in a biology class.

08- 19

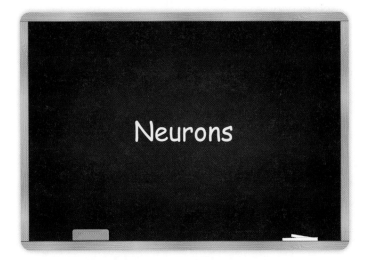

Biology

Neurons

6 What is the lecture mainly about?

(A) How neurons communicate

(B) The genetic makeup of neurons

(C) Where neurons come from

(D) Common problems with neurons

7 According to the professor, what are neurons composed of?
Click on 2 answers.

(A) Axons

(B) Mitochondria

(C) Ganglia

(D) Dendritic trees

8 How are neurons able to transmit information?

(A) Via target neurons

(B) Via the brain

(C) Via synapses

(D) Via the blood stream

9 Why does the professor mention the cerebellum?

    Ⓐ To describe one of its functions

    Ⓑ To compare it with another part of the brain

    Ⓒ To explain how large it is

    Ⓓ To say that its importance is not known

10 What does the professor imply about neurons in children?

    Ⓐ They do not increase in children.

    Ⓑ They develop slowly in children.

    Ⓒ Thet boost children's immune systems.

    Ⓓ They reduce in number as children grow.

11 Listen again to part of the lecture. Then answer the question.
Why does the professor say this: 🎧

    Ⓐ To tell the students to look at the screen

    Ⓑ To answer a question that a student asks

    Ⓒ To repeat an important point he made

    Ⓓ To be sure the students understand him

Vocabulary Check-Up

A Choose the correct words that match the definitions.

1	thermal	•	• Ⓐ	rare; uncommon
2	piece	•	• Ⓑ	something written that is put forward for consideration
3	organism	•	• Ⓒ	perfect
4	academic	•	• Ⓓ	a time when an economy does poorly
5	recession	•	• Ⓔ	to fill with fear
6	proposal	•	• Ⓕ	an article
7	ideal	•	• Ⓖ	to surpass
8	dedicate	•	• Ⓗ	a lifeform
9	choir	•	• Ⓘ	a group of people who sing together
10	intimidate	•	• Ⓙ	to say out loud or officially
11	extraordinary	•	• Ⓚ	pertaining to school or scholastics
12	emergency	•	• Ⓛ	relating to or caused by heat
13	purify	•	• Ⓜ	to commit to a goal or objective; to devote
14	exceed	•	• Ⓝ	a condition of urgent need
15	announce	•	• Ⓞ	to cleanse; to clean

B Complete the sentences by filling in the blanks with the words in the box.

Ⓐ bump up	Ⓑ slip	Ⓒ underclassman	Ⓓ indefinitely	Ⓔ credit

1 She is still a(n) _____ but will be junior next year.

2 Your grade is starting to _____, so work harder.

3 Some students try to get extra _____ on their assignments.

4 The teacher will not _____ grades when students ask.

5 The game has been postponed _____.

Actual Test

Actual Test

Listening Section Directions

09-01

This section measures your ability to understand conversations and lectures in English.

The Listening section is divided into separately timed parts. In each part, you will listen to 1 conversation and 1 or 2 lectures. You will hear each conversation or lecture only **one** time.

After each conversation and lecture, you will answer questions about it. The questions typically ask about the main idea and supporting details. Some questions ask about a speaker's purpose or attitude. Answer the questions based on what is stated or implied by the speakers.

You may take notes while you listen. You may use your notes to help you answer the questions. Your notes will not be scored.

If you need to change the volume while you listen, click on the **Volume** icon at the top of the screen.

In some questions, you will see this icon: 🎧 This means that you will hear, but not see, part of the question.

Some of the questions have special directions. These directions appear in a gray box on the screen.

Most questions are worth 1 point. If a question is worth more than 1 point, it will have special directions that indicate how many points you can receive.

A clock at the top of the screen will show you how much time is remaining. The clock will not count down while you are listening. The clock will count down only while you are answering the questions.

PART 1

Listening Directions

09-02

In this part, you will listen to 1 conversation and 1 lecture.

You must answer each question. After you answer click on **Next**. Then click on **OK** to confirm your answer and go on to the next question. After you click on **OK**, you cannot return to previous questions.

You may now begin this part of the Listening section. You will have **7 minutes** to answer the questions.

Click on **Continue** to go on.

09-03

1 Why did the man ask to see the student?

    Ⓐ To ask her to show him her room

    Ⓑ To provide her with options regarding her room

    Ⓒ To discuss a violation of a rule with her

    Ⓓ To announce his need to conduct an inspection

2 According to the man, what is true about Mastodon Hall?

    Ⓐ It is a dormitory with multiple floors.

    Ⓑ It is the largest dormitory on campus.

    Ⓒ It is scheduled to be remodeled soon.

    Ⓓ It is the oldest dormitory at the school.

3 What does the student need to do by Friday?

    Ⓐ Remove an appliance

    Ⓑ Sign up for a class

    Ⓒ Change dorm rooms

    Ⓓ Find a new roommate

4 What will the student probably do next?

    Ⓐ Visit the student housing office

    Ⓑ Look for a storage area

    Ⓒ Search for off-campus housing

    Ⓓ Return to her dorm room

5 Listen again to part of the conversation. Then answer the question.
What does the student mean when she says this: 🎧

    Ⓐ She does not want to argue anymore.

    Ⓑ The man wins the game they are playing.

    Ⓒ The man should stop bothering her.

    Ⓓ She will do what the man requests.

09-04

Ragtime

6 What is the lecture mainly about?

(A) The history of ragtime

(B) The influence of ragtime on American music

(C) The similarities between ragtime and classical music

(D) The influence of ragtime on piano playing styles

7 What is the professor's opinion of ragtime?

(A) It was the first real American music genre.

(B) It is not as good as jazz.

(C) It is too difficult for him to play on the piano.

(D) It is better than classical music.

8 Why does the professor discuss sheet music?

(A) To explain why it became outdated

(B) To distinguish ragtime from jazz

(C) To prove that it limited the spread of ragtime

(D) To say it made ragtime difficult to record

9 What influence did the stride piano have?

- Ⓐ It made jazz easier to play.
- Ⓑ It made jazz complex and distinctive.
- Ⓒ It made jazz the most popular music of the 1920s.
- Ⓓ It made jazz a clear successor to the Delta blues.

10 What does the professor imply about the future of ragtime?

- Ⓐ It will eventually die out.
- Ⓑ It will never be as good as when it first started.
- Ⓒ It will continue to influence new forms of music.
- Ⓓ It will never live up to jazz.

11 What did the revival of ragtime in the 1950s do for the genre?

- Ⓐ Many new ragtime songs were recorded.
- Ⓑ It became the most popular genre of the age.
- Ⓒ More ragtime concerts were held.
- Ⓓ Many original ragtime artists were finally recognized.

PART 2

Listening Directions

09-05

In this part, you will listen to 1 conversation and 2 lectures.

You must answer each question. After you answer click on **Next**. Then click on **OK** to confirm your answer and go on to the next question. After you click on **OK**, you cannot return to previous questions.

You may now begin this part of the Listening section. You will have **10 minutes** to answer the questions.

Click on **Continue** to go on.

VOLUME

09-06

1 What is the student's problem?

   Ⓐ She is not interested in the professor's topic.

   Ⓑ She needs an extension on the paper she is writing.

   Ⓒ She is not ready to give a presentation to the class.

   Ⓓ She is unable to find information on a topic.

2 Why does the student mention the Andromeda Galaxy?

   Ⓐ She knows nothing about it.

   Ⓑ She would like to write about it.

   Ⓒ She thinks it is a boring topic.

   Ⓓ She read about it in the textbook.

3 What can be inferred about the dwarf planets in the Kuiper Belt?

   Ⓐ They were recently discovered by astronomers.

   Ⓑ They are suggested by the student as a potential topic.

   Ⓒ They are a topic nobody is already writing on.

   Ⓓ They are well known to the student.

4 What is indicated about the report?
Click on 2 answers.

   Ⓐ It must be at least ten pages long.

   Ⓑ It must be typed on a computer.

   Ⓒ It must be submitted online.

   Ⓓ It must include a bibliography.

5 Listen again to part of the conversation. Then answer the question.
What does the professor imply when he says this: 🎧

   Ⓐ He does not want the student to write about ancient Greece.

   Ⓑ He thinks the student did not do enough research.

   Ⓒ He believes that Canopus is a fascinating star.

   Ⓓ He thinks the ancient Egyptians knew a lot about Canopus.

VOLUME

09-07

Botany

6 What is the lecture mainly about?

   Ⓐ Southeast Asia

   Ⓑ The Venus flytrap plant

   Ⓒ Tetra stigma vines

   Ⓓ Rafflesia plants

7 Why does the professor explain passive carnivores?

   Ⓐ To point out how many of them there are

   Ⓑ To identify the rafflesia as one

   Ⓒ To compare them with the tetrastigma vine

   Ⓓ To say they are only found in Southeast Asia

8 What are pitchers?

   Ⓐ They are roots.

   Ⓑ They are flowers.

   Ⓒ They are leaves.

   Ⓓ They are flies.

9 How does a pitcher plant get nutrients?

(A) By removing them from other plants

(B) By consuming lifeforms

(C) By extracting them from the soil

(D) By using photosynthesis

10 What does the professor say about the *Rafflesia arnoldii*?

(A) Most people cannot stand its smell.

(B) It has the biggest flower in the world.

(C) Some people have grown it in cold climates.

(D) It has bright red flowers.

11 What can be inferred about the *Rafflesia arnoldii*?

(A) It only grows in soil that is very dry.

(B) It can be grown in places around the world.

(C) It has a life cycle of only a few weeks.

(D) Few people ever see its flower in person.

VOLUME

09-08

History of Science

12 What is the main topic of the lecture?

    (A) Gutenberg's printing press

    (B) Newspaper printing

    (C) Nineteenth-century printing

    (D) Computerized printing

13 Why does the professor explain what an alloy is?

    (A) To respond to a student's inquiry

    (B) To describe why alloys are strong

    (C) To detail the manufacturing process

    (D) To say which metals were hard to find

14 What was the result of people using the Linotype printing press?

    (A) It cost less than older models.

    (B) It required more people to operate.

    (C) It changed the publishing industry.

    (D) It was cleaner than older models.

15 According to the professor, what is a counterpunch?

    Ⓐ A writing process

    Ⓑ A type of alloy

    Ⓒ A type of printing press

    Ⓓ A device that cuts other punches

16 What is the professor's attitude toward the students?

    Ⓐ She is fairly unhelpful regarding explanations.

    Ⓑ She would like them to ask better questions.

    Ⓒ She thinks they should know the information already.

    Ⓓ She is willing to answer their questions.

17 What does the professor imply about the Linotype printing press?

    Ⓐ It was a process anyone could do with no training.

    Ⓑ It was easier to use than modern-day printing methods.

    Ⓒ It required a craftsman throughout the entire difficult process.

    Ⓓ It was a much slower process than the Gutenberg printing press.

Appendix

Mastering Word List

This part provides lists of important vocabulary words in each unit. They are essential words for understanding any academic scripts. Many of the words are listed with their derivative forms so that students can expand their vocabulary in an effective way. These lists can be used as homework assignments.

UNIT 01 — Listening for Main Ideas

Step A

- [ ] acid
- [ ] amphibian
- [ ] assignment
- [ ] background
- [ ] barcode
- [ ] beeswax
- [ ] camouflage
- [ ] circulation
- [ ] copper
- [ ] description
- [ ] engraver
- [ ] esophagus
- [ ] etching
- [ ] gastric
- [ ] hatch
- [ ] havoc
- [ ] heartburn
- [ ] intestine
- [ ] Mediterranean
- [ ] nutrient
- [ ] permission
- [ ] prudent
- [ ] reptile
- [ ] seismic
- [ ] sphincter
- [ ] suffrage
- [ ] swipe
- [ ] tectonic

Step B

- [ ] *n.* affiliation
- [ ] *v.* affiliate
- [ ] *adj.* affiliated

- [ ] *n.* amendment
- [ ] *v.* amend
- [ ] *adj.* amendable

- [ ] *n.* association
- [ ] *v.* associate
- [ ] *adj.* associative
- [ ] *adv.* associatively

- [ ] *n.* digest

- [ ] *v.* digest
- [ ] *adj.* digestive
- [ ] *adv.* digestively

- [ ] *n.* disconnection
- [ ] *v.* disconnect
- [ ] *adj.* disconnected
- [ ] *adv.* disconnectedly

- [ ] *n.* eligibility
- [ ] *adj.* eligible
- [ ] *adv.* eligibly

- [ ] *n.* exposure
- [ ] *v.* expose
- [ ] *adj.* exposed

- [ ] *n.* extraction
- [ ] *v.* extract
- [ ] *adj.* extractive

- [ ] *n.* familiarity
- [ ] *v.* familiarize
- [ ] *adj.* familiar
- [ ] *adv.* familiarly

- [ ] *n.* identity
- [ ] *v.* identify
- [ ] *adj.* identifiable
- [ ] *adv.* identifiably

- [ ] *n.* recognition
- [ ] *v.* recognize
- [ ] *adj.* recognizable
- [ ] *adv.* recognizably

- [ ] *n.* removal
- [ ] *v.* remove
- [ ] *adj.* removable

- [ ] *n.* reservation
- [ ] *v.* reserve
- [ ] *adj.* reserved
- [ ] *adv.* reservedly

- [ ] *n.* revolution
- [ ] *v.* revolutionize
- [ ] *adj.* revolutionary
- [ ] *adv.* revolutionarily

- [ ] *n.* theory
- [ ] *v.* theorize
- [ ] *adj.* theoretical
- [ ] *adv.* theoretically

UNIT 02 — Listening for Main Purpose

Step A

- [ ] advent
- [ ] botany
- [ ] carnivorous
- [ ] continue
- [ ] conversion
- [ ] dispute
- [ ] enzyme
- [ ] flourish
- [ ] flytrap
- [ ] hotspot
- [ ] intense
- [ ] landfill
- [ ] nitrogen
- [ ] obsolete
- [ ] pioneer
- [ ] pollution
- [ ] potential
- [ ] premise
- [ ] recyclable
- [ ] sedimentary
- [ ] spew
- [ ] sufficient
- [ ] swampland
- [ ] trigger
- [ ] tripod
- [ ] victim

Step B

- [ ] *n.* action
- [ ] *v.* act
- [ ] *adj.* active
- [ ] *adv.* actively

- [ ] *n.* advance
- [ ] *v.* advance
- [ ] *adj.* advanced

- [ ] *n.* availability
- [ ] *adj.* available
- [ ] *adv.* availably

- [ ] *n.* economy
- [ ] *v.* economize
- [ ] *adj.* economic

□ *adv.* economically

□ *n.* effect
□ *v.* effect
□ *adj.* effective
□ *adv.* effectively

□ *n.* extraction
□ *v.* extract
□ *adj.* extractive

□ *n.* fame
□ *adj.* famous
□ *adv.* famously

□ *n.* finance
□ *adj.* financial
□ *adv.* financially

□ *n.* flexibility
□ *v.* flex
□ *adj.* flexible
□ *adv.* flexibly

□ *n.* industry
□ *adj.* industrial
□ *adv.* industrially

□ *n.* motor
□ *v.* motorize
□ *adj.* motored

□ *n.* nerve
□ *adj.* nervous
□ *adv.* nervously

□ *n.* pace
□ *v.* pace
□ *adj.* paced

□ *n.* pollution
□ *v.* pollute

□ *n.* precision
□ *adj.* precise
□ *adv.* precisely

□ *n.* preference
□ *v.* prefer
□ *adj.* preferable
□ *adv.* preferably

□ *n.* shame
□ *v.* shame
□ *adj.* shameful
□ *adv.* shamefully

□ *n.* succession
□ *v.* succeed
□ *adj.* successive
□ *adv.* successively

□ *n.* theory
□ *v.* theorize
□ *adj.* theoretical
□ *adv.* theoretically

UNIT **03** Listening for Major Details

Step A

□ allegiance
□ ancestry
□ aristocrat
□ arsenal
□ blockade
□ chastise
□ confederate
□ distinction
□ dock
□ evolve
□ federalism
□ functional
□ heritage
□ hierarchy
□ immigrant
□ influx
□ invasion
□ jargon
□ monarch
□ predominantly
□ snowplow
□ supreme
□ territory
□ ultimatum
□ vassal
□ vault
□ withdraw
□ zoning

Step B

□ *n.* approval

□ *v.* approve
□ *adj.* approving
□ *adv.* approvingly

□ *n.* balance
□ *v.* balance
□ *adj.* balanced

□ *n.* chat
□ *v.* chat
□ *adj.* chatting

□ *n.* colony
□ *v.* colonize
□ *adj.* colonial
□ *adv.* colonially

□ *n.* completion
□ *v.* complete
□ *adj.* complete
□ *adv.* completely

□ *n.* creation
□ *v.* create
□ *adj.* creative
□ *adv.* creatively

□ *n.* distinction
□ *v.* distinguish
□ *adj.* distinct
□ *adv.* distinctly

□ *n.* domination
□ *v.* dominate
□ *adj.* dominating
□ *adv.* dominatingly

□ *n.* evolution
□ *v.* evolve
□ *adj.* evolutionary

□ *n.* extension
□ *v.* extend
□ *adj.* extensive
□ *adv.* extensively

□ *n.* infusion
□ *v.* infuse

□ *n.* motive
□ *v.* motivate
□ *adj.* motive

□ *n.* option
□ *v.* opt

- [ ] *adj.* optional
- [ ] *adv.* optionally

- [ ] *n.* predominance
- [ ] *v.* predominate
- [ ] *adj.* predominant
- [ ] *adv.* predominantly

- [ ] *n.* shift
- [ ] *v.* shift
- [ ] *adj.* shifted

- [ ] *n.* uniqueness
- [ ] *adj.* unique
- [ ] *adv.* uniquely

UNIT 04 — Understanding the Function of What Is Said

Step A

- [ ] accomplish
- [ ] adopt
- [ ] alert
- [ ] astonishing
- [ ] axis
- [ ] clockwise
- [ ] confused
- [ ] coyote
- [ ] decoration
- [ ] dioxide
- [ ] elite
- [ ] emergency
- [ ] emit
- [ ] eruption
- [ ] famine
- [ ] fin
- [ ] fulfill
- [ ] genus
- [ ] grassland
- [ ] lava
- [ ] longitudinal
- [ ] marmot
- [ ] peninsula
- [ ] poisonous
- [ ] prey
- [ ] primary
- [ ] shrink

- [ ] sophisticated
- [ ] treaty

Step B

- [ ] *n.* ascent
- [ ] *v.* ascend
- [ ] *adj.* ascendable

- [ ] *n.* descent
- [ ] *v.* descend
- [ ] *adj.* desendible

- [ ] *adj.* clockwise
- [ ] *adv.* clockwise

- [ ] *n.* cultivation
- [ ] *v.* cultivate
- [ ] *adj.* cultivatable

- [ ] *n.* evidence
- [ ] *adj.* evidential
- [ ] *adv.* evidentially

- [ ] *n.* grammaticality
- [ ] *adj.* grammatical
- [ ] *adv.* grammatically

- [ ] *n.* identity
- [ ] *v.* identify
- [ ] *adj.* identical
- [ ] *adv.* identically

- [ ] *n.* manipulation
- [ ] *v.* manipulate
- [ ] *adj.* manipulative
- [ ] *adv.* manipulatively

- [ ] *n.* ozone
- [ ] *adj.* ozonic

- [ ] *n.* perfection
- [ ] *v.* perfect
- [ ] *adj.* perfect
- [ ] *adv.* perfectly

- [ ] *n.* person
- [ ] *v.* personify
- [ ] *adj.* personal
- [ ] *adv.* personally

- [ ] *n.* politics
- [ ] *adj.* political
- [ ] *adv.* politically

- [ ] *n.* similarity
- [ ] *adj.* similar
- [ ] *adv.* similarly

- [ ] *n.* technology
- [ ] *adj.* technological
- [ ] *adv.* technologically

- [ ] *n.* toxicity
- [ ] *adj.* toxic

UNIT 05 — Understanding the Speaker's Attitude

Step A

- [ ] accomplish
- [ ] anarcho-syndicalism
- [ ] angst
- [ ] antique
- [ ] apocalypse
- [ ] appendectomy
- [ ] archaeological
- [ ] conduct
- [ ] constable
- [ ] criticism
- [ ] dedicate
- [ ] deliberate
- [ ] depict
- [ ] deputy
- [ ] drastic
- [ ] egotistical
- [ ] entrench
- [ ] existentialism
- [ ] expire
- [ ] formalism
- [ ] hemisphere
- [ ] inspection
- [ ] mannerism
- [ ] marvel
- [ ] oscillation
- [ ] peasant
- [ ] peculiar
- [ ] prospective
- [ ] shipshape

Step B

- [ ] *n.* complaint
- [ ] *v.* complain
- [ ] *adj.* complaining
- [ ] *adv.* complainingly

- [ ] *n.* contribution
- [ ] *v.* contribute

- [ ] *n.* couple
- [ ] *v.* couple
- [ ] *adj.* coupled

- [ ] *n.* entrenchment
- [ ] *v.* entrench
- [ ] *adj.* entrenched

- [ ] *n.* expiration
- [ ] *v.* expire
- [ ] *adj.* expired

- [ ] *n.* evaluation
- [ ] *v.* evaluate
- [ ] *adj.* evaluative

- [ ] *n.* impression
- [ ] *v.* impress
- [ ] *adj.* impressive
- [ ] *adv.* impressively

- [ ] *n.* inconvenience
- [ ] *v.* inconvenience
- [ ] *adj.* inconvenient
- [ ] *adv.* inconveniently

- [ ] *n.* intellect
- [ ] *v.* intellectualize
- [ ] *adj.* intellectual
- [ ] *adv.* intellectually

- [ ] *n.* intersection
- [ ] *v.* intersect
- [ ] *adj.* intersected

- [ ] *n.* note
- [ ] *v.* note
- [ ] *adj.* notable
- [ ] *adv.* notably

- [ ] *n.* oscillation
- [ ] *v.* oscillate
- [ ] *adj.* oscillatory

- [ ] *n.* possession
- [ ] *v.* possess

- [ ] *adj.* possessive

- [ ] *n.* presentation
- [ ] *v.* present
- [ ] *adj.* presentational
- [ ] *adv.* presentationally

- [ ] *n.* proof
- [ ] *v.* prove
- [ ] *adj.* proved

- [ ] *n.* prospect
- [ ] *v.* prospect
- [ ] *adj.* prospective
- [ ] *adv.* prospectively

- [ ] *n.* recovery
- [ ] *v.* recover
- [ ] *adj.* recovered

- [ ] *n.* reference
- [ ] *v.* refer
- [ ] *adj.* referential
- [ ] *adv.* referentially

UNIT 06 Understanding Organization

Step A

- [ ] abiotic
- [ ] absorb
- [ ] affluent
- [ ] angiosperm
- [ ] anther
- [ ] argon
- [ ] blacksmith
- [ ] botany
- [ ] cerebral
- [ ] cognitive
- [ ] compulsory
- [ ] configuration
- [ ] criminology
- [ ] deciduous
- [ ] entomology
- [ ] external
- [ ] flyby
- [ ] forbearer
- [ ] forensic
- [ ] fungus

- [ ] gamete
- [ ] gymnosperm
- [ ] habitable
- [ ] literacy
- [ ] microorganism
- [ ] optimally
- [ ] pollination
- [ ] urgently

Step B

- [ ] *n.* absorption
- [ ] *v.* absorb
- [ ] *adj.* absorbed
- [ ] *adv.* absorbedly

- [ ] *n.* affect
- [ ] *v.* affect
- [ ] *adj.* affective
- [ ] *adv.* affectively

- [ ] *n.* circle
- [ ] *v.* circle
- [ ] *adj.* circular
- [ ] *adv.* circularly

- [ ] *n.* complement
- [ ] *v.* complement
- [ ] *adj.* complementary
- [ ] *adv.* complementarily

- [ ] *n.* completion
- [ ] *v.* complete
- [ ] *adj.* complete
- [ ] *adv.* completely

- [ ] *n.* declaration
- [ ] *v.* declare
- [ ] *adj.* declarative
- [ ] *adv.* declaratively

- [ ] *n.* digestion
- [ ] *v.* digest
- [ ] *adj.* digestive
- [ ] *adv.* digestively

- [ ] *n.* education
- [ ] *v.* educate
- [ ] *adj.* educational
- [ ] *adv.* educationally

- [ ] *n.* effect
- [ ] *v.* effect

- *adj.* effective
- *adv.* effectively

- *n.* emphasis
- *v.* emphasize
- *adj.* emphatic
- *adv.* emphatically

- *n.* help
- *v.* help
- *adj.* helpful
- *adv.* helpfully

- *n.* pat
- *v.* pat

- *n.* primary
- *adj.* primary
- *adv.* primarily

- *n.* rearrangement
- *v.* rearrange
- *adj.* rearranged

- *n.* representation
- *v.* represent
- *adj.* representative

- *n.* reservation
- *v.* reserve
- *adj.* reserved

- *n.* retrieval
- *v.* retrieve

- *n.* rub
- *v.* rub

- *n.* season
- *adj.* seasonal
- *adv.* seasonally

- *n.* shift
- *v.* shift

- *n.* slowness
- *v.* slow
- *adj.* slow
- *adv.* slowly

- *n.* substitute
- *v.* substitute

- *n.* system
- *v.* systemize
- *adj.* systemic

- *adv.* systemically

- *n.* transfer
- *v.* transfer

Step A

- afflict
- ape
- apparatus
- artistry
- astounding
- authenticity
- blubber
- broadband
- captivity
- contaminate
- contentious
- contractual
- corrupt
- echolocation
- enduring
- genuine
- hibernation
- hoax
- insulate
- memorable
- Paleolithic
- predatory
- pregnancy
- prototypical
- province
- pulse
- sensory
- temporarily

Step B

- *n.* academy
- *adj.* academic
- *adv.* academically

- *n.* apparentness
- *adj.* apparent
- *adv.* apparently

- *n.* benefit
- *v.* benefit
- *adj.* beneficial
- *adv.* beneficially

- *n.* brutality
- *v.* brutalize
- *adj.* brutal
- *adv.* brutally

- *n.* communication
- *v.* communicate
- *adj.* communicative
- *adv.* communicatively

- *n.* corruption
- *v.* corrupt
- *adj.* corrupt
- *adv.* corruptly

- *n.* depiction
- *v.* depict
- *adj.* depictive

- *n.* enjoyment
- *v.* enjoy
- *adj.* enjoyable
- *adv.* enjoyably

- *n.* intensity
- *v.* intensify
- *adj.* intense

- *n.* isolation
- *v.* isolate
- *adj.* isolated

- *n.* maintenance
- *v.* maintain
- *adj.* maintainable

- *n.* perfect
- *v.* perfect
- *adj.* perfect
- *adv.* perfectly

- *n.* process
- *v.* process
- *adj.* processed

- *n.* skill
- *adj.* skillful
- *adv.* skillfully

- *n.* type

□ *v.* typify
□ *adj.* typical
□ *adv.* typically

□ *n.* variety
□ *v.* vary
□ *adj.* various
□ *adv.* variously

UNIT 08 Making Inferences

Step A

□ apparatus
□ cancel
□ cerebellum
□ dendrite
□ devotee
□ dialect
□ disinfect
□ elaborate
□ endotherm
□ enthusiasm
□ excitatory
□ extremist
□ filter
□ grassroots
□ grizzly
□ homeostasis
□ hypothermia
□ inhibitory
□ innate
□ intimidate
□ microbe
□ parallel
□ pathogen
□ radiation
□ rehearsal
□ skull
□ surge
□ understaffed
□ vertebrate

Step B

□ *n.* constant

□ *adj.* constant
□ *adv.* constantly

□ *v.* continue
□ *adj.* continuous
□ *adv.* continuously

□ *n.* deliberateness
□ *v.* deliberate
□ *adj.* deliberate
□ *adv.* deliberately

□ *n.* depth
□ *v.* deepen
□ *adj.* deep
□ *adv.* deeply

□ *n.* diminishment
□ *v.* diminish
□ *adj.* diminishing
□ *adv.* diminishingly

□ *n.* diversity
□ *v.* diversify
□ *adj.* diverse
□ *adv.* diversely

□ *n.* electricity
□ *adj.* electric
□ *adv.* electrically

□ *n.* environment
□ *adj.* environmental
□ *adv.* environmentally

□ *n.* excess
□ *v.* exceed
□ *adj.* excessive
□ *adv.* excessively

□ *n.* final
□ *v.* finalize
□ *adj.* final
□ *adv.* finally

□ *n.* form
□ *v.* form
□ *adj.* formal
□ *adv.* formally

□ *n.* mind
□ *v.* mind
□ *adj.* mindful
□ *adv.* mindfully

□ *n.* possibility
□ *adj.* possible
□ *adv.* possibly

□ *n.* respect
□ *v.* respect
□ *adj.* respected
□ *adv.* respectedly

□ *n.* satisfaction
□ *v.* satisfy
□ *adj.* satisfying
□ *adv.* satisfyingly

□ *n.* stability
□ *v.* stabilize
□ *adj.* stable
□ *adv.* stably

MEMO

How to
Master Skills for the
TOEFL® iBT
LISTENING

Answers, Scripts, and Translations

Intermediate

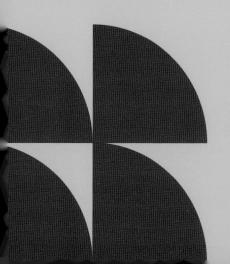

How to
Master Skills for the

Second Edition

TOEFL® iBT

LISTENING Intermediate

Answers, Scripts,
and Translations

DARAKWON

Listening for Main Ideas

Basic Drill · p.14

Drill 1 Ⓐ

Script 🎧 01-02

W Student: Professor Landon, I need to talk to you about my presentation.

M Professor: Sure, Susan. What's going on?

W: I'd like to change my topic. I'm having trouble finding information on the subject I chose.

M: Well, there is only one week before you have to speak. Do you think you can do it?

W: Yes, I can. I've already got a new subject picked out, and there's plenty of information on it.

M: Okay. Then you have my permission to change it. But you need to email me a description of your new topic. Please do that before tomorrow morning.

해석

W Student: Landon 교수님, 발표와 관련해서 교수님께 말씀을 드려야 할 것 같아요.

M Professor: 그래요, Susan. 무슨 일인가요?

W: 주제를 바꾸고 싶어서요. 제가 선택한 주제와 관련된 정보를 찾는데 어려움을 겪고 있어요.

M: 음, 발표를 하기 전까지 일주일 밖에 남지 않았어요. 그럴 수 있다고 생각하나요?

W: 네, 그래요. 새 주제를 이미 골라 놓았는데, 그에 관한 정보는 많이 있어요.

M: 좋아요. 그렇다면 바꾸는 것을 허락할게요. 하지만 새로운 주제에 대해 제게 이메일로 설명을 해야 해요. 내일 오전까지 그렇게 해 주세요.

Drill 2 Ⓒ

Script 🎧 01-03

W Dining Services Employee: All right, the first thing you need to do is register for your meal plan.

M Student: How can I do that?

W: There's an office at the main dining hall on campus. Take your student identification card and a credit card. The meal plans are expensive.

M: But what if I don't eat that much food?

W: That doesn't matter. All first-year students are

required to get a plan for at least two meals a day. So it would be a really good idea if you ate at a dining hall at least two meals a day. That way, you will actually get your money's worth.

M: So how much is this meal plan going to cost me?

W: I'm not sure because it changes from semester to semester. There's a pricing guide at the dining hall office.

해석

W Dining Services Employee: 좋아요, 제일 먼저 하셔야 할 일은 급식을 신청하는 것이에요.

M Student: 어떻게 하면 되나요?

W: 교내의 가장 큰 식당 건물에 사무실이 있어요. 학생증과 신용카드를 가지고 가세요. 급식은 비싼 편이라서요.

M: 하지만 제가 식사를 그다지 많이 하지 않는 경우에는요?

W: 그건 상관없어요. 신입생들은 모두 하루에 최소 2회의 급식을 신청해야 해요. 그러니 교내 식당에서 하루에 최소한 두 번 식사를 하는 것이 좋을 거예요. 그래야 실제로 돈이 아깝지 않을 테니까요.

M: 그러면 그러한 급식을 신청할 때 얼마를 내야 하나요?

W: 학기마다 다르기 때문에 잘 모르겠군요. 교내 식당의 사무실에 요금 안내문이 있어요.

Drill 3 Ⓑ

Script 🎧 01-04

M Student: Hello. How can I sign up for a club?

W Student Activities Office Employee: You should just contact the president of the club. Which club are you interested in?

M: I'd like to join the chess club. However, I can't find any information on it.

W: Ah, there's no chess club here anymore. Not enough students were interested in it, so the club closed down last year.

M: That's too bad. Do you have a list of clubs that are on campus? I'd love to do an extracurricular activity, but I'm not sure what's available.

W: Sure. Here's a handout. It has the phone number of the president of each club, so you can contact the person in charge if you want to join a club.

해석

M Student: 안녕하세요. 어떻게 하면 동아리에 가입할 수 있나요?

W Student Activities Office Employee: 동아리의 회장에게 연락을 하기만 하면 되죠. 어떤 동아리에 관심이 있나요?

M: 저는 체스 동아리에 가입하고 싶어요. 하지만 그에 대한 정보를 찾을 수가 없네요.

W: 아, 체스 동아리는 더 이상 존재하지 않아요. 체스에 관심이 있는 학생의 수가 충분하지 않아서 체스 동아리는 작년에 없어졌어요.

M: 안 되었군요. 교내에 있는 동아리의 리스트를 가지고 계신가요? 과외 활동을 하고 싶은데, 가입이 가능한 동아리가 어떤 것인지 잘 몰라서요.

W: 물론이죠. 여기 유인물을 드릴게요. 각 동아리 회장들의 전화 번호가 나와 있기 때문에 가입하고 싶은 클럽이 있는 경우에는 책임자에게 연락을 할 수 있을 거예요.

Drill 4 ⓒ

Script 🎧 01-05

M Professor: The Earth has frequent natural disasters. Natural disasters are acts of nature that create havoc among the planet's creatures. One kind of natural disaster is a tsunami. A tsunami is a giant tidal wave that starts in the ocean. It causes major flooding wherever it hits. It can even sink entire islands so that they no longer can be seen from the surface of the water. One reason why tsunamis happen is underwater earthquakes. These quakes create disturbances in the water and cause large swells. These swells create waves, which move until they hit land.

해석

M Professor: 지구에서는 많은 자연 재해가 발생합니다. 자연 재해는 지구의 생물들에게 엄청난 피해를 가져다 주는 자연의 활동이죠. 자연 재해 중 하나가 쓰나미입니다. 쓰나미는 바다에서 생기는 거대한 파도예요. 쓰나미가 강타하는 곳마다 엄청난 홍수가 발생합니다. 심지어 섬 전체를 가라앉혀서 수면에서 사라지게 만들 수도 있죠. 쓰나미를 일으키는 원인 중 하나는 해저 지진입니다. 이러한 지진 때문에 바닷물이 요동치고 거대한 놀이 발생합니다. 이러한 놀이 파도를 일으키는데, 이 파도가 이동해서 육지를 강타하게 되죠.

Drill 5 ⓓ

Script 🎧 01-06

W Professor: Women worldwide had to fight for the right to vote. Most governments thought that women couldn't make decisions about politics. In the 1800s, women started to fight against this. They became active in fighting for women's suffrage. Oh, suffrage means the right to vote. The first country to grant women the right to vote was New Zealand. This happened in 1892. Over the next hundred years, many more countries gave women voting rights. Many women around the world can now vote if they want to, but there are still countries that don't allow women to vote. Many battles in this fight have been won, but the fight for women's voting rights is not over.

해석

W Professor: 전 세계의 여성들은 투표권을 얻기 위해 투쟁해야 했습니다. 대부분의 정부들은 여성들이 정치에 관한 결정을 내릴 수 없다고 생각했어요. 1800년대, 여성들은 이에 대한 투쟁을 시작했습니다. 참정권을 얻기 위해 적극적으로 투쟁에 참여했죠. 오, 참정권이란 투표에 참여할 수 있는 권리를 말합니

다. 여성에게 참정권을 부여한 최초의 국가는 뉴질랜드였어요. 1892년의 일이었죠. 그 후 100년에 걸쳐 보다 많은 국가들이 여성들에게 참정권을 부여했어요. 전 세계의 많은 여성들이 원하는 경우 투표를 할 수 있게 되었으나 아직까지도 여성들에게 투표를 허용하지 않는 국가들이 있습니다. 이러한 투쟁에서 많은 승리를 거두었지만, 여성의 투표권을 얻기 위한 투쟁은 아직 끝나지 않았어요.

Drill 6 ⓑ

Script 🎧 01-07

W Professor: The digestive system is vital for keeping humans and other animals alive. It lets animals take in food and extract nutrients. These nutrients are important to keeping animals healthy. In humans, the digestive tract is made up of the mouth, the esophagus, the stomach, the small intestine, and the large intestine. Food is broken down in the mouth, the esophagus, and the stomach. Nutrients are taken out of food in the small intestine. Food waste then goes through the large intestine. Here, more nutrients are pulled out or extracted. Finally, waste is passed out of the body through the colon. This is the bottom part of the large intestine. Without the digestive system, we wouldn't be alive.

해석

W Professor: 소화기는 인간 및 기타 동물이 생활하는데 대단히 중요해요. 소화기 덕분에 동물들은 음식물을 섭취하고 영양소를 흡수할 수가 있죠. 이러한 영양소는 동물의 건강 유지에 중요한 역할을 합니다. 인간의 경우, 소화관은 입, 식도, 위, 소장, 그리고 대장으로 이루어져요. 음식물은 입, 식도, 그리고 위에서 잘게 부숴집니다. 음식물의 영양분은 소장에서 흡수되고요. 그런 다음에 음식물 찌꺼기는 대장을 통과합니다. 여기에서 더 많은 영양소가 흡수되거나 추출되죠. 마지막으로, 결장을 통해 음식물 찌꺼기가 몸 밖으로 빠져 나갑니다. 결장은 대장의 가장 아랫부분이에요. 소화기가 없다면 우리는 살 수 없을 것입니다.

Exercises with Mid-Length Conversations

Exercise 1   1 ⓑ   2 ⓓ   p.16

Script 🎧 01-08

W Student: Excuse me. I have a problem with my room.

M Student Housing Office Employee: Sure. What's wrong with it?

W: The key doesn't work. I just picked it up, but the door won't open.

M: That's strange. Which dorm do you live in?

W: I'm in room 342 in Milton Hall. My roommate's key works fine, but mine doesn't.

M: Okay. I can have a new key made for you in about one hour. Do you have your student ID card with you?

W: Sure. Uh . . . here it is. What is this going to cost me?

M: It won't cost you anything at all. It's our mistake, so we'll pay for it. Why don't you be back at your dorm room at 3:30? I'll be over there with a key for you then.

W: Thanks so much. I really appreciate it.

해석

W Student: 실례합니다. 제 방에 문제가 있어서요.

M Student Housing Office Employee: 그렇군요. 어떤 문제가 있나요?

W: 키가 작동을 하지 않아요. 조금 전에 키를 받았는데, 문이 열리지가 않는군요.

M: 이상하네요. 어떤 기숙사에서 살고 있나요?

W: Milton 홀 342호에 살아요. 제 룸메이트의 키는 작동이 잘 되지만, 제 것은 그렇지가 않아요.

M: 좋아요. 약 한 시간 후에 새로운 키를 만들어 드릴 수 있어요. 학생증을 가지고 있나요?

W: 그럼요. 어⋯ 여기 있어요. 그렇게 하면 비용이 얼마나 들까요?

M: 아무런 비용이 들지 않을 거예요. 저희 실수이기 때문에 저희가 비용을 지불할 거예요. 3시 30분에 기숙사 방에 가 있는 것이 어떨까요? 그때 제가 키를 가지고 그곳으로 갈게요.

W: 정말 고맙습니다. 정말 감사해요.

🖉 Summary Note

A

❶ cost

❷ fine

B

The student visits the student housing office. She tells the man there that her dorm key does not work. It will not open the door. She says her roommate's key is fine. The man asks the student for her ID card and says he can make a new key for her. He says it will not cost anything to get a new key. He will deliver the key to the student at 3:30 in the afternoon.

Exercise 2   1 Ⓐ   2 Ⓓ   p.18

Script 🎧 01-09

W Bookstore Employee: How's it going? Can I help you with anything?

M Student: Yeah, I hope so. I was looking for this book that I need for my, um, my research methods class. The professor wants us to start reading this book now and going over the material, but I can't seem to find it on the shelves.

W: All right, let me see if I can help you with that. What's the title of the book? Oh, and if you have the author, that would be really helpful, too.

M: Okay, hold on. I have to find where I wrote it down. Hmm . . . The title of the book is *Methods of Educational Research*. And the author is, um, Wiersma.

W: All right, let me enter that information into the computer to see if we have it in stock. Um, Wiersma, did you say? And *Methods of Educational Research*?

M: Yeah, that's it.

W: Wow, those disappeared quickly. We had a brand-new shipment come in yesterday—fifty books—and they were gone by this morning.

M: Oh, no! I knew I should have come by yesterday. I just got so carried away with school supply shopping. Are you expecting to get more in?

W: Hmm . . . Yes, I think we're going to get another shipment in about a week. But it's going to be significantly smaller. I think just twenty books or so.

M: Oh, man! I need to have two chapters read by next week. I don't know what I'm going to do. What a horrible way to start the semester!

W: I have a suggestion. You could put your name down to reserve one of the copies that'll be in, and in the meantime, maybe you could check the library to see if it has a copy on reserve. But if you're going to do that, you should probably do it quickly because I'm sure a lot more students are going to be in your position.

M: Yeah, I guess I'll try that. Um, okay, so where do I reserve a copy of the textbook?

W: We can do that right here. But remember that you have to pick up the book within one week of delivery, or you'll lose your reservation, and it'll go to someone else.

M: All right. Thanks for all your help.

해석

W Bookstore Employee: 안녕하세요? 제가 도와 드릴까요?

M Student: 예, 그래 주시면 좋겠어요. 제, 음, 제 연구 방법 수업에 필요한 이 책을 찾고 있는 중이에요. 교수님께서는 저희들이 이 책을 읽고 내용을 검토해 보기를 원하시는데, 서가에서 찾을 수가 없네요.

W: 좋아요, 제가 도움을 드릴 수 있는지 볼게요. 책 제목이 어떻게 되죠? 오, 저자 이름을 알아도 제게 큰 도움이 될 거예요.

M: 그래요, 잠깐만요. 어디다 써 놨는지 찾아 봐야해서⋯ 책 제목은 *교육 연구 방법*이에요. 그리고 저자는 음, 위어스마고요.

W: 좋아요, 정보를 컴퓨터에 입력해서 그 책이 있는지 확인해 볼게요. 음, 위어스마라고 했죠? 그리고 *교육 연구 방법*이고요?

M: 예, 맞아요.

W: 와, 빨리 나갔네요. 어제 새 책이 50권 들어왔는데, 오늘 아침에 다 나갔어요.

M: 오, 이런! 어제 왔어야 했군요. 학용품을 사느라 정신이 팔려 있었네요. 더 들어올 것으로 생각하시나요?

W: 음⋯ 네, 약 일주일 후에 더 들어올 것 같아요. 하지만 물량이 훨씬 적을 거예요. 스무 권 정도 될 것 같군요.

M: 오, 세상에! 다음 주까지 두 챕터는 읽어야 해요. 어떻게 해야 할지 모르겠군

요. 이번 학기는 시작부터 엉망이네요!

W: 제가 한 가지 제안을 할게요. 우선 이름을 적어서 입고될 책 중 하나를 예약해 두고, 그 동안은 도서관에서 대출이 가능한 도서가 있는지 확인해 보시면 될 거예요. 만약 그럴 생각이라면, 분명 학생과 같은 처지인 학생들이 훨씬 많을 테니, 아마도 서둘러야 할 거예요.

M: 예, 그렇군요. 그렇게 할게요. 음, 그럼, 책 예약은 어디서 하면 되나요?

W: 여기에서 저희가 해 드릴 수 있어요. 하지만 배송 후 일주일 이내에 대출을 해야 하고, 그렇지 않으면 예약이 무효가 되어서 책이 다른 학생에게 넘어 갈 것이라는 점을 기억하세요.

M: 좋아요. 도와 주셔서 감사합니다.

✏️ Summary Note

A

❶ needs a textbook

❷ the library's copy

B

A student is looking for a book at the campus bookstore. The woman informs him that the textbook is out of stock. She says a new shipment will arrive in a week. The student panics because his professor has already assigned two chapters to read. The woman makes a suggestion. She thinks the student should see if the book is on reserve at the library. That way, the student can do his reading without getting behind while he waits for the new shipment of textbooks.

Exercise 3 1 Ⓐ 2 Ⓒ p.20

Script 🎧 01-10

W Librarian: All first-year students are required to do a one-on-one orientation with a librarian or a librarian's aide their first semester.

M Student: Thank you.

W: The first thing I'm going to do is walk you through how to borrow books from the library. What you need to do first is make sure your identification card is registered at the front desk. The circulation desk employee will, um, scan your card and then assign you a barcode that will be swiped every time you borrow a book.

M: But why is that attached to my student ID card? I mean, couldn't I get a separate library card? That's how things were at my public library back home.

W: It's really important for your library card to have a photograph of you on it for, um, for identification purposes. Only students, professors, and people affiliated with the university are allowed to borrow books from this library. So by attaching a barcode to your student ID, we're pretty much ensuring that you belong to this

university. Plus, since your ID already has your picture on it, we don't have to worry about anyone else using your ID and taking out books.

M: I guess I understand that. It's just a little weird to me to have one card for everything here. I mean, it already has my meal plan and a cash account on it, and it lets me back into my dorm.

W: Well, that's kind of a good thing. You don't end up carrying around a lot of cards.

M: It's kind of bad, too. If I lose it, I can't do anything. I guess I have to be really careful.

W: I guess you do. It's not so hard. Don't worry.

M: Thanks. Okay, so the first thing I have to do before I can borrow books is, um, take my student ID to the circulation desk for a barcode?

W: That's right. Once you do that, you can start borrowing books.

해석

W Librarian: 모든 신입생들은 첫 학기에 사서나 보조 사서로부터 일대일 오리엔테이션을 받아야 해요.

M Student: 감사합니다.

W: 제일 먼저 도서관에서 어떻게 대출을 하는지 알려 드릴게요. 우선 학생증을 프론트 데스크에 등록해야 해요. 대출 데스크의 직원이, 음, 학생증을 스캔 한 다음에 책을 대출할때마다 인식에 사용될 바코드를 발급해 줄 거예요.

M: 하지만 그것이 왜 학생증에 부착되나요? 제 말은, 따로 도서 대출 카드를 만들 수는 없나요? 제가 살던 곳의 공공 도서관에서는 그렇게 해 주었거든요.

W: 본인 확인을 위해서는, 음, 도서 대출 카드에 학생의 사진을 부착하는 일이 정말로 중요해요. 학생, 교수, 그리고 대학과 관련이 있는 사람들만이 이곳 도서관에서 책을 빌릴 수가 있죠. 그래서 학생증에 바코드를 부착함으로써 학생이 이 학교의 소속이라는 점을 저희가 확인할 수 있어요. 게다가, 학생증에는 이미 사진이 붙어 있으니 학생의 학생증으로 다른 사람이 책을 대출하는 일에 대해서도 걱정할 필요가 없고요.

M: 이해가 가는군요. 여기에서는 하나의 카드로 모든 일을 처리한다는 것이 약간 이상하기는 하지만요. 제 말은, 학생증으로 급식도 먹고, 현금도 찾고, 그리고 물론 이 카드로 기숙사에도 들어가고요.

W: 음, 그건 좋은 점이죠. 카드를 여러 장씩 가지고 다니지 않아도 되니까요.

M: 나쁜 점도 있어요. 잃어버리는 경우에는 아무것도 할 수가 없잖아요. 정말로 주의해야 할 것 같아요.

W: 그래야겠네요. 그렇게 어려운 일은 아닐 거예요. 걱정하지 마세요.

M: 감사합니다. 좋아요, 그러면 제가 책을 빌리기 전에 제일 먼저 해야 할 일은, 음, 대출 데스크로 학생증을 가서 바코드를 받는 일이군요?

W: 맞아요. 그렇게 하고 난 다음에 책을 빌릴 수 있어요.

✏️ Summary Note

A

❶ the student's ID card

❷ a lot of accounts

B

A librarian is informing the student about the book borrowing process. She tells him the first step is to get a barcode attached to his student identification card. She says it is important to have photo identification when borrowing books because only people affiliated with the university are allowed to borrow books. The student worries about having another account attached to his ID card because it already holds his money accounts and meal plan. He's afraid he will lose it. The librarian reassures him that he will be fine.

Exercise 4 1 (A) 2 (A) p.22

Script 🎧 01-11

W Student: Hi, Professor Carlos. I was wondering if I could ask you for some advice.

M Professor: Of course. What can I do for you?

W: Well, I was going over my financial situation, and I'm really aggravated about it because I just don't think I'm going to be able to afford to stay here for more than a year. And I really would prefer not to transfer. I mean, I love it here.

M: Okay, well, I'm sure we can figure something out. Um, have you filled out a financial aid form yet?

W: No, I don't think so.

M: All right. Then that's your first task. That form will help determine your eligibility for loans and, um, need-based scholarships. Actually, I'm certain you have to complete that form even if you're going for a merit-based scholarship.

W: Where can I get it? And who do I turn it into? And what kind of information does it ask for?

M: I'm pretty sure you can pick it up at the financial assistance office. That is where you should return it as well. Actually, I think the financial assistance office has set up an interface so that you can complete the form via the Internet.

W: Really? Wow, that's so convenient!

M: Yes, it really is. Um, just find the site for the university's financial assistance office, and you can probably hyperlink to the form from there.

W: I think I'll do that right now. Wait. Do you know what kind of information I'll need to fill out the form?

M: Um, I think it would be most prudent to fill out the form with a copy of last year's tax returns. That should have all the information you'll need.

W: Okay. I have a copy of that in my room.

M: And if you submit the form within the next couple of days, you might be eligible for some of the departmental

scholarships we're awarding for next semester. We have both need- and merit-based scholarships available.

W: That's excellent! Thank you so much.

해석

W Student: 안녕하세요, Carlos 교수님. 조언을 좀 구할 수 있을까 해서요.

M Professor: 그래요. 어떻게 도와 드릴까요?

W: 음, 제가 경제적인 문제를 겪고 있는데, 1년 이상 이곳에 더 머무를 여력이 없을 것 같아서 정말로 걱정이 커요. 그리고 전학을 가고 싶지는 않고요. 그러니까, 이곳이 정말 마음에 들거든요.

M: 좋아요, 그럼. 분명 방법을 찾을 수 있을 거예요. 음, 그런데 학자금 융자 신청서는 작성했나요?

W: 아니요, 하지 않았어요.

M: 그렇군요. 그렇다면 그것이 가장 먼저 할 일이에요. 신청서를 내면 학생에게 융자와, 음, 재정 보조 장학금을 신청할 자격이 있는지 알 수 있을 거예요. 사실 성적 장학금 신청을 하는 경우에도 신청서를 작성해야 하는 것으로 알고 있어요.

W: 어디에서 얻을 수 있나요? 그리고 누구한테 제출하면 될까요? 그리고 어떤 내용을 적어야 하죠?

M: 신청서는 분명 재정 지원 사무실에서 받을 수 있을 거예요. 제출도 그곳에 하면 되고요. 사실 재정 지원 사무실에서는 인터넷으로도 서류 작성이 가능하도록 인터페이스를 마련해 둔 것으로 알고 있어요.

W: 정말인가요? 오, 정말 편리하겠군요!

M: 네, 그래요. 음, 재정 지원 사무실의 사이트만 찾으면 되고, 아마도 그곳에서 하이퍼링크로 신청서를 작성할 수 있을 거예요.

W: 지금 당장 신청해야 할 것 같아요. 잠시만요. 신청서에 어떤 내용을 적어야 하는지 아시나요?

M: 음, 작년 소득세 신고서 사본을 첨부해서 신청서를 작는 것이 가장 현명한 일일 거예요. 거기에 필요한 정보가 다 들어 있을 테니까요.

W: 알겠습니다. 제 방에 사본이 있어요.

M: 그리고 이틀 이내에 신청서를 제출한다면 다음 주에 수여될 몇몇 학과 장학금의 대상자가 될 수도 있어요. 재정 보조 장학금과 성적 장학금 모두 가능하고요.

W: 잘 됐네요! 정말 감사합니다.

✏️ Summary Note

A

❶ a financial aid form
❷ scholarships

B

The student asks the professor for advice about receiving financial aid. Her professor tells her that to get a loan or a scholarship, she must fill out the financial aid form. The form can be found at the financial assistance office or online. The professor urges her to fill out the form as soon as possible. He says this because there are departmental scholarships available for the following semester. The student is very grateful for her professor's help and advice.

Exercise 1 1 Ⓑ 2 Ⓑ p.24

Script 🎧 01-12

M1 Professor: So we've talked about Rembrandt and his life and a bit about his work. He was a really famous painter and engraver. The thing is that his talents in those activities aren't what made him so famous. Rembrandt pretty much revolutionized the art of etching. We talked a bit about that technique before. Remember? Who can tell me what etching is?

W Student: Doesn't it involve burning an image onto a metal plate?

M1: That's right. The artist usually has a copper plate that he coats or covers with an acid-resistant substance. Um, this stuff is usually made of beeswax and resin, and this substance is called bitumen. Altogether, it's called the etching ground. What the artist does is cover the copper plate with the ground compound—all that stuff I just mentioned—and he carves a design through it with a sharp tool. You have to carve pretty deep because you want to get through the ground to uncover the copper underneath. Then, the artist exposes the plate to acid, the parts that are uncovered by the ground get eaten away, and the metal is recessed into those areas, creating channels. Who knows what's done with the metal plates afterward?

M2 Student: They're used to make prints, right?

M1: Great job. Yes, after the ground compound is removed, ink is poured into the parts that have been eaten away. These channels hold ink really well. Then, the plate is pressed onto moist paper, and you get a print. Rembrandt was a genius when it came to etchings. I think that after a while, etchings were all he did. Um, let me see. Does anyone recognize this etching?

M2: I know that one. It's in a museum in Washington, D.C. Um, I think it's called *Woman and Arrow*.

M1: Pretty close. It's called *The Woman with the Arrow*. Rembrandt created this etching in 1661.

해석

M1 Professor: 우리는 렘브란트와 그의 삶, 그리고 간단히 그의 작품에 대해 논의해 보았습니다. 그는 정말로 유명한 화가이자 조각가였어요. 하지만 중요한 사실은 그러한 활동에서의 그의 재능 때문에 그가 유명해진 것이 아니라는 점이에요. 렘브란트는 에칭 기법에 혁명을 가져다 주었어요. 전에 그러한 기법에 대해 잠깐 논의를 한 적이 있었죠. 기억이 나시나요? 에칭이 무엇인지 누가 말해 볼까요?

W Student: 금속판에서 이미지를 부식시키는 것과 관련이 있지 않나요?

M1: 맞아요. 화가들은 주로 구리판을 사용해서 내산성 물질을 구리판에 칠하거나 입힙니다. 음, 그러한 재료는 보통 밀랍과 수진으로 이루어지며, 이러한 물질

은 역청이라고 불리죠. 이를 모두 합쳐 에칭 그라운드라고 부릅니다. 화가들은 제가 방금 언급한 모든 재료들, 즉 그라운드 화합물을 구리판에 입힌 후에 날카로운 도구를 이용해서 그곳에 디자인을 새깁니다. 아래쪽에 있는 구리가 드러나도록 판을 뚫으려면 매우 깊게 새겨야 하죠. 그런 다음 화가가 판을 산에 노출시키면 그라운드로 덮여 있지 않은 부분들이 부식되어 이러한 영역에서는 금속이 파이게 되는데, 이로써 홈이 만들어집니다. 그 후 금속판으로 무엇을 하는지 아는 사람이 있나요?

M2 Student: 그것을 가지고 프린트를 하죠, 맞죠?

M1: 잘 대답했어요. 네, 그라운드 화합물을 제거한 후 부식된 부분에 잉크를 붓습니다. 그러한 홈에는 잉크가 잘 들어가게 되죠. 그런 다음에 판을 촉촉한 종이에 찍으면 판화를 얻게 됩니다. 에칭에 관한 한 렘브란트는 천재였어요. 한동안 렘브란트는 에칭에만 전념했던 것 같아요. 음, 잠시만요. 이러한 에칭 작품을 아는 사람이 있나요?

M2: 하나 알고 있습니다. 워싱턴 DC의 박물관에 있는 작품이죠. 음, *여인과 화살*이라고 생각해요.

M1: 거의 정답이네요. *화살을 든 여인*이라는 작품입니다. 렘브란트가 1661년에 그 에칭 작품을 만들었어요.

✏️ Summary Note

A

❶ ground compound
❷ channels
❸ moist paper

B

Etchings are created by covering a copper plate with a ground compound. Then, the artist cuts an image into the compound until the copper plate is exposed underneath. Next, the artist pours acid over the compound. The parts of the copper plate that are covered with the compound remain untouched. The other parts get eaten away by the acid. This creates channels. The artist removes the compound and pours ink into the channels. Finally, the plate is pressed onto moist paper. This creates a print.

Exercise 2 1 Ⓑ 2 Ⓒ p.26

Script 🎧 01-13

W Professor: After food is swallowed, the digestive process keeps going in the esophagus. The esophagus is basically a long tube. It pretty much goes straight up and down from your mouth to your stomach. At the top of the esophagus is the upper sphincter, which is a ring-like muscle. It stays closed most of the time and for good reason. After you swallow, the upper sphincter opens to let food in. Then, it closes right away so that the food doesn't come back out.

Um, so once food is let into the esophagus, a process starts that's called peristalsis. This is the wave-like movements of the muscles. During peristalsis, the muscles in the esophagus push the food down the tube. Picture a toothpaste tube. To get toothpaste out of the tube, you have to squeeze from one end to the other. That's what peristalsis is like except that there's a wave-like motion from the top of the tube to the bottom. The food is pushed in front of the wave till it reaches the bottom of the esophagus. At the bottom of the, um, the esophagus, is the lower sphincter. When food gets to that point, the lower sphincter opens up to let food pass into the stomach. Then, it closes really fast so that the acids from the stomach can't get into the esophagus.

And speaking of acids getting into the esophagus, those acids are what cause the feeling called heartburn. Heartburn doesn't actually have anything to do with the heart. Actually, um, heartburn takes place in the esophagus. It's what happens when the lower sphincter gets weak. Gastric acids from the stomach enter the esophagus. They cause a burning feeling. These acids don't cause problems in the stomach because the stomach has, um, well, it has a lining, kind of like armor, that keeps it from getting hurt. The esophagus doesn't have that kind of lining or armor, so gastric acids can really harm it.

해석

W Professor: 음식물을 삼키면 식도에서 소화 과정이 계속되죠. 기본적으로 식도는 긴 모양의 관입니다. 입에서 위까지 거의 일직선으로 이어져 있어요. 식도의 위쪽에는 고리 모양의 근육인 상부 괄약근이 있습니다. 이는 대부분의 경우 닫혀 있는데, 그럴 만한 타당한 이유가 있습니다. 음식물을 삼키면 음식물이 들어갈 수 있도록 상부 괄약근이 열립니다. 그런 다음에는 음식물이 다시 나오지 못하도록 바로 닫히죠.

음, 일단 음식물이 식도로 들어가면 연동 운동이라고 불리는 과정이 시작됩니다. 이는 근육이 파도처럼 움직이는 것이에요. 연동 운동이 일어나는 동안 식도의 근육들이 음식물을 식도 아래쪽으로 내려 보냅니다. 치약 튜브를 떠올려 보세요. 튜브에서 치약을 짜내려면 치약의 한쪽 끝에서 반대쪽 끝으로 치약을 짜내야 합니다. 식도의 위에서 아래로 파도와 같은 움직임이 일어난다는 점을 제외하면 그것이 바로 연동 운동의 작동 방식이에요. 파도의 앞쪽에 있는 음식이 밀려나서 식도의 가장 아랫부분에 도달합니다. 식도의, 음, 아랫부분에는 하부 괄약근이 있어요. 음식물이 이 지점에 도달하면 하부 괄약근이 열려서 음식물이 위로 들어가게 되죠. 그런 다음에는 위산이 식도로 역류하지 않도록 곧바로 닫힙니다.

그리고 식도로 역류하는 위산에 대해 말하자면, 이 산이 속쓰림 증상을 일으킵니다. 속쓰림은 사실 심장과는 아무런 관련이 없어요. 실제로, 음, 속쓰림은 식도에서 발생합니다. 하부 괄약근이 약해지면 이런 일이 발생해요. 위에서 나온 위산이 식도로 들어갑니다. 이들이 속쓰림을 일으키죠. 이 위산은 위에서는 아무 문제를 일으키지 않는데, 그 이유는 위에, 음, 위를 다치지 않게 해 주는 일종의 갑옷과 같은 위벽이 있기 때문입니다. 식도에는 그러한 종류의 위벽이나 갑옷이 없기 때문에 위산이 피해를 일으킬 수 있어요.

📝 Summary Note

A

❶ the mouth and the stomach
❷ Heartburn
❸ Burning

B

After food leaves the mouth, digestion goes on in the esophagus. The esophagus is a long tube that connects the mouth and the stomach. Food enters the esophagus through the upper sphincter. Then, the food is pushed through the esophagus by a process called peristalsis. Peristalsis happens when the muscles squeeze food down the tube. Food leaves the esophagus through the lower sphincter. If the lower sphincter is weak, a person can get heartburn.

Exercise 3 1 ⓓ 2 ⓐ p.28

Script 🎧 01-14

M1 Professor: The next chapter in our book discusses earthquakes. Um, well, I hope you've all read this chapter because I will be asking questions from the chapter for participation points today. Okay, to begin, the authors talk about plate tectonic theory as a pretty widely accepted explanation for earthquakes. Who can tell me what this theory states? Yes, go ahead . . .

W Student: I think the authors wrote that plate tectonic theory is the idea that the Earth's surface is made up of these large plates that are kind of disconnected. I think they move against one another.

M1: Very good. Yes, the Earth's surface is not one solid piece of land. Um, it's made up of these plates that move against each other. The worst earthquakes tend to happen where one plate is kind of pushed under another. These quakes start really deep in the ground. Other quakes, um, less severe quakes, happen where the plates slide against each other. How many major earthquake zones are there?

M2 Student: Three.

M1: And what are they?

M2: Um, one lies around the Pacific Ocean. Another is called the, um, the trans-Asiatic belt. That one goes across the Mediterranean countries and then across Asia. And the third, the third one is in the Atlantic Ocean and is called the mid-ocean ridges.

M1: Excellent. Does anyone have questions about plate tectonic theory?

W: What about earthquakes that don't happen in these zones? I mean, aren't there ever earthquakes that, um, that don't occur around a seismic zone?

M1: Great question. Yes, I think that sometimes earthquakes do happen away from, um, seismic zones. These ones are tough to figure out though. Quakes that don't occur along plate boundaries are called, um, intraplate earthquakes. I don't think scientists have figured out the causes for those yet, but I think they do agree that, um, there's a lot of ground stress where these quakes happen.

M1 Professor: 우리 교재의 다음 장은 지진에 관한 것이에요. 음, 그러니까, 제가 이번 장에 관한 질문을 해서 오늘 수업에 대한 참여 점수를 매길 것이기 때문에 모두들 이번 장을 읽어 오셨기를 바랍니다. 좋아요, 우선, 저자들은 지진의 원인을 설명하는 것으로 널리 알려진 판 구조론에 대해 논의하고 있습니다. 이 이론이 무엇을 주장하는지 누가 말해 볼까요? 네, 말씀해 보세요…

W Student: 저자들의 설명에 따르면 판 구조론은 지구의 표면이 거대한 판으로 이루어져 있다는 아이디어인데, 이러한 판들은 분리되어 있어요. 이 판들은 서로 반대 방향으로 이동하고 있다고 알고 있습니다.

M1: 잘 했어요. 네, 지구의 표면은 단단한 하나의 땅 덩어리가 아닙니다. 음, 서로 방대 방향으로 이동하는 판들로 이루어져 있죠. 가장 강력한 지진은 하나의 판이 다른 지판 밑으로 밀려 들어갈 때 발생하는 경향이 있어요. 이러한 지진은 아주 깊은 지하에서 시작되죠. 다른 지진들은, 음, 보다 강하지 않은 지진들은 판들이 서로 부딪혀 미끄러질 때 나타납니다. 주요 지진대는 몇 개일까요?

M2 Student: 세 개입니다.

M1: 어떤 것들이죠?

M2: 음, 하나는 태평양 주변에 있어요. 다른 하나는, 음, 횡아시아 지진대라는 것이고요. 지중해 국가들을 가로질러 아시아에까지 걸쳐 있죠. 그리고 세 번째는, 세 번째 것은 대서양에 있는데, 중앙 해령 지진대라고 불립니다.

M1: 훌륭해요. 판 구조론에 관해 질문할 사람이 있나요?

W: 이 지진대에서 발생하지 않는 지진들은 어떤가요? 제 말은, 음, 지진대 주변이 아닌 곳에서 지진이 일어나는 경우는 없나요?

M1: 좋은 질문이에요. 네, 때로는, 음, 지진대에서 멀리 떨어진 곳에서도 지진이 발생하는 것으로 알고 있어요. 하지만 그러한 지진들은 알아내기가 힘들죠. 판의 경계를 따라 일어나지 않는 지진들을, 음, 판 내부 지진이고 부르죠. 과학자들은 아직 이러한 지진의 원인은 밝혀내지 못했지만, 음, 이러한 지진이 발생하는 지역에 엄청난 지중 응력이 존재한다는 점은 과학자들이 다들 인정하는 것으로 알고 있어요.

✏️ Summary Note

A

❶ fault lines
❷ rub against
❸ these quakes occur

B

One theory about why earthquakes happen is called plate tectonic theory. The Earth's surface is made up of plates that move against one another. The most severe quakes happen when one plate gets pushed underneath another one. Less severe quakes happen when plates rub against each other. Scientists do not really know what causes them. There are three major earthquake zones on the Earth. But sometimes earthquakes happen away from seismic zones due to ground stress.

Exercise 4   1 (B)   2 (A)   p.30

Script 🎧 01-15

W Professor: A thing to note about the women's suffrage movement in this country is that women were fighting, um, I guess you could say it was a tough battle. Oh, by the way, suffrage means the right to vote. There had been a long history of women not having the right to vote. Even in the earliest democracies, in ancient Greece and Rome, women couldn't vote. And experts say that these times gave us the best thoughts and ideas of all time.

Anyway, let's just say that women had a lot of history to break down before they could vote. So women in Great Britain and the United States fought for the right to vote during the 1800s and the 1900s. Women in Great Britain struggled in the same way American women did for this right. However, we're just going to look at American women and what they did. So the women's suffrage movement started in the U.S. around the same time as the anti-slavery movement. Um, that would have been during the, um, the mid-1800s. So this is what happened. A group of female activists started pushing for anti-slavery laws. And while they were doing this, they found that women's issues in America also needed to be looked at.

These women realized that something wasn't right about how women were treated. So this is what they did. They held a couple of meetings in different parts of the country to attract women in those regions into the cause. Now, the problem was that there was no way to give women the right to vote nationally. A state could give this right to women. But that would only affect women in that state. Because of this, these women believed that it was vital to get an amendment, or change, to the Constitution to give women the right to vote. This would give women the right to vote pretty much nationwide. So what they did was start a group called the National Woman's Suffrage Association. The purpose of the, um, the NWSA was to get an amendment to the Constitution.

W Professor: 우리 나라의 여성 참정권 운동에 관해 한 가지 주목할 점은 여성들이 투쟁을, 음, 이렇게도 말할 수 있을 것 같은데, 힘든 싸움을 했다는 것이에요. 오, 그건 그렇고 참정권이란 투표에 참여할 수 있는 권리를 말합니다. 역사의 오랜 기간 동안 여성들은 투표할 권리를 갖지 못했어요. 고대 그리스와 로마와 같은 최초의 민주주의 국가에서조차 여성들은 투표를 할 수가 없었죠. 그리고 전문가들은 모든 시대를 통틀어 이 시기에 가장 훌륭한 사고와 아이디어가 등장했다고 주장합니다.

어쨌든, 여성들이 투표를 할 수 있게 되기까지 수 차례 역사가 바뀌었다고 해 두죠. 그래서 영국과 미국의 여성들은 1800년대와 1900년대에 투표권을 얻기 위해 투쟁했습니다. 영국의 여성들 역시 미국의 여성들과 마찬가지로 이러한 권리를 얻기 위해 같은 방식으로 투쟁했어요. 하지만 우리는 미국의 여성들과 그들이 한 일에 대해서만 살펴보고자 합니다. 자, 미국에서의 여성 참정권 운동은 노예제 폐지 운동과 비슷한 시기에 시작되었어요. 음, 아마도 1800년대, 음, 중반이었을 거예요. 이제 어떤 일이 있었는지 알려 드리죠. 한 무리의 여성 운동가들이 노예제 폐지 법안을 요구하기 시작했어요. 그리고 그렇게 하는 동안에 미국의 여성과 관련된 문제들도 살펴볼 필요가 있다는 점도 알게 되었죠.

이러한 여성들은 여성들의 처우와 관련해서 잘못된 점이 있다는 것을 깨닫게 되었어요. 그래서 다음과 같은 일을 했어요. 그들은 미국의 여러 지역에서 두어 차례의 모임을 개최해서 해당 지역의 여성들을 이러한 운동에 끌어들였어요. 자, 문제는 전국적으로 여성에게 투표할 권리를 줄 수 있는 방법이 없다는 점이었어요. 하나의 주만이 여성들에게 그러한 권리를 줄 수 있었죠. 하지만 이는 그 주에 있는 여성들에게만 적용되었습니다. 이 때문에, 이들 여성들은 여성들에게 투표권을 부여하기 위해서는 헌법을 수정, 혹은 개정하는 일이 필수적이라고 생각했어요. 그러면 거의 전국적으로 여성들에게 투표권이 주어지게 되겠죠. 그래서 이들은 전국 여성 참정권 협회라는 모임을 조직했습니다. 음, 이 NWSA의 목적은 헌법을 수정하는 것이었죠.

✏ Summary Note

A

❶ have the right to vote
❷ nationally
❸ give women the right to vote

B

There is a long history of a lack of voting rights for women. In the mid-1800s, American women started fighting for their right to vote. This started during the anti-slavery movement. While women were fighting for rights for others, they realized that they did not have many rights themselves. American women started meeting about what to do. They realized that the only way that all American women would get the right to vote would be to push for an amendment to the Constitution. So they created the National Woman's Suffrage Association for that purpose.

Integrated Listening & Speaking   p.32

Script 🎧 01-16

M Professor: Rembrandt was a famous artist in the 1600s. He did paintings and engravings, but he was most famous for his etchings. Etching is a technique that involves burning an image onto a metal plate. Usually, a copper plate is used. It can be done by applying a ground compound to a copperplate. The ground compound is made up of beeswax, resin, and bitumen. Then, the artist carves an image into the ground deep enough to reach the copper. The plate is exposed to acid, and the image gets burned into the plate. The artist then removes the ground compound and pours ink into the channels created by the acid. The plate is pressed onto moist paper. The image from the plate is transferred to the paper, creating a print.

1 a. The process explained is etching.
  b. The lecture explains how to do an etching.

2 a. The first step is to apply a ground compound to the plate.
  b. First, a person must put a ground compound on the plate.

3 a. What happens last is the plate is pressed on moist paper.
  b. The last step is when the artist presses the plate on moist paper.

Script 🎧 01-17

W Professor: The esophagus is an important part of the digestive system. It is a long tube that connects the mouth and the stomach. After it leaves the mouth, food enters the esophagus through the upper sphincter. From there, a process called peristalsis pushes food down the tube. This process happens when muscles in the esophagus squeeze food down. When the food reaches the bottom of the esophagus, it goes to the stomach from the esophagus through the lower sphincter. A disease of the esophagus is called heartburn. Heartburn happens because the lower sphincter is weak. This lets acids from the stomach enter the esophagus and cause a burning feeling. The esophagus cannot handle that because it does not have the special lining, or armor, that the stomach has. Stomach acids can destroy the esophagus because of this.

1 a. The esophagus connects the mouth and the stomach.
  b. The mouth and the stomach are connected by the esophagus.

2 a. Food enters through the upper sphincter.
  b. The upper sphincter lets food into the esophagus.

3 a. Heartburn feels like burning.
  b. Heartburn causes a burning sensation.

Mini TOEFL iBT Practice Test   p.34

1 ⓓ	2 ⓑ	3 ⓒ	4 ⓑ	5 ⓓ
6 ⓒ	7 ⓐ	8 ⓑ	9 ⓓ	10 ⓐ
11 ⓓ				

[1-5]

W Student: Hi, Professor Jackson. I was wondering if I could ask you something.

M Professor: Of course. How may I be of assistance?

W: I'm taking your developmental psychology class.

M: Right. I recognize you from the lectures. You sit in the first couple of rows, right?

W: Yes, that's me. Anyway, I'm taking this class with you, and I didn't do so well on the first exam. Well, I guess I did okay, but I'm not really satisfied with my grade. So I wonder if you might be able to help me figure out how to bring it up for the next exam.

M: What did you get on the exam?

W: I got a B–. But I studied really hard, and I really need an A in this class for my graduate school application.

M: A B– isn't bad for the first exam. But since you're determined, let's figure out how you can get an A on the next two exams. That should bring you pretty close to an A for the class. And if you participate in class, I'll take that into account. I mean, participation does count for, um, ten percent of your grade.

W: Okay, I'll try to participate more.

M: Great! That's an easy step to take. So what did you do to study for this exam?

W: Well, I went over all of my lecture notes a few times and paid attention to definitions and theories. I also memorized Piaget's stages of development.

M: Well, that's a good start. And Piaget definitely came up on the exam a few times. What about the textbook? How did you review that material?

W: I went over what I had highlighted when reading earlier this semester. And I took notes on that stuff, and I, um, reviewed the notes a few times.

M: It sounds like you did everything right. Hmm . . . What you should do for the next exam is talk to my teaching assistant for the class. I've given her old copies of exams from previous semesters, so you should try to practice with those. And if you miss some of the stuff on those exams, then you know what you need to work on for the actual one.

W: Really? I can do that? I never knew that was an option!

M: You can certainly do that.

W: Great! And all the TA's information is on the syllabus, right?

M: Yes, it is. Email her before the next exam, but give yourself at least a week in case she doesn't get back to you right away.

W: Thanks, Professor. I promise to participate more in class as well.

M: Great! Student participation is my favorite part of my job. Good luck with everything!

해석

W Student: Jackson 교수님, 안녕하세요. 여쭤 볼 것이 있는데 괜찮으신지 궁금합니다.

M Professor: 그럼요. 어떻게 도와 드릴까요?

W: 저는 교수님의 발달 심리학 수업을 듣고 있어요.

M: 그래요. 알아 보겠군요. 맨 앞자리 쪽에 앉죠, 그렇죠?

W: 네, 맞아요. 어쨌든, 제가 교수님 수업을 듣고 있는데, 첫 번째 시험을 잘 못 봤어요. 음, 그럭저럭 보긴 했지만, 저는 제 성적에 정말로 만족할 수가 없어요. 그래서 다음 시험에서 성적을 올릴 수 있는 방법을 찾는데 교수님께서 도움을 주실 수 있는지 궁금합니다.

M: 지난 번 시험 성적이 어땠죠?

W: B–를 받았어요. 하지만 저는 정말 열심히 공부했고, 대학원에 진학하기 위해서는 이번 수업에서 꼭 A를 받아야 해요.

M: 첫 시험에서의 B–는 나쁜 성적이 아니에요. 하지만 학생 각오가 그렇다니 다음 두 번의 시험에서는 A를 받는 법을 같이 알아보죠. 그러면 이번 수업에서의 학점이 A에 상당히 가까워질 테니까요. 그리고 학생이 수업에 활발하게 참여한다면 제가 그것도 고려할 거예요. 제 말은, 수업 참여도가, 음, 성적의 10%를 차지하니까요.

W: 알겠습니다. 더 열심히 참여할게요.

M: 좋아요! 그것이 쉬운 방법이죠. 그러면 이번 시험을 위해서 어떻게 공부했나요?

W: 음, 수업에서 필기한 것을 모두 몇 차례 훑어보았고, 정의와 이론들에 신경을 썼어요. 또한 피아제의 발달 단계도 외웠고요.

M: 음, 시작은 좋았군요. 그리고 피아제는 확실이 시험에서 여러 차례 등장했고요. 교재는 어땠나요? 교재의 내용은 어떻게 공부했죠?

W: 이번 학기에 읽기 과제를 하면서 강조 표시를 해 두었던 부분들을 검토했어요. 그리고 그에 대한 필기를 했고, 음, 필기한 부분을 여러 번 복습했죠.

M: 해야 할 건 다 한 것처럼 들리네요. 흠… 다음 시험에서 학생이 해야 할 일은 수업 조교와 이야기를 나누는 것이에요. 조교에게 지난 학기의 시험지들을 주었으니 그걸로 모의 시험을 보세요. 그리고 시험에서 틀린 문제가 생기는 경우, 실제 시험에서는 학생이 공부해야 하는 부분이 무엇인지 알게 될 거예요.

W: 정말요? 그래도 되나요? 그런 방법이 있다는 건 생각도 못했어요!

M: 당연히 그래도 되죠.

W: 잘 됐네요! 그리고 조교의 연락처는 전부 강의 계획서에 나와 있죠, 그렇죠?

M: 네, 그래요. 다음 시험 보기 전에 조교에게 이메일을 보내고, 바로 답장을 받지 못할 수도 있으니 적어도 일주일 정도 여유를 두고 보내세요.

W: 감사합니다, 교수님. 그리고 수업에도 더 열심히 참여할게요.

M: 좋아요! 학생 참여야말로 제 일에서 제가 가장 좋아하는 부분이죠. 모든 일에 행운이 따르길 빌어요!

[6-11]

M Professor: All right, class. Today, we're going to talk about reptiles. Now, as you probably remember,

Answers, Scripts, and Translations **11**

reptiles are cold-blooded animals that hatch from eggs and have scales. Does this sound familiar to everyone? Okay, good. Now, I think the best thing to do would be to provide some examples of reptiles. Let me see . . . Please raise your hand if you've ever heard of an animal called the horned toad. Okay, so many of you have heard of this creature. I see some questions in your eyes. You are probably wondering why we're going to talk about the horned toad since I just mentioned that we'll be discussing reptiles.

As you all know, a toad is an amphibian. That's an animal which starts its life living in water with gills and ends up living on land with lungs. So here is the issue with the horned toad: it's not actually a toad at all! The horned toad is actually a lizard. It's a reptile. The reason people confuse it for a toad is that it is kind of round. So from now on, if you hear of someone talking about a horned toad, let that person know that it's actually a lizard.

Additionally, the horned toad doesn't actually have horns. The things that look like horns are really just spiny scales. These scales act as protection for the lizard. If an animal is trying to eat the lizard, it will puff up, kind of like a balloon, and that will make the scales stick out. And when these spiny scales are sticking out, it's hard for other animals to swallow the lizard.

The horned toad has other ways of protecting itself. One of these is camouflage. Does everyone remember what camouflage is? No? Okay, well, camouflage is when an animal blends into its surroundings. The horned toad does this really well. It usually lives in deserts, and it is a, um, a brownish color. Its color allows it to blend into the desert background.

Some kinds of horned toads have yet another way of protecting themselves. Now, this is kind of gross, but some of them can shoot blood out of the corners of their eyes. This really confuses their predators. This blood also contains a substance that, um, that doesn't taste good. That makes animals that might have wanted to eat the horned toad not want to eat it anymore.

해석

M Professor: 좋습니다, 여러분. 오늘은 파충류에 관해 논의할 예정이에요. 자, 아마 여러분도 기억하시겠지만, 파충류는 알에서 부화하고 비늘을 가지고 있는 냉혈 동물입니다. 모두들 잘 알고 있겠죠? 그래요, 좋습니다. 자, 제일 좋은 방법은 몇 가지 파충류의 예를 들어보는 것이겠죠. 봅시다… 뿔두꺼비라는 동물에 대해 들어본 적이 있는 사람은 손을 들어 주세요. 좋아요, 많은 분들이 이 생물에 대해 들어 보셨군요. 여러분의 눈에서 의아해 하는 눈빛이 보이네요. 방금 제가 파충류에 대해 논의할 것이라고 했는데 왜 뿔두꺼비 이야기를 하는지 궁금하신 것 같군요.

여러분 모두가 알고 있는 것처럼, 두꺼비는 양서류입니다. 아가미가 있어서 물속에서 삶을 시작하지만 허파가 있기 때문에 결국 육지에서 생활하게 되는 동물이죠. 따라서 뿔두꺼비의 문제는 다음과 같습니다. 이는 사실 두꺼비가 아니에

요! 뿔두꺼비는 사실 도마뱀입니다. 파충류죠. 사람들이 이를 두꺼비로 착각하는 이유는 몸이 동그랗기 때문입니다. 그러니 이제부터는 누군가 뿔두꺼비에 관해 얘기하는 것을 듣는 경우, 그 사람에게 그것은 사실 도마뱀이라고 알려 주세요.

어쨌든, 뿔두꺼비에게는 사실 뿔이 없습니다. 뿔처럼 보이는 것은 실제로 뾰족한 비늘이에요. 이 비늘은 이 도마뱀의 방어 수단으로 기능합니다. 어떤 동물이 이 도마뱀을 잡아 먹으려고 하면, 도마뱀은 몸을 마치 풍선처럼 부풀려서 비늘이 바깥으로 튀어나오게 만듭니다. 그리고 이러한 비늘이 밖으로 나와 있으면 다른 동물들이 도마뱀을 삼키기가 힘들어지죠.

뿔두꺼비들은 또 다른 보호 수단도 가지고 있습니다. 그중 하나가 위장이죠. 위장이 무엇인지 모두들 기억하고 있죠? 아닌가요? 좋아요, 음, 위장이란 동물이 자신의 몸을 주변 환경과 비슷하게 만드는 것입니다. 뿔두꺼비는 위장을 정말 잘해요. 보통 사막에서 사는데, 음, 갈색을 띠어요. 이러한 색깔 때문에 사막의 주변 환경과 잘 섞입니다.

일부 종류의 뿔두꺼비들은 또 다른 보호 수단도 가지고 있어요. 자, 좀 그렇긴 한데, 어떤 녀석들은 눈 옆으로 피를 뿜어낼 수도 있습니다. 이렇게 해서 포식자들을 대단히 혼란스럽게 만들죠. 또한 이 피에는, 음, 이상한 맛이 나는 물질이 들어 있습니다. 이로써 이 도마뱀을 잡아 먹으려 했던 동물들이 더 이상 잡아 먹으려고 하지 않게 되죠.

Vocabulary Check-Up p.39

A
1 Ⓝ	2 Ⓛ	3 Ⓚ	4 Ⓔ	5 Ⓓ
6 Ⓕ	7 Ⓙ	8 Ⓗ	9 Ⓐ	10 Ⓖ
11 Ⓒ	12 Ⓑ	13 Ⓜ	14 Ⓞ	15 Ⓘ

B
| 1 Ⓑ | 2 Ⓓ | 3 Ⓐ | 4 Ⓒ | 5 Ⓔ |

UNIT 02 Listening for Main Purpose

Basic Drill p.42

Drill 1 Ⓓ

Script 🎧 02-02

M Student: Professor Prokofiev, I have a problem. I think I might have to withdraw from school.

W Professor: Withdraw? Why do you need to do that?

M: The price of tuition keeps going up, and my family can't afford to pay it.

W: Ah, I understand. Well, you're an outstanding student with good grades. Why don't you apply for a scholarship?

M: How can I do that?

W: Go to the financial aid office in Barton Hall. Talk to someone there and describe your situation. You'll be asked to fill out some forms, and then you'll be considered for a scholarship.

M: Wow. Thanks. But . . . do you really think I have a chance to get one?

W: It's highly likely. If you need a recommendation for your application, just ask me. Okay?

해석

M Student: Prokofiev 교수님, 제게 문제가 있어서요. 학교를 그만두어야 할 것 같아요.

W Professor: 그만둔다고요? 왜 그래야 하나요?

M: 등록금이 계속 오르고 있는데, 저희 가족이 등록금을 감당할 수가 없어요.

W: 아, 이해가 되는군요. 음, 학생은 성적이 우수한 학생이잖아요. 장학금을 신청해 보는 것이 어떨까요?

M: 어떻게 하면 되죠?

W: Barton 홀에 있는 재정 지원 사무실로 가세요. 그곳 사람에게 이야기를 해서 학생의 상황을 설명하세요. 몇 가지 서류를 작성하라는 요청을 받게 될 텐데, 그러면 학생은 장학금 후보에 오를 거예요.

M: 와, 감사합니다. 하지만… 실제로 제가 장학금을 탈 수 있을 것이라고 생각하시나요?

W: 그럴 가능성이 높죠. 신청에 추천서가 필요한 경우에는 저한테 요청하세요. 알겠죠?

Drill 2 ⓒ

Script 🎧 02-03

W Student: Hi, Professor Tomlin. May I ask you for some advice?

M Professor: Sure. What's the problem?

W: I've been working really hard in your class, but I'm having trouble understanding the material in the textbook.

M: Well, the material is a little complicated. I've actually had quite a few students ask me for advice about it. So I think what you should do is take notes on the material while you're going over it. You know, uh, write down key words, concepts, and such. And if that doesn't work, you could always go to the learning center. Someone there can help you with other tactics.

W: Oh, okay. Thanks a lot. Uh . . . do you know how much the learning center charges?

M: Its services are free of charge.

해석

W Student: 안녕하세요, Tomlin 교수님. 교수님께 조언을 구해도 될까요?

M Professor: 물론이죠. 무슨 문제인가요?

W: 수업은 정말 열심히 듣고 있는데, 교재 내용을 이해하기가 어려워서요.

M: 음, 내용이 약간 복잡한 편이에요. 실제로 제게 조언을 구했던 학생들이 상당수 있었죠. 그래서 학생도 교재를 공부를 하는 동안 그 내용에 대해 메모를 해야 할 거예요. 알다시피, 어, 핵심어, 개념, 그리고 기타 등등을 적으세요. 그리고 그래도 소용이 없으면 학습 지원 센터에 가보도록 해요. 그곳의 누군가가 다른 방법들을 알려 줄 수 있을 거예요.

W: 오, 알겠어요. 정말 감사합니다. 어… 학습 지원 센터의 비용은 얼마인지 아시나요?

M: 그곳 서비스는 무료예요.

Drill 3 Ⓐ

Script 🎧 02-04

W Student: Good morning. I'm considering studying abroad next semester, but . . .

M Study Abroad Office Employee: But what?

W: Well, I'm concerned about getting credit for the classes I take abroad. Is that a problem?

M: That's a good question. The best thing to do is to attend a university that ours has a partnership with.

W: Why is that?

M: In most cases, the classes students take at those schools automatically get transferred here. So you get credit for them. If you go to a school that we don't have a partnership with, you might not get credit for every class you take.

W: Ah, I see. That's very helpful. Thanks a lot.

해석

W Student: 안녕하세요. 다음 학기에 유학을 생각 중인데요, 하지만…

M Study Abroad Office Employee: 하지만 무엇인가요?

W: 음, 해외에서 듣는 수업의 학점이 인정되는지 걱정이 되어서요. 문제가 되나요?

M: 좋은 질문이군요. 가장 좋은 것은 우리 학교와 파트너쉽을 맺고 있는 대학에 다니는 것이죠.

W: 왜 그런가요?

M: 대부분의 경우, 그러한 학교에서 학생들이 듣는 수업은 자동으로 이곳에서도 인정을 받아요. 그러니 그에 대한 학점을 얻게 되죠. 우리와 파트너쉽을 맺고 있지 않은 학교를 다니는 경우에는 학생이 듣는 모든 수업의 학점이 인정받지 못할 수도 있어요.

W: 아, 그렇군요. 큰 도움이 되었어요. 정말 감사합니다.

Drill 4 Ⓓ

Script 🎧 02-05

M Professor: Technology is useful to humans for many reasons. Unfortunately, it has also been used by humans to harm the environment. Pollution is one way in which the environment is harmed by people. For example, the factories that people build to produce goods emit smoke into the air. Many factories dump waste that they produce into rivers and the ocean. Additionally, cars, trains, and ships spew smoke into the air. Humans also use computers a lot. New computers come out all the time and make old computers obsolete. Computers are not recyclable, so we have to throw them away. This fills up landfills.

해석

M Professor: 기술은 여러 가지 이유에서 인간에게 유용합니다. 안타까운 일은 기술이 인간에 의해 환경을 파괴시키는 일에도 사용되고 있다는 점이에요. 인간에 의해 환경이 파괴되는 한 가지 방식은 오염입니다. 예를 들어 제품 생산을 위해 지어진 공장들이 공기 중으로 매연을 배출합니다. 많은 공장들이 공장에서 나오는 폐기물을 강과 바다에 버리고 있죠. 뿐만 아니라 자동차, 기차, 그리고 선박들도 공기 중으로 매연을 뿜어냅니다. 사람들은 또한 컴퓨터를 많이 사용합니다. 항상 새로운 컴퓨터가 나옴으로써 기존 컴퓨터는 구식이 되어 버리죠. 컴퓨터는 재활용이 불가능하기 때문에 이를 버릴 수 밖에 없어요. 그래서 매립지가 가득 차게 됩니다.

Drill 5 (B)

Script 🎧 02-06

W Professor: The trickle-down effect in economics is a disputed theory. It states that big businesses should be allowed to do as they please because lower-level businesses will flourish from their successes. They should not be regulated or taxed by the government. Many economic theorists believe that this theory is only supported by certain economists. Others think that it's really not a valid theory at all. They don't believe that big businesses should be allowed to do whatever they want. Instead, they think that the government should regulate these businesses. They claim that big businesses should be taxed so that the money will be able to go to those who need it most.

해석

W Professor: 경제학에서 낙수 효과는 논란의 여지가 많은 이론이에요. 이는 대기업이 성공하면 중소기업들도 번성하기 때문에, 대기업들로 하여금 하고 싶은 대로 놔두어야 한다는 주장입니다. 대기업을 정부가 규제하거나 대기업에 세금을 부과해서는 안 되는 것이죠. 많은 경제학자들은 이 이론을 특정 경제학자들만 지지한다고 생각해요. 이 이론이 현실과 동떨어진 이론이라고 생각하는 학자들도 있고요. 이들은 대기업이 하고 싶은 것을 하도록 놔두어서는 안 된다고 생각합니다. 대신 정부가 이러한 기업들을 규제해야 한다고 생각하죠. 대기업들에게 세금을 부과해서 이를 가장 필요로 하는 사람들에게 그 돈이 갈 수 있도록 해야 한다고 생각합니다.

Drill 6 (D)

Script 🎧 02-07

M Professor: The 1930s brought about a change in the film industry. This change greatly affected all in the industry, especially the actors. Before the 1930s, film was silent. It wasn't until the 1930s that the advent of "talkies" brought sound to cinema. Before the 1930s, actors like Charlie Chaplin were really popular. The films that Chaplin starred in are some of the most famous films from the silent film era. However, once sound was introduced into the film industry, Charlie Chaplin no longer got film roles. While he was a great actor in silent films, he was not good at doing speaking parts. His physical comedy did not translate well into sound. This sort of thing happened to many actors when the conversion from silent film to talkies took place.

해석

M Professor: 1930년대 영화 산업에 변화가 일어났습니다. 이러한 변화는 영화 산업의 모든 것, 특히 배우들에게 커다란 영향을 미쳤어요. 1930년대 이전에는 영화들이 무성 영화였습니다. 1930년대 이후 "유성 영화"가 등장함으로써 영화에 소리가 들어가게 되었죠. 1930년대 이전에는 찰리 채플린과 같은 배우들이 매우 유명했습니다. 채플린이 주연한 영화들은 무성 영화 시대에서 만들어진 가장 유명한 영화에 속합니다. 하지만 영화 산업에 소리가 도입되자 찰리 채플린은 더 이상 역할을 맡지 못했어요. 무성 영화에서는 훌륭한 배우였지만 발성에 있어서는 뛰어나지 못했거든요. 신체를 이용한 그의 코미디는 소리로 잘 전달되지 않았습니다. 무성 영화가 유성 영화로 바뀌면서 많은 배우들에게 이러한 일들이 일어났습니다.

Exercises with Mid-Length Conversations

Exercise 1 1 (B) 2 (D) p.44

Script 🎧 02-08

W Professor: Ivan, thanks for coming here. I need to speak with you about something important. I'm a bit concerned about your class performance.

M Student: What do you mean? I got a B on the midterm exam.

W: Yes, but I was expecting more from you. Your advisor told me that you're an excellent student, so I was expecting higher than a B from you.

M: Ah, I see. Well . . .

W: Yes?

M: To be honest, I didn't study much for the exam. I had to work at my part-time job until after midnight the night before the test, so . . .

W: What kind of job do you have that makes you work so late?

M: I work at Nate's Pizza as a delivery driver. I had to substitute for the other driver that night, and Nate's doesn't close until two in the morning.

W: I see. Do you finish late every shift you work?

M: Yes, but I normally just work there on Friday and Saturday nights. I only had to work on a Tuesday night because the other driver was sick. I was doing him a favor.

W: Okay. I guess that explains your performance.

M: I will do my best on the final exam and the paper. I will try to get my grade up.

W: I'm glad to hear you say that. You can still pull out an A in this class if you ace both of them.

M: That's great news. Thank you for saying that.

해석

W Professor: Ivan, 와 줘서 고마워요. 학생과 중요한 일에 대한 이야기를 해야 해서요. 저는 학생의 수업 성적이 약간 걱정스러워요.

M Student: 무슨 말씀이신가요? 저는 중간고사에서 B를 받았는데요.

W: 그렇기는 하지만 저는 학생에게서 더 많은 것을 기대하고 있었어요. 학생의 지도 교수님께서 학생이 뛰어난 학생이라고 말씀하셨기 때문에 B보다 높은 성적을 기대하고 있었죠.

M: 아, 알겠어요. 그게…

W: 네?

M: 솔직하게 말씀을 드리면, 제가 시험 준비를 많이 하지 못했어요. 시험 전날 자정 이후에도 아르바이트를 해야 했기 때문에, 그래서…

W: 무슨 일을 하길래 그렇게 늦게까지 일을 하나요?

M: Nate's Pizza에서 배달 기사로 일을 하고 있어요. 그날 밤 다른 기사의 일을 대신해야 했는데, Nate's는 오전 2시 이후에야 문을 닫죠.

W: 그렇군요. 근무를 할 때마다 늦게 끝나나요?

M: 네, 하지만 보통은 금요일과 토요일 밤에만 일을 해요. 다른 기사가 아팠기 때문에 화요일 밤에 일을 했던 것이고요. 제가 그의 부탁을 들어 주고 있었죠.

W: 그래요. 그러면 학생의 성적이 설명이 되는 것 같군요.

M: 기말고사와 보고서는 최선을 다해서 준비할게요. 성적을 올리도록 노력하겠습니다.

W: 그렇게 말하다니 기쁘군요. 두 경우 모두 높은 성적을 받는다면 이번 수업에서 A를 받을 수 있을 거예요.

M: 좋은 소식이군요. 말씀해 주셔서 감사합니다.

📝 Summary Note

A

❶ part-time job

❷ final exam and paper

B

The professor tells the student she is concerned about his test performance. She was told he is an excellent student, but he got a B on the midterm exam. The student says that he had to work until after midnight the night before the exam, so he could not study for it much. He explains that he

delivers food for a restaurant. He had to substitute for the other driver the night before the test. He promises to do well on the final exam and the paper and to improve his grade.

Exercise 2 1 Ⓐ 2 Ⓒ
p.46

Script 🎧 02-09

W Professor: Hi. Can I help you?

M Student: Hi, Professor Madison. My name is John Smith. I wonder if I can ask you something.

W: Of course, John.

M: I know our final exam is in a week. And I know generally professors don't have to get the final grades in for two weeks afterward. But the thing is that I've applied for a study abroad position that starts in four weeks, and I need to have all my grades in really early to be accepted to the program. So I wonder if you can grade my exam early so that I can complete the application process on time.

W: Hmm . . . When is the application deadline?

M: A week and a half from today. Three days after the final exam to be precise.

W: And which study abroad program is this?

M: I'm doing a program in Rome. If I'm there for a semester, it'll take care of my classics minor.

W: Wow, that sounds so exciting. So you're taking care of your minor first? And then you'll finish your major?

M: Yes. I'm already a little ahead on my finance major, so I can afford to take a semester just focusing on the minor. Plus, it's a great way to travel and to get a little international perspective.

W: I absolutely agree. I think all students should do a study abroad program. Anyway, back to your question. I'll make a note of your situation and copy that to my teaching assistant. One of us will make sure to grade your exam first and get your grade to the Registrar's office.

M: Thank you so much. I really appreciate it.

W: No problem. Glad to help. Good luck on the exam and in Rome.

M: Thanks!

해석

W Professor: 안녕하세요. 무슨 일이죠?

M Student: 안녕하세요, Madison 교수님. 제 이름은 John Smith예요. 여쭤볼 것이 있어서요.

W: 그래요, John.

M: 일주일 후에 기말고사가 있다고 알고 있어요. 그리고 보통은 교수님들께서 시험 후 2주 동안은 최종 성적을 공개하실 필요가 없는 것으로 알고 있습니다.

하지만 문제는 제가 4주 후에 시작하는 해외 유학 프로그램에 지원했는데, 그 프로그램에 들어가려면 제 전체 성적을 일찍 알아야 해요. 그래서 제가 시간 내에 지원을 마칠 수 있도록 교수님께서 제 시험 성적을 일찍 매겨 주실 수 있는지 궁금합니다.

W: 흠… 신청 마감이 언제인가요?

M: 오늘부터 1.5주 후예요. 정확하게는 기말고사 끝나고 3일 후이고요.

W: 그리고 어떤 해외 유학 프로그램인가요?

M: 로마에서의 프로그램에 참여할 거예요. 한 학기 동안 그곳에 있으면서 부전공인 고전학을 공부할 예정이고요.

W: 와, 정말 재미있을 것 같군요. 그러니까 부전공을 먼저 공부하는 것이죠? 그런 다음에 전공 공부를 마치려고요?

M: 네. 전공인 재정학은 조금 앞서 가고 있기 때문에 한 학기 동안은 부전공에만 초점을 맞춰도 될 것 같아요. 또한 여행을 하면서 국제적인 시각을 약간 키울 수 있는 좋은 기회이기도 하고요.

W: 전적으로 동의해요. 저는 모든 학생들이 해외 유학을 경험해야 한다고 생각해요. 어쨌든, 학생의 질문으로 돌아가죠. 제가 학생의 상황에 대한 메모를 한 후 이를 복사해서 수업 조교에게 보낼게요. 우리 두 사람 중 한 명이 학생 시험지를 제일 먼저 채점한 후에 학생 성적을 학적과에 알리도록 할게요.

M: 정말 고맙습니다. 정말 감사해요.

W: 천만에요. 도와 줄 수 있어서 다행이군요. 시험에서도 로마에서도 행운이 있기를 빌어요.

M: 감사합니다!

📝 Summary Note

A

❶ grades
❷ international perspective

B

The student asks his professor for a favor. He is applying for a study abroad program in Rome. He needs his professor to turn in his grade early to meet the application deadline. The professor is pleased that her student is taking an opportunity to go abroad. The student is excited about learning new things and gaining a new perspective. The professor says she will make a note and inform her teaching assistant to get the student's grade to the Registrar's office.

Exercise 3 1 ⒟ 2 ⒝   p.48

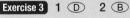 **Script** 🎧 02-10

M Dining Services Office Employee: Can I help you?

W Student: Yes, I heard that there are job openings here at the dining hall. Do you still have openings?

M: Yes, we do. Are you looking for a job?

W: Yes, I am.

M: Okay, the way things work around here is that students who are eligible for work-study usually have first

dibs at the jobs. After that, we start hiring people who aren't eligible for work-study. Are you eligible for work-study?

W: Yes, I am. The financial aid office actually sent me here. The person there said you might be hiring dining hall staff and that this would probably be the most flexible place to work around my classes.

M: Well, we definitely work around students' schedules here. So I'm going to give you an application to fill out. Just let me know what you want to do in terms of whether you want to cook, serve, clean, work the register, or whatever. You rank the different positions in your order of preference. Oh, you also need to let us know what your availability is. You know, what days and hours you can work. Then, we'll match your preferences and availability with what we need.

W: Okay.

M: So if you want, you can just take a seat at one of the tables and fill out the application right away.

W: Great. Oh, how long after I turn in the application will I find out if I'm going to be hired?

M: You'll surely be hired if your availability matches what we need. You'll probably get a call by tomorrow.

W: Wonderful. Thanks. All right, I'll turn this in as soon as I'm done.

해석

M Dining Services Office Employee: 제가 도와 드릴까요?

W Student: 네, 식당에서 사람을 구한다고 들었어요. 아직도 구하고 있는 중인가요?

M: 네, 그래요. 일자리를 찾고 있나요?

W: 네, 맞아요.

M: 좋아요, 이곳에서는 원칙적으로 근로 장학생 자격이 있는 학생들에게 주로 일자리에 대한 우선권을 부여해요. 그런 다음에 근로 장학생 자격이 없는 사람들을 고용하고요. 근로 장학생인가요?

W: 네, 맞아요. 사실 재정 지원 사무실에서 이곳으로 가라고 했어요. 그곳 직원 분께서는 식당에서 직원을 뽑고 있을 수도 있는데, 아마도 이곳이 수업을 들으면서 제가 가장 유연하게 일할 수 있는 곳일 것이라고 하시더군요.

M: 음, 이곳에서는 절대적으로 학생 시간표에 맞춰 일을 하죠. 그러면 제가 작성해야 할 신청서를 줄게요. 어떤 일을 하고 싶은지, 즉 요리, 서빙, 청소, 계산, 혹은 그 어떤 일이던 하고 싶은 일을 알려 주세요. 여러 가지 일들을 선호 순서에 따라 순위를 매겨 주시고요. 오, 언제 근무가 가능한지도 알려 주셔야 해요. 알겠지만, 어떤 요일에 몇 시간 동안 일을 할 수 있는지요. 그러면 학생이 선호하는 일과 가능한 근무 시간을 저희에게 필요한 일과 근무 시간에 맞춰 보도록 할게요.

W: 좋아요.

M: 그러면 원하는 경우, 테이블 중 한곳에 앉아서 지금 바로 신청서를 작성해도 좋아요.

W: 그럴게요. 오, 신청서를 낸 후 언제쯤 채용 여부를 알 수 있나요?

M: 학생이 근무 가능한 시간이 우리에게 필요한 경우라면 틀림없이 채용이 될 거예요. 아마 내일 정도 전화를 받게 될 거예요.

W: 잘 되었군요. 감사합니다. 좋아요. 작성을 마치는 대로 제출할게요.

✏️ Summary Note

A

❶ an application

❷ availability

B

A student is inquiring about positions at the dining hall. The man tells her that the dining hall is still hiring and asks if she is eligible for work-study. He says that work-study students are hired first. The student confirms that she is eligible. The employee tells the student that she needs to fill out an application and indicate her position preferences and hours of availability. Then, the dining hall staff will match their needs with the student's preferences and availability. The student will find out if she has a job by tomorrow.

Exercise 4 1 ⓒ 2 True: ① ② False: ③ ④   p.50

Script 🎧 02-11

W Student: Hi, Professor Denver. You want to see me?

M Professor: Yes, I do. Remember how you asked for advice on getting your grade in my class up a couple of months ago?

W: Yes, I do. And I want to thank you again for your advice.

M: Not a problem. You've done pretty well so far. Your exam scores have improved a lot. The only thing that hasn't really gotten better is your class participation. I'm kind of surprised about that. It's a really easy way to get an extra ten percent on your grade.

W: I've tried, Professor. I just get really nervous talking in front of the class.

M: Why is that?

W: I just don't want to make a mistake in front of everyone.

M: Don't worry about that. You really understand the material, you know. It shows from your test scores. You're doing well in the class otherwise. Besides, we've got such a small class.

W: I know. I just can't seem to bring myself to raise my hand.

M: This isn't usually my style, but if you'd like, I can call on you at first a couple of times. Then, maybe after you answer a couple of questions, you'll be more comfortable raising your hand.

W: Well, I guess. I mean, we could try.

M: That's really all I ask. If you participate, you might

be able to bring your grade up to an A by the time the semester's over.

W: Oh, wow. I didn't know I was so close.

M: You are. It would be a shame if this was what was holding you back.

W: Okay, uh, I promise to do my best.

해석

W Student: 안녕하세요, Denver 교수님. 저를 찾으셨나요?

M Professor: 네, 그래요. 학생이 두 달 전에 찾아 와서 수업 성적을 올릴 수 있는 방법에 관해 조언을 구했던 일이 기억나요?

W: 네, 그래요. 그리고 교수님 조언에 다시 한 번 감사를 드리고 싶어요.

M: 천만에요. 지금까지 무척 잘하고 있어요. 시험 성적이 많이 올랐어요. 진전이 없는 유일한 부분은 수업 참여도예요. 사실 그 점에 대해서는 좀 놀랐어요. 성적에서 10퍼센트의 추가 점수를 받을 수 있는 정말로 쉬운 방법이잖아요.

W: 저도 노력은 하고 있어요, 교수님. 급우들 앞에서 말을 할 때 정말로 긴장이 많이 되어서요.

M: 왜 그렇죠?

W: 모든 사람들 앞에서 실수를 하고 싶지는 않거든요.

M: 그 점은 걱정하지 말아요. 알겠지만, 학생은 수업 내용을 잘 이해하고 있어요. 학생의 시험 성적으로 알 수 있죠. 그 외의 부분에서는 잘 하고 있어요. 게다가 인원도 매우 적은 수업이고요.

W: 저도 알아요. 하지만 손을 들 수가 없는걸요.

M: 이렇게 하는 것이 제 스타일은 아니지만, 처음 몇 번은 제가 학생을 호명할 수 있어요. 그러면 두어 번 대답을 하고 난 후에 손을 드는 일이 보다 편해질 거예요.

W: 음, 그럴 수도 있겠군요. 제 말은, 그렇게 하면 될 것 같아요.

M: 제가 요청하는 것은 그것이 다예요. 수업 참여만 잘하면 학기가 끝날 때쯤 학생 성적이 A로 올라갈 수 있을 거예요.

W: 오, 와우. 제 점수가 A에 근접해 있다는 점은 제가 몰랐네요.

M: 실제로 그래요. 이러한 일로 뒷덜미를 잡히면 안타까운 일이 될 거예요.

W: 잘 알겠어요, 어, 최선을 다하겠다고 약속드릴게요.

✏️ Summary Note

A

❶ participating in class

❷ call on student

B

The professor tells the student to participate more in class. He says that she is doing really well and that her test scores have improved a lot. The only thing she has not improved in is class participation. The student feels nervous about speaking in front of the class. The professor suggests calling on her a couple of times. Then, when she is more comfortable talking in front of the class, she can volunteer answers on her own. The professor finally tells the student that she can probably get an A in the class.

Exercises with Mid-Length Lectures

Exercise 1 1 Ⓒ 2 Ⓐ p.52

Script 🎧 02-12

W Professor: We all know that there are three types of rocks. They are sedimentary rocks, igneous rocks, and metamorphic rocks. Sedimentary rocks are formed when sediment comes together over the course of many years and forms rocks. Limestone and shale are two examples of sedimentary rocks. Igneous rocks are volcanic rocks. You know, uh, they form when volcanoes erupt. Volcanoes eject lava, which cools and hardens over time. Granite and pumice are both volcanic rocks. Metamorphic rocks form when other types of rocks are transformed through intense heat and pressure. Marble is a kind of metamorphic rock, and so are soapstone and slate.

Now, uh, what's interesting is that there is something called the rock cycle. You see, rocks constantly undergo change. These changes may occur over the course of millions of years, but they still occur. Here, uh, let me give you an example of how the rock cycle works.

A volcano erupts, and lava pours out onto the ground. After a while, the hot lava cools off and hardens, becoming igneous rock. Well, as time passes, the igneous rocks are slowly eroded by the weather. The wind and the rain both combine to break down the rock into tiny pieces of sediment. This sediment stays together and is buried by other rocks and soil. Over time, the sediment combines and hardens, becoming rock. This is sedimentary rock. Millions of more years may pass, and the sedimentary rock gets covered with more layers of rock and soil. It gets pushed down farther into the ground. The pressure and the heat increase, which transforms the sedimentary rock into metamorphic rock. Later, when the volcano erupts again, the metamorphic rock melts and becomes lava, which goes back up to the surface, and the cycle starts all over again.

해석

W Professor: 우리 모두는 세 가지 유형이 암석이 존재한다는 점을 알고 있습니다. 퇴적암, 화성암, 그리고 변성암이 그것이죠. 퇴적암은 여러 해 동안 퇴적물이 쌓여서 암석을 형성시킬 때 나타납니다. 두 가지 예가 석회암과 이판암이고요. 화성암은 화산암입니다. 아시다시피, 어, 이들은 화산이 폭발할 때 만들어져요. 화산이 용암을 분출해서 시간이 지나면 용암이 식어서 굳습니다. 화강암과 부석 모두 화산암이고요. 변성암은 다른 종류의 암석이 극도의 열과 압력으로 인해 변형될 때 나타납니다. 대리석이 변성암의 한 종류이며, 동석과 점판암도 마찬가지죠.

자, 어, 흥미로운 점은 암석 순환이라는 것이 존재한다는 사실이에요. 아시다시피 암석은 끊임없이 변합니다. 이러한 변화는 수백만 년에 걸쳐 일어날 수도 있고, 지금도 일어나고 있습니다. 자, 어, 암석 순환이 어떻게 이루어지는지 예를 들어 볼게요.

화산이 폭발하면 용암이 지면으로 흘러 나옵니다. 이후 뜨거운 용암이 식어서 단단해지면 화성암이 만들어지죠. 음, 시간이 지나면서 화성암은 기후에 의해 서서히 침식됩니다. 바람과 비로 인해 바위가 작은 조각의 퇴적물로 부숴집니다. 이러한 퇴적물이 모여서 다른 암석 및 토양 아래에 묻히게 되죠. 시간이 지나면 이 퇴적물이 합쳐지고 단단해져서 암석이 됩니다. 이것이 퇴적암이에요. 이후 수백만 년이 지나면 이 퇴적암이 암석과 토양으로 이루어진 더 많은 층으로 덮이게 됩니다. 보다 깊은 땅속으로 들어가게 되는 것이죠. 압력과 열이 증가함에 따라 퇴적암이 변성암으로 바뀌게 됩니다. 이후 화산이 다시 폭발하면 변성암이 녹아 용암이 되고, 이 용암은 다시 표면 위로 올라가게 되는데, 이로써 또 다시 순환이 시작됩니다.

📝 Summary Note

A

❶ volcanic eruptions
❷ heat and pressure
❸ lava

B

The professor says that there are three types of rocks. Sedimentary rocks are formed from sediment while igneous rocks are volcanic. Metamorphic rocks form when heat and pressure change other types of rocks. Then, the professor talks about the rock cycle. A volcano erupts, and lava comes out and then hardens. Over time, the rock is eroded and breaks down into sediment. The sediment combines and forms sedimentary rock. It is then pushed down into the ground, where it becomes metamorphic rock. Then, the volcano erupts, and the metamorphic rock melts and becomes lava.

Exercise 2 1 Ⓑ 2 Ⓓ p.54

Script 🎧 02-13

M1 Professor: The next topic we have to discuss is the trickle-down effect. Now this is a theory that has been highly debated in economic circles. It's pretty complicated, but maybe we can figure it out together. Now, who can define the trickle-down effect? Yes?

W Student: Okay, I'm not sure about this, but I think the premise of the theory is that by large businesses doing well and making profits, everybody else does well, too. I mean, because the businesses spread their profits throughout the economy.

M1: Absolutely right. Now, it is still quite an abstract concept. So we're going to use an example that isn't quite the same, but it'll help us get an idea of the trickle-down effect. Okay. So let's say we have an author. This author writes a bestselling novel. Of course, the author will make a lot of money. But who else makes money?

Any ideas?

M2 Student: Um . . . the publishing company?

M1: Definitely. The publishing company will also make a lot of money because it will be printing many copies of the book. All right, who else will make money?

W: The booksellers will definitely make money off a bestseller. They charge a mark-up, right?

M1: Right again. If a book is in high demand, and most bestsellers are, the booksellers can make a profit because of the mark-up price. They pay a certain amount of money to the publishing house for the books. Then, they charge their customers more. That way, they're making a profit. Let me see . . . Another industry that would stand to gain from an author writing a bestseller is the shipping industry. The books have to get from the publishing house to the bookstore. So shipping companies would get business from that and profit. Anyway, are there any questions about this?

해석

M1 Professor: 다음으로 논의할 주제는 낙수 효과입니다. 현재 이 이론은 경제학계에서 굉장히 논란이 되고 있는 이론이에요. 꽤 복잡하기는 하지만 함께 알아보도록 하죠. 자, 낙수 효과의 정의를 말해 볼 사람이 있나요? 네?

W Student: 네, 정확하지는 않지만, 그 이론의 전제는 대기업이 잘 운영되어 이익을 냄으로써 그 밖의 모든 사람들 또한 이익을 얻는다는 것으로 알고 있어요. 제 말은, 대기업의 이윤이 경제 전체로 퍼져나가기 때문에 그런 것이죠.

M1: 정확하군요. 자, 이 이론은 꽤 추상적인 개념입니다. 그래서 완전히 들어맞지는 않지만 낙수 효과에 대한 개념을 이해하는데 도움이 될 예를 하나 들어 보죠. 좋아요. 한 작가를 가정해 볼게요. 이 작가는 베스트셀러 소설 작가예요. 물론 작가는 많은 돈을 벌게 될 것입니다. 하지만 누가 또 돈을 벌까요? 아는 사람이 있나요?

M2 Student: 음… 출판사인가요?

M1: 그렇습니다. 출판사가 책을 인쇄하기 때문에 출판사 또한 많은 돈을 벌게 될 거예요. 좋아요, 누가 또 돈을 벌까요?

W: 책을 파는 사람들도 분명 베스트셀러로 돈을 벌 거예요. 가격을 올려 받으니까요, 맞죠?

M1: 잘 대답했어요. 어떤 책에 대한 수요가 높으면, 대부분의 베스트셀러들이 그렇듯이, 책을 파는 사람들은 가격을 인상시켜 이윤을 남길 수가 있어요. 이들은 일정 금액을 출판사에 지불하고 책을 매입합니다. 그런 다음 소비자에게 보다 많은 금액을 청구하죠. 그럼으로써 이윤을 남깁니다. 생각해 보면… 베스트셀러 소설을 쓰는 작가 때문에 돈을 버는 또 다른 업계는 운송업계입니다. 출판사에서 서점까지 책을 운송해야 하니까요. 그래서 운송 회사들은 그로 인해 비지니스를 하고 이윤을 얻게 되죠. 그러면, 이에 대한 질문이 있나요?

✏ Summary Note

A

❶ Publisher
❷ Booksellers

B

The trickle-down effect is a debated economic theory. It

concerns how the actions of one business can affect many others in a country's economy. An example of how this theory works can be an author who writes a bestselling novel. The author will make money off the book. Other companies that will profit from the book are the publisher, the booksellers, and the shippers.

Exercise 3 1 ⓒ 2 Ⓐ   p.56

Script 🎧 02-14

M Professor: Today, we're going to talk about how filmmaking was done before the 1930s. Before the 1930s, most filmmaking was done using what were called crank cameras. There were two types of cameras back then. There were motorized cameras and crank cameras. When using crank cameras, a person had to crank the film forward by hand. Motorized cameras would forward the film automatically. But the motors on these cameras were so big and bulky that they were really hard to carry around. Instead, filmmakers used crank cameras.

How these crank cameras worked was the cameraman would either hold the camera or have the camera on a tripod. Just so you know, women didn't make films during this era, so we can call the person holding the camera a cameraman. The cameraman would aim the lens at the scene he was trying to record. Then, he would crank the handle on the camera to advance the film. Now, this process could be pretty difficult. The cameraman had to crank the handle at a uniform pace so that the movie didn't seem rushed or delayed, which took lots of practice. But once the cameraman had mastered this skill, he could alter the pace to make special effects. For example, an experienced cameraman could decrease the number of cranks for a scene. This would make the actions on film look rushed and kind of disconnected.

In addition, for a good part of this time, films were shot on a single reel. This meant most films were pretty short—fifteen to twenty minutes usually. Then, right before the First World War, which started in 1914, filmmakers pioneered the double-reel process. This allowed for much longer films. This was also where the icon of the double-reel camera that we see everywhere comes from.

해석

M Professor: 오늘은 1930년대 이전의 영화 제작 방식에 대해 논의할 예정입니다. 1930년대 이전에는 크랭크 카메라를 이용해서 대부분의 영화를 제작했어요. 그 당시에는 두 종류의 카메라가 있었습니다. 바로 전동 카메라와 크랭크 카메라였죠. 크랭크 카메라를 사용하는 경우, 사람이 손으로 필름을 감아야 했어요. 전동 카메라는 자동으로 필름이 감겼고요. 하지만 이들 카메라에 장착된 모

터는 부피가 너무 커서 가지고 다니기가 정말로 힘들었습니다. 그래서 그 대신 영화 제작자들은 크랭크 카메라를 사용했죠.

이 크랭크 카메라를 사용하는 방법은 카메라맨이 들고 찍거나 삼각대 위에 올려놓고 찍는 두 가지 방식 중 하나였어요. 아시다시피 당시에는 여성들이 영화를 만들지 않았기 때문에 카메라를 들고 있는 사람을 카메라맨이라고 불러도 됩니다. 카메라맨은 촬영하고자 하는 장면을 향해 카메라를 들었습니다. 그리고는 카메라 손잡이를 돌려 필름을 감았죠. 자, 이러한 과정은 꽤 힘들었어요. 카메라맨은 영화 속도가 빨라지거나 느려지지 않도록 일정한 속도로 손잡이를 돌려야 했는데, 이는 많은 연습을 필요로 하는 일이었습니다. 하지만 일단 이러한 기술을 익히고 나면 카메라맨은 크랭크 돌리는 속도를 조절해서 특수 효과를 만들어 낼 수가 있었죠. 예를 들어 노련한 카메라맨은 한 장면에서 손잡이를 돌리는 횟수를 줄일 수 있었어요. 그렇게 하면 영화 속 움직임이 빠르고 단속적인 것처럼 보이게 되었죠.

또한 이 시기에는 대부분 영화가 싱글릴로 촬영되었습니다. 이 말은 대부분의 영화들이, 보통 15분에서 20분정도로, 상당히 짧았다는 뜻이에요. 그러다가 1914년에 시작된 1차 세계 대전 직전에 영화 제작자들이 처음으로 더블릴을 이용해 촬영을 하기 시작했습니다. 이로써 훨씬 더 긴 영화들이 만들어졌어요. 또한 우리가 어디서나 볼 수 있는 더블릴 카메라의 아이콘도 여기에서 비롯된 것입니다.

📝 Summary Note

A

❶ advance film

❷ special effects

B

Filmmaking before the 1930s used two types of cameras: motorized cameras and crank cameras. Filmmakers generally used crank cameras because they were easier to carry. The cameramen would turn the handle on them to advance the film. This was difficult and took a lot of practice. When a cameraman mastered this skill, he could alter the pace to make special effects. During most of this era, films were shot on a single reel. Then, just before 1914, the double-reel process was introduced. This is where the double-reel film icon comes from.

Exercise 4 1 ⓓ 2 ⓑ p.58

Script 🎧 02-15

W1 Professor: Now that we know a bit about jazz music, I'm going to talk about some jazz musicians. Personally, I think there's no better place to start than with one of my favorites, Duke Ellington. He was born in North Carolina, but he didn't become famous till he moved to . . . Does anyone know?

M Student: New York City! He played in Harlem, right?

W1: That's right. Duke Ellington got his first New York City gig at the Cotton Club in Harlem. Harlem was a hotspot for up-and-coming music and musicians back

then. That's where Duke Ellington started to be well known. So after his first gig at the Cotton Club, Duke Ellington got a weekly radio show. And that spread his music everywhere. Then, a bunch of famous individuals started to go to the Cotton Club as well. This made the Cotton Club the most famous jazz club in Harlem. The Duke made two major contributions to jazz. First of all, he brought jazz music to all corners of the world. His band traveled everywhere around the world. Secondly, he wrote and recorded hundreds of jazz hits. Can anyone name any famous Duke Ellington songs?

W2 Student: Um . . . "Take the 'A' Train."

W1: Yes. "Take the 'A' Train" is probably his most famous song. It's about the subway line you take in New York City to get up to Harlem and the Cotton Club. Some of the Duke's other famous songs are "Rockin' in Rhythm," "Satin Doll," "New Orleans," and "Crescendo in Blue."

해석

W1 Professor: 재즈 음악에 대해서 약간 살펴보았으니 이제 재즈 뮤지션들에 대한 이야기를 하고자 합니다. 개인적으로 제가 가장 좋아하는 재즈 뮤지션 중의 한 명인 듀크 엘링턴으로 시작하는 것이 가장 좋을 것 같군요. 그는 노스캐롤라이나에서 태어났지만, 유명해진 것은 이사를 간 후인데… 어디로 갔는지 아는 사람이 있나요?

M Student: 뉴욕시요! 할렘에서 연주를 했어요, 맞죠?

W1: 맞아요. 듀크 엘링턴은 할렘의 코튼 클럽에서 첫 뉴욕시 공연을 가졌습니다. 할렘은 당시 유망한 음악 및 뮤지션들로 활기가 넘쳤던 곳이었죠. 바로 이곳에서 듀크 엘링턴이 유명해지기 시작했어요. 코튼 클럽에서 첫 번째 공연을 마친 뒤 듀크 엘링턴은 주 1회의 라디오 프로그램에 출연했어요. 그리고 이로 인해 그의 음악이 모든 곳에 퍼지게 되었죠. 그 후 여러 유명한 인사들 또한 코튼 클럽을 찾기 시작했어요. 이로써 코튼 클럽은 할렘에서 가장 유명한 재즈 클럽이 되었습니다. 듀크는 재즈에 두 가지 커다란 기여를 했어요. 우선 그는 재즈 음악을 세계 곳곳에 알렸습니다. 그의 밴드는 전 세계 모든 곳을 돌아다녔죠. 두 번째로 그는 수백 곡의 재즈 히트곡을 쓰고 녹음했어요. 듀크 엘링턴이 쓴 유명한 곡을 말해 볼 사람이 있나요?

W2 Student: 음… "A열차로 가자"입니다.

W1: 네. "A열차로 가자"가 아마도 가장 유명한 곡일 거예요. 할렘과 코튼 클럽에 가기 위해 뉴욕시에서 타야 하는 지하철에 관한 곡이죠. 듀크의 다른 유명한 곡들로는 "락킹 인 리듬," "새틴 돌," "뉴올리언스," 그리고 "크레센도 인 블루"가 있습니다.

📝 Summary Note

A

❶ Cotton Club

❷ around the world

B

Duke Ellington was a famous jazz musician from the early twentieth century. He was born in North Carolina and got his first big gig in New York City at the Cotton Club. This gig made him famous. It also made the Cotton Club the most famous jazz club in Harlem. Ellington and his band traveled all around the world. His most famous song is called "Take the 'A' Train."

Integrated Listening & Speaking p.60

A

Script 🎧 02-16

W Professor: There are three types of rocks. Sedimentary rocks are formed from sediment while igneous rocks are volcanic. Metamorphic rocks form when heat and pressure change other types of rocks. The rock cycle shows how rocks change from one form to another over time. A volcano erupts, and lava comes out and then hardens. Over time, the rock is eroded and breaks down into sediment. The sediment combines and forms sedimentary rock over a long period of time. It is then pushed down into the ground. As it gets farther into the ground, it is exposed to intense heat and pressure, so it becomes metamorphic rock. Then, the volcano erupts, and the metamorphic rock melts and becomes lava.

1 a. The purpose of this lecture is to describe three different kinds of rocks.
   b. The topic of this lecture is three types of rocks.

2 a. The rock cycle shows how rocks change from one type to another over time.
   b. It is the way that rocks can change their types over time.

3 a. It becomes metamorphic rock when it is exposed to intense heat and pressure.
   b. That happens when it is underground and is exposed to intense heat and pressure.

B

Script 🎧 02-17

M Professor: Filmmaking before the 1930s was very different from filmmaking today. During that time, there were two types of cameras: motorized cameras and crank cameras. Filmmakers generally used crank cameras because they were easier to carry. Motorized cameras were big and bulky. Crank cameras were placed on a tripod, and the cameraman would turn the handle on the camera to advance the film. This was a difficult skill to master and took a lot of practice. When the cameraman had mastered this skill, he could alter the pace to make special effects. For example, he could crank slower to make the action in the film look

disconnected. In addition, during most of this era, films were shot on a single reel. Then, just before 1914, the double-reel process was introduced. This is where the double-reel film icon comes from.

1 a. The professor explains how filmmaking was done before the 1930s.
   b. The lecture is about what filmmaking was like before the 1930s.

2 a. Filmmakers didn't use motorized cameras because they were big, bulky, and difficult to carry around.
   b. Filmmakers preferred crank cameras because they were lighter than motorized cameras.

3 a. Cameramen created special effects by changing the pace of the crank.
   b. Special effects were created by adjusting the crank's speed.

Mini TOEFL iBT Practice Test   p.62

1 ⓓ	2 ⓒ	3 ⓐ	4 ⓑ	5 ⓑ
6 ⓑ	7 ⓑ, ⓓ	8 ⓒ	9 ⓓ	10 ⓑ
11 ⓑ				

[1-5]

Script 🎧 02-18

M Student: Excuse me. Where can I check these books out?

W Librarian: You have to go downstairs to the circulation desk. It's at the bottom of the stairs to the right.

M: Oh, okay. How long can I keep the books?

W: Our general lending time is four weeks. Most students find that sufficient.

M: What if I need them for more time though?

W: You can always renew them. There are a couple of ways you can do that. You can bring the books back and renew them at the circulation desk. Or you can extend them online. You just have to create an account on the library's website. One of the options on that page is "Renew Library Materials."

M: That sounds easy enough.

W: Yeah, it really isn't that complicated. It's pretty easy to take care of if that's what you need.

M: Great. Oh, my roommate said there might be a time when I need to turn the books in earlier. Is that true?

W: Yes, it is. That doesn't happen very often, but every now and then, someone will need a book you've checked out. If that happens, the person can recall it, which means that the person can request it. Now, a person can't do that unless you've had the book for more than a week.

M: So what exactly does that mean?

W: If one of the books you borrow gets recalled, you'll get an email. So make sure you check your email daily. After that, you'll have twenty-four hours to return the book.

M: What happens if I can't bring it back within twenty-four hours?

W: You have to figure out a way to do that. Otherwise, you get charged a really steep fee. It ends up being ten dollars a day.

M: Oh, wow. That's a lot of money. But what if I still need the book? Then what happens?

W: You have to bring it in, and the person who recalled it will pick it up. But after a week, you can recall it yourself.

M: Really?

W: Yeah. So it's not such a huge deal. Besides, it hardly ever happens. So check out your books and don't worry about it.

해석

M Student: 실례합니다. 이 책들을 어디에서 대출하면 되나요?

W Librarian: 아래층 대출 데스크로 가셔야 해요. 계단 아래 오른쪽에 있어요.

M: 오, 그렇군요. 대출 기간은 어떻게 되죠?

W: 일반적으로 대출 기간은 4주예요. 대부분의 학생들에게 그 정도면 충분하죠.

M: 하지만 시간이 더 필요한 경우에는 어떻게 하나요?

W: 언제든지 갱신할 수 있어요. 두 가지 방법으로 그렇게 할 수 있죠. 책을 다시 가지고 와서 대출 데스크에서 갱신을 할 수 있어요. 아니면 온라인으로 기간을 연장할 수도 있고요. 도서관 웹사이트에서 계정을 만들기만 하면 되죠. 해당 페이지의 옵션 중 하나가 "도서관 자료 갱신"이에요.

M: 상당히 쉬울 것 같군요.

W: 그래요, 전혀 복잡하지 않아요. 갱신을 해야 하는 경우에 무척 편리하게 갱신을 할 수 있죠.

M: 잘 되었군요. 오, 제 룸메이트 말로는 책을 더 빨리 반납해야 되는 경우도 있다고 하던데요. 그게 사실인가요?

W: 네, 그래요. 자주 있는 일은 아니지만 가끔씩 누군가 학생이 대출한 책을 필요로 하는 경우가 있을 수 있어요. 그런 경우에는 그 사람이 리콜을 할 수 있는데, 이는 그 사람이 책 반납을 요청할 수 있다는 뜻이에요. 자, 학생이 책을 일주일 이상 가지고 있지 않은 경우에는 그럴 수가 없고요.

M: 그러면 그것이 정확히 어떤 의미인가요?

W: 만약 학생이 빌린 책 중 한 권에 대해 리콜이 이루어지면 학생은 이메일을 받게 될 거예요. 그러니 매일 이메일을 확인하도록 하세요. 그 후에는 24시간 이내에 책을 반납해야 하고요.

M: 24시간 이내에 반납하지 않으면 어떻게 되나요?

W: 어떻게든 반납해야 해요. 그렇지 않으면 적지 않은 연체료를 내게 될 테니까요. 하루에 10달러예요.

M: 오, 이런. 큰 금액이군요. 하지만 책이 계속 필요한 경우에는요? 그러면 어떻게 되죠?

W: 일단 책을 반납해야 하고, 리콜을 한 학생이 책을 가져갈 거예요. 하지만 일주일 후에는 학생이 그 책을 리콜할 수가 있죠.

M: 정말인가요?

W: 예. 그렇기 때문에 그처럼 걱정할 일은 아니에요. 게다가 그런 일은 거의 일어나지도 않고요. 그러니 책을 대출하시고 그에 대해서는 걱정하지 마세요.

[6-11]

Script 🎧 02-19

M1 Professor: We're going to continue our botany unit with a discussion about the Venus flytrap. Now, the Venus flytrap is a carnivorous plant. It's kind of strange that a plant would use animals for food since this usually happens the other way around. But the Venus flytrap does. So . . . who can tell me what a Venus flytrap eats?

M2 Student: Flies!

M1: Of courses. But flies aren't the only thing it eats. What else?

W Student: Spiders?

M1: Very good. Basically, the Venus flytrap will eat any insect or spider that gets caught in its leaves. The way it works is that it has some trigger hairs on the ends of its leaves. If something touches these hairs in rapid succession twice, the leaves will close on the bug, forming a trap. Now, why do you think the plant waits till something touches the hairs twice?

W: Um, because it may not be a bug?

M1: Well, yes. Say it's raining. If the flytrap didn't wait for the second touch, it would remain closed through an entire rainstorm, and it wouldn't get any food. When the trap closes, it remains closed for a few hours. And if there's nothing in the trap, that's a lot of potential food that the flytrap has missed out on. So let's say the plant catches a spider. The leaves of the trap close and end up sealing the spider in. The trap becomes something like a stomach. Then, the flytrap starts to digest the spider by secreting enzymes into the trap. This process takes about ten days. That's a long time just to digest a single animal. Then, the trap will open again and await its next victim. Now why do you think the plant needs to eat bugs?

M2: It needs food.

M1: Close but not exactly. It needs the nutrients in bugs' bodies. The Venus flytrap is often found in swamplands, uh, and the soil in these places is not rich in nutrients. So it must find another way to get the nutrients it requires, particularly nitrogen and some minerals and vitamins. It gets all of its energy from the sun, but unlike other plants, it can't extract nutrients from the soil because the soil simply doesn't have enough. So the plant has to eat bugs. It's quite an ingenious way to solve a problem if you ask me.

해석

M1 Professor: 오늘은 파리지옥에 관한 논의로 식물 단원을 계속 공부해 볼게요. 자, 파리지옥은 식충 식물입니다. 식물이 동물을 먹이로 삼는다는 것은 다소 특이한 일인데, 보통은 그 반대의 경우에 해당되죠. 하지만 파리지옥은 그렇게 합니다. 그러면… 파리지옥이 잡아먹는 동물이 무엇인지 누가 말해 볼까요?

M2 Student: 파리입니다!

M1: 당연하겠죠. 하지만 파리만 잡아먹는 것은 아니에요. 또 무엇을 잡아먹을까요?

W Student: 거미요?

M1: 아주 잘 대답했어요. 기본적으로 파리지옥은 파리지옥의 잎에 들어온 곤충이나 거미를 잡아먹습니다. 잎 끝에 달려 있는 털을 이용해서 그렇게 하죠. 무언가 빠르게 이 털을 두 번 연속해서 건드리면 잎이 곤충을 감싼 채 닫히는데, 이로써 덫이 만들어집니다. 자, 왜 파리지옥은 털을 두 번 건드릴 때까지 기다린다고 생각하나요?

W: 음, 곤충이 아닐 수도 있기 때문에요?

M1: 음, 그래요. 비가 온다고 합시다. 만약 파리지옥이 두 번째 터치를 기다리지 않는다면 비가 내리는 동안 계속 닫혀 있어서 어떤 먹이도 잡을 수가 없을 거예요. 잎이 닫히는 경우에는 몇 시간 동안 계속 닫혀 있습니다. 그리고 덫 안에 아무것도 없는 경우, 파리지옥이 놓친 잠재적인 먹잇감들이 많다는 뜻이 되죠. 그러면 파리지옥이 거미를 잡는다고 해 봅시다. 덫의 잎이 닫히고 거미가 잎 안에 갇힙니다. 덫은 위와 같은 기능을 하게 되죠. 그런 다음 파리지옥은 덫 안에 효소를 분비함으로써 거미를 소화시키기 시작합니다. 이러한 과정은 약 10일에 걸쳐 이루어져요. 한 마리를 소화시키는데 꽤 오랜 시간이 걸리죠. 그 후 다시 덫이 열리고 다음 먹이를 기다리게 됩니다. 자, 파리지옥은 왜 곤충을 잡아먹어야 한다고 생각하나요?

M2: 먹이가 필요하니까요.

M1: 정답에 가깝기는 하지만 정확하지는 않아요. 파리지옥은 곤충의 신체에 들어 있는 영양분을 필요로 합니다. 파리지옥은 종종 습지에서 찾아볼 수 있는데, 어, 이러한 곳의 토양에는 영양분이 많지가 않죠. 그래서 다른 방법을 찾아서 필요한 영양분을, 특히 질소와 일부 무기질 및 비타민들을, 얻어야만 합니다. 파리지옥은 태양으로부터 모든 에너지를 얻지만, 다른 식물들과 달리 토양에서 영양분을 얻지는 못하는데, 그 이유는 단지 토양에 영양분이 충분하지 않기 때문이에요. 그래서 이 식물은 곤충을 잡아먹어야 합니다. 만약 제게 묻는다면, 이는 문제를 해결하는 매우 기발한 방식인 것이죠.

Vocabulary Check-Up
p.67

A

1 ⓞ	2 ⓖ	3 ⓙ	4 ⓛ	5 ⓓ
6 ⓒ	7 ⓑ	8 ⓗ	9 ⓔ	10 ⓕ
11 ⓘ	12 ⓚ	13 ⓜ	14 ⓝ	15 ⓐ

B

1 ⓑ	2 ⓓ	3 ⓒ	4 ⓔ	5 ⓐ

Basic Drill
p.70

Drill 1 ⓒ

Script 🎧 03-02

M Security Guard: Excuse me. I need to see your school ID before you can enter.

W Student: Well, that's the problem. I lost my purse, and my ID was in it. What can I do?

M: That's not a problem. Just show me some other form of photo ID.

W: Umm, everything was in my purse, including my driver's license and credit cards.

M: I see, but I can't let you in. Do you have any other ID?

W: Yeah! I have a passport. It's in my room.

M: Uh, you know you can't get to your room without your ID?

W: Are you kidding?

M: Okay, I will follow you to your room. Then, you can show me your passport.

해석

M Security Guard: 실례합니다. 들어가려면 제가 학생증을 확인해야 해요.

W Student: 음, 그게 문제예요. 제가 지갑을 잃어버렸는데, 그 안에 학생증이 있었어요. 어떻게 해야 하나요?

M: 문제될 것 없어요. 사진이 부착된 다른 신분증을 보여 주세요.

W: 음, 운전면허증과 신용카드를 포함해서 전부 지갑 안에 있었어요.

M: 알겠습니다만 들여보낼 수가 없어요. 다른 신분증은 없나요?

W: 그래요! 여권이 있어요. 제 방에 있어요.

M: 어, 신분증 없이는 방에 들어갈 수 없다는 거 아시죠?

W: 정말인가요?

M: 좋아요, 제가 방까지 따라가죠. 그런 다음에 제게 여권을 보여 주세요.

Drill 2 ⓒ

Script 🎧 03-03

W Professor: Hello, Matt. Come here.

M Student: Yes?

W: I want to tell you that your paper on American federalism was excellent. I think you should try to get it published.

M: Really?

W: Yes. You make some good points that haven't been discussed very much. If you want, I will send it to a friend who is the editor of *Politics Magazine*. What do you think?

M: That would be great.

W: Have you thought about attending graduate school? I really think you have a future in political science.

M: I have thought about it a bit.

W: You should seriously consider it. You are a great writer, and you always produce good work.

M: Okay. Thanks.

해석

W Professor: 안녕하세요, Matt. 이쪽으로 오세요.

M Student: 네?

W: 미국의 연방 제도에 관한 학생의 보고서가 훌륭했다는 이야기를 하고 싶어요. 잡지에 게재를 하는 것도 좋을 것 같아요.

M: 정말인가요?

W: 그래요. 학생은 그다지 논의되지 않는 몇 가지 좋은 논점들을 제시했어요. 원하는 경우, 제가 *Politics Magazine*의 편집자인 제 친구에게 보내 볼게요. 어떻게 생각하나요?

M: 좋을 것 같아요.

W: 대학원 진학에 대해 생각해 본 적이 있나요? 학생이 정치학을 공부하면 정말로 앞날이 밝을 것 같아서요.

M: 약간 생각은 해 봤어요.

W: 진지하게 고려해 보세요. 학생은 글도 잘 쓰고 성적도 항상 우수한 편이니까요.

M: 그럴게요. 고맙습니다.

Drill 3 Ⓓ

Script 🎧 03-04

W Admissions Office Employee: Hello. Can I help you with something?

M Student: Yes, I just need to tell you I am going to miss orientation. So when can I get the information I will miss?

W: Why are you going to miss it?

M: I am going to take a trip to New York with a friend.

W: That's it? You need to attend orientation. You will take a tour of campus, learn about the school, figure out your classes, and get your room assignment. It's very important to attend.

M: Really? I didn't know that. I thought it wasn't a big deal. Okay, I will cancel my trip.

W: That's a good decision. Make sure you are here before nine o'clock.

해석

W Admissions Office Employee: 안녕하세요. 제가 도와 드릴 일이 있을까요?

M Student: 네, 제가 오리엔테이션에 참석을 못 할 것 같다는 말씀을 드려야 해서요. 그러면 제가 놓치게 될 내용들을 언제 알 수 있나요?

W: 왜 참석을 하지 못하시나요?

M: 친구와 함께 뉴욕으로 여행을 갈 예정이거든요.

W: 그것이 다인가요? 오리엔테이션에는 참석하셔야 해요. 캠퍼스를 견학하고, 학교에 대해 배우고, 수업을 알아보고, 그리고 방 배정도 받게 될 거예요. 참석하는 것이 중요해요.

M: 정말인가요? 제가 몰랐군요. 별일 아니라고 생각했어요. 좋아요, 여행을 취소할게요.

W: 결정 잘 하셨어요. 9시 전에 꼭 이곳으로 오셔야 해요.

Drill 4 Ⓓ

Script 🎧 03-05

M Professor: The Cuban Missile Crisis is recognized as the peak of the Cold War. At the time, the Soviet Union had a severe disadvantage in its nuclear arsenal compared to the United States. In an attempt to catch up with the U.S., Nikita Khruschev ordered nuclear missiles to be based in Cuba. President Kennedy feared having nuclear weapons based only ninety miles from American territory. Kennedy decided to use a naval blockade of Cuba as well as an ultimatum, and preparations for a full invasion were made. To solve the crisis, Khruschev and Kennedy agreed publicly to have the missiles withdrawn in return for an American promise not to invade Cuba. In secret, Kennedy also agreed to withdraw American missiles from Turkey.

해석

M Professor: 쿠바 미사일 위기는 냉전의 정점으로 여겨집니다. 그 당시 소련의 핵전력은 미국에 비해 심각한 열세를 보였어요. 미국을 따라잡기 위해 니키타 흐루쇼프는 쿠바에 핵미사일의 기지 건설을 명령했죠. 케네디 대통령은 미국 영토에서 불과 90마일 밖에 떨어지지 않은 곳에 핵무기 기지가 생긴다는 점을 두려워했습니다. 케네디는 쿠바의 해상을 봉쇄할 뿐만 아니라 최후 통첩을 내리기로 결정했고, 전면전에 대한 준비가 이루어졌습니다. 위기를 해결하기 위해 흐루쇼프와 케네디는 미국이 쿠바를 침략하지 않는다는 약속에 대한 대가로서 미사일을 철수시키기로 공개적으로 합의했습니다. 비공개적으로는 터키에서 미국의 미사일 또한 철수하는 것에 케네디가 합의해 주었죠.

Drill 5 Ⓒ

Script 🎧 03-06

W Professor: Perhaps the most famous building in America is the Empire State Building. The building represents the country's transition into the modern era not only in its size but also in its design. For example, its well-known shape was designed because of the New York City Zoning Law of 1916. This reduced the sizes of shadows in the city. The top of the 102-story building was originally intended to be a dock for airships. This idea was abandoned after a few failed tests, but the building retained its shape. It was also done in the Art Deco style, which was extremely popular when the building was erected.

해석

W Professor: 아마도 미국에서 가장 유명한 건물은 엠파이어 스테이트 빌딩일 거예요. 이 건물은 규모뿐만 아니라 설계에 있어서도 미국이 현대에 진입했다는 점을 나타냅니다. 예를 들어 이 유명한 건물 형태는 1916년의 뉴욕시 조닝법 때문에 설계되었어요. 이로 인해 도시에 드리우는 그림자의 면적이 줄어들었죠. 102층 건물의 꼭대기는 원래 비행선의 격납고로 사용될 계획이었어요. 몇 번의 실험 끝에 그러한 아이디어는 철회되었지만, 건물의 형태는 유지되었죠. 또한 이 건물은 건물이 세워질 당시 매우 인기가 있었던 아르 데코 양식으로 지어졌습니다.

Drill 6 (B), (C)

Script 🎧 03-07

M Professor: Sociologists often call the United States a melting pot. In a melting pot, all the parts melt and are mixed together to form something new. The United States is a country made by immigrants. Its original settlers were from England, France, and Germany. Later, large numbers of immigrants from Ireland, Italy, China, and Latin America made new homes in the United States. All of these people have added to the mixed American culture. For example, Chinese and Mexican foods are very popular. Many Americans have also studied Spanish and can understand a good amount of the language. Many cities hold large parades for St. Patrick's Day, a popular Irish holiday.

해석

M Professor: 사회학자들은 종종 미국을 용광로라고 부릅니다. 용광로에서는 모든 부분들이 녹고 섞여서 새로운 것이 만들어지죠. 미국은 이민자들로 이루어진 나라예요. 최초의 정착민들은 영국인, 프랑스인, 그리고 독일인들이었습니다. 이후 아일랜드, 이탈리아, 중국, 그리고 라틴 아메리카 국가에서 수많은 이민자들이 미국에 정착했고요. 이러한 모든 사람들이 혼합된 미국 문화에 유입되었습니다. 예를 들어 중국 음식과 멕시코 음식은 매우 인기가 높습니다. 또한 다수의 미국인들이 스페인어를 배우고 있고 스페인어를 상당 부분 이해할 수 있어요. 아일랜드에서 인기 있는 휴일인 성 패트릭 데이에는 여러 도시에서 거대한 행진이 이루어집니다.

Exercise 1   1 (D)   2 (B)   p.72

Script 🎧 03-08

M Professor: Hi, Susan. You wanted to speak to me about something?

W Student: Yes, I was wondering if I could talk to you about the term paper due in two weeks.

M: Sure. What's up?

W: My sister is getting married next weekend, and I'm the maid of honor, so this week is a little crazy. I was wondering if I could get an extension on the term paper.

M: How much do you have written already? With a paper this size, I would expect that you would have the majority of it taken care of by now.

W: I have taken care of most of it. The delay has been in two of my sources. I needed to request them from a library across the state, and it is taking a really long time for them to get here. I requested the books almost a month ago. And they're really important to my paper. I just feel that it would be incomplete without those sources.

M: So when do you expect the sources to arrive?

W: According to the library, they should be here tomorrow. But I won't have time to go through them until next week.

M: Well, if you turn in your outline and your paper as it is tomorrow in class, I can grant you a one-week extension.

W: Thanks so much! But there is a problem.

M: What problem?

W: Well, tomorrow I have to meet my sister about her wedding. I am going to leave at 6:00 AM, so I will miss all my classes tomorrow. What can I do?

M: In that case, why don't you just email me the paper and the outline? You should have my email address because I put it on the class syllabus.

W: Ah, okay. I can do that. Thanks.

해석

M Professor: 안녕하세요, Susan. 저와 이야기하고 싶은 것이 있다고요?

W Student: 네, 2주 후 마감인 기말 보고서에 대해 이야기를 나눌 수 있는지 궁금했거든요.

M: 그래요. 무슨 일이죠?

W: 언니가 다음 주말에 결혼을 하는데, 제가 대표 들러리라서 이번 주에 정말 정신이 없어요. 그래서 기말 보고서의 작성 기간을 연장할 수 있는지 궁금했어요.

M: 지금까지 얼만큼 작성했죠? 이 정도 분량의 보고서라면 지금쯤 대부분 작성했을 것으로 생각되는군요.

W: 대부분 작성했어요. 늦어지는 부분은 두 개의 자료와 관련해서예요. 주 반대

편에 있는 도서관에 자료를 요청해야 했는데, 이곳에 도착하기까지 정말로 긴 시간이 걸리고 있어요. 거의 한 달 전에 도서를 요청했거든요. 그리고 그 도서들은 제 보고서에 정말로 중요한 것이에요. 그 자료들이 없으면 보고서 작성을 완료할 수 없을 것 같아요.

M: 그러면 그 자료들이 언제 도착할 것으로 예상하나요?

W: 도서관 말에 따르면 내일 이곳에 도착할 거예요. 하지만 다음 주까지는 자료를 살펴볼 시간이 없어요.

M: 음, 내일 수업 시간까지 개요와 보고서를 제출하면 마감을 일주일 연장시켜 줄게요.

W: 정말 감사합니다! 그런데 문제가 하나 있어요.

M: 어떤 문제인가요?

W: 음, 내일은 결혼 문제로 언니를 만나야 해요. 오전 6시에 떠날 예정이라서 내일은 수업을 다 빠지게 될 거예요. 어떻게 하면 될까요?

M: 그런 경우라면, 보고서와 개요를 이메일로 보내는 것이 어떨까요? 강의 계획에서 적어 두었으니 제 이메일 주소를 알 수 있을 거예요.

W: 아, 좋습니다. 그렇게 할게요. 감사합니다.

✏️ Summary Note

A

❶ getting married
❷ waiting on two books

B

The student asks for an extension on her term paper. Her sister is getting married, and she does not have time to finish the paper before the deadline. The professor wonders how much work the student has done so far. The professor says that the paper is mostly written, but she is waiting for two more books from the library to finish. The professor tells her to email what she has written and her outline by tomorrow, and she will get a one-week extension.

Exercise 2 1 Ⓒ 2 Ⓐ   p.74

Script 🎧 03-09

M Student: Excuse me. May I ask you a question?

W Housing Office Employee: Sure. How can I help you?

M: I was just wondering how old this dorm is.

W: It's really old. It was built the same year that the college opened.

M: Well, I was wondering what the protocol for painting my room is. Right now, it's a gross pale green color, and I just want to make it more livable.

W: I definitely understand your wanting to repaint your room. But you have to get all paint approved by the Housing Department. And you also have to repaint it the original color at the end of the year.

M: Really? That's so much work. Why do I need to get paint approved?

W: We just need to make sure you're using paint that is safe. You know, it should be lead-free and stuff.

M: Oh, well that makes sense. How long does that process usually take?

W: Depending on how busy they are, it can take up to a month.

M: Really? That's such a long time for an eight-month stay.

W: Yeah, it is. Most students just end up putting up wall hangings and posters. It saves a lot of time and effort. And there isn't nearly as much red tape around that.

M: Yeah, I can understand that. I might end up doing the same thing.

W: It's certainly a much simpler process.

M: Yeah, I guess I'll try that. Can I submit the paperwork with the Housing Department and then cancel later if the posters look okay? If they don't look good, then I will have already started the request process.

W: I don't see any problem with that. It's a good idea. Go for it.

M: Okay. Thanks for your help.

해석

M Student: 실례합니다. 뭐 좀 물어봐도 될까요?

W Housing Office Employee: 물론이죠. 어떻게 도와 드릴까요?

M: 이 기숙사가 얼마나 오래 전에 지어졌는지 궁금해서요.

W: 정말로 오래 전에 지어졌죠. 대학이 문을 연 해에 지어졌으니까요.

M: 음, 제 방을 칠하는데 어떤 원칙이 있었는지 궁금했어요. 현재 제 방의 색깔은 전체적으로 옅은 초록색인데, 보다 주거에 적합한 색으로 바꾸면 좋겠어요.

W: 방을 다시 칠하고 싶어하는 마음은 이해하고도 남아요. 하지만 모든 페인트는 기숙사 사무실에서 승인을 받아야 해요. 그리고 연말에 원래의 색으로 다시 페인트칠을 해야 하고요.

M: 정말인가요? 보통 일이 아니군요. 페인트는 왜 승인을 받아야 하나요?

W: 사용할 페인트가 안전한지 확인해야 하니까요. 알겠지만, 납 성분 등이 없어야 하죠.

M: 오, 이해가 가는군요. 그러한 절차에 보통 시간이 얼마나 걸리나요?

W: 그들이 얼마나 바쁜지에 따라 다른데, 길게는 한 달이 걸릴 수도 있어요.

M: 정말인가요? 8개월 지내는 것에 비하면 정말로 긴 시간이군요.

W: 예, 그래요. 대부분의 학생들은 벽걸이용 천과 포스터를 붙여요. 많은 시간과 노력을 절약할 수 있죠. 그리고 그에 대해서는 규제가 거의 없고요.

M: 네, 이해가 가네요. 저도 결국 똑같이 하게 될 것 같군요.

W: 분명 그 편이 훨씬 쉬울 거예요.

M: 예, 그렇게 해 보죠. 일반 기숙사 사무실에 서류를 낸 후 포스터가 괜찮게 보이면 나중에 취소를 할 수도 있나요? 괜찮게 보이지 않는 경우에는 이미 신청 절차가 시작되어 있을 테니까요.

W: 그에 대해서는 문제가 없을 것 같아요. 좋은 생각이네요. 그렇게 하세요.

M: 좋아요. 도와 주셔서 감사합니다.

📝 Summary Note

A

❶ hang posters and wall hangings

❷ he will hang posters

B

The student does not like the color of his dorm room. He wants to paint it a different color. The housing office employee says he must get the paint choice approved by the Housing Department. This process can take up to a month. According to the woman, most students just put up posters and wall hangings instead. The student thinks that that might be easier to do.

Exercise 3 1 ⓒ 2 Ⓑ, Ⓓ p.76

Script 🎧 03-10

M Student: Professor Waddle, do you have some time to speak to me?

W Professor: Of course, Pierre. I always have time for one of my best students. What's up?

M: As you know, I'm going to be a senior next semester. I've been thinking about my future, but I'm not really sure what I should do.

W: Have you thought about graduate school?

M: I'm not really interested in that. I'd prefer to get a job.

W: Okay. Your major in Economics, so you have a lot of options. You could work at a bank or another type of financial institution.

M: Yeah, but that's the problem. I don't actually enjoy my major anymore, and I don't think I want to do anything related to economics in the future.

W: I see . . . Well, it's probably too late to change majors unless you want to stay here for a fifth year.

M: That's a good point. But I'm also getting a minor in history. I checked the requirements, and I might be able to change the major into a minor.

W: How many more classes would you have to take?

M: Five more, including a seminar.

W: That's possible, but you should probably stay here this summer and take a history class or two then.

M: That's a good idea. Should I talk to someone in the History Department as well?

W: Definitely. You'll need an advisor there if you're going to change your major.

해석

M Student: Waddle 교수님, 잠시 이야기를 나눌 수 있는 시간이 있으신가요?

W Professor: 그럼요, Pierre. 가장 뛰어난 학생 중 한 명을 위한 시간은 언제나 있죠. 무슨 일인가요?

M: 아시겠지만 저는 다음 학기에 4학년이 되어요. 제 장래에 대해 생각 중인데, 무엇을 해야 할지 정말로 잘 모르겠어요.

W: 대학원에 대해 생각해 본 적은 있나요?

M: 그쪽은 정말로 관심이 없어요. 오히려 취직을 하고 싶어요.

W: 그래요. 학생은 경제학을 전공하고 있으니 선택할 수 있는 것들이 많아요. 은행이나 기타 금융 기관에서 일을 할 수도 있죠.

M: 그렇기는 한데, 그것이 문제예요. 저는 사실 더 이상 전공을 좋아하지 않아서 앞으로 경제학과 관련된 일을 하고 싶지는 않거든요.

W: 알겠어요… 음, 이곳에서 5년째 있는 것을 원하지 않는 이상 전공을 바꾸기에는 너무 늦은 것 같군요.

M: 맞는 말씀이에요. 하지만 저는 역사를 부전공으로 삼고 있어요. 조건을 확인해 보았는데, 제 전공을 부전공으로 바꿀 수는 있을 것 같았어요.

W: 몇 개의 수업을 더 들어야 하나요?

M: 세미나 수업 하나를 포함해서 다섯 개를 더 들어야 해요.

W: 그러면 가능은 하겠지만, 아마도 이번 여름을 이곳에서 보내면서 역사 수업을 한두 개 들어야 할 거예요.

M: 좋은 아이디어군요. 제가 역사학과의 누군가와 이야기를 해야 할까요?

W: 물론이죠. 전공을 변경하려면 그쪽 지도 교수님이 필요할 거예요.

📝 Summary Note

A

❶ get a job

❷ economics

B

The student is not sure what he wants to do in the future. He does not want to attend graduate school, but he would prefer to find a job. However, he does not like his major anymore, so he wants to stop doing economics. The professor thinks it may be too late to change majors since the student will be a senior next semester. However, the student can change his minor in history to a major by taking five more classes. The professor suggests taking summer school classes and talking to a professor in the History Department.

Exercise 4 1 Ⓐ, ⓒ 2 Ⓓ p.78

Script 🎧 03-11

W Professor: Tim, may I have a moment of your time, please?

M Student: Of course. What can I do for you?

W: I want to talk about your assignment.

M: Really? Did you like it?

W: Well, the story was okay, and our class is a creative writing class, but there is a lot of room for improvement.

M: Oh . . . Okay. What did I do badly?

W: First of all, your story was not balanced. Your main character talks way too much. At times, I thought I was reading a play. Do you know why?

M: No.

W: Because in a play, the writer only writes what people say and only a tiny bit about their actions, and then the actors do the rest. Are you writing a play?

M: No, I wasn't. I just . . .

W: Remember that you need to describe things. Tell me what is going on. For example, your main character says, "What a wonderful tree." I know it was a wonderful tree because he says so, but tell me why it was a wonderful tree. Describe it to me.

M: Ah, okay. Is there anything else?

W: Yes, there is. I believe that only the main character talks. The others don't contribute at all. Let everyone else have some dialog. You might want to add some more characters, too.

M: Yes, ma'am, I understand. Less talking by the main character.

W: Your favorite book series is *The Lord of the Rings*, right? Do you know one reason why it's so beloved by people? One reason is that the author made many unique characters. They all participate in the action, and they all make their own individual contributions. That is what you should try to do.

해석

W Professor: Tim, 잠시 시간을 낼 수 있나요?

M Student: 그럼요. 어떻게 도와 드릴까요?

W: 과제에 대해 이야기를 하고 싶어요.

M: 정말이요? 마음에 드셨어요?

W: 음, 줄거리는 괜찮았는데, 우리 수업은 창의적인 글쓰기 수업이라 개선의 여지가 많아요.

M: 오… 그렇군요. 제가 무엇을 잘못했나요?

W: 우선, 줄거리의 균형이 맞지 않아요. 주인공의 대사가 너무 많아요. 때때로 희곡을 읽고 있는 것 같았어요. 그 이유를 아나요?

M: 아니요.

W: 희곡에서는 작가가 사람들이 하는 말만 쓰고 행동에 관해서는 아주 약간만 쓰는데, 배우들이 나머지를 처리하기 때문이죠. 희곡을 쓰는 중인가요?

M: 아니요, 그렇지 않아요. 저는 그냥…

W: 상황을 묘사해야 한다는 점을 기억해요. 무슨 일이 일어나고 있는지 이야기 하세요. 예를 들어 주인공이 "정말 멋진 나무구나."라고 말을 해요. 그가 그렇게 말했기 때문에 그것이 멋진 나무라는 점은 알겠지만, 왜 멋진 나무인지는 알려 줘야 해요. 설명을 하세요.

M: 아, 알겠어요. 다른 문제도 있나요?

W: 네 있어요. 주인공의 대사만 있다고 생각해요. 다른 인물들은 전혀 말을 하지 않죠. 그 밖의 모든 사람들도 대화에 참여하도록 만드세요. 등장 인물을 추가하고 싶을 수도 있을 거예요.

M: 네, 교수님, 이해했어요. 주인공의 대사를 줄이라는 점이요.

W: 학생이 가장 좋아하는 시리즈가 *반지의 제왕*이죠, 그렇죠? 사람들이 그 책을 좋아하는 한 가지 이유를 알고 있나요? 그 한 가지 이유는 작가가 독특한 인물들을 많이 만들었기 때문이에요. 그들 모두 액션에 참여해서 각자의 역할을 하죠. 학생이 해야 할 일이 바로 그것이에요.

📝 Summary Note

A

❶ talks too much

❷ do not talk enough

B

The professor tells the student why his creative writing assignment is not good. She says that the main character talks so much that the story is like in a play. He needs to have more description. In addition, he must make the other characters talk more. They do not talk enough. She uses the example of *The Lord of the Rings* to tell him he needs more characters and, through their words, make them come to life.

Exercises with Mid-Length Lectures

Exercise 1   1 Ⓑ   2 Ⓓ   p.80

Script 🎧 03-12

M1 Professor: Since we've been talking about the Civil War for a while, it's about time for us to talk about another important thing related to it. We're going to shift gears a bit and talk about the Gettysburg Address. Who can tell me who gave the Gettysburg Address?

W Student: That's easy. Everyone knows it was Abraham Lincoln.

M1: That's right. President Lincoln gave the Gettysburg Address. Now who can tell me when he gave this address?

M2 Student: Didn't he make the speech after the Battle of Gettysburg? I think the week after the battle, right?

M1: No, not quite. I know it makes sense that he would give the Gettysburg Address soon after the Battle of Gettysburg, but actually, he gave it almost half a year after the Battle of Gettysburg was fought. Lincoln made the speech at the battleground at Gettysburg. That's why it's called the Gettysburg Address. Now there are a number of reasons why this speech is famous. Probably the most important reason is its content. Lincoln spoke about the importance of freedom in the nation. One thing that we have to note is that whenever he talked about the United States, he called it a "nation," not a "union." Can anyone tell me why this distinction is important?

M2: Well, probably because he wanted to make it a point not to exclude the Confederate States. By saying "nation," he was making a point that the Union states and the Confederate states were both part of the same country. That country was formed by the same people, and they're all basically the same people.

M1: Excellent. That's exactly right. By talking about everyone as a nation, he made sure to include everyone who was fighting the war. This helped motivate the North as well as welcome back the South after the war.

해석

M1 Professor: 한동안 남북 전쟁에 관해 논의했으니 이제 그와 관련된 또 다른 중요한 일에 대해 논의할 때입니다. 약간 방향을 바꾸어서 게티스버그 연설에 대해 이야기를 해 보죠. 누가 게티스버그 연설을 했는지 말해 볼까요?

W Student: 쉽네요. 에이브러햄 링컨이었다는 것은 누구나 알고 있죠.

M1: 맞았어요. 링컨 대통령이 게티스버그 연설을 했죠. 그럼 언제 이 연설을 했는지 누가 말해 볼까요?

M2 Student: 게티스버그 전투 후에 연설을 하지 않았나요? 전투가 끝나고 그 다음 주였던 것으로 알고 있는데요, 맞나요?

M1: 아니요, 그렇지 않습니다. 상식적으로는 게티스버그 전투가 끝나고 얼마 지나지 않아서 연설을 했을 것 같지만, 게티스버그 전투가 끝나고 거의 반년이 지나서야 연설을 하게 되었어요. 링컨은 게티스버그 전투가 일어났던 곳에서 연설을 했습니다. 바로 이러한 점 때문에 이를 게티스버그 연설이라고 부르는 것이죠. 자, 이 연설이 유명한 여러 가지 이유가 있습니다. 아마도 가장 중요한 이유는 연설의 내용 때문일 거예요. 링컨 대통령은 미국에서 자유의 중요성에 대해 이야기했어요. 한 가지 주목할 점은 그가 미국에 관해 이야기를 할 때마다 미국을 "연방"이 아닌 "국가"라고 지칭했다는 점입니다. 왜 이러한 구분이 중요한지 아는 사람 있나요?

M2: 음, 아마도 남부 연합의 주들을 배제하지 않겠다는 점을 강조하고 싶었던 것 같아요. "국가"라고 말함으로써 북부 연방과 남부 연합이 모두 같은 나라의 일부라는 점을 강조했던 것이죠. 그 나라가 같은 사람들에 의해 만들어졌고, 그들 모두 기본적으로 같은 사람들이니까요.

M1: 훌륭해요. 정확합니다. 모든 사람들을 한 민족이라고 말함으로써 전쟁에 참가했던 모든 사람들을 포용하려 했던 것이죠. 이는 종전 후 북부를 고무시키고 남부를 다시 따뜻하게 맞이하는데 도움이 되었습니다.

📝 Summary Note

A

❶ Abraham Lincoln

❷ battleground

❸ freedom

B

The Gettysburg Address was a famous speech given by President Abraham Lincoln. He gave this speech on the

battleground at Gettysburg half a year after that battle was fought. The Gettysburg Address is famous mostly because of its content. In this address, Lincoln talked about the importance of freedom in the nation. The language he used was very important. The reason is that he did not exclude soldiers from either side of the war.

Exercise 2   1 ⓑ   2 ⓑ, ⓒ   p.82

Script 🎧 03-13

W1 Professor: Let's move forward in our discussion on architecture and cover Turkey. Now, Turkey was once a part of the Ottoman Empire, so when we talk about Turkish architecture from a long time ago, we are generally referring to Ottoman architecture. Who can tell me what years the Ottoman Empire lasted from?

W2 Student: I am not sure, but didn't it start about 500 B.C. and fall about 500 A.D.?

W1: You're thinking of the Roman Empire, which did play a huge role in the founding of the Ottoman Empire, but that is not correct. Anyone else?

M Student: It lasted a really long time, didn't it? From about 1300 to 1920, didn't it?

W1: Yes, that's exactly right. But the architecture of the Ottoman Empire flourished during the fourteenth and fifteenth centuries. Who can tell me some of the key characteristics of Ottoman architecture?

W2: It used a lot of domes, didn't it?

W1: Yes, it did. The Ottomans actually made the dome a really popular architectural structure. Okay, anyone else?

M: Um . . . I think I read something about vaults.

W1: Great. Vaults are very much Ottoman architectural structures. In addition to domes and vaults, the Ottomans also used a lot of semi-domes and columns. Now, if you'll remember, the Greeks originally popularized the column. But it's such a functional structure that many groups of people have used it throughout history. What the Ottomans did with these structures is that they used them to make mosques more beautiful. Before the Ottomans, mosques were usually big, open, and dull places. But the Ottomans designed mosques to be splendid in appearance. You can see examples of their mosques all around Turkey.

M: I heard that their houses had doors on the roof. Is that correct?

W1: It is correct, but we will talk about that next week.

해석

W1 Professor: 이제 건축에 대한 논의를 진전시켜 터키를 살펴보도록 하죠. 자, 터키는 한때 오스만 제국의 일부였기 때문에 오래 전의 터키 건축을 이야기

하는 경우에는 일반적으로 이를 오스만 건축이라고 지칭해요. 오스만 제국이 몇 년도부터 존재했는지 아는 사람이 있나요?

W2 Student: 정확하지는 않지만 기원전 500년경에 세워져서 기원후 500년경에 사라지지 않았나요?

W1: 학생은 로마 제국을 생각하는 것 같은데, 로마 제국이 오스만 제국의 설립에 커다란 역할을 하기는 했지만 정답은 아니에요. 다른 사람?

M Student: 정말로 오랫동안 존재했죠, 그렇죠? 1300년경부터 1920년까지요, 그렇지 않나요?

W1: 네, 정확히 맞췄어요. 하지만 오스만 제국의 건축은 14세기와 15세기에 번성했습니다. 오스만 건축의 주요 특징을 말해볼 사람이 있나요?

W2: 돔이 많이 사용되었어요, 그렇지 않나요?

W1: 네, 그래요. 실제로 오스만 사람들은 건축물로 돔을 정말 많이 사용했어요. 좋아요, 다른 사람?

M: 음… 아치형 천장에 대해 읽은 것 같아요.

W1: 잘했어요. 아치형 천장도 오스만 건축물의 큰 특징입니다. 돔과 아치형 천장 이외에도 오스만 사람들은 세미돔과 원형 기둥을 많이 사용했어요. 자, 기억할지 모르겠는데, 원형 기둥은 원래 그리스인들이 주로 사용했습니다. 하지만 워낙 실용적인 구조물이었기 때문에 역사적으로 여러 민족들이 이를 사용했죠. 오스만 사람들은 이러한 구조물을 가지고 모스크를 보다 아름답게 만들었습니다. 오스만 사람들이 있기 전에는 모스크가 보통 크고, 개방되어 있고, 단조로운 공간이었어요. 하지만 오스만 사람들은 모스크가 멋지게 보이도록 설계했습니다. 이러한 모스크의 예는 터키 전역에서 찾아볼 수 있어요.

M: 주택 지붕에 문이 달려 있다고 들었습니다. 맞나요?

W1: 맞는 말이지만, 그에 대해서는 다음 주에 이야기할게요.

✏️ Summary Note

A

❶ Domes

❷ splendid structures

B

Turkish architecture usually means Ottoman architecture. The Ottoman Empire lasted from 1300 to 1920, and its architecture flourished during the fourteenth and fifteenth centuries. The Ottomans popularized the use of domes, vaults, and semi-domes. What the Ottomans mostly used these structures for was to create beautiful mosques. Before the Ottomans, mosques were really plain and boring. Afterward, they were very lovely in appearance.

Exercise 3 1 Ⓑ 2 Ⓐ p.84

Script 🎧 03-14

W Professor: Last week, we talked about the United States being a melting pot, where all the different immigrants mix together to create something new. Well, everything has exceptions, including our melting pot, right? In the Mississippi River Valley, there is a large area that is part melting pot and part garden salad. In Louisiana, or more specifically, New Orleans, there have been a few major cultural influences that are different from the rest of the United States. Unlike the rest of the United States, which was colonized by England and Spain, New Orleans was predominantly a French settlement. It was also a unique slave culture.

While the rest of the U.S. was a melting pot, mixing all its parts to create something new, New Orleans became a garden salad. Right now, you are asking yourself what I mean by garden salad, aren't you? A garden salad has many parts that are combined to make a new flavor. Each piece retains its original identity, but combined, they make something new and hopefully better. This contrasts with the melting pot because in a melting pot, all of the pieces lose their identity to form something new.

So in New Orleans, there was a French beginning with French culture, food, language, and lifestyle. Added in over the centuries was a bit of a Spanish influence, when Spain controlled the territory for about fifty years after the French and Indian War. After that was the American and English influence after President Jefferson bought the territory from France. And last was an influx of Latino culture from Mexico and the Caribbean.

The result now is that New Orleans has a distinct culture apart from the United States. Because of their French ancestry, people from New Orleans have different jargon, such as they say, "I'm making groceries," instead of, "I am grocery shopping." Again, this is due to the French influence. In French, the direct translation is "to make groceries," not "to buy or go shopping."

해석

W Professor: 지난 주에는 다양한 이민자들이 모두 섞여 새로운 것을 만들어 내는, 용광로로서의 미국에 대해 이야기했습니다. 음, 우리의 용광로를 포함해서 모든 것에는 예외가 있기 마련이죠, 그렇죠? 미시시피 리버 밸리에는 부분적으로는 용광로이면서 부분적으로는 가든샐러드에 해당되는 넓은 지역이 존재합니다. 루이지애나에는, 보다 구체적으로는 뉴올리언즈에는, 미국의 나머지 지역과 상이한 문화적 영향들이 일부 남아 있어요. 영국과 스페인의 식민지였던 미국의 나머지 지역들과 달리 뉴올리언즈에는 주로 프랑스인들이 거주를 했죠. 또한 그 곳에는 독특한 노예 문화가 있었습니다.

미국의 나머지 지역들이 모든 성분이 섞여 새로운 것을 만들어 내는 용광로였다면 뉴올리언즈는 가든샐러드였어요. 지금 여러분은 가든샐러드가 무엇인지 자문하고 있죠, 그렇지 않나요? 가든샐러드의 많은 부분들은 섞여서 새로운 맛을 냅니다. 각 부분들은 자신의 정체성을 유지하지만, 섞이는 경우 보다 새롭고, 바람직하게는, 더 뛰어난 무언가를 만들어 내죠. 이는 용광로와 대조적인 것으로, 용광로에서는 모든 부분들이 정체성을 잃고 새로운 무언가를 만들어 냅니다.

그래서 뉴올리언즈는 프랑스 문화, 프랑스 음식, 프랑스어, 그리고 프랑스적인 생활 방식으로 시작되었어요. 프렌치 인디언 전쟁 후 50년 동안 스페인이 이 지역을 지배했던 때에는 수 세기에 걸쳐 스페인의 영향도 약간 받았고요. 그 후 제퍼슨 대통령이 프랑스로부터 이 지역을 매입하면서 미국과 영국의 영향을 받게 되었습니다. 그리고 마지막으로 멕시코와 카리브 지역으로부터 라틴 문화가 유입되었죠.

그 결과 뉴올리언즈에는 미국과는 구별되는 독특한 문화가 존재합니다. 프랑스인 계통이기 때문에 뉴올리언즈 출신의 사람들은 다른 용어를 사용하는데, 예컨대 "나는 식료품을 살 거야."라는 말 대신 "나는 식료품을 만들 거야."라고 말을 합니다. 마찬가지로 이 역시 프랑스의 영향 때문이에요. 이를 프랑스어로 그대로 옮기는 경우 "사거나 구입하다"가 아니라 "식료품을 만든다"가 됩니다.

✏️ Summary Note

A

❶ slave culture

❷ Latin countries

B

Most of the United States is considered a melting pot because the different immigrants mix together. In the Mississippi River Valley, New Orleans is different from the rest of the United States. It is a garden salad. Its different pieces have retained their identities. New Orleans was heavily influenced from its French beginnings. Later, Spanish, American, English, and Latin immigrants all added to the culture of the city. One example of this difference is the jargon. The local jargon has a heavy French influence.

Exercise 4 1 ⓒ 2 ⓓ   p.86

Script 🎧 03-15

M Professor: Let's keep talking about the idea of a language evolving. I talked about how war changes a language because one culture can dominate another and infuse aspects of its language into a new language. Now, I will talk about another way a language can change. It is . . . can anyone guess . . . ? Technology.

One example is, hmm, a cellphone. Cellphones have changed and are currently changing the way we communicate with each other. Only fifty years ago, phone conversations were considered private affairs. For example, if I was at your house, and your phone rang, I would leave the room so that you could have a private conversation. With cellphones, people have conversations everywhere. I mean, uh, at restaurants, on dates, umm, and even on public transportation, you can see people chatting away.

Now people are talking about what was considered private in public. We talk about work, people we dislike, our relationships, and our plans in front of complete strangers. The things we now talk about on the phone would have been considered extremely rude to say in public fifty years ago. Back then, you would be chastised by someone for talking about your boyfriend or girlfriend or a party you went to the night before.

Um, what else? We are changing how we talk as well. We all get phone bills, so talking on the phone means

you are using money. So the faster you talk, the less money you use. This means we often start and end our phone conversations quickly. Before, we would take our time on the phone, ask someone how that person is doing, chit chat for a bit, and then get to the point. We would slowly end the conversation and often say bye two or three times. Now, we just say the point and then maybe say goodbye, and the conversation is over. That would have been so rude only twenty years ago.

해석

M Professor: 언어 진화의 개념에 대해 계속해서 논의해 보죠. 문화는 다른 문화를 지배할 수 있고 자신의 언어를 주입시켜 새로운 언어를 만들어 낼 수 있기 때문에, 우리는 전쟁이 어떻게 언어를 변화시키는지에 대해 논의해 보았습니다. 자, 언어가 변화하는 또 다른 방식에 대해 논의해 볼게요. 그것은… 아는 사람이 있을까요…? 기술입니다.

한 가지 예가, 흠, 휴대 전화죠. 휴대 전화는 우리의 커뮤니케이션 방식을 변화시켰고 지금도 변화시키고 있습니다. 불과 50년 전만 해도 전화 통화는 사적인 것으로 간주되었어요. 예를 들어 제가 여러분의 집에 있는데 전화가 울리는 경우, 저는 여러분이 사적인 대화를 나눌 수 있도록 자리를 비켜 줄 것입니다. 휴대 전화로는 어디에서나 통화가 가능합니다. 제 말은, 어, 식당에서, 데이트하는 동안, 음, 심지어는 대중 교통에서도 사람들이 통화하는 모습을 볼 수가 있죠.

요즘 사람들은 한때 사적인 것으로 생각되었던 것들을 공개적으로 이야기합니다. 완전히 모르는 사람 앞에서 일, 우리가 싫어하는 사람, 우리의 관계, 그리고 우리의 계획을 이야기하죠. 현재 우리가 전화로 이야기하는 것들을 50년 전으로 돌아가서 공개적으로 이야기한다면 매우 예의에 어긋나는 일로 간주될 거예요. 그 당시에는 남자 친구나 여자 친구, 혹은 전날 밤에 갔던 파티에 대해 이야기하면 누군가에게 비난을 받았을 것입니다.

음, 또 무엇이 있을까요? 우리가 말을 하는 방식도 바뀌었습니다. 우리 모두 전화 요금 고지서를 받고 있는데, 전화 통화는 돈이 나가고 있다는 점을 의미하죠. 따라서 말을 빨리 할 수록 돈을 덜 쓰게 됩니다. 이는 종종 우리가 전화 통화를 빨리 시작하고 끝낸다는 점을 의미해요. 전에는 여유를 가지고 통화를 하고, 그 사람의 안부를 묻고, 이런저런 잡담을 하고 난 뒤에야 본론으로 들어가곤 했죠. 전화 통화는 천천히 종료되었고, 두세 차례 작별 인사를 하는 경우도 종종 있었고요. 이제는 요점만 이야기한 후 작별 인사를 하면 통화가 끝납니다. 20년 전만 해도 이는 대단히 무례한 일이었을 것입니다.

✏️ Summary Note

A

❶ save money

❷ quicker

B

English is an evolving language. One way a language can evolve is through technology. Cellphones have changed how we speak. Cellphones allow us to speak in public places. This has changed what we consider private. Many things we discuss in public were once considered private and should not be spoken in public. People also talk quickly on cellphones to save money. This has shortened conversations. We often do not greet people the same as we did, and we end conversations without saying bye.

Integrated Listening & Speaking   p.88

Script 🎧 03-16

> **W Professor:** Turkish architecture is actually Ottoman architecture because the Ottoman Empire heavily influenced the style of the Turks. The Ottoman Empire lasted from 1300 to 1920, but its architectural peak came in the fourteenth and fifteenth centuries. Some characteristics of Ottoman architecture are domes, semi-domes, vaults, and columns. They used these designs to make mosques more beautiful. Before they added these designs, mosques were big, open, dull spaces. Even today, the mosques of Turkey still have Ottoman-style domes and columns. Another example of Ottoman influence on Turkish architecture is having a door on the roofs of houses.

1 a. The biggest influence on Turkish architecture was the Ottoman Empire.

   b. The Ottoman Empire was a very big influence on the development of Turkish architecture.

2 a. The peak of Ottoman architecture was the fourteenth and fifteenth centuries.

   b. The height of architecture in the Ottoman Empire started in the year 1300 and ended about 1500.

3 a. Some common characteristics of Turkish architecture are domes, semi-domes, vaults, and columns.

   b. Domes, semi-domes, vaults, and columns are very popular designs in Turkish architecture.

Script 🎧 03-17

> **W Professor:** Parts of the Mississippi Valley, specifically the city of New Orleans, are different from the rest of the United States. New Orleans is compared to a garden salad because all of the cultural influences have kept their old identity. Like in a garden salad, all the pieces keep their tastes, but combined, they make a new flavor. The rest of the United States is compared to a melting pot. New pieces are added, and they lose their identity when they combine with the rest of the pot and create something new. Because of the people's French heritage, in New Orleans, the jargon is different. For example, they say "making groceries" instead of "going shopping."

1 a. The city has its own culture, and the new pieces keep their old identity while adding to the city's culture.

   b. The city's culture is made of many pieces that retain their original identity but still add to the culture of the city.

2 a. All of the pieces become part of American culture and lose their original culture.

   b. The pieces no longer have an original identity and become part of the culture of America.

3 a. The people of New Orleans say "making groceries" because of their French heritage.

   b. Due to their French origins, people in New Orleans say things like "making groceries."

Mini TOEFL iBT Practice Test   p.90

1 Ⓑ	2 Ⓒ	3 Ⓒ	4 Ⓒ, Ⓓ	5 Ⓓ
6 Ⓓ	7 Ⓐ, Ⓓ	8 Ⓐ	9 Ⓓ	10 Ⓒ
11 Ⓐ				

[1-5]

Script 🎧 03-18

> **M Student Services Center Employee:** Hello. Can I help you?
>
> **W Student:** Yes, please. I just have a few questions.
>
> **M:** Sure. I will see if I can answer them.
>
> **W:** Okay. First of all, I have a car on campus, and I just want to make sure I understand all the fees. I got the guidebook, and I downloaded it on my computer, but I am not sure if I understand everything completely.
>
> **M:** Of course. Some of those rules are a bit strange to people outside of our state.
>
> **W:** Yeah, first, it says I have to park on alternating sides of the road. What exactly does that mean?
>
> **M:** Okay, here in Minnesota, it snows a lot. So the snowplows need to have open paths to plow. City law says you must park on alternating sides of the road. This means, on even dates, for example, today, is the 20th, so you must park on the even side of the road. One side of the road will have addresses like 910, 912, and 914, and the other side will be 911, 913, and 915. So you must park on the even side. Does this make sense?
>
> **W:** Yes, I understand. But then I must move my car every day?
>
> **M:** Yes, that's what it means.
>
> **W:** Wow, that can get pretty annoying. When? Just during winter? When there is snow on the ground?
>
> **M:** Nope, always. Even in the summer you must do this. You should also remember that if you park at 10:00 PM on the 13th of the month, think about the next day. The next day would be the 14th, so you must be on the even side of the street. It can get a bit confusing. What is your

next question?

W: Well, I just got my car, so I don't have a parking permit. How much time do I have until I need it?

M: Oh, you should buy it now. A semester pass costs thirty dollars, and a year-long pass costs fifty dollars.

W: I don't have enough money right now. What can I do?

M: You can park off campus. You can also hope security doesn't notice you, or you can drive your car back home until you buy a pass.

W: I see. I think I'll have enough money in a few days, so I will take my chances until then. Thanks.

해석

M Student Services Center Employee: 안녕하세요. 도와 드릴까요?

W Student: 네, 부탁드려요. 몇 가지 질문이 있어서요.

M: 그래요. 제가 답을 드릴 수 있을지 보죠.

W: 좋아요. 먼저, 제가 교내에 차를 가지고 다니는데, 모든 요금제를 제대로 이해하고 있는지 확인하고 싶어요. 안내서를 보고 컴퓨터에 다운로드했지만, 제가 모든 것을 완벽히 이해한 것 같지가 않아서요.

M: 그럴 거예요. 우리 주에 살지 않는 사람들에게는 몇몇 규정들은 약간 낯설 거예요.

W: 예, 우선, 도로 양쪽에 번갈아가면서 주차를 해야 된다고 적혀 있더군요. 그것이 정확히 무슨 의미인가요?

M: 그래요, 이곳 미네소타에서는 눈이 많이 내려요. 그래서 제설차가 제설 작업을 하기 위해서는 길이 뚫려 있어야 하죠. 시에서 정한 법에 따르면 도로 양쪽에 번갈아가면서 주차를 해야 해요. 무슨 말인가 하면, 예를 들어 오늘이 20일이니까 도로의 짝수 쪽에 주차를 해야 하죠. 도로의 한쪽에는 910, 912, 914와 같은 주소가 적혀 있고, 다른 한쪽에는 911, 913, 915가 적혀 있을 거예요. 그러니 짝수 쪽에 주차해야 해요. 이해가 되시나요?

W: 네, 이해했어요. 하지만 그렇다면 매일 차를 이동시켜야 하나요?

M: 네, 그런 의미죠.

W: 와, 상당히 불편할 수 있겠네요. 언제인가요? 겨울 동안만인가요? 도로에 눈이 있을 때인가요?

M: 아니요, 항상이에요. 여름에도 그렇게 해야 하죠. 또한 13일 오후 10시에 주차를 한 경우에는 다음 날도 생각해야 한다는 점을 기억하세요. 다음 날은 14일이 될 테니까 도로의 짝수 편에 차가 있어야 해요. 꽤 헷갈릴 수 있어요. 다음 질문은 무엇인가요?

W: 음, 얼마 전에 차를 구입했기 때문에 주차 허가증이 없어요. 허가증을 받으려면 얼마나 기다려야 하나요?

M: 오, 지금 사셔야 해요. 한 학기 주차권은 30달러이고, 1년 주차권은 50달러예요.

W: 지금 당장은 돈이 없어요. 어떻게 해야 하나요?

M: 학교 밖에 주차를 할 수 있어요. 또한 보안 요원이 보지 못하기를 바랄 수도 있고, 주차권을 구입하기 전까지 차를 집에 다시 가져다 놓을 수도 있죠.

W: 알겠어요. 며칠 후에 충분한 돈이 생기니까 그때까지는 위험을 감수해야 할 것 같군요.

[6-11]

W Professor: Before the rise of the nation-state and absolute monarchies, Europe went through a period known as feudalism. Like democracy, feudalism had many forms and varied by location and time period. Let me see . . . Feudalism originated by mixing Roman law with Germanic tradition. The Germanic warriors that lived about 3,000 years ago had a tradition of electing a supreme warrior as leader. After battles, he would collect all of the spoils and distribute them fairly among all the warriors. Feudalism is defined by three principal terms. They are lord, vassal, and fief.

Okay, in feudalism, a lord was a person that owns land. He temporarily gave this land to another person, called a vassal. The land given was called a fief. The vassal entered this contract so that he could obtain land. Land sizes varied from the size of a small farm to huge counties. The vassal gained revenues generated by the land, usually in the form of farming products.

What did the lord get? At this time, there were no standing armies. There were no professional soldiers. The vassal swore allegiance to the lord. In times of trouble, the lord could call upon the vassal to fight for the lord. This guaranteed the lord's security.

Other details were often included in feudal deals. For example, since the lord still owned the land and merely lent the land to the vassal, the lord had to maintain the land and defend it. The vassal, many times, would be required to grind his wheat and bake his bread in the ovens and mills owned by the lord, who would then collect taxes.

The vassals also acted as counselors to the lord. During times of crisis, the lords would often hold meetings by calling together all the vassals to help them decide major decisions, such as to go to war or not.

Ah, lastly, feudalism had many levels. What I mean is that a king could be a lord, giving aristocrats large lands, who then became his vassals. Those aristocrats were lords themselves, so they divided up their land to lesser vassals. At the top of this hierarchy was the emperor, who was the lord to his vassal kings. It was a very effective way of ruling lands for many years.

Feudalism declined when lords became strong enough to maintain standing armies and did not require the services of their vassals.

해석

W Professor: 민족 국가와 절대 왕정이 등장하기 전에 유럽은 봉건제의 시기를 거쳤어요. 민주주의와 마찬가지로 봉건제 역시 여러 가지 형태로 존재했으며 장소와 시간에 따라 종류가 다양했습니다. 봅시다… 봉건제는 로마법과 게르만의 전통이 혼합되어 탄생했어요. 약 1300년 전에 살았던 게르만 전사들에게는

최고의 전사를 지도자로 뽑는 전통이 있었습니다. 전투가 끝난 후 지도자는 모든 전리품을 한곳에 모아 이를 모든 전사들에게 공평하게 분배했어요. 봉건제는 세 가지 용어로 정의할 수 있습니다. 군주, 봉신, 그리고 봉토가 그것이죠.

좋아요, 봉건제에서 군주는 토지를 소유한 사람이었습니다. 군주는 일시적으로 봉신이라는 다른 사람에게 자신의 토지를 나누어 주었어요. 주어진 토지는 봉토라고 불렸고요. 봉신은 이러한 계약을 맺음으로써 토지를 얻을 수 있었습니다. 토지는 작은 농장에서부터 거대한 주에 이르기까지 크기가 다양했습니다. 봉신은 토지에서 발생하는 수익을 보통 농작물의 형태로 얻었죠.

군주는 무엇을 얻었을까요? 이 당시에는 상비군이 없었습니다. 직업 군인도 없었고요. 봉신은 군주에게 충성을 맹세했습니다. 위기 상황이 발생하면 군주는 봉신에게 자신을 위해 싸우도록 요구할 수 있었죠. 이로써 군주의 안전이 보장되었습니다.

기타 세부 사항들이 종종 봉건 계약에 포함되었어요. 예를 들어서 토지는 여전히 군주의 소유였고 단지 이 토지가 봉신에게 임대된 것이었기 때문에 군주가 토지를 관리하고 보호해야 했어요. 봉신은, 여러 차례, 오븐과 군주의 소유물인 제분소를 이용하여 자신의 밀을 빻고 빵을 구워야 했는데, 그리고 난 뒤에는 군주가 세금을 징수했습니다.

또한 봉신은 군주의 상담자의 역할도 했어요. 위기 상황에서 군주들은, 예컨대 전쟁을 할 것인지 말 것인지에 관한 중요한 결정을 내리기 위해, 종종 모든 봉신들을 소환하여 회의를 하곤 했습니다.

아, 마지막으로 봉건제에는 여러 단계가 있었어요. 제 말은, 왕이 군주가 되어 귀족들에게 많은 토지를 줄 수 있었고, 그러면 귀족들은 봉신이 되는 것이었죠. 이 귀족들은 그들 스스로가 군주가 되어 자신의 토지를 아래 봉신들에게 나누어 주었습니다. 이러한 위계의 가장 꼭대기에는 황제가 있었는데, 황제는 자신의 봉신인 왕들의 군주가 되었습니다. 이는 여러 해 동안 매우 효과적인 통치 방식이었어요.

군주들이 상비군을 보유할 정도로 강력해지고 봉신들의 부역이 필요하지 않게 되자 봉건제는 쇠퇴했습니다.

Vocabulary Check-Up
p.95

A
1 ⓔ 2 ⓑ 3 ① 4 ⓓ 5 ⓖ
6 ① 7 ⓐ 8 ⓜ 9 ① 10 ⓚ
11 ⓞ 12 ⓗ 13 ⓒ 14 ⓝ 15 ⓕ

B
1 ⓔ 2 ⓑ 3 ⓐ 4 ⓒ 5 ⓓ

UNIT 04 Understanding the Function of What Is Said

Basic Drill ·· p.100

Drill 1 Ⓐ

Script 🎧 04-02

> **W Student:** Hi. I registered last year to have the same roommate again this year, but I have a new roommate. What happened?
>
> **M Student Housing Office Employee:** What are your name and room number?
>
> **W:** My name is Emily Davis. I live in Emerson 216.
>
> **M:** Okay, I have your registration form here. Look here. You didn't fill it out completely.
>
> **W:** Really? What is wrong with it?
>
> **M:** You didn't put your roommate's last name on the form. It just has her first name. We didn't know who your roommate was.
>
> **W:** Couldn't you just look up who I lived with last year?
>
> **M:** Well, that is your job. But if your new roommate agrees and your old roommate wants to move in, you can do that. But they must change rooms by tomorrow.
>
> **W:** Okay, I will talk to my roommate now. Thank you!

해석

W Student: 안녕하세요. 올해도 같은 룸메이트와 지내겠다고 작년에 신청했는데 새 룸메이트가 배정되었어요. 어떻게 된 일인가요?

M Student Housing Office Employee: 학생 이름과 방 번호가 어떻게 되죠?

W: 제 이름은 Emily Davis예요. Emerson 216호에서 살고요.

M: 좋아요, 신청서가 여기 있군요. 여기를 보세요. 학생이 신청서를 제대로 작성하지 않았네요.

W: 정말이요? 어디가 잘못되었나요?

M: 신청서에 룸메이트의 성을 적지 않았어요. 이름만 있죠. 학생의 룸메이트가 누군지 저희가 알 방법이 없었어요.

W: 제가 작년에 누구와 살았는지 찾아보실 수 없으셨나요?

M: 음, 그건 학생이 할 일이죠. 하지만 새 룸메이트가 동의하고 이전 룸메이트가 함께 살고 싶어한다면 그럴 수는 있어요. 하지만 내일까지는 방을 바꿔야 해요.

W: 좋아요, 지금 제 룸메이트와 이야기해 볼게요. 감사합니다!

Drill 2 Ⓓ

M Student: Hello Professor Smith. Can I talk to you?

W Professor: Sure. What can I do for you?

M: I wonder if I can get an extension on the report due tomorrow. I don't need much time, just maybe two more days.

W: I told the class that's not possible on the first day of the semester. I don't permit work to be turned in late.

M: I remember, but I was hoping you would understand. I need the time because I work so much. My parents don't pay any of my tuition, and I don't have a scholarship here.

W: I understand that must be difficult for you, but I already explained my policy.

M: Okay. I understand. I'll make sure that you get the paper tomorrow.

W: Good luck.

M Student: 안녕하세요, Smith 교수님. 말씀을 나눌 수 있을까요?

W Professor: 물론이죠. 어떻게 도와 드릴까요?

M: 내일까지 제출해야 하는 보고서의 기한을 연장할 수 있는지 궁금합니다. 많이는 아니고 이틀 정도 시간이 더 필요해서요.

W: 그건 불가능하다고 제가 수업 첫날에 얘기했을 텐데요. 보고서를 늦게 제출하는 것은 용납할 수 없어요.

M: 저도 기억하고 있지만, 교수님께서 이해를 해 주셨으면 좋겠어요. 제가 아르바이트를 너무 많이 하기 때문에 시간이 필요해요. 부모님께서 등록금을 내 주시지 못하는데, 이곳에서 장학금도 받지 못하고 있어요.

W: 틀림없이 힘든 상황인 것은 알겠지만, 이미 제 방침을 설명했어요.

M: 알겠습니다. 이해해요. 꼭 내일 보고서를 제출하도록 할게요.

W: 행운을 빌어요.

M1 Professor: Hi, John. I want to talk to you about your papers.

M2 Student: Is something wrong with them?

M1: I have noticed a few common problems in all of your papers.

M2: Please tell me so I can correct them.

M1: Of course. First, you have lots of grammar mistakes. These are not excusable. Double-check these, use your grammar guidebook, and have it proofread. You shouldn't be making any grammar mistakes at all.

M2: Okay, I usually write my papers at night, so I am tired, but I can fix that. What's the other problem?

M1: Your thesis is never clear. It is very important that your thesis be clear and simple. I didn't understand your thesis on your last paper until page two. It needs to be explained clearly in the introduction.

M2: I have always had trouble with that. I will work harder on my thesis.

M1 Professor: 안녕하세요, John. 학생 보고서에 대한 이야기를 하고 싶어서요.

M2 Student: 무슨 문제라도 있나요?

M1: 보고서 전체에 몇 가지 공통된 문제가 있다는 것을 알게 되었어요.

M2: 말씀하시면 수정하도록 하겠습니다.

M1: 그래요. 우선, 문법과 관련된 실수들이 많아요. 이러한 실수는 용납할 수 없는 것들이죠. 다시 한 번 확인하고 문법 교재도 참고해서 교정을 보세요. 문법과 관련된 실수는 전혀 없어야 해요.

M2: 그렇군요, 제가 보통 밤에 보고서를 작성하는데 피곤해서요. 고칠 수 있습니다. 다른 문제는 무엇인가요?

M1: 주제가 전혀 명확하지 않아요. 주제를 간단 명료하게 만드는 것이 매우 중요해요. 지난 번 학생 보고서에서도 2페이지를 읽기 전까지 제가 주제를 이해할 수 없었어요. 주제가 서론에서 명확하게 설명되어 있어야 해요.

M2: 항상 그 부분에서 어려움을 겪어 왔어요. 주제에 더욱 신경을 쓰겠습니다.

M Professor: Many people think that tomatoes are vegetables, but they really are not. Tomatoes are actually fruits. The definition of a fruit is the sweet-tasting part of a plant that contains the seeds. **Unlike fruits, vegetables are the parts of plants that are eaten without seeds.** Usually, it is a root or leaf, like carrots or spinach. A tomato has seeds, and people eat the part of the plant around the seeds. Most people think tomatoes are vegetables because they are not sweet and they taste like vegetables.

M Professor: 많은 사람들은 토마토가 채소라고 생각하지만 사실은 그렇지 않습니다. 토마토는 실제로 과일이에요. 과일에 대한 정의는 단맛이 나는 식물의 부분으로, 여기에는 씨앗이 포함되어 있습니다. 과일과 달리 채소는 씨앗이 들어 있지 않은, 먹을 수 있는 식물의 부분입니다. 보통, 당근이나 시금치와 같이 뿌리나 잎인 것이죠. 토마토에는 씨가 있고, 사람들은 이 식물에서 씨가 있는 주변을 먹습니다. 대부분의 사람들은 토마토가 달지 않고 채소와 같은 맛이 나기 때문에 토마토가 채소라고 생각하죠.

W Professor: Scientists divide the depths of the ocean into two different layers. The top is called the <u>surface</u> layer. Below the surface layer is <u>deep water</u>. The surface layer's depth varies but is usually a few hundred meters. The surface layer is the part of the ocean that is affected by wind, rain, waves, tides, and other <u>weather</u> events. **All of these factors constantly mix the surface layer and make it less dense than deep water.** The part of the ocean that divides deep water and the surface layer is called the <u>pycnocline</u>. The <u>gradual</u> movement of the surface layer is called the current. The current does not affect deep water.

해석

W Professor: 과학자들은 바다를 깊이에 따라 서로 다른 두 개의 층으로 구분해요. 맨 위층은 표층이라고 불립니다. 표층 아래에는 심해가 있고요. 표층의 깊이는 다양하지만 보통 수백 미터 정도입니다. 표층은 바다에서 바람, 비, 파도, 조수, 그리고 기타 기상 상황의 영향을 받는 부분이에요. 이러한 모든 요인들이 표층을 항상 섞어 놓기 때문에 표층은 심해보다 밀도가 낮습니다. 심해와 표층을 구분하는 바다의 부분은 밀도 경사라고 불려요. 표층의 점진적인 운동은 해류라고 불리고요. 해류는 심해에 영향을 끼치지 않습니다.

Drill 6 Ⓒ

Script 🎧 04-07

M Professor: The <u>monarch butterfly</u> is easily <u>recognizable</u> in summertime. Interestingly, it's one of the most poisonous insects in the world. The reason is that it <u>consumes</u> milkweed, which is itself a poisonous plant. Over time, <u>predators</u> have learned to avoid the monarch butterfly. Its bright <u>coloring</u> makes it <u>easy</u> for animals to identify. Now, uh, many other butterflies employ something called mimicry. So they look <u>very similar</u> to the monarch butterfly. **This action helps keep them safe.** Which butterflies <u>resemble</u> the monarch? Well, the queen butterfly is. So is the viceroy butterfly. The regal fritillary and the phaon crescent are two others that many animals mistake for the monarch butterfly.

해석

M Professor: 제왕나비는 여름에 쉽게 알아볼 수 있습니다. 흥미롭게도 제왕나비는 전 세계에서 가장 독성이 강한 곤충 중 하나예요. 그 이유는 제왕나비가 독성을 지닌 식물인 밀크위드를 먹기 때문이죠. 오랜 시간에 걸쳐 포식자들은 제왕나비를 피해야 한다는 점을 알게 되었습니다. 제왕나비의 밝은 색깔 때문에 동물들이 이를 알아채기가 쉽습니다. 자, 어, 기타 여러 나비들이 의태라는 것을 이용합니다. 따라서 제왕나비와 매우 비슷하게 보이죠. 이러한 행동으로 인해 안전이 보장될 수 있습니다. 어떤 나비가 제왕나비와 비슷할까요? 음, 여왕나비가 그렇습니다. 총독나비도 마찬가지고요. 리갈나비와 파온크레센트나비 역시 여러 동물들이 제왕나비로 착각하는 나비들이죠.

Exercises with Mid-Length Conversations

Exercise 1 1 Ⓐ 2 Ⓓ p.102

Script 🎧 04-08

W Student: Hello. I need to get some copies of <u>my transcript</u>, but I'm not sure what to do.

M Registrar's Office Employee: It's simple. Just fill out this form here, and we'll <u>do the rest</u>.

W: Great. So <u>they'll be ready</u> in a few minutes?

M: Sorry. It takes us around twenty-four hours <u>to prepare them</u>. We're pretty busy these days and have lots of <u>similar requests</u> to deal with.

W: Okay. I understand. <u>How much</u> does it cost?

M: <u>Each copy</u> of your transcript costs six dollars. That fee includes the cost of <u>mailing them</u> to whichever school or organization you're planning on sending it to.

W: Oh, <u>I didn't realize</u> you would mail them for me. That's great.

M: Sure. You just need to write <u>the addresses of the</u> places you want us to send them to on that form.

W: Um . . . **I guess I'll have to come back tomorrow.**

M: That's all right. Just take the form back to your dorm, <u>fill it out</u>, and bring it here when you can.

W: That's fine. I'm not really <u>in a big hurry</u>. Oh, do you <u>take cash</u>?

M: Not anymore. We only accept <u>credit cards</u>.

W: Okay. Thanks for letting me know. I'll make sure I <u>have my card</u> when I come tomorrow. Thanks a lot.

M: You're welcome. Have a nice day.

해석

W Student: 안녕하세요. 성적표 사본이 몇 장 필요한데, 어떻게 해야 할지 잘 모르겠어요.

M Registrar's Office Employee: 간단해요. 여기 이 양식을 작성하시기만 하면 저희가 나머지를 처리해 드릴게요.

W: 잘 되었군요. 그러면 몇 분 후에 준비가 될까요?

M: 죄송해요. 준비하기까지 24시간 정도가 걸려요. 저희가 요즘 상당히 바쁘기도 하고, 처리해야 할 그와 비슷한 요청들이 많아서요.

W: 그렇군요. 이해가 가요. 비용은 얼마나 드나요?

M: 성적표 사본 한 장당 6달러의 비용이 들어요. 이 요금에는 학생이 보내려고 하는 학교나 기관에 우편으로 보내는 비용도 포함되어 있죠.

W: 오, 우편으로 보내 주신다는 점은 제가 몰랐네요. 잘 되었군요.

M: 그래요. 그 양식에 보내고자 하는 장소의 주소만 적으면 되죠.

W: 음… 내일 다시 와야 할 것 같아요.

M: 그러세요. 기숙사로 양식을 가지고 가서 작성을 한 후 가능한 시간에 이곳으로 가지고 오세요.

W: 그렇게 할게요. 사실 크게 급한 일은 아니라서요. 오, 현금도 받으시나요?

M: 이제는 받지 않아요. 신용카드만 받고 있죠.

W: 그렇군요. 알려 주셔서 감사합니다. 내일 올 때 잊지 않고 카드를 가지고 올게요. 정말 고맙습니다.

M: 천만에요. 좋은 하루 보내세요.

✎ Summary Note

A

❶ 24 hours

❷ credit card

B

The student needs some copies of her transcript, and the man says that it will take twenty-four hours to prepare them. He adds that she can write the addresses of the places where they should send the transcript to on the form. The student says she did not realize the Registrar's office would do that. The man says to take the form back to her dorm, fill out it, and return later. The student asks about paying with cash, but the man says that the office only accepts credit cards.

Exercise 2   1 ⓓ   2 ⓓ   p.104

Script 🎧 04-09

M Student: Hello, Professor Winthrop. May I talk to you?

W Professor: Go ahead.

M: I'm curious about the grade on the report we just got back.

W: Is there a problem?

M: You gave me a B, but I think I deserved a higher grade. I thought I was going to get an A.

W: Why don't you tell me why you think you deserve an A?

M: First, there were only two grammatical mistakes in the report, so you shouldn't have knocked me down for that. My thesis was very clear. My thesis was that England actually won the War of 1812. I supported it with a lot of evidence, I cited all my work, and I fulfilled your page requirements, so I don't understand how you gave me a B.

W: Okay, how about telling me what was not good in that paper?

M: Yes, sometimes my writing is not clear, I know that's not one of my strong points. I didn't use very many primary sources. I know you wanted us to use that, but I couldn't find a lot.

W: First, your paper stated that England won the War of 1812. You also pointed out all the military and political victories England had as well as the treaty that ended the war, right?

M: Yes.

W: Well, the assignment was to describe how a war affected the people of the countries fighting it. Did you talk about the people of Canada, America, or England?

M: No, I didn't.

W: That is why you got a B. Understand?

M: Ah, yes. I see your point.

해석

M Student: 안녕하세요, Winthrop 교수님. 말씀을 나눌 수 있을까요?

W Professor: 얘기해 보세요.

M: 방금 받은 보고서의 점수에 대해 궁금한 점이 있어서요.

W: 문제가 있나요?

M: 제게 B를 주셨는데, 저는 제가 더 높은 점수를 받을 자격이 있다고 생각해요. A를 받을 것으로 생각하고 있었죠.

W: 왜 A를 받을 자격이 있는지 제게 이야기해 볼까요?

M: 우선, 보고서에 문법적인 실수가 두 개 밖에 없었기 때문에 그로 인한 감점은 없어야 했죠. 제 주제는 매우 분명했어요. 제 주제는 1812년 전쟁에서 실제로 영국이 승리했다는 것이었죠. 이를 많은 증거로 뒷받침했고, 보고서 전반에 걸쳐 자료를 인용했고, 페이지 분량 조건도 지켰기 때문에, 저는 교수님께서 제게 왜 B를 주셨는지 이해가 가지 않아요.

W: 좋아요, 그 보고서에서 모자란 부분을 이야기해 볼까요?

M: 네, 제 글이 때때로 명확하지가 않아요. 그것이 제 강점이 아니라는 점은 저도 알고 있어요. 1차 자료들도 그다지 많이 사용하지 않았고요. 교수님께서 저희가 그러한 자료를 사용하기를 바란다는 점은 알고 있지만, 많이 찾을 수가 없었어요.

W: 우선, 학생의 보고서는 1812년 전쟁에서 영국이 승리했다고 주장했어요. 학생은 또한 영국이 거둔 모든 군사적 그리고 정치적 승리와 함께 전쟁을 끝낸 조약도 언급했고요, 그렇죠?

M: 네.

W: 음, 과제는 전쟁에 참전한 국가의 사람들에게 전쟁이 어떠한 영향을 끼쳤는지 설명하라는 것이었어요. 캐나다, 미국, 혹은 영국의 국민들에 대해 논의했나요?

M: 아니요, 그러지 않았어요.

W: 그것이 바로 학생이 B를 받은 이유예요. 이해가 되나요?

M: 아, 네. 무슨 말씀인지 알겠습니다.

✎ Summary Note

A

❶ grammatical mistakes

❷ primary sources

❸ Did not discuss people

B

A student talks to a professor about his grade on a paper. He believes his paper was good, and he deserved an A on it. He tells the professor why his paper was good. He had few grammatical errors, a clear thesis, and lots of evidence, he cited his work, and he wrote the appropriate length. The professor asks him the details of his paper, which was about the War of 1812. The student did not do the assignment properly because he did not discuss the people affected by the war.

Exercise 3 1 Ⓐ 2 Ⓓ   p.106

Script 🎧 04-10

> **W Student:** Hello, Professor Gray. I have an appointment with you.
>
> **M Professor:** Sure. Your name is Heather, right?
>
> **W:** Yes, I want to change my major, but I was told I must get permission from you.
>
> **M:** You are majoring in history, right?
>
> **W:** Yes, but I want to change to chemistry. What do I need to do?
>
> **M:** First, tell me why you want to change.
>
> **W:** When I was a freshman, I really liked history, so I decided to study it. In fact, I still like it a lot. I am sure I will keep taking history classes. But I have been thinking about my financial future a lot lately. **Honestly, history doesn't seem like a good major.**
>
> **M:** Keep going.
>
> **W:** I've recently become interested in being a doctor, so I have decided I go to medical school. History won't help me get into medical school, but chemistry will.
>
> **M:** How long have you thought about this?
>
> **W:** Hmm, about six weeks. My cousin is in medical school, and we talked about what it would take to get in and become a doctor.
>
> **M:** Okay, that is good, but what will you do with your degree if you don't get into medical school?
>
> **W:** I have thought about that, too. There is big demand for nurses. I also am getting a minor in education, so I could be a teacher. Or I could be a temporary teacher until I get into medical school.
>
> **M:** Have you taken any chemistry classes?
>
> **W:** Yes, I have. I got an A in general chemistry and a B+ in chemical analysis. I actually have a note from a chemistry professor supporting me.
>
> **M:** Sounds good. Let's get you changed.

해석

W Student: 안녕하세요, Gray 교수님. 교수님과 약속이 되어 있어서요.

M Professor: 그래요. 학생 이름이 Heather죠, 맞나요?

W: 네, 저는 전공을 바꾸려고 하는데, 교수님의 허락이 필요하다는 말을 들어서요.

M: 역사를 전공하고 있죠, 그렇죠?

W: 네, 하지만 화학으로 바꾸고 싶어요. 어떻게 하면 되나요?

M: 우선, 왜 전공을 바꾸려고 하는지 얘기해 보세요.

W: 1학년 때에는 역사가 정말 좋아서 역사를 공부하기로 결심을 했죠. 사실 지금도 역사를 무척 좋아해요. 역사 수업도 계속해서 꼭 들을 생각이고요. 하지만 최근에 제 미래의 재정적인 상황에 대해 생각해 보았어요. 솔직히 말씀을 드리면, 역사는 좋은 전공처럼 보이지 않더군요.

M: 계속 얘기해 보세요.

W: 저는 최근에 의사가 되는 것에 관심을 갖게 되어서 의대에 진학하기로 결심했어요. 의대 입학에는 역사가 도움이 안 되겠지만, 화학은 도움이 될 거예요.

M: 그에 대해 얼마나 오랫동안 생각해 보았나요?

W: 음, 6주 정도요. 제 사촌이 의대를 다니는데, 의대에 들어가고 의사가 되기 위해 무엇이 필요한지 이야기를 나누어 봤어요.

M: 좋아요. 그건 좋지만, 의대에 입학을 하지 못한다면 학생 학위로 무엇을 할 건가요?

W: 그 점에 대해서도 생각해 봤어요. 간호사에 대한 수요도 많잖아요. 제 부전공이 교육학이기 때문에 교사가 될 수도 있고요. 아니면 의대에 입학하기 전까지 기간제 교사 일을 할 수도 있을 거예요.

M: 화학 수업을 들은 적은 있나요?

W: 네, 있어요. 일반 화학에서는 A를 받았고 화학 분석에서는 B+를 받았어요. 실제로 한 화학과 교수님께서 저를 격려해 주신 메모도 가지고 있어요.

M: 좋아요. 그럼 전공을 바꾸기로 하죠.

📝 Summary Note

A

> ❶ a nurse or a teacher
>
> ❷ chemistry

B

A student made an appointment to talk to her advisor. She is currently a history major, but she wants to change to become a chemistry major. She needs permission to change her major. The advisor asks her some basic questions to make sure she is making the right decision. The advisor determines the student has thought about it long enough, the change will help her future, and the student has performed well. The advisor decides the change in majors is good for the student and grants her permission.

Exercise 4 1 Ⓒ 2 Ⓑ   p.108

Script 🎧 04-11

> **W Student:** Professor Lawson, I have a question about today's class.
>
> **M Professor:** Sure, Lily. What is it?
>
> **W:** I'm a bit confused about something you said about Roman roads. You mentioned that some of the roads they built still exist today. But, uh, but that's not actually

possible, is it? I mean, they built those roads around 2,000 years ago.

M: It actually is possible. The Romans, you see, were master builders. Just look at how many of their old buildings are still standing.

W: Oh . . . That's a good point.

M: To get back to the roads, the Romans had a very sophisticated way of making them.

W: How so?

M: Well, they didn't just level the ground and then put stones on the ground. Instead, there were several steps Roman builders took to make them. The result was strong roads that were used by Roman legions, merchants, and travelers all throughout the empire.

W: It sounds fascinating. Would you mind if I wrote my term paper about the roads?

M: Not at all. I think it's a great topic. In fact, you're the first student in nine or ten years to choose that topic.

W: Thanks. I'm looking forward to doing research on how they made the roads.

M: You should also focus on how the Romans used the roads. You see, the high quality of the roads was one reason that the empire was able to stay together for so long.

W: I'll be sure to do that. Thanks, sir.

해석

W Student: Lawson 교수님, 오늘 수업과 관련해서 질문이 하나 있어요.

M Professor: 그래요, Lily. 무엇인가요?

W: 로마의 도로에 대해 말씀하신 것 중에서 이해가 잘 가지 않는 것이 있어요. 로마인들이 건설한 도로 중 일부가 오늘날에도 존재한다고 말씀하셨잖아요. 하지만, 어, 실제로 그건 가능하지 않은 일이에요, 그렇죠? 제 말은, 로마인들이 약 2,000년 전에 그 도로들을 건설했으니까요.

M: 실제로 가능한 일이에요. 로마인들은, 알다시피, 뛰어난 건축가들이었어요. 얼마나 많은 오래된 건물들이 여전히 남아 있는지 보세요.

W: 오… 좋은 지적이군요.

M: 도로로 다시 돌아가면, 로마인들은 매우 정교한 방법으로 도로를 건설했어요.

W: 어떻게요?

M: 음, 단지 지면을 평평하게 만든 후 지면에 돌을 올려 놓았던 것이 아니에요. 대신 로마의 건축가들은 몇 차례의 단계를 거쳐 도로를 건설했어요. 그 결과 튼튼한 도로가 만들어졌고, 이는 로마 제국 전역에서 로마의 군대, 상인, 그리고 여행객들에 의해 이용되었죠.

W: 훌륭하군요. 제가 기말 보고서에 로마 도로에 관한 글을 써도 될까요?

M: 그럼요. 멋진 주제라고 생각해요. 사실 그러한 주제를 고른 학생은 9년 혹은 10년 동안 학생이 처음이에요.

W: 고맙습니다. 그들이 어떻게 도로를 건설했는지 빨리 조사해 보고 싶어요.

M: 로마인들이 도로를 어떻게 사용했는지에 대해서도 초점을 맞추어야 해요. 알겠지만, 도로의 높은 품질은 로마 제국이 그처럼 오랫동안 존속할 수 있었던

한 가지 이유였으니까요.

W: 꼭 그렇게 할게요. 감사합니다, 교수님.

✎ Summary Note

A

❶ Roman roads
❷ sophisticated

B

The student asks the professor how it is possible that Roman roads are still in existence since they were built 2,000 years ago. The professor says that the Romans were master builders as some of the old buildings are still standing. He notes that the Romans used sophisticated methods to build roads. They used several steps to make the roads. The student asks if she can write her term paper about Roman roads, and the professor agrees with her suggestion.

Exercises with Mid-Length Lectures

Exercise 1 1 Ⓓ 2 Ⓓ   p.110

Script 🎧 04-12

W Professor: Today, we are going to talk about the controls of an airplane. Umm, but as you know, I like to talk a bit about the history of things. People generally credit the Wright brothers for having accomplished the first manned flight of an airplane. **Their work is astonishing when you consider they had to do all their own research and there were no precedents for them to look at.** Even something as simple as controlling the airplane had to be imagined, tested, developed, and perfected.

Over the past 100 years, the technology of airplanes has changed, but the controls are still similar. Today, airplanes have three basic turns: turning up and down, turning left and right, and spinning. Airplanes turn by manipulating fins that are designed in their wings. When a pilot moves the fins in the air stream, they react with the air pressure to turn the aircraft.

You see, an airplane has three axes. A turn in the lateral axis can make the plane move up or down. A turn in the longitudinal axis can make the plane spin or roll. The third axis is the vertical axis. This turns the plane left or right.

Each axis has its own set of fins on the aircraft. To make a turn on the lateral or vertical axis, a pilot only needs to turn the fins in the direction of the desired turn. For example, if the pilot wants to turn left, he would turn the vertical axis left. The air stream that flows around the aircraft would change, and the aircraft would turn right.

In order to turn on the longitudinal axis, the pilot must do something a little different. For this axis, a turn is achieved by manipulating the fins in the same direction. To achieve a spin, the fins go in opposite directions. For example, to spin clockwise, the right fin would turn down, so the right side of the aircraft would drop. The left fin would turn right, so the left side of the aircraft would rise. With one side rising and one side dropping, the aircraft then would perform a spin or roll.

해석

W Professor: 오늘은 비행기의 조종 방식에 대해 이야기하려고 해요. 음, 그런데 아시다시피, 역사적인 이야기를 약간 하고자 합니다. 일반적으로 사람들은 비행기로 최초의 유인 비행을 한 사람이 라이트 형제라고 알고 있어요. 자신들이 모든 연구를 직접 해야 했고 그들이 참고할 만한 선례가 없었다는 점을 감안하면, 그들의 업적은 놀라운 것입니다. 심지어 비행기를 조종하는 것 같은 간단한 일도 상상을 하고, 실험을 해서, 발전시키고, 완성시켜야 했어요.

지난 100년 동안 항공기 기술은 변했지만 조종 방식은 거의 그대로 입니다. 오늘날 비행기는 세 가지 기본적인 방향 전환, 즉 상하 선회, 좌우 선회, 그리고 스피닝을 해요. 비행기는 날개에 달려 있는 핀을 조작해서 방향을 전환합니다. 조종사가 기류 속에서 핀을 움직이면 이들이 기압에 반응하여 비행기가 방향을 전환하게 되는 것이죠.

아시다시피 비행기에는 세 개의 축이 있어요. 횡축을 움직이면 비행기가 위아래로 움직일 수 있죠. 종축을 움직이는 경우에는 비행기가 스피닝이나 롤링을 할 수 있고요. 세 번째 축은 수직축입니다. 이 축은 비행기를 왼쪽이나 오른쪽으로 선회하게 만들죠.

항공기의 축은 각각 자신들의 핀들을 가지고 있습니다. 횡축 또는 수직축으로 방향을 전환하기 위해서는 조종사가 원하는 방향으로 핀을 움직이기만 하면 되죠. 예를 들어, 조종사가 좌회전을 하고자 한다면 수직축을 왼쪽으로 돌리면 됩니다. 그러면 항공기 주변에 흐르는 기류가 바뀌어 항공기가 오른쪽으로 방향을 틀게 되어요.

종축으로 방향을 전환하고자 하는 경우, 조종사는 약간 다르게 해야 합니다. 이 축의 경우 핀을 조작해서 동일한 방향으로 두어야 방향을 전환할 수 있습니다. 스피닝을 하려면 핀들이 반대 방향으로 움직여야 해요. 예를 들어 시계 방향으로 스피닝을 하기 위해서는 오른쪽 핀이 아래로 내려가서 항공기의 왼쪽 면이 올라가야 합니다. 한쪽은 올라가고 한쪽은 내려가면 항공기가 스피닝이나 롤링을 하게 되는 것이죠.

📝 Summary Note

A

❶ left or right
❷ spins
❸ turns up or down

B

Airplanes have three axes. Each axis has its own set of fins built into the aircraft's wings. The fins turn and react with the air stream to enable the airplane to turn. Three basic turns are capable. The airplane can turn up or down on the lateral axis, it can turn left or right on the vertical axis, and it can

spin on the longitudinal axis. For the first two types of turns, the fins turn in the direction of the desired turn. For a spin, the fins turn in opposite directions.

Exercise 2 1 ⓓ 2 ⓐ, ⓓ p.112

Script 🎧 04-13

M1 Professor: We have studied the causes of volcanoes. Now, I want to discuss the effects volcanoes have on the Earth. We can classify the effects into three different categories. Can anyone take a guess what they are?

W1 Student: Well, I am sure one of them is lava or is related to lava.

M1: Yes, you are right. There are a few different kinds of lava flows. All of them can completely destroy the immediate environment, but later they are very beneficial to plant life. Lava, when it is not hot, is a great fertilizer for plants. Volcanoes also emit lots of ash. But we will get into that tomorrow. What other categories are there besides lava and similar emissions?

M2 Student: What about other kinds of emissions, like gases? Volcanoes emit toxic gases, right?

M1: Yes, volcanoes emit many toxic and harmful gases, such as sulfur dioxide. Of course, not all the gases released are harmful, like water vapor, but others wreak havoc on our atmosphere. When sulfur dioxide reaches the atmosphere and reacts to change into sulfuric acid, it increases the Earth's albedo. What is the albedo?

W1: The albedo reflects the sun's heat. That reaction increases the Earth's albedo.

M1: Yes, why?

W1: Doesn't that mean volcanoes can actually reverse the effects of global warming and cool the Earth down?

M1: Very good. The eruptions of the past half century have actually increased the albedo enough to cool the surface of the Earth by half a degree Fahrenheit. But many of the gases emitted also destroy parts of the ozone layer and can create acid rain. What other effects are there?

M2: In the movies, all the animals run away before a volcano.

M1: You almost got it. There are volcanic side effects. There are events that occur because of volcanoes but are not emitted from volcanoes. Any guesses?

W2 Student: Earthquakes. Earthquakes and volcanoes occur near faults and often accompany each other. Sometimes volcanoes cause small earthquakes.

M1: Yes, there are also hot springs, geysers, fumaroles, and mud pots.

M1 Professor: 화산의 원인에 대해서는 공부해 보았습니다. 이제 화산이 지구에 미치는 영향에 대해 논의해 보고 싶군요. 어떤 영향을 미치는지 의견을 말해 볼 사람이 있나요?

W1 Student: 음, 한 가지 영향은 분명 용암이거나 용암과 관련된 것으로 알고 있어요.

M1: 네, 맞았어요. 용암류에는 몇 가지 종류가 있습니다. 이들 모두 주변 환경을 완전히 파괴해 버릴 수 있지만, 나중에는 식물에게 매우 유익하게 되죠. 용암은, 뜨겁지 않은 경우, 식물에게 좋은 비료가 됩니다. 화산은 또한 많은 재를 분출해 냅니다. 하지만 그에 대해서는 내일 살펴볼 거예요. 용암 및 그와 비슷한 분출물 이외에 또 어떤 것들이 있을까요?

M2 Student: 가스와 같은 다른 종류의 배출물은 어떨까요? 화산은 독성 가스를 분출합니다, 그렇죠?

M1: 네, 화산은 이산화황과 같은 해롭고 유독한 여러 가스를 분출해요. 물론 수증기와 같이 분출되는 모든 가스가 유해한 것은 아니지만, 기타 가스들은 대기에 극심한 피해를 입힙니다. 이산화황이 대기와 만나 반응을 일으키면 황산으로 변하는데, 이로써 지구의 알베도가 증가하게 됩니다. 알베도는 무엇일까요?

W1: 알베도는 태양열을 반사시키는 정도입니다. 그러한 반응으로 지구의 알베도가 증가하게 되죠.

M1: 그래요, 왜 그렇죠?

W1: 그렇게 되면 화산이 실제로 지구 온난화의 효과를 상쇄시켜 지구를 차갑게 만들 수 있기 때문이 아닌가요?

M1: 아주 잘 대답했어요. 실제로 지난 반 세기 동안 있었던 화산 분출로 알베도가 증가해서 지구의 표면 온도가 화씨 0.5도 정도 감소했어요. 하지만 방출되는 많은 가스들로 인해 오존층의 일부가 파괴되고 있으며, 그로 인해 산성비가 내릴 수도 있어요. 다른 효과로는 어떤 것이 있을까요?

M2: 영화에서는 화산이 불출하기 전에 모든 동물들이 도망을 가던데요.

M1: 거의 정답이군요. 화산의 부작용이 존재합니다. 화산 때문에 일어나는 현상이 존재하지만, 화산에서 분출되는 것은 아니죠. 짐작이 가는 사람이 있나요?

W2 Student: 지진이요. 지진과 화산은 단층 근처에서 발생하는데, 종종 함께 일어나죠. 때로는 화산이 소규모의 지진을 일으키기도 하고요.

M1: 네, 그리고 온천, 간헐천, 분기공, 그리고 머드 포트도 있습니다.

✏️ Summary Note

A

❶ Fertilizer

❷ ozone

❸ geysers

B

Volcanoes have three basic types of effects on the Earth. First, volcanoes produce lava. Lava can destroy or severely damage anything that lies in its path. Later, lava works as a good fertilizer. Second, volcanoes emit several gases into the atmosphere. Some of the gases are beneficial. They can help increase the albedo. Other gases can damage the ozone layer or create acid rain. Last, there are several other side effects, such as geysers and earthquakes.

Exercise 3 1 ⓓ 2 ⓑ p.114

Script 🎧 04-14

W Professor: Today, we are going to compare two different species that are the same genus. The two animals we will compare are the Olympic marmot and the Bobak marmot. First, they live a world apart. The Olympic marmot lives in a small area in North America. It lives on the Olympic Peninsula in the state of Washington. Excluding Alaska, it is the northwesternmost part of the United States. Oh, yeah, and Hawaii is farther west. The Bobak marmot's home is on the other side of the world in the steppes of Russia and Central Asia. Even though they are both marmots, they prefer different areas to live. The Olympic lives in alpine meadows near the Olympic Mountains. The Bobak marmot is not like most marmots and lives in rolling grasslands and has also been known to live near cultivated fields.

Let's go on to defense calls. All species of marmots have calls and whistles to alert others of predators. The Olympic marmot has much more developed calls though. Most research shows that the Bobak marmot only has one call. This call communicates any and all forms of predators. Some studies have hinted that its call can change depending on the terrain. In flat areas, the call is slow. In rugged terrain, the calls tend to be faster.

Umm, okay, the Olympic marmot's calls are much more advanced. Its calls are categorized as ascending, descending, flat, and trills. The different calls are used to designate the type of predator, for example, a bird of prey or a bear. The trills are believed to be used for very dangerous situations.

The Olympic marmot's natural enemies are mainly the coyote and the puma and, to a lesser extent, birds of prey and bobcats. The Bobak marmot's natural enemies are similar animals: large cats and packs of hunting canines. This may sound strange, but the Bobak marmot has been a source of emergency food for many Russian people. In times of extreme hardship and famine, the Bobak marmot has been used by people to provide both food and clothing. Due to this, you can guess that the Olympic marmot is less shy around people.

W Professor: 오늘은 동일한 속에 속하는 두 개의 서로 다른 종을 비교해 볼 거예요. 비교할 두 동물은 올림픽마멋과 보박마멋입니다. 우선 이들은 서로 떨어져 있는 곳에서 살아요. 올림픽마멋은 북미의 좁은 지역에서 서식합니다. 워싱턴주의 올림픽반도에서 서식을 하죠. 알래스카를 제외하면 이곳은 미국에서 가장 북서쪽 지역이에요. 오, 그래요, 더 서쪽에는 하와이가 있군요. 보박마멋의 서식지는 지구의 반대편인 러시아와 중앙아시아의 스텝 지방에 있습니다. 이들 모두 마멋이지만 선호하는 거주 지역은 서로 달라요. 올림픽마멋은 올림픽산맥 근처 고산 지대의 초원 지역에서 서식하죠. 보박마멋은 대부분의 마멋과는 달리 완만한 경사가 있는 초원 지대에 사는데, 또한 경작지 근처에서도 사는 것으로도 알

려져 있습니다.

울음소리로 넘어가 보죠. 모든 마멋종들은 울음소리 또는 날카로운 소리로 다른 개체들에게 포식자를 경고해 줍니다. 하지만 올림픽마멋의 울음소리는 훨씬 발달되어 있어요. 대부분의 연구에 따르면 보박마멋은 한 가지의 울음소리만 냅니다. 이 소리는 온갖 종류의 포식자들을 모두 알려 주어요. 일부 연구들은 지형에 따라 이러한 소리가 변할 수도 있다는 점을 암시합니다. 평지에서는 울음소리가 느립니다. 울퉁불퉁한 곳에서는 울음소리가 보다 빨라지는 경향을 보이죠.

음, 그래요, 올림픽마멋의 울음소리는 훨씬 발달되어 있어요. 이들의 소리는 올라가는 소리, 내려가는 소리, 높낮이가 일정한 소리, 그리고 떨리는 소리로 구분됩니다. 각기 다른 소리는, 예컨대 맹금류 또는 곰과 같이, 포식자의 종류를 나타내기 위해 사용되어요. 떨리는 소리는 가장 위험한 상황을 알릴 때 사용되는 것으로 알려져 있습니다.

올림픽마멋의 천적은 주로 코요테와 퓨마이며, 보다 적기는 하지만, 맹금류와 밥캣도 이들의 천적이에요. 보박마멋의 천적도 유사한 동물들로, 몸집이 큰 고양이과 동물과 사냥을 하는 개과 동물 무리들이 여기에 해당됩니다. 이상하게 들릴 수도 있지만, 많은 러시아인들이 보박마멋을 비상 식량으로 사용해 왔어요. 극심한 고난의 시기 및 기근이 찾아오면 사람들은 보박마멋을 이용해 음식 및 의복을 구했습니다. 이러한 점에서 올림픽마멋이 사람들을 덜 무서워한다는 점을 짐작하실 수 있을 거예요.

✏ Summary Note

A

❶ complex
❷ rolling grasslands
❸ clothes

B

Two different species of marmots are the Olympic marmot and the Bobak marmot. The Olympic marmot lives near the Olympic Mountains in the Olympic Peninsula in the state of Washington. The Bobak marmot lives in open grasslands in Central Asia and Russia. Both animals have calls to warn other marmots of a predator, but the Olympic marmot's calls are more advanced and recognize different kinds of predators. The Bobak marmot has been eaten by Russian people during famine, and it has also been used as a source of fur for clothes.

Exercise 4 1 ⓒ 2 ⓐ p.116

Script 🎧 04-15

M1 Professor: Let's talk about what some people consider the **most popular sport in the United States.** Football was derived from soccer. Versions of soccer were played all over the world. The Chinese played a game called *cuju* over 2,200 years ago. Native Americans were playing a game like soccer before Europeans arrived in the Americas.

W Student: How much influence did the Native Americans have on football? Did settlers play with them?

M1: I am sure settlers and Native Americans played, but that had almost no influence on the development of football. Football became popular due to elite college students playing the game around the 1820s. It was mainly an unorganized version of mob-style soccer. Harvard played a game similar to rugby. In 1874, McGill University of Montreal played Harvard. Harvard adopted the Canadian version of football, which was much more similar to today's football. Harvard spread that style of football to other schools, who were playing a soccer-style game.

M2 Student: Do you mean Canadians were playing American-style football before Americans?

M1: Not quite. They were playing a game similar to rugby, but they did influence the development of football. By 1883, a coach named Walter Camp made some major changes to the game, such as reducing the number of players from fifteen to eleven, adding the line of scrimmage, and adding a rule that if the ball is not moved five yards after three downs, the other team would gain control of the ball. This rule was created to thwart Yale's strategy of controlling the ball without attempting to score.

W: Didn't Harvard and Yale dislike each other?

M1: Football was very dangerous. Harvard invented the flying wedge, which almost killed seven Yale players in one game. Eighteen players were killed in 1905. This led to more changes, such as the forward pass and adding a fourth down. After this, the game became pretty similar to the football that is played today.

해석

M1 Professor: 몇몇 사람들이 미국에서 가장 인기 있는 스포츠라고 생각하는 것에 대해 이야기를 해 보죠. 미식축구는 축구에서 유래되었어요. 전 세계 각지에서 다양한 형태의 축구가 행해지고 있습니다. 중국에서는 2,200년도 더 전에 쿠주라고 불렸던 경기를 했어요. 유럽인들이 미 대륙에 도착하기 전에 미 원주민들도 축구와 비슷한 경기를 하고 있었죠.

W Student: 미 원주민들이 미식축구에 얼마나 많은 영향을 끼쳤나요? 정착민들도 그들과 경기를 했나요?

M1: 분명 정착민들과 미 원주민들이 경기를 했을 것으로 생각되지만, 그러한 점은 미식축구의 발달에 거의 영향을 끼치지 못했어요. 미식축구는 1820년대 무렵 경기를 하던 엘리트 대학생들 때문에 인기가 높아졌죠. 주로 무질서하고 몰려다니는 식의 축구였어요. 하버드 대학에서 럭비와 비슷한 경기를 했습니다. 1874년 몬트리얼의 맥길 대학이 하버드 대학과 경기를 하게 되었어요. 하버드 대학은 오늘날의 미식 축구와 훨씬 더 유사했던 캐나다식의 축구를 도입하게 되었죠. 하버드 대학은 이러한 방식의 축구를, 축구와 비슷한 방식의 경기를 하고 있던 다른 대학들에게 전파시켰습니다.

M2 Student: 캐나다인들이 미국인들보다 먼저 미식축구를 했다는 말씀이신 가요?

M1: 꼭 그렇지는 않아요. 캐나다인들은 럭비와 비슷한 경기를 하고 있었지만, 이들이 미식축구의 발달에 영향을 끼쳤죠. 1883년경 월터 캠프라는 코치가 경기에, 예컨대 선수 수를 15명에서 11명으로 줄이고, 스크리미 선을 추가하고, 세

번의 다운 후에 공을 5야드 이상 이동시키지 않으면 상대팀에게 공을 넘겨 주는 규칙을 추가하는 등의 변화를 가져왔습니다. 위 규칙은 득점 시도 없이 공을 가지고 있으려는 예일 대학의 전략을 무력화시키기 위해 만들어진 것이었어요.

W: 하버드대와 예일대는 서로를 싫어하지 않았나요?

M1: 미식 축구는 대단히 위험했습니다. 하버드는 플라잉 웨지를 고안해 냈는데, 이 때문에 한 경기에서 7명의 예일대 선수가 죽을 뻔 하기도 했어요. 1905년에는 18명의 선수가 사망을 했죠. 이로 인해 포워드 패스 및 네 번째 다운이 추가되는 등의 더 많은 변화들이 생겨났어요. 그 후에 경기가 오늘날 실시되고 있는 미식축구 경기와 상당히 비슷해졌습니다.

📝 Summary Note

A

❶ Walter Camp
❷ many deaths

B

American football is derived from European soccer. In the 1820s, American universities made the sport popular, but they played a game similar to soccer. Harvard played a game more like rugby. Harvard then played a Canadian football team and adopted the Canadian style of football. Harvard passed on this style to other American universities. Walter Camp changed the game even further by adding downs and the line of scrimmage and by reducing the number of players. The large number of deaths resulted in more changes, like the forward pass and a fourth down.

Integrated Listening & Speaking   p.118

A

Script 🎧 04-16

M Professor: Volcanoes have three different kinds of effects on the Earth. The first category is the lava and the ash that are emitted from the volcano. Lava can cause lots of damage to the surrounding environment. Later, after it has cooled, lava is a good fertilizer for plants. The second category is the different gas emissions from the volcano. Many of the gases emitted are toxic or harmful to the ozone layer, like sulfur dioxide. Other gases help increase the albedo in the ozone layer, and that causes the Earth's temperature to cool. The third category is the side effects the volcano can have, such as earthquakes, geysers, and hot springs.

1 a. The gas emissions from volcanoes increase the albedo.
b. The albedo is increased by the gas emissions from volcanoes.

2 a. Lava destroys the surrounding environment and then serves as a good fertilizer for plants when it cools.
b. At first, lava can destroy the surrounding environment, and then it helps plants by being a good fertilizer after it cools.

3 a. One of the gases emitted from a volcano is sulfur dioxide.
b. During an eruption, volcanoes will emit gases such as sulfur dioxide.

B

Script 🎧 04-17

W Professor: I'd like to discuss the differences between two animals. They are different species but the same genus. The first is the Olympic marmot, which lives on the Olympic Peninsula in the state of Washington. The other is the Bobak marmot. The Bobak marmot lives in Central Asia and Russia. The Olympic marmot lives in alpine meadows near mountains. The Bobak marmot lives in rolling grasslands and near cultivated fields. Both animals have a call to alert other marmots of the presence of predators. The Bobak marmot has one call for all predators. The Olympic marmot has several calls to distinguish different types of predators. The Bobak marmot has been used as a source of food and clothes by some people.

1 a. The Olympic marmot lives in alpine meadows near mountains.
b. The Olympic marmot's home is close to mountains in alpine meadows.

2 a. The purpose of the marmot's calls is to warn other marmots of predators.
b. The marmot will call other marmots because a predator is nearby.

3 a. The Bobak marmot has served people as an emergency source of food and clothes.
b. People have used the Bobak marmot to eat and make clothes during times of emergencies.

Mini TOEFL iBT Practice Test   p.120

1 Ⓑ	2 Ⓐ	3 Ⓓ	4 Ⓒ	5 Ⓒ
6 Ⓓ	7 Ⓓ	8 Ⓐ	9 Ⓑ	10 Ⓓ
11 Ⓑ				

Script 🎧 04-18

M Student: Excuse me, Professor Donovan. Could I have a moment of your time?

W Professor: Sure, Peter. But just a moment. I've got to teach my seminar in about five minutes.

M: Thanks so much. This shouldn't take too long.

W: Great. So . . . what brings you here?

M: I just got offered an internship at a local company, but I'm not sure if I should accept it.

W: Really? Why would you turn it down?

M: Well, the company is Landis Manufacturing. You've probably heard of it. The internship is in the Public Relations Department, so it's exactly what I want. However . . .

W: However what?

M: I'm still waiting to hear from three other companies that I applied to. I'd much rather do an internship at any of them since they are located in my hometown. That way, I can live at home.

W: Why don't you ask Landis to wait a bit?

M: That's the problem. My contact there told me that the company needs a response by tomorrow, or the position will get offered to someone else.

W: Did you speak with the other companies?

M: I did. All three of them told me that they were going to make a final decision by next Monday. **One of them hinted that I would probably be pleased with the results.**

W: That's a good sign. So what are you going to do?

M: I don't really like being pressured into a decision, so I'm probably going to turn down the Landis offer since the company is unwilling to let me wait a few days. I think that's the best thing to do.

W: It sounds like you've made up your mind. And just so you know, I agree with your decision. Okay, uh, time's up.

해석

M Student: 실례합니다. Donovan 교수님. 잠시 시간을 내 주실 수 있으신가요?

W Professor: 물론이죠, Peter. 하지만 잠깐 동안만이에요. 약 5분 후에 세미나 수업에 가야 해서요.

M: 정말 감사합니다. 오래 걸리지 않을 거예요.

W: 잘 되었군요. 그러면… 무슨 일 때문에 온 거죠?

M: 인근의 한 회사로부터 인턴쉽 자리를 제안받았는데, 제가 이를 수락해야 할지 잘 모르겠어요.

W: 정말인가요? 왜 거절하려고 하죠?

M: 음, 그 회사는 Landis Manufacturing이에요. 아마도 들어본 적이 있으실 거예요. 인턴쉽 자리는 홍보부 자리라서, 정확히 제가 원하는 것이죠. 하지만…

W: 하지만 뭔가요?

M: 저는 제가 지원한 세 곳의 다른 회사로부터 답변을 기다리고 있는 중이에요. 이들은 제 고향에 있기 때문에 그중 한 곳의 인턴쉽 자리를 선택하는 편이 나을 것 같아요. 그러면 집에서 지낼 수 있으니까요.

W: Landis 측에 잠시 기다려 달라고 요청해 보는 건 어때요?

M: 그것이 문제예요. 그곳 직원은 제게 내일까지 회사에 답을 주지 않으면 다른 사람에게 그 자리를 제안할 것이라고 말했어요.

W: 다른 회사들과는 얘기를 했나요?

M: 했어요. 세 곳 모두 다음 주 월요일에 최종 결정을 내릴 것이라고 말하더군요. 그중 한 곳은 제가 결과에 아마도 만족할 것이라는 힌트를 주기도 했고요.

W: 좋은 징조네요. 그러면 어떻게 할 건가요?

M: 저는 압박을 받아서 결정을 내리는 것을 정말 좋아하지 않는데, Landis는 제게 며칠 더 기다릴 수 있는 시간을 주지 않으려 하기 때문에 그 회사의 제안은 아마도 거절하게 될 것 같아요. 그것이 최선이라고 생각해요.

W: 이미 마음을 정한 것처럼 들리는군요. 그리고 알겠지만 저도 학생 결정에 찬성이에요. 좋아요, 어, 시간이 다 되었군요.

Script 🎧 04-19

W Professor: Let's talk about current American houses. Current American houses are very different from the housing styles of the past a few hundred years. The biggest change in housing style comes from the locations of houses. 100 years ago, people lived in the countryside or in cities. Lately, however, there has been a trend of people moving into suburbs. Why is this important?

M Student: Well, the suburbs are cheaper, and there are fewer people.

W: How are the suburbs cheaper? Do you mean buying a pizza at a lower price affects houses?

M: Of course not. Hmm, well, the cost of land is cheaper.

W: Yes. Exactly. Land costs a lot less in suburbs. Land is also more available there. That means houses can get bigger without needing to build more stories. There are two big things there. First, there are no more homes built above stores. Those second-story homes are only located in the cities. Next, houses can be built on larger areas of land for cheaper prices. This means more people can afford large homes. What technological developments have changed American homes since the turn of the century?

M: I am sure there are many. There have been many changes in the kitchen.

W: Not really the kitchen, but you are close. Fireplaces have been replaced by heaters, meaning most homes don't have fireplaces, or they are just for decoration. Many American families now have more than one car, so they frequently have multi-car garages. There have been social changes as well. The middle of the twentieth century gave rise to the nuclear family. In addition, as farming became less popular, households have shrunk. The average family has only two or three kids. Now bedrooms are bigger and more personal. Many families have fewer people at home but bigger houses, so bedrooms often have only one or two people in them. This is a big contrast to the bedrooms on farms or in cities with several people in one room.

M: Why do all the houses in suburbs seem to be identical?

W: The reason is that they are built very quickly. There is a huge demand by people who want to move out of the cities, so houses are not individually designed and built. Developers build several houses at the same time by using a similar style for each one. That is more efficient.

해석

W Professor: 현재의 미국 주택에 대해 논의해 보죠. 현재의 미국 주택은 몇 백 년 전의 주택 스타일과 크게 다릅니다. 주택 스타일의 가장 큰 변화는 주택의 위치에서 비롯되고 있어요. 100년 전에는 사람들이 시골이나 도시에서 살았습니다. 하지만 최근에는 사람들이 교외로 옮겨 가는 경향을 보이고 있죠. 이러한 점이 왜 중요할까요?

M Student: 음, 교외가 더 저렴하고 사람들도 더 적으니까요.

W: 어째서 교외가 더 저렴할까요? 더 낮은 가격에 피자를 사먹을 수 있다는 점이 주택에 영향을 끼친다는 뜻인가요?

M: 물론 아니죠. 음, 그러니까, 땅값이 더 싸잖아요.

W: 네. 정확해요. 교외의 땅값이 훨씬 저렴합니다. 구할 수 있는 땅도 더 많고요. 이는 층수를 높일 필요 없이 주택을 더 넓게 지을 수 있다는 점을 의미해요. 여기에는 두 가지 중요한 사실이 있습니다. 먼저, 상가 위에 더 이상 주택을 짓지 않습니다. 2층에 있는 주택은 도시에만 존재해요. 다음으로, 보다 저렴한 가격으로 보다 넓은 대지 위에 집을 지을 수가 있어요. 이는 보다 많은 사람들이 넓은 주택을 소유할 수 있다는 점을 의미하죠. 세기가 바뀐 이후로 미국의 주택에 어떤 기술적인 변화들이 일어났을까요?

M: 틀림없이 여러 가지가 있을 것으로 생각해요. 주방에서 많은 변화들이 이루어졌죠.

W: 사실 주방은 아니지만 정답에 가까웠어요. 벽난로는 히터로 대체되었는데, 이는 대부분의 가정에 더 이상 벽난로가 존재하지 않거나 이들이 단지 장식용으로 사용된다는 점을 의미합니다. 미국의 다수 가족들이 현재 한 대 이상의 차를 소유하고 있기 때문에 여러 대의 차를 수용할 수 있는 차고가 있는 경우도 많습니다. 뿐만 아니라 사회적인 변화도 있었어요. 20세기 중반에 핵가족이 생겨났습니다. 또한 농사를 짓는 경우가 줄어들면서 세대의 크기도 줄어들었어요. 평균적인 가정의 경우 자녀수가 두 명 내지 세 명이죠. 현재 침실은 더 커졌고 보다 사적인 공간이 되었어요. 주택에 거주하는 가족 구성원 수도 줄어들었기 때문에 침실에는 한 명이나 두 명만 거주하는 경우가 많습니다. 이는 한 방에 여러 명이 지내는 농장 혹은 도시의 침실과 큰 대조를 이루죠.

M: 왜 교외에 있는 집들은 모두 똑같이 생겼나요?

W: 매우 빠르게 지어졌기 때문입니다. 도시를 벗어나고자 하는 사람들에 의한 수요가 막대하기 때문에 주택들이 개별적으로 설계되고 지어지지 못해요. 개발업자들은 비슷한 스타일을 사용해서 동시에 여러 채의 주택을 짓습니다. 그게 더 효과적이죠.

Vocabulary Check-Up

p.125

A
1	ⓞ	2	Ⓑ	3	Ⓖ	4	Ⓔ	5	Ⓓ
6	Ⓘ	7	Ⓐ	8	Ⓙ	9	Ⓒ	10	Ⓜ
11	Ⓝ	12	Ⓛ	13	Ⓕ	14	Ⓗ	15	Ⓚ

A
| 1 | Ⓔ | 2 | Ⓑ | 3 | Ⓓ | 4 | Ⓒ | 5 | Ⓐ |

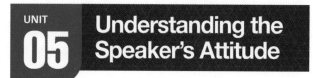

UNIT 05 Understanding the Speaker's Attitude

Basic Drill

p.128

Drill 1 Ⓐ

Script 🎧 05-02

M Dormitory Security Officer: Hello. Is there something that I can help you with?

W Student: I sure hope so. I just tried to gain access to my room, but the key card won't work. I don't know what the problem is. Here is the card.

M: Hmm . . . It doesn't appear to be damaged at all. When did it last work?

W: The card worked fine about an hour ago. Do you think that you could come up to my room and see if you can get it to work properly?

M: I'm not permitted to leave this spot until my replacement arrives.

W: Ah, I see. I'll try the student housing office and see if someone there can assist me.

해석

M Dormitory Security Officer: 안녕하세요. 제가 도와 드릴 일이라도 있나요?

W Student: 도와 주시면 좋겠어요. 조금 전에 제 방에 들어가려고 했는데, 카드키가 작동하지 않더군요. 무슨 문제인지 모르겠어요. 카드는 여기 있고요.

M: 흠… 손상된 부분은 전혀 없어 보이네요. 마지막으로 작동한 건 언제였나요?

W: 약 한 시간 전에는 잘 작동했어요. 제 방으로 오셔서 제대로 작동하는지 확인해 주실 수 있으신가요?

M: 교대가 올 때까지는 제가 자리를 비울 수가 없어요.

W: 아, 그러시군요. 그럼 기숙사 사무실에 가서 그곳에 있는 분이 도움을 주실 수 있는지 알아볼게요.

Script 🎧 05-03

M Student: Professor Andre, I need to speak to you about my interview project.

W Professor: Yes, Paul? What's going on?

M: As you know, I was scheduled to interview Nelson Waterford, the mayor of the city, tomorrow. However, his office just called me and canceled because he's going to be out of town for a week.

W: That's terrible news, especially since this assignment is due on Friday.

M: What can I do?

W: Let me make a couple of calls. I know some people in the city government. I'll arrange for you to interview someone else tomorrow. I'll email you as soon as I get some results.

해석

M Student: Andre 교수님, 제 인터뷰 프로젝트와 관련해서 말씀을 나눠야 할 것 같아요.

W Professor: 네, Paul? 무슨 일인가요?

M: 아시겠지만, 저는 내일 우리 시의 시장인 Nelson Waterford 씨와 인터뷰를 하기로 되어 있었어요. 하지만 그분께서 일주일 동안 시에 계시지 않을 예정이라 조금 전에 시장실에서 제게 전화를 해서 약속을 취소시켰어요.

W: 이번 과제의 마감일이 금요일이라는 점에서 특히 좋지 않은 소식이로군요.

M: 제가 어떻게 하면 될까요?

W: 제가 전화를 한두 통 해 볼게요. 시청에서 근무하는 몇몇 사람들을 알고 있거든요. 학생이 내일 다른 사람과 인터뷰를 할 수 있도록 자리를 마련해 보죠. 결과를 알게 되는 대로 학생에게 이메일을 보낼게요.

Script 🎧 05-04

M Professor: Hi, Jennifer. Can I speak to you for a moment?

W Student: Sure, Professor Kline. What is it?

M: Let's take a look at this report you handed in yesterday. I can't accept it from you.

W: Oh, but why? I worked so hard on it.

M: That may be the case, but you forgot two very important requirements. First of all, you didn't cite your sources.

W: Aha, I see. I can go back and do that easily.

M: Secondly, this paper is single spaced. I specifically told you I needed your reports to be double spaced because I need the extra space to write my comments between the lines.

W: Okay. I'll fix it right away and hand it back to you after lunch.

해석

M Professor: 안녕하세요, Jennifer. 잠깐 이야기할 시간이 있나요?

W Student: 물론이죠, Kline 교수님. 무슨 일이신가요?

M: 어제 학생이 제출한 이 보고서를 살펴보죠. 제가 받을 수가 없어요.

W: 오, 왜죠? 저는 열심히 했는데요.

M: 그렇기는 하겠지만, 대단히 중요한 두 가지 요건을 잊었더군요. 우선, 학생은 출처를 밝히지 않았어요.

W: 아, 알겠습니다. 다시 가서 금방 해 올 수 있어요.

M: 두 번째로, 이 보고서의 줄 간격은 1이에요. 제가 줄 사이에 코멘트를 달 수 있도록 추가적인 공간이 필요하기 때문에 줄 간격을 2로 해 달라고 특별히 얘기를 했잖아요.

W: 알겠습니다. 바로 수정을 해서 점심 시간 이후에 다시 가져다 드릴게요.

Script 🎧 05-05

W Professor: Today, I want to tell you about Avram Noam Chomsky. He was born in Philadelphia in 1928. He most notably created the theory of generative grammar. This is considered to be one of the most significant contributions to the field of theoretical linguistics. But Chomsky is far better known for his political activism than his work in linguistics. He has strongly criticized the foreign policies of the United States and other governments. He describes himself as a libertarian socialist and sympathizer of anarcho-syndicalism. Chomsky is a key intellectual figure in left-wing politics in the United States. Between 1980 and 1992, Chomsky was the most cited living scholar. He is the eighth-most cited scholar overall.

해석

W Professor: 오늘은 아브람 노암 촘스키에 대해 공부하도록 하겠습니다. 그는 1928년 필라델피아에서 태어났어요. 생성 문법 이론을 만든 것으로 가장 잘 알려져 있죠. 이 이론은 이론언어학 분야에 가장 큰 공헌을 한 이론 중 하나라고 여겨지고 있습니다. 하지만 촘스키는 언어학에서의 업적보다 정치적인 활동으로 훨씬 더 잘 알려져 있어요. 그는 미국 및 다른 정부들의 외교 정책을 강력히 비판해 왔습니다. 그는 스스로를 자유주의적인 사회주의자이면서 무정부주의적 노동 운동의 지지자라고 설명해요. 촘스키는 미국의 좌파 성향의 인물들 중 핵심적인 지성인입니다. 1980년과 1992년 사이에는 현존하는 학자 중에서 가장 많이 인용된 학자였어요. 종합적으로는 여덟 번째로 많이 인용되고 있습니다.

Script 🎧 05-06

M Professor: That was a really big earthquake that hit

Asia yesterday, wasn't it? Do you know what impressed me? It was the fact that very few buildings collapsed. And not one single skyscraper fell down. Why is that? Well, those skyscrapers are marvels of modern engineering. You see, uh, most of the buildings constructed nowadays are essentially earthquake proof. They may sway back and forth, but they don't collapse. One reason for this is that the materials used are able to resist earthquakes better. Additionally, the foundations of the buildings are very flexible, which enable them to absorb seismic waves.

해석

M Professor: 어제 아시아에서 정말로 강력한 지진이 일어났죠, 그렇지 않나요? 제가 어떤 점에 큰 감명을 받았는지 아시나요? 무너진 건물이 거의 없었다는 사실이었어요. 그리고 고층 빌딩은 단 한 채도 무너지지 않았죠. 왜 그런걸까요? 음, 그러한 고층 건물들은 경이로운 현대 공학의 산물입니다. 아시다시피, 어, 오늘날 지어지는 대부분의 건물들은 필수적으로 내진 설계가 되어 있어요. 앞뒤로 흔들릴 수는 있지만 무너지지는 않죠. 그와 같은 한 가지 이유는 사용되는 자재들이 지진에 보다 잘 견딜 수 있기 때문이에요. 게다가 건물 토대가 매우 유연하기 때문에 건물들이 지진파를 흡수할 수 있습니다.

Drill 6 (A)

Script 🎧 05-07

M Professor: I want to spend some time discussing the manager-employee relationship. There are various styles of management that a manager can employ to accomplish his goals. Let's consider two very different styles of management. An autocratic manager makes all of the decisions. The advantage of this style is that all of the decisions are consistent. A danger of this style is that employees may become overly dependent on the manager. The opposite of the autocratic style is the laissez-faire style. This kind of manager simply allows the employees to manage themselves. This can bring out the best in highly creative individuals. But in many cases, it is not deliberate and is the result of poor management.

해석

M Professor: 잠시 관리자와 직원의 관계에 대해 논의해 보고자 해요. 관리자가 자신의 목표를 이루기 위해 사용할 수 있는 다양한 관리 방식이 존재합니다. 서로 크게 다른 두 가지 관리 방식에 대해 살펴보죠. 전제 군주와 같은 관리자는 모든 결정을 혼자서 내립니다. 이러한 방식의 장점은 모든 결정에 일관성이 있다는 점이에요. 이러한 방식의 위험성은 직원들이 관리자에게 지나치게 의존할 수도 있다는 점입니다. 전제 군주적인 관리 방식과 반대되는 것은 자유 방임형 방식이에요. 이러한 유형의 관리자는 직원들이 스스로 알아서 하도록 놔둡니다. 매우 창의적인 개인들이 있는 경우에는 이 방법이 최선의 결과를 낳을 수 있어요. 하지만 많은 경우, 이는 의도된 것이 아니며 부실한 관리의 결과입니다.

Exercises with Mid-Length Conversations

Exercise 1 1 (B) 2 (D) p.130

Script 🎧 05-08

W Student: Hi, Professor Caruso. May I have a moment of your time?

M Professor: Hello, Mary. What's up?

W: I'm working on my final project for my international business development class. I have to assemble a presentation as if it were a campaign to increase tourism for Guatemala. Since you're a professor of Latin American studies, I was hoping you might have some supplements that I could add to my presentation to spruce it up. You know, like some posters or brochures.

M: Hmm, let me think for a second. Well, I have an ancient Mayan spearhead and some examples of Stone Age pottery. Would those archaeological antiques be of any use if I loaned them to you?

W: Uh, those sound interesting. But I was hoping for something more modern. I was thinking you might have some big laminated posters, some enlarged photographs, or maybe some information about the tourism industry.

M: Aha, I see. You're doing a booth to educate people about visiting Guatemala. Okay, I can help. But I don't have the materials here. Let me give you the telephone number for the Guatemalan Consulate downtown. I know the deputy ambassador there. I'm sure she would be happy to furnish you with some public relations materials. I know the consulate has packets of posters and brochures that it hands out for free.

W: Thank you so much. That sounds like just what I need. I'll call your friend right away.

M: Sure, let me just check my rolodex here for Marta's phone number. I'll call her and put in a good word for you. She's always very helpful when I refer students. Let me tell you about one time. Last year, we took a study trip there, and two of my students lost their passports. There was a mix-up with immigration, and I called her. She got it all sorted out for us.

W: Wow, it's good to have connections.

M: You bet it is.

해석

W Student: 안녕하세요, Caruso 교수님. 잠깐 시간을 내 주실 수 있으신가요?

M Professor: 안녕하세요, Mary. 무슨 일이죠?

W: 저는 국제 비즈니스 개발 수업의 기말 프로젝트를 하고 있는 중이에요. 과테말라의 관광업을 증진시키기 위한 캠페인을 하는 것처럼 발표를 해야 하죠. 교수

님께서 라틴 아메리카학 교수님이시기 때문에 제 발표를 돋보이게 할 수 있는 보충 자료를 교수님께서 가지고 계시기를 바라고 있었어요. 아시겠지만, 포스터나 소책자같은 것이요.

M: 흠, 잠깐 생각해 볼게요. 음, 고대 마야의 창촉과 석기 시대의 그릇 샘플들이 좀 있어요. 그러한 고고학 유물들을 학생에게 빌려 주면 쓸모가 있을까요?

W: 어, 흥미롭게 들리네요. 하지만 저는 보다 현대적인 것을 기대하고 있었어요. 코팅된 대형 포스터, 확대된 사진, 혹은 관광업과 관련된 정보를 가지고 계실지도 모른다고 생각했어요.

M: 아하, 알겠어요. 사람들에게 과테말라 관광에 대해 알려 줄 부스를 운영할 예정이군요. 좋아요, 제가 도울 수 있어요. 하지만 여기에는 자료가 없어요. 시내에 있는 과테말라 영사관의 전화번호를 알려 줄게요. 제가 그곳의 부대사를 알고 있어요. 그녀가 기꺼이 홍보용 자료를 줄 것이라고 확신해요. 영사관에 무료로 배포하는 포스터와 소책자 세트가 있는 것으로 알고 있어요.

W: 정말 고맙습니다. 제게 꼭 필요한 정보처럼 들리는군요. 바로 전화해 봐야겠네요.

M: 그래요, 여기 명함 파일에서 Marta의 전화번호를 찾아볼게요. 제가 그녀에게 전화를 해서 학생을 위한 말을 해 둘게요. 제가 학생들 얘기를 하면 그녀가 항상 큰 도움을 주거든요. 한 번은 이런 적도 있었어요. 작년에 우리가 그곳으로 현장 학습을 갔는데, 두 명의 학생이 여권을 잃어 버렸어요. 출입국 심사 때 혼선이 생겨서 제가 그녀에게 전화를 걸었죠. 그랬더니 그녀가 다 해결해 주었어요.

W: 와, 아는 사람이 있다는 것은 좋은 일이에요.

M: 당연하죠.

✏ Summary Note

A

❶ her presentation

❷ posters and brochures

B

The student tells the professor that she is working on her final project for her international business development class. She needs to make a campaign to increase tourism to Guatemala. She asks her professor if he has any supplements she could use in the presentation. He offers her some archaeological antiques, but those are not what she is looking for. Then, he offers to connect her with the Guatemalan Consulate. He says that it will probably have some materials for her to use. Finally, he tells her a story about the time when his friend at the Guatemalan Consulate helped him.

Exercise 2 1 ⓑ 2 ⓒ p.132

Script 🎧 05-09

W Student: Pardon me, but I think I need to speak with someone in this office.

M Housing Office Employee: Sure. You can talk to me.

W: Great. Thanks. I just received this notice in my mailbox. Could you take a look at it, please?

M: Okay . . . Hmm . . . According to this, you need to pay a fine of fifty dollars.

W: Yeah, but, uh . . . why do I have to pay a fine? The notice doesn't explain what this is for.

M: It doesn't . . . ? Oh, yeah. You're right. Just a moment while I type your case number into the computer.

W: Sure.

M: Okay. Apparently, there was an inspection of your room three days ago. Do you remember that?

W: Yes, the RA told me about it, but I wasn't there when it happened.

M: Okay. Anyway, during the inspection, the person from the housing office noticed that a chair was missing from your room. So the fine is to pay for a replacement chair.

W: Um . . . There wasn't a chair in the room when I moved in after the semester started a month ago. I actually came here and asked about that, but nobody ever brought me a new chair.

M: That's peculiar. Let me check on that . . . Okay, uh, I just typed your name into the computer, and what you said is absolutely correct. This is completely our fault. I'm going to personally deliver a chair to your room right after lunch ends.

W: And the fine?

M: **Consider it gone.** I'm very sorry for the inconvenience. I'll make sure something like this doesn't happen again.

해석

W Student: 실례지만 이곳 사무실에 계신 분과 이야기를 해야 할 것 같은데요.

M Housing Office Employee: 그래요. 저한테 말씀하세요.

W: 잘 되었군요. 고맙습니다. 조금 전에 우편함에서 이 고지서를 받았어요. 한 번 봐 주시겠어요?

M: 그러죠… 흠… 여기에 따르면 50달러의 벌금을 내야 하는군요.

W: 그런데, 하지만, 어… 제가 왜 벌금을 내야 하죠? 고지서에는 무엇 때문인지 나와 있지 않거든요.

M: 나와 있지 않다고요…? 오, 그러네요. 학생 말이 맞아요. 잠시 기다리시면 제가 컴퓨터에 학생의 케이스 번호를 입력할게요.

W: 알겠어요.

M: 좋아요. 보아하니 3일 전에 학생 방에 대한 점검이 이루어졌군요. 기억하나요?

W: 네, 기숙사 조교가 그에 대해 말을 해 주었지만, 저는 그때 그곳에 없었어요.

M: 좋아요. 어쨌든 점검을 하는 동안 기숙사 사무실 직원이 학생 방에서 의자가 하나 없어졌다는 점을 알게 되었어요. 그래서 벌금은 의자를 다시 가져다 두기 위한 비용과 관련된 것이죠.

W: 음… 한 달 전 이번 학기가 시작된 후 제가 기숙사에 들어 왔을 때 의자는 방에 없었어요. 실제로 제가 이곳으로 와서 그에 대해 문의했지만, 제게 새 의자를 가져다 준 분은 없었어요.

M: 이상하군요. 제가 확인해 보죠… 그래요, 어, 학생의 이름을 컴퓨터에 입력해

보니 학생이 말한 것이 분명 사실이군요. 전적으로 저희 잘못이네요. 점심 시간 직후에 제가 직접 학생의 방에 의자를 가져다 드릴게요.

W: 그러면 벌금은요?

M: 끝난 일이죠. 불편을 끼쳐 드려 정말 죄송해요. 다시는 이러한 일이 일어나지 않도록 주의할게요.

✎ Summary Note

A

> **❶** $50 fine
>
> **❷** no chair
>
> **❸** Removes the fine

B

The student visits the student housing office because she got a notice indicating she must pay a fine of fifty dollars. However, she does not know what the fine is for. The man checks and says that the fine is for a chair that was found missing during an inspection. The student says that there was no chair when she moved in and that she already asked about it. The man confirms the student is right. He promises to deliver her a chair and removes the fine.

Exercise 3 1 ⓒ 2 ⓓ p.134

Script 🎧 05-10

M Student: Professor Simmons, how are you doing? I haven't seen you since last year.

W Professor: Hey, Fred. Long time, no see. I had an appendectomy last summer. I was in the hospital for two weeks. But I'm fully recovered now and feeling great. My body is one-hundred-percent shipshape. So how are you? I hear you're a student-teacher these days.

M: That's right. I'm teaching the freshmen introduction to modern literature course.

W: That's what I heard. As a matter of fact, that's why I called and asked you to meet me here today. The university has assigned me to observe your class next week on Tuesday, and I wanted to tell you in person.

M: Oh, really? Did I do something wrong? Was there a complaint?

W: No, nothing of the sort. It's just a routine yearly evaluation that the university does on all new student-teachers.

M: Hmm, okay. I'm just surprised because I would think someone would have told me about it earlier.

W: Well, you know, the university administration likes to use the element of surprise sometimes. They want me to observe your normal teaching style. Speaking of which, what are you teaching this semester?

M: I'll email you my syllabus and lesson plans before you come. But in brief, I'm doing a compare-and-contrast unit, during which we read a novel and then watch the Hollywood adaptation and discuss the difference.

W: That sounds really interesting. Which books and movies are you doing?

M: First, we're reading and watching William Golding's *Lord of the Flies*. Then, we're going to do Shakespeare's *Hamlet* with the Kenneth Brannaugh film adaptation. After that, if we have enough time, we'll take a look at Joseph Conrad's *Heart of Darkness* with Francis Ford Coppola's *Apocalypse Now* for the film portion.

W: Wow! That's a heavy syllabus.

M: Do you think it's overambitious?

W: Maybe a little.

해석

M Student: Simmons 교수님, 어떻게 지내셨나요? 지난 해에 뵙고 처음 뵙네요.

W Professor: 안녕하세요, Fred. 오랜만이에요. 저는 지난 여름에 맹장 수술을 받았어요. 2주간 입원해 있었죠. 하지만 지금은 완전히 회복해서 아주 좋아요. 몸이 100퍼센트 회복되었죠. 학생은 어떻게 지냈나요? 요즘 교생 업무를 하고 있다고 들었어요.

M: 맞아요. 신입생들에게 현대 문학 개론 수업을 가르치고 있죠.

W: 저도 그렇게 들었어요. 사실 그것이 바로 제가 학생에게 연락해서 오늘 만나자고 한 이유예요. 대학측이 제게 다음 주 화요일에 학생 수업을 참관하라고 해서 학생에게 직접 이야기하고 싶었거든요.

M: 오, 그런가요? 제가 잘못한 것이 있었나요? 불만 사항이 나왔나요?

W: 아니요, 그런 건 아니에요. 모든 신입 교생에 대해 대학측이 매년 하고 있는 정기적인 평가일 뿐이에요.

M: 흠, 그렇군요. 저는 좀 놀랐는데, 누군가 그에 대해 더 일찍 말해 줄 수도 있었다는 생각이 드는군요.

W: 음, 알다시피 대학 행정부는 때때로 일을 기습적으로 벌이는 것을 좋아하죠. 그들은 제가 학생의 일상적인 교수법을 관찰하기를 바라고 있어요. 말이 나왔으니까 말인데, 이번 학기엔 어떤 내용을 가르치나요?

M: 수업에 들어오시기 전에 강의 요강과 수업 계획서를 이메일로 보내 드릴게요. 하지만 짧게 말씀을 드리면, 저는 비교와 대조 단원을 다루고 있는데, 저희는 한 편의 소설을 읽고 할리우드의 각색물을 본 후 그 차이점에 대해 토론을 해요.

W: 정말 흥미롭게 들리는군요. 어떤 책과 영화를 다루고 있나요?

M: 먼저 윌리엄 골딩의 *파리대왕*을 읽고 시청 중이에요. 그 다음에는 셰익스피어의 *햄릿*과 케네스 브래너의 영화를 같이 살펴볼 거예요. 그 후 시간이 남으면 조셉 콘라드의 *암흑의 핵심*과 그에 대한 영화인 프란시스 포드 코폴라 감독의 *지옥의 묵시록*을 살펴볼 것이고요.

W: 와! 계획이 엄청나군요.

M: 욕심이 과하다고 생각하시나요?

W: 약간 그런 것 같아요.

Summary Note

A

❶ comparisons and contrasts

❷ the Hollywood adaptation

B

The professor tells the student that he was in the hospital for an appendectomy. He says his body is fully recovered now. The student says he enjoys being a student-teacher. The professor says that the university administration is sending him to observe the student's class. The professor asks the student what he is teaching. The student responds that he is taking a unit that compares and contrasts novels and their Hollywood adaptations. The student wonders if the professor thinks this syllabus is overambitious. The professor says it may be.

Exercise 4 1 Ⓐ 2 Ⓒ   p.136

Script 🎧 05-11

M Student Activities Office Employee: Good morning. How are you doing today?

W Student: I'm great. Thanks. How are you?

M: I'm doing all right. So . . . what brings you to the office today?

W: One of my friends told me she is serving as a host for a high school student who's going to be visiting in a couple of weeks. That sounds kind of interesting, so I thought I would ask if you need any volunteers.

M: I'm so glad you showed up just now.

W: Oh . . . Okay. So what can I do?

M: On the weekend of October 15 and 16, we're going to have around 200 prospective students in high school visiting us. We try to put them up in dorms so that they can experience campus life.

W: Ah, okay. I've got a roommate, but she's fine with having someone stay with us for the weekend.

M: Great. First . . . do you like the school?

W: Sure. I love it here.

M: That's good. We don't want any students staying with people who are having unpleasant experiences at school. They might get a bad impression of the school.

W: That makes sense. So what do I need to do?

M: Just sign your name here and provide your phone number. We'll find someone to stay with you and call you in a couple of days. Why don't you take this pamphlet, which explains what we hope you can do while the student is here?

W: Sounds good to me.

해석

M Student Activities Office Employee: 안녕하세요. 오늘 어떠신가요?

W Student: 좋아요. 고마워요. 선생님은요?

M: 저도 좋아요. 그러면… 무슨 일로 사무실에 오신 건가요?

W: 제 친구 중 한 명이 2주 후 방문 예정인 고등학생을 위해 호스트를 역할을 맡을 것이라고 말해 주더군요. 흥미로운 일처럼 들려서 혹시 자원봉사자가 필요한지 여쭤봐야겠다고 생각했어요.

M: 제때 나타나 주셔서 정말 기쁘네요.

W: 오… 그렇군요. 그러면 제가 어떻게 하면 되나요?

M: 10월 15일과 16일 주말에 고등학교에 재학 중인 약 200명의 예비 대학생들이 방문할 거에요. 그들이 캠퍼스 생활을 경험할 수 있도록 기숙사에서 지내도록 할 예정이죠.

W: 아, 그렇군요. 제게는 룸메이트가 있지만, 주말 동안 다른 사람과 같이 지내는 것을 그녀도 좋아할 거예요.

M: 잘 되었군요. 먼저… 학교가 마음에 드시나요?

W: 그럼요. 이곳이 정말 마음에 들어요.

M: 좋아요. 학교에서 불쾌한 경험을 하고 있는 사람과 학생들을 같이 머물게 하고 싶지는 않거든요. 학교에 대한 나쁜 인상을 줄 수 있으니까요.

W: 이해가 가요. 그러면 제가 어떻게 하면 되나요?

M: 여기에 학생 이름을 적고 전화번호를 알려 주시기만 하면 돼요. 저희가 학생과 지낼 사람을 찾아서 이틀 후에 연락을 드릴 거예요. 예비 대학생이 이곳에 있는 동안 학생이 했으면 하는 사항들이 나와 있는 이 팜플렛을 가져 가는 것이 어떨까요?

W: 좋아요.

Summary Note

A

❶ prospective student

❷ name and phone number

B

The student tells the man that one of her friends will be hosting a visiting high school student, and she wants to do the same thing. The man is happy the student showed up. He says that around 200 prospective students in high school will be visiting. The school needs students who like the school to act as hosts. The student says that she likes the school and that her roommate is fine with someone staying with them. The man asks the student to sign her name and phone number and states that she will be contacted later. He gives her a pamphlet containing the school's expectations and asks her to read it.

Exercises with Mid-Length Lectures

Exercise 1   1 Ⓐ   2 Ⓓ   p.138

Script 🎧 05-12

W1 Professor: Today, we are going to discuss the construction of one of the world's most famous tourist attractions. It's located in the middle of Paris, France.

W2 Student: You're talking about the Eiffel Tower, designed by Gustave Eiffel and built between 1887 and 1889.

W1: That's absolutely correct. The Eiffel Tower today remains the tallest structure in Paris, standing 300 meters high. The iron structure of the tower weighs a total of 7,300 tons. It required 300 workers to join together 18,038 pieces of puddle iron with three and a half million rivets to erect the tower.

M Student: That doesn't sound like such a big deal.

W1: In a way, you're right. By today's standards, building that kind of structure would be quite easy. But at the time, it was the tallest structure in the world. It held the record for over forty years. The tower was erected to be the entrance arch for the 1898 World's Fair in Paris. Did you know that only one worker died during construction? He was killed when he fell down the elevator shaft.

W2: Well, as famous as it is, I still think it looks like the skeleton of a building.

W1: You wouldn't be the only one who has thought the tower was an eyesore. Many members of the French public did not approve of the tower. One famous novelist even ate his lunch at a restaurant near the tower because he felt it was the only place in Paris where he could eat without having to see it.

   Furthermore, the city government of Paris had an agreement with Gustave Eiffel that after twenty years, rights to the tower would be theirs, at which time they would tear it down. But since it proved to be a valuable antenna for radio communications, the city allowed Eiffel's permit to expire. By that time, the tower was so firmly entrenched in French culture that they could not tear it down.

해석

W1 Professor: 오늘은 세계에서 가장 유명한 관광지 중 한 곳의 건축물에 대해 논의할 예정입니다. 프랑스 파리의 한 가운데 위치해 있죠.

W2 Student: 구스타브 에펠이 설계하고 1887년과 1889년 사이에 지어진 에펠탑을 말씀하시는 것이군요.

W1: 정확하게 맞췄어요. 에펠탑은 높이가 300미터로 오늘날까지 파리에서 가장 높은 구조물이에요. 철로 만들어진 이 탑의 무게는 총 7,300톤이고요. 300명의 인부가 350만개의 리벳을 이용해 18,038개의 철 조각을 결합시켜서 탑을 세웠습니다.

M Student: 그렇게 대단한 일로 들리지는 않는데요.

W1: 어떤 면에서 보면 학생 말이 맞아요. 오늘날의 기준에서는 그런 구조물을 만드는 일이 꽤 쉬운 일일 거예요. 하지만 당시에는 에펠탑이 세계에서 가장 높은 구조물이었어요. 그 기록은 40년 넘게 유지되었고요. 이 탑은 1898년 파리 만국 박람회의 출입구로서 세워졌어요. 공사 기간 동안 단 한 명의 인부만 사망했다는 점을 알고 있었나요? 승강기 통로에서 떨어져 목숨을 잃었습니다.

W2: 음, 유명하긴 해도 저에게는 건물의 뼈대처럼 보이는 것 같군요.

W1: 학생 말고도 에펠탑이 보기 흉하다고 생각하는 사람들이 많이 있을 거예요. 많은 프랑스 사람들이 에펠탑을 마음에 들어 하지 않았어요. 심지어 한 유명한 소설가는 에펠탑 근처에 있는 한 식당에서 점심을 먹었는데, 그 이유는 그곳이 에펠탑을 보지 않으면서 식사를 할 수 있는 유일한 장소라고 생각했기 때문이었죠.

   뿐만 아니라 파리시는 구스타브 에펠로부터 20년 후 언제라도 탑을 허물 수 있는 권리가 자신들에게 있다는 합의를 받아냈습니다. 하지만 에펠탑이 라디오 방송의 안테나 역할을 훌륭히 해냈기 때문에 파리시는 에펠과의 합의를 종료시켰어요. 당시 에펠탑이 프랑스 문화에서 너무나 확고하게 자리잡고 있었기 때문에 이를 허물 수가 없었습니다.

✏️ Summary Note

A

❶ 300
❷ 3,500,000

B

The Eiffel Tower was designed by Gustave Eiffel. It is still the tallest structure in Paris. The iron structure of the tower weighs 7,300 tons. It required 300 workers to join 18,038 pieces of puddle iron and three and a half million rivets to erect the tower. It held the record for tallest building in the world for over forty years. The Eiffel Tower was the entrance arch for the 1898 World's Fair. Only one worker died during its construction. By the time the tower's permit expired, it was so firmly entrenched in French culture that the government could not tear it down.

Exercise 2   1 Ⓓ   2 Ⓐ   p.140

Script 🎧 05-13

M Professor: Companies that want to sell more goods and services typically invest in marketing. This enables them to get word about their products out both to existing and potential customers. In the past, most marketing was either word of mouth, as people told others about a business and its products, or print based. In other words, marketing appeared in various newspapers, magazines, and journals or as printed advertisements. Of course, once radio and television were developed, marketing was done utilizing them, too.

   Nowadays, thanks to the Internet, there are many more types of marketing that companies can engage in. One primary advantage of using the Internet is that a business can market its products literally to anyone with an Internet connection. So rather than merely focusing on local or national customers, businesses can market their products to people all around the world. This can help businesses grow tremendously if they take advantage of this opportunity.

What are some different types of online marketing? Well, let's think for a moment . . . Content marketing is one. This may utilize videos, blogs, and e-guides as businesses provide their customers with information about their products, which may convince people to purchase these goods or services. Another type is social media marketing. There are many popular social media sites used by hundreds of millions of people around the world. This type of marketing can be extremely effective at times.

Influencer marketing is yet another type of Internet-based marketing method. You all know what influencers are, right? Well, many businesses hire influencers to promote their products. Some influencers may have hundreds of thousands—or even millions—of followers, and the most, uh, influential ones can be extremely successful at marketing products. **Some companies should strongly consider employing them.** In just a moment, I'm going to give you a couple of examples of these. But first, I want to continue talking about different online marketing methods. A fourth one I'd like to discuss now is email marketing. Can anyone tell me what that is?

해석

M Professor: 더 많은 제품과 서비스를 판매하고자 하는 기업들은 일반적으로 마케팅에 투자를 합니다. 이로써 현재의 고객 및 잠재적인 고객 모두에게 자신의 제품들을 알릴 수가 있죠. 과거에 대부분의 마케팅은, 사람들이 기업이나 제품에 대해 다른 사람에게 말을 하는 형태로서, 구두로 이루어지거나, 혹은 인쇄물로 이루어졌습니다. 다시 말해 다양한 신문, 잡지, 그리고 저널에서, 혹은 인쇄물 광고로서 마케팅을 볼 수 있었죠. 물론 라디오와 텔레비전이 개발된 후에는 이들을 활용한 마케팅이 이루어졌어요.

오늘날에는 인터넷 덕분에 기업들이 활용할 수 있는 마케팅 수단이 보다 많아졌습니다. 인터넷을 이용할 때의 주요 이점은 기업이 문자 그대로 인터넷에 연결된 누구에게나 자신의 제품을 마케팅할 수 있다는 점이에요. 그래서 기업들이 역내 혹은 국내 고객들에게만 초점을 맞추지 않고 전 세계 모든 사람들을 대상으로 제품을 마케팅할 수가 있죠. 이러한 기회를 이용하는 경우 기업들은 막대한 성장을 이룰 수가 있습니다.

온라인 마케팅 유형에는 어떤 것들이 있을까요? 음, 잠시 생각해 보조… 콘텐츠 마케팅이 그중 하나입니다. 이는 동영상, 블로그, 그리고 인터넷 사용 설명서를 활용하여 기업들이 자사 제품의 정보를 고객들에게 제공해 주는 것으로, 이를 통해 해당 제품이나 서비스를 구입하도록 사람들을 설득시킬 수 있습니다. 또 다른 유형으로는 소셜 미디어 마케팅이 있어요. 전 세계적으로 수억 명의 사람들이 다수의 유명 소셜 미디어 사이트를 이용하고 있죠. 이러한 유형의 마케팅은 때때로 대단히 효율적일 수 있습니다.

인플루언서 마케팅 역시 인터넷을 기반으로 한 마케팅 유형 중 하나예요. 모두들 인플루언서가 무엇인지 아시죠, 그렇죠? 음, 많은 기업들이 인플루언서를

이용하여 자신들의 제품을 홍보합니다. 일부 인플루언서들에게는 수만 명, 심지어는 수백만 명의 팔로워들이 있을 수도 있으며, 대부분의, 어, 영향력 있는 인플루언서들은 매우 성공적으로 제품을 마케팅할 수 있어요. 몇몇 기업들은 이들을 이용하는 것을 적극적으로 고려해야 합니다. 잠시 후 이에 대한 두어 가지 예를 알려 드리죠. 하지만 먼저 다양한 온라인 마케팅 방식에 대한 이야기를 계속하려고 합니다. 논의하고자 하는 네 번째 방법은 이메일 마케팅이에요. 이것이 무엇인지 말해 볼 사람이 있나요?

✏ Summary Note

A

❶ Printed advertisements
❷ Social media marketing
❸ Influencer marketing

B

The professor states that businesses use marketing to get word out about their products. In the past, word of mouth, print-based marketing, and marketing on radio and television were used. Today, there are many more types of marketing thanks to the Internet. Content marketing uses videos, blogs, and e-guides to provide information about products. Social media marketing can be effective since hundreds of millions of people use social media. Influencer marketing uses influencers with large audiences to promote products. A fourth one is email marketing.

Exercise 3 1 Ⓑ 2 Ⓑ   p.142

Script 🎧 05-14

M Professor: I'd like to provide you with overviews of the El Nino and La Nina weather phenomena. These patterns are not easy to understand, so pay close attention.

The El Nino Southern Oscillation, or just El Nino for short, is a global coupled ocean-atmosphere phenomenon. Pacific Ocean signatures such as El Nino and La Nina are major temperature fluctuations in surface waters of the tropical eastern part of the Pacific Ocean. El Nino signifies a rise of 0.5° Celsius or more and La Nina a drop of the same that is sustained for a period longer than five months.

Many of the countries most affected by El Nino are developing nations on the continents of South America and Africa. Their economies are largely dependent on the agricultural and fishing sectors as major sources of food, employment, and foreign exchange. New capabilities for predicting these events can have a great socio-economic impact.

These episodes usually occur irregularly every two to seven years. They usually last for one or two years. The effects of El Nino are very wide ranging. Many places experience weather that is the reverse of their normal climate. Some areas even experience terrible flooding due to excess rainfall or forest fires because of heavy drought. Aside from the drastic weather changes around the Southern Hemisphere, the fishing and manure industries in South America are heavily affected.

In the normal Pacific pattern, equatorial winds gather. Then, warm water pools toward the west. Cold water upswells along the South American coast. Since fish follow the cool nutrient-rich water, this brings them up the coast, where they support the local fishing industry. When El Nino takes effect, the warm water flows toward the South American coast. The absence of cold upswelling increases warming and sends the fish population out to sea instead of along the coast. These conditions are severely damaging to local fishing industries.

The causes of El Nino and La Nina temperature changes are still undiscovered. But many scientists are dedicating their careers to better understanding this global weather phenomenon.

해석

M Professor: 기상 현상인 엘니뇨와 라니냐에 대해 대략적으로 알려 드리고자 합니다. 이러한 패턴은 이해하기 쉽지 않으니 잘 들어 주세요.

엘리뇨 남방 진동, 혹은 줄여서 엘니뇨는 해양 및 대기와 관련된 전 지구적인 현상입니다. 태평양에서 특징적으로 일어나는 엘니뇨 및 라니냐는 열대 지역에 해당되는 태평양의 해수면 온도가 크게 요동치는 현상이에요. 엘니뇨가 발생하는 경우 다섯 달이 넘는 기간 동안 수온이 섭씨 0.5도 이상 상승하며, 라니냐가 발생하는 경우에는 그와 동일한 정도로 수온이 내려갑니다.

엘리뇨의 영향을 가장 많이 받은 국가들 중 다수가 남아메리카 및 아프리카 대륙의 개발도상국들입니다. 이들의 경제는 식량 수급, 고용 창출, 그리고 외화 획득을 가능하게 만드는 농업과 어업에 크게 의존하고 있죠. 이러한 기상 현상을 예측할 수 있는 새로운 능력은 막대한 사회경제적 영향을 끼칠 수 있을 거예요.

이러한 일들은 2년에서 7년 간격으로 불규칙하게 일어납니다. 보통 1년이나 2년 정도 지속되고요. 엘니뇨의 효과는 매우 다양합니다. 여러 지역에서 정상적인 날씨와 반대되는 날씨를 경험하죠. 일부 지역에서는 비가 과도하게 내려서 끔찍한 홍수가 발생하기도 하고, 혹은 극심한 가뭄으로 인해 산불이 나기도 합니다. 남반구 주변에서 일어나는 극심한 기후 변화를 제외하고라도 남아메리카의 어업과 비료 산업이 그로 인해 막대한 영향을 받고 있어요.

태평양의 정상적인 패턴에서는 적도풍이 모입니다. 그러면 따뜻한 물이 서쪽으로 흐르게 되죠. 차가운 물은 남아메리카 해안을 따라 솟아오르게 됩니다. 어류는 영양분이 풍부한 차가운 물을 따라 이동하기 때문에 그로 인해 어류들이 해안가로 몰려들게 되며, 이로써 지역 어업이 발달하게 되죠. 엘니뇨가 발생하면 따뜻한 물이 남아메리카 해안 쪽으로 흐르게 됩니다. 차가운 물이 솟아오르지 않기 때문에 수온이 상승하게 되고, 어류들은 해안가 대신 바다로 나아가게 됩니다. 이러한 상황은 지역 어업에 막대한 피해를 입히고 있죠.

엘니뇨 및 라니냐에 따른 수온 변화의 원인은 아직 밝혀지지 않고 있어요. 하지만 많은 과학자들이 이러한 전 지구적인 기후 현상을 더 잘 이해하기 위해 매진하고 있습니다.

📝 Summary Note

A

❶ developing nations

❷ local fishing industries

B

El Nino and La Nina signify a temperature change of 0.5° Celsius higher or lower than normal for more than five months. Countries on the continents of South America and Africa are the most affected by El Nino. These episodes occur irregularly every two to seven years. They reverse normal climates. An example of El Nino in action is when warm water flows toward the South American coast. The absence of cold water upswelling sends the fish population out to sea. This is due to the fact that fish follow the cool nutrient-rich water. The causes of El Nino are still not fully understood by scientists.

Exercise 4 1 Ⓐ 2 Ⓒ   p.144

Script 🎧 05-15

M1 Professor: I'd like to start this class with a question. Who here can tell me which great philosopher said, "I think; therefore, I am"?

W Student: I've heard that before. Was it . . . Jean Paul Sartre?

M1: That's a good guess, but no. This philosopher lived almost three hundred years before Jean Paul Sartre. His name is Rene Descartes. He is considered the founder of modern philosophy.

M2 Student: Was he an existentialist?

M1: No, he wasn't. Descartes was a natural philosopher. He was also a mathematician. His love for math and philosophy intersected. He felt math could be used to prove truth about the universe. But it's interesting that you brought up the existentialists. That's an important group from modern Western philosophy. Let's talk about an early existentialist named Soren Kierkegaard.

Soren Kierkegaard was a Danish philosopher who lived in the 1800s. He made a very important statement on truth. He said, "All truth is subjective."

W: Does that mean that up is down, black is white, and two plus two equals five?

M1: No, his viewpoint was not that drastic. Kierkegaard just thought that each person experienced a different version of the truth based on the perspective from where they were standing. For example, two men are looking at a glass of water. One man says the glass of water is half empty. The other man says the glass is half full. Their opinions seem to be conflicting. Are they? No, they are both right. Each man possesses his own truth. Neither one is more right or more wrong. Their truths are simply subjective. This was a precursor to the existentialist view that each person is alone in their relationship with the rest of the universe. This viewpoint, called the doctrine of Solipsism, has gotten a lot of criticism from other branches of philosophy. It's accused of being selfish and egotistical.

M2: But it makes sense to me.

M1: Sure. Existentialism and teen angst have always gone hand in hand.

해석

M1 Professor: 이번 수업은 질문으로 시작해 보죠. "나는 생각한다. 고로 존재한다."라고 말한 위대한 철학자가 누구인지 아는 사람이 있나요?

W Student: 전에 들어본 적이 있어요. 그게… 장 폴 사르트르인가요?

M1: 시도는 좋았지만 아니에요. 이 철학자는 장 폴 사르트르보다 거의 300년 이전에 살았어요. 그의 이름은 르네 데카르트입니다. 근대 철학의 창시자로 여겨지고 있죠.

M2 Student: 그가 실존주의자였나요?

M1: 아니요, 아니었어요. 데카르트는 자연철학자였습니다. 또한 수학자이기도 했죠. 수학과 철학을 똑같이 좋아했어요. 그는 수학을 사용해서 우주의 진리를 입증할 수 있다고 생각했죠. 하지만 학생이 실존주의자를 언급한 것은 흥미롭네요. 실존주의는 근대 서양 철학에서 비롯된 중요한 부류예요. 쇠렌 키에르케고르라는 초기 실존주의자에 대해 논의해 봅시다.

쇠렌 키에르케고르는 1800년대에 살았던 덴마크의 철학자였어요. 그는 진리에 관해 매우 중요한 주장을 했죠. "모든 진리는 주관적인 것이다."라는 말을 했어요.

W: 그 말은 위가 아래이고, 검정색이 하얀색이고, 2 더하기 2가 5라는 뜻인가요?

M1: 아니요, 그의 견해가 그렇게 극단적인 것은 아니었어요. 키에르케고르는 각자가 자신의 입장에 따른 관점에 기반해서 각기 다른 형태의 진리를 경험한다고 생각했어요. 예를 들어 두 사람이 물이 든 컵을 바라보고 있어요. 한 사람은 물컵의 반이 비었다고 말합니다. 다른 한 사람은 물컵의 반이 차 있다고 말하고요. 이들의 견해는 상반되는 것처럼 보입니다. 그런가요? 아니에요, 두 사람 다 맞습니다. 각자에게 각자의 진실이 있는 것이죠. 둘 중에서 더 맞고 더 틀린 사람은 없어요. 이들의 진리가 주관적인 것뿐이에요. 이는 우주의 나머지 부분과의 관계에 있어서 각각의 사람들은 혼자라는 실존주의적 견해의 배경이 되었습니다. 유아론의 교리라고 불렸던 이러한 견해는 다른 철학 분야로부터 많은 비판을 받아 왔어요. 이기적이고 자기본위적이라고요.

M2: 하지만 말이 되는 것 같아요.

M1: 그래요. 실존주의와 십대의 불안은 항상 붙어 다니죠.

✏️ Summary Note

A

❶ subjective
❷ a different version
❸ criticism

B

The professor begins the lecture with the quote, "I think; therefore, I am." It is from Rene Descartes. Descartes was a natural philosopher. He was also a mathematician who believed math could be used to prove truth about the universe. Soren Kierkegaard was an early existentialist. He said, "All truth is subjective." The professor and the students then discuss the meaning of truth to individual people. Kierkegaard's statement on truth led to the doctrine of Solipsism, that all individuals are alone with the rest of the universe. Solipsism has suffered much criticism from other branches of philosophy for being selfish and egotistical.

Integrated Listening & Speaking p.146

A

 Script 🎧 05-16

> **M Professor:** Businesses use marketing because they want to get word out about their products to existing and potential customers. In the past, word of mouth, print-based marketing, and marketing on radio and television were used by businesses. Today, there are many more types of marketing thanks to the Internet. Content marketing uses videos, blogs, and e-guides to provide information about products. Social media marketing can be effective since hundreds of millions of people use a variety of different social media sites. Influencer marketing uses influencers with large audiences to promote products and can be very effective. A fourth one is email marketing.

1 a. Businesses use marketing because they want to get word out about their products to existing and potential customers.
   b. In order to get word out about their products to existing and potential customers, businesses use marketing.

2 a. It uses videos, blogs, and e-guides to provide information about products.
   b. Videos, blogs, and e-guides are used to provide information about products in content marketing.

3 a. It can be very effective since some influencers have large audiences.
   b. Due to the large audiences some influencers have, it can be very effective.

B

 Script 🎧 05-17

> **M Professor:** The quote, "I think; therefore, I am," is

from Rene Descartes. He was a natural philosopher. Descartes was also a mathematician. He believed math could be used to prove truth about the universe. Soren Kierkegaard was an early existentialist. He made the statement, "All truth is subjective." The meaning of truth to individual people is discussed. Kierkegaard's important statement on truth led to the doctrine of Solipsism. This is the view that all individuals are alone with the rest of the universe. Other branches of philosophy have criticized Solipsism for being selfish and egotistical.

1 a. The professor begins the lecture by saying, "I think; therefore, I am."
   b. "I think; therefore, I am" is the famous statement which the professor begins his lecture with.

2 a. He believed that math could be used to prove truth about the universe.
   b. The truth about the universe could be proved with math.

3 a. All truth is subjective.
   b. Every truth on the Earth is subjective.

Mini TOEFL iBT Practice Test   p.148

1 Ⓑ	2 Ⓐ	3 Ⓒ	4 Ⓓ	5 Ⓑ
6 Ⓑ,Ⓒ	7 Ⓓ	8 Ⓓ	9 Ⓑ	10 Ⓓ
11 Ⓒ				

[1-5]

Script 🎧 05-18

W Student: Excuse me. Is this the Biology Department office?

M Biology Department Office Employee: Yes, it is. Are you looking for someone?

W: As a matter of fact, I am. I was hoping to speak with Professor Paulson.

M: He should be having office hours right now. His office is on the second floor of this building in room 217. You can take the stairs up. They're to the right once you go out the door.

W: Uh, actually, I was already up at his office, but the door is locked. I knocked on the door, but nobody answered. A student told me that she saw Professor Paulson walking down the stairs a few minutes ago, so I was hoping you might know where he is.

M: I'm sorry, but I couldn't tell you. What do you need to speak with him about?

W: Uh, I heard from one of my friends that he is looking

to hire a student as a lab assistant. He needs someone to conduct research on the starfish that he keeps in his lab.

M: Starfish? That's odd. Professor Paulson doesn't study them. The last I heard, he's conducting research on crossbreeding various types of tropical fruit trees.

W: Huh . . . Maybe I got the professor's name wrong. I could have sworn that it started with a P though.

M: Ah, I know who you want. You want to speak to Professor Pokorny. He was in the office the other day talking about the research he's doing on starfish. But, uh, I don't know about any available jobs in his lab.

W: Ah, Pokorny. That's right. Thanks. Do you know if he's here?

M: He is on campus today, but I believe he's teaching a class right now. It's scheduled to end around three o'clock.

W: That's just fifteen minutes from now. Does he normally return to his office when he's done?

M: Yes, he does.

W: Great. I'll just wait for him outside his office.

M: Um . . . You might not want to do that. Professor Pokorny always attends a staff meeting on Thursday afternoons. It starts just a bit after three. So he's going to be in a rush as soon as he finishes class. You probably won't make a good impression on him if you wait outside his office.

W: What should I do then? I really want this job.

M: Be here early in the morning around seven thirty or eight. He arrives early every Friday, and he really respects students who get up early enough in the morning to talk to him before classes start.

해석

W Student: 실례합니다. 여기가 생물학과 사무실인가요?

M Biology Department Office Employee: 네, 맞아요. 찾으시는 분이 있나요?

W: 사실 그래요. Paulson 교수님과 이야기를 했으면 좋겠어요.

M: 지금은 사무실 근무 시간일 거예요. 그분 사무실은 이 건물 2층에 있는 217호죠. 계단을 올라가시면 돼요. 계단은 나가시면 오른쪽에 있고요.

W: 어, 사실 이미 그분 사무실에는 다녀왔는데 문이 잠겨 있더군요. 노크를 했지만 아무런 답이 없었어요. Paulson 교수님께서 몇 분 전에 계단을 내려갔다고 한 학생이 이야기를 해 줘서 그분이 어디 계신지 혹시 아시기를 바라고 있었죠.

M: 죄송하지만 저도 모르겠어요. 그분과 무엇에 대해 이야기를 하셔야 하나요?

W: 어, 제 친구 중 한 명이 그분께서 실험실 조교를 맡을 학생을 채용하고 싶어 하신다고 말했어요. 그분 실험실에서 진행 중인 불가사리 연구에 사람이 필요하다고요.

M: 불가사리요? 이상하군요. Paulson 교수님께서는 불가사리에 대한 연구를 하지 않으시는데요. 최근에 들은 바에 따르면, 다양한 열대 과수의 교배에 대해 연구를 하실 거예요.

W: 허… 제가 교수님의 이름을 잘못 알고 있을 수도 있겠네요. 하지만 P로 시작한다는 점은 맹세할 수 있어요.

M: 아, 누구를 만나고 싶어하는지 알겠어요. Pokorny 교수님과 이야기를 하고 싶겠군요. 며칠 전 사무실에서 그분께서 하고 계신 불가사리에 대한 연구에 대해 말씀을 하셨거든요. 하지만, 어, 실험실의 일자리에 대해서는 잘 모르겠어요.

W: 아, Pokorny요. 맞아요. 고마워요. 그분이 여기에 계신지 알고 계시나요?

M: 오늘은 교내에 계시는 날이지만, 지금은 수업 중으로 알고 있어요. 수업은 3시 정도에 끝날 예정이고요.

W: 지금부터 15분 후이군요. 수업이 끝나면 보통 사무실로 돌아오시나요?

M: 네, 그래요.

W: 잘 되었네요. 그분 사무실 밖에서 기다리고 있을게요.

M: 음… 그러지 않는 것이 좋을 것 같군요. Pokorny 교수님께서는 목요일 오후마다 교직원 회의에 참석하세요. 회의는 3시 조금 지나서 시작하죠. 그래서 수업을 마치는 대로 서둘러 가셔야 할 거예요. 학생이 그분 사무실 밖에서 기다린다면 아마도 그분께 좋은 인상을 남기지는 못할 거예요.

W: 그럼 제가 어떻게 해야 할까요? 정말로 이번 일자리를 얻고 싶거든요.

M: 아침 일찍 오전 7시 30분이나 8시 정도에 여기로 오세요. 매주마다 금요일에는 일찍 도착을 하시는데, 수업이 시작되기 전 자신과 이야기를 하려고 아침 일찍 일어나는 학생들을 정말로 높이 평가하시죠.

[6-11]

Script 🎧 05-19

W Professor: Realist painting arose in the late 1500s when Caravaggio went against the prevailing European style of Mannerism, which flaunted figures in graceful but unlikely poses. Caravaggio painted normal people, in real tones of flesh and blood, awkward and ugly, as they truly appeared in real life.

Now, Edgar Degas was both a Realist and Impressionist. Looking at his work creates a perfectly natural bridge between one school of painting to the other. Degas was one of the founding painters of the Impressionist movement. This movement began as a loose association of painters in Paris. The name of the movement comes from Claude Monet's painting *Impression, Sunrise*. The characteristics of this movement are visible brushstrokes, light colors, open composition, emphasis on the changing qualities of light, ordinary subject matter, and unusual visual angles. The influence of this movement spread to music and literature.

Interestingly, it was a group of French realist landscape painters called the Barbizon School who directly led to the Impressionists. The Realist nature scenes of John Constable influenced a younger generation of painters to abandon formalism and to draw their inspiration directly from nature. One of these painters, Jean Francois Millet, extended the idea from landscapes to figures. He depicted peasant figures, peasant life, and their work in the fields. In his painting *The Gleaners*, Millet portrays three peasant women working hard at the harvest. The painting depicts no drama and no story; there are simply three women working hard.

Now, I want to share with you my favorite Impressionist painting. This . . . is Georges Seurat's *Sunday Afternoon on the Island of La Grande Jatte*. This incredible painting simply depicts different people from different classes of society enjoying a sunny afternoon in the park. If you look closely, you'll see that all of the color is applied in points, or unmixed dots, instead of brushstrokes. It allows the eye of the viewer to blend the colors optically instead of having them blended on the canvas. It took Seurat two years to complete and now hangs in the Art Institute of Chicago. Now, uh, here's another painting by Seurat. Let's look at it.

해석

W Professor: 사실주의 회화는 1500년대 후반에 등장했는데, 이때는 유럽에서 인기를 끌던 양식인 매너리즘에 카라바조가 반기를 들기 시작한 때로, 매너리즘은 우아하지만 현실에서 보기 힘든 자세를 취한 인물들을 과장해서 나타냈어요. 카르바조는 실제 피부 및 피를 나타내는 색조로 평범한 사람들을, 현실에서 보이는 그대로, 어색하면서도 추하게 표현했습니다.

자, 에드가 드가는 사실주의 화가이자 인상주의 화가였어요. 그의 작품을 보면 두 학파 사이의 완벽하게 자연스러운 다리가 드러납니다. 드가는 인상주의 운동의 선구적인 화가 중 한 명이었어요. 이 운동은 파리에 있는 화가들로 이루어진 느슨한 모임에서 탄생했습니다. 이 운동의 이름은 클로드 모네의 회화 작품인 *인상, 해돋이*에서 비롯되었죠. 이 운동의 특징은 눈에 띄는 붓터치, 밝은 색깔, 탁 트인 구성, 변화하는 빛에 대한 강조, 일상적인 소재, 그리고 특이한 시각입니다. 이 운동은 음악과 문학에도 영향을 끼쳤죠.

흥미롭게도 직접적으로 인상주의를 이끌어 낸 것은 바르비종이라고 불렸던 프랑스의 사실주의 풍경화가 그룹이었어요. 존 콘스터블가 그린 사실주의적인 풍경들이 보다 젊은 세대의 화가들에게 영향을 끼쳐 이들로 하여금 형식주의를 버리고 자연으로부터 직접 영감을 얻도록 만들었죠. 이러한 화가 중 한 명이었던 장 프랑수와 밀레는 그러한 아이디어를 풍경에서 인물로 확장시켰습니다. 그는 농부, 농부의 삶, 그리고 들판에서의 그들의 노동을 묘사했어요. 밀레는 자신의 그림 *이삭 줍는 여인*들에서 세 명의 여성 농부가 열심히 일하는 모습을 보여 줍니다. 이 그림은 어떠한 드라마도, 어떠한 스토리도 나타내지 않아요. 단지 열심히 일하고 있는 세 명의 여인만 있을 뿐이죠.

자, 제가 제일 좋아하는 인상주의 회화를 소개하고 싶군요. 바로… 조르쥬 쇠라의 *그랑드자트섬의 일요일* 오후입니다. 이 놀라운 그림은 출신이 각기 다른 계급의 사람들이 공원에서 화창한 오후를 즐기고 있는 모습을 보여 줍니다. 자세히 보면 모든 색들이, 붓을 놀리지 않고서, 포인트로, 즉 섞이지 않은 점으로 표현되어 있다는 것을 알 수 있어요. 이로써 관객의 눈이, 캔버스에 혼합되어 있는 색을 보는 대신, 색들을 시각적으로 혼합시킵니다. 쇠라가 이 그림을 완성하기까지 2년이 걸렸으며, 이 그림은 현재 시카고 미술관에 전시되어 있어요. 자, 어, 쇠라의 또 다른 그림이 있습니다. 보시죠.

Vocabulary Check-Up

p.153

A	1 Ⓜ	2 Ⓞ	3 Ⓝ	4 Ⓓ	5 Ⓑ
	6 Ⓚ	7 Ⓕ	8 Ⓗ	9 Ⓘ	10 Ⓖ
	11 Ⓙ	12 Ⓒ	13 Ⓐ	14 Ⓛ	15 Ⓔ
B	1 Ⓒ	2 Ⓐ	3 Ⓓ	4 Ⓑ	5 Ⓔ

UNIT 06 Understanding Organization

Basic Drill ·········· p.158

p.158

Drill 1 Ⓒ

 Script 🎧 06-02

W Student: Hi, Professor Higgins. I was hoping I could ask you some questions about declaring a double major.

M Professor: Oh, hi, Mary. Sure, I can spare a few minutes. I've had a lot of students do double majors in my department. What subjects were you thinking about focusing on?

W: I was thinking that I'd like to do a double major in criminology, in your department, and sculpture.

M: Hmm, criminology and sculpture. That's a social science and a fine art. That could be a problem. You see, the best double majors are two subjects that complement each other. For example, majors in criminology and forensic science go together well if you want to become a forensic detective.

해석

W Student: 안녕하세요, Higgins 교수님. 복수 전공을 하는 것에 대해 몇 가지 질문을 하면 좋을 것 같아서요.

M Professor: 오, 안녕하세요, Mary. 물론이죠, 몇 분 시간을 낼 수 있어요. 우리 과에서 복수 전공을 하는 학생들이 많죠. 어떤 과목에 초점을 맞추려고 생각했나요?

W: 교수님 학과의 범죄학과 조각을 복수 전공할까 생각 중이었어요.

M: 흠, 범죄학과 조각이라. 사회 과학과 순수 미술이군요. 문제가 될 수 있겠어요. 알겠지만 최선의 복수 전공은 서로 보완 관계에 있는 두 개의 과목이에요. 예를 들어 법의학 수사관이 되고 싶다면 범죄학과 법의학이 서로 잘 어울리죠.

Drill 2 Ⓓ

 Script 🎧 06-03

M Student: Hi. I wonder if you can help me find Plato's *Dialogues*. I have to do a report on the *Republic*.

W Librarian: Okay, let me check. Hmm, all of our copies seem to be out.

M: Oh, no. They must have been checked out by the other students in my class. This report is due in two days.

W: You should have reserved a copy if you knew you'd

need it.

M: Reserve a copy? I didn't know I could do that. How?

W: Do you see that desk over there by the water fountain?

M: Sure.

W: That's the reservations desk. The clerk there will reserve any book you ask her to. All you have to do is fill out a reservation card. Then, when the book comes in, a librarian will set it aside and call you.

M: Wow, wish I'd known that!

해석

M Student: 안녕하세요. 플라톤의 *대화*를 찾는데 도움을 주실 수 있는지 궁금하군요. 제가 *국가*에 대한 보고서를 써야 해서요.

W Librarian: 그래요, 한번 찾아보죠. 흠, 소장본이 모두 대출된 것 같네요.

M: 오, 이런. 분명 수업을 같이 듣는 다른 학생들이 대출했을 거예요. 이번 보고서의 마감일이 이틀 후이거든요.

W: 필요할 줄 알았으면 예약을 했어야 해요.

M: 예약이요? 예약을 할 수 있는지 모르고 있었어요. 어떻게요?

W: 저쪽 분수 옆에 데스크가 보이나요?

M: 그럼요.

W: 그곳이 예약 데스크예요. 그곳 직원에게 요청하면 어떤 책이라도 예약할 수 있어요. 예약 신청서를 작성하기만 하면 되죠. 그러면 책이 들어오는 대로 사서가 그 책을 따로 보관해 두고 학생에게 전화를 할거예요.

M: 와, 미리 알았으면 좋았겠군요!

Drill 3 Ⓐ

 Script 🎧 06-04

W Student: Hello. Do you work here?

M Dining Services Employee: I sure do. How can I help you?

W: I heard you might be hiring cashiers.

M: We've actually just hired two new cashiers. That position is filled. But I'm sure there are jobs for kitchen workers. We always need more of those.

W: Oh, yeah? What does that entail?

M: Washing dishes, cleaning up before and after lunch, that sort of thing.

W: Hmm, that doesn't sound like my cup of tea. I think I'm going to have to keep looking around.

M: Sure, I don't blame you. Another place you might look is the bulletin board at the student center. I heard you can always find different jobs there.

W: Thanks. I'll try there.

해석

W Student: 안녕하세요. 이곳에서 일을 하시나요?

M Dining Services Employee: 그래요. 어떻게 도와 드릴까요?

W: 계산원을 구한다는 이야기를 들어서요.

M: 사실 조금 전에 두 명의 계산원을 새로 고용했어요. 그 자리는 채워졌죠. 하지만 주방 근무자 자리는 분명 있을 거예요. 주방 근무자는 항상 더 필요하거든요.

W: 오, 그런가요? 무슨 일을 하게 되나요?

M: 설거지, 점심 시간 전후에 하는 청소, 뭐 그런 것들이죠.

W: 흠, 저한테 맞는 일은 아닌 것처럼 들리네요. 계속 찾아봐야 할 것 같아요.

M: 그래요, 그럴 수 있죠. 학생 센터에 있는 게시판도 살펴 보세요. 그곳에서는 항상 다양한 일자리들을 찾아볼 수 있다고 들었거든요.

W: 고마워요. 가 볼게요.

Drill 4 Ⓒ

Script 🎧 06-05

W Professor: Right now, I'd like to talk about my favorite heavenly body, the comet. It is a small body that orbits the sun. It also exhibits a coma, or atmosphere, and a tail. These are primarily due to the effects of solar radiation upon the comet's nucleus. The nucleus is a minor body composed of rock, dust, and ice. Due to their origins in the outer solar system and the fact that they are heavily affected by close approaches to the major planets, comets' orbits are constantly changing. Some comets are destroyed when they near the sun while others are thrown out of the solar system forever.

해석

W Professor: 자, 오늘은 제가 제일 좋아하는 천체인 혜성에 대해 논의하고자 해요. 혜성은 태양계 주위를 도는 작은 물체입니다. 또한 코마, 즉 대기와 꼬리도 보여 주죠. 이들은 기본적으로 태양 복사가 혜성의 핵에 끼치는 영향 때문에 나타납니다. 핵은 암석, 먼지, 그리고 얼음으로 이루어진 크지 않은 몸체이에요. 태양계 외부에서 생긴다는 점과 주요 행성들에 가까워질 수록 막대한 영향을 받는다는 사실 때문에, 혜성의 궤도는 계속해서 바뀝니다. 일부 혜성들은 태양과 가까워지면 파괴되기도 하며, 영원히 태양계 밖으로 밀려나는 혜성들도 있죠.

Drill 5 Ⓐ

Script 🎧 06-06

M Professor: Let's talk about something everybody likes on their pizza but not growing between their toes: fungus. Fungi are eukaryotic organisms that digest food externally. Then, they absorb the nutrient molecules into their cells. Along with bacteria, fungi are the primary decomposers of dead organic matter in most terrestrial ecosystems. Many fungi have important symbiotic relationships with various other organisms. Mycorrhizal symbiosis between plants and fungi is particularly important. Over ninety percent of all plant species

---

engage in some sort of mycorrhizal relationship with fungi and are dependent on that relationship for survival. As I mentioned a moment ago, fungi are also used extensively by humans.

해석

M Professor: 오늘은 피자에 있으면 모든 사람들이 좋아하지만 발가락 사이에 생기면 좋아하지 않은 것에 대해 얘기해 보죠. 바로 균류입니다. 균류는 음식물을 체외에서 소화시키는 진핵생물이에요. 그런 다음에 세포 안으로 양분을 흡수하죠. 박테리아와 마찬가지로 균류도 대부분의 토양 생태계에서 죽은 유기물을 분해하는 1차 분해자입니다. 많은 균류들이 다양한 유기체들과 중요한 공생 관계를 맺고 있어요. 식물과 균류 사이의 균근 공생 관계는 특히 중요하죠. 모든 식물 종 중 90퍼센트 이상이 특정 형태로 균류와 균근 공생 관계를 맺고 있으며, 그러한 관계에 의지해 살아가고 있습니다. 조금 전에 말씀을 드렸던 것처럼, 균류는 인간에 의해서도 광범위하게 이용되고 있습니다.

Drill 6 Ⓑ

Script 🎧 06-07

W Professor: I hope you listen carefully today because I want everyone to remember what I tell you. Although traditional studies of memory began in the realm of philosophy, the late nineteenth and early twentieth centuries put memory with the paradigms of cognitive psychology. In recent decades, it has become one of the principal pillars of a new branch of science that represents a marriage between cognitive psychology and neuroscience called cognitive neuroscience. There are several ways to classify memories, including those based on duration, nature, and retrieval of information. From an information processing perspective, there are three main stages in the retrieval of memory. These are encoding, storage, and recall.

해석

W Professor: 제가 드리는 말씀을 모두들 잘 기억하기를 바라기 때문에 오늘은 주의 깊게 들어 주시면 좋겠습니다. 기억에 관한 전통적인 연구는 철학 분야에서 시작되었지만, 19세기 후반과 20세기 초에 기억은 인지 심리학의 패러다임에 들어가게 되었어요. 최근에는 인지 심리학과 인지 신경 과학이라는 신경 과학이 결합된 새로운 과학 분야의 중심 개념 중 하나가 되었죠. 기억을 분류하는 몇 가지 방법이 존재하는데, 여기에는 지속 기간, 특성, 그리고 정보의 인출에 따른 방법들이 포함됩니다. 정보 처리의 관점에서 볼 때 기억의 인출에는 세 가지 주요 단계가 있습니다. 바로 부호화, 저장, 그리고 회상입니다.

Exercises with Mid-Length Conversations

Exercise 1 1 Ⓓ 2 Ⓑ   p.160

Script 🎧 06-08

M Student: Hi. Who should I talk to about changing my

---

class timetable for this semester?

W Registrar's Office Employee: You can talk to me about it. I'm the Registrar's assistant.

M: Great. You're just the person I need to talk to. I want to join the recreational hockey league. So I'm going to have to shift my calculus class to Tuesday mornings, my intro to modern literature course to the night class, and maybe drop Chemistry 101.

W: Hmm, that sounds like a lot of rearranging. Are you sure you want to do that just to join the hockey league?

M: Oh, totally, for sure. Hockey versus Chemistry 101 . . . Which one would you choose?

W: Do you want to graduate with a useful degree in four years?

M: Yeah, but that's not for years. I need to get some exercise this winter. That seems more important right now.

W: Okay, I'm looking at your schedule here, and I see some problems. First of all, the night class for intro to modern literature is full. There's no way you can get in there.

M: Oh, that stinks.

W: Secondly, you can transfer to the Tuesday morning calculus class. But I have to warn you that it's an accelerated class. That means that the professor will move through the book a lot faster than the low-level class you're currently in. Are you prepared to keep up with the increased course speed? Is calculus one of your strong suits?

M: Well, no, but maybe I could . . .

W: Finally, about dropping Chemistry 101. Your major is Microbiology. You have to have Chemistry 101 as a prerequisite to take most of the other classes in your major. If you drop it this semester, it'll hold you up from taking any other courses in your major next semester. You could set your entire education back a year just to play recreational hockey. Do you really want to do that?

M: Hmm, I guess I'd better not. Thanks anyway.

W: No problem. Have a nice day!

해석

M Student: 안녕하세요. 이번 학기 시간표를 변경하는 것에 관해서는 어느 분께 말씀을 드려야 하나요?

W Registrar's Office Employee: 저한테 말씀하세요. 저는 학적과 행정 조교예요.

M: 잘 됐네요. 제가 이야기를 드려야 할 분이셨군요. 저는 레크리에이션 하키 리그에 참가하고 싶어요. 그래서 미적분 수업을 화요일 오전으로, 현대 문학 개론 수업을 야간 수업으로 옮기고, 그리고 화학 101 수업은 아마도 수강 철회를 해야 할 것 같아요.

W: 흠, 많이 바꾸어야 할 것 같군요. 단지 하키 리그에 참가하기 위해서 그렇게

하려는 것이 확실한가요?

M: 오, 그럼요, 물론이죠. 하키 대 화학 101… 어떤 걸 고르시겠어요?

W: 4년 후 도움이 될 학위를 가지고 졸업하고 싶으세요?

M: 그래요, 하지만 몇 년씩 하겠다는 것은 아니에요. 이번 겨울에만 운동을 하면 되는 것이죠. 지금으로서는 그것이 더 중요하게 보여요.

W: 좋아요, 여기 학생 시간표를 보니 몇 가지 문제가 있네요. 먼저, 현대 문학 개론의 야간 수업은 이미 정원이 다 찼어요. 들어갈 방법이 없어요.

M: 오, 안 되었군요.

W: 둘째, 화요일 오전 미적분 수업으로 바꾸는 것은 가능해요. 하지만 그 수업은 속성 과정이라는 점을 경고해 드릴게요. 다시 말해 교수님께서 지금 듣는 낮은 레벨의 수업에서보다 훨씬 더 빠르게 책을 살펴보실 것이라는 점을 의미하죠. 빠른 속도의 수업을 따라갈 준비가 되어 있나요? 학생이 미적분을 잘하는 편인가요?

M: 음, 그건 아니지만, 아마 할 수 있을지도…

W: 마지막으로, 화학 101 수업을 철회하는 것에 관해서요. 학생의 전공은 미생물학이잖아요. 기타 대부분의 전공 수업을 듣기 위해서는 필수 과목으로서 화학 101 수업을 반드시 들어야 해요. 만약 이번 학기에 이 수업을 철회하면 다음 학기에 기타 전공 과목 수업을 듣지 못하는 문제가 생길 거예요. 레크리에이션 하키 경기를 하기 위해 전체 학사 일정을 1년 늦출 수는 있어요. 정말 그렇게 하고 싶나요?

M: 흠, 그러지 않는 편이 좋을 것 같군요. 어쨌든 감사합니다.

W: 천만에요. 좋은 하루 되세요!

✏ Summary Note

A

❶ hockey recreational league
❷ too advanced
❸ prerequisite class

B

A student wants to change his schedule so that he can join a recreational hockey league. He wants to shift his classes to different times. He also wants to drop his Chemistry 101 class. The assistant tells him that the classes he wants to change into are either full or too advanced for him. She also tells him that he might not be able to graduate in four years if he drops Chemistry 101. The student changes his mind and decides not to play hockey.

Exercise 2 1 Ⓓ 2 Ⓑ p.162

Script 🎧 06-09

W Student: Good morning, Professor Johanssen. May I have a word with you, please?

M Professor: Hello. Oh . . . I remember you. You took my class in microeconomics last semester. I seem to recall that you did very well in it. But . . . I'm afraid I don't remember your name.

W: I'm Amy Riley, sir.

M: Ah, that's right. I should have remembered that. So what can I do for you today, Amy?

W: Well, uh, this is the start of my sophomore year, so I need to declare a major. I really enjoyed the class that I took with you, and I thought you were a great professor.

M: Thank you for saying that.

W: I'd therefore like to declare economics my major and ask you to be my academic advisor. Would that be possible?

M: Of course, it's possible. But I need to ask you . . . Are you sure that you want to major in economics?

W: Yes, sir. I am. I am actually taking two economics classes this semester. The first is with Professor Monroe while the second one is with, um, Professor Parkins.

M: Ah, those should be good classes. Both of them are very good lecturers.

W: Yes, I'm learning a lot in each class. So, uh, I need to fill out a form and have you sign it, right?

M: That's correct, but I'm afraid that I don't have this form in my office.

W: Don't worry. I brought it with me. I just need to get your signature and the signature of my freshman advisor. I plan to do that right after I leave your office.

M: I'm glad to see that you've already got the form. Let me just find a pen somewhere.

해석

W Student: 안녕하세요, Johanssen 교수님. 교수님과 이야기를 나눌 수 있을까요?

M Professor: 안녕하세요. 오… 기억이 나는군요. 지난 학기에 제 미시경제학 수업을 들었죠. 학생의 수업 성적이 매우 좋았던 것으로 기억해요. 그런데… 안타깝지만 학생의 이름은 기억이 나지 않는군요.

W: 저는 Amy Riley입니다, 교수님.

M: 아, 맞아요. 제가 기억했어야 하는데. 그러면 어떻게 도와 주면 될까요, Amy?

W: 음, 어, 이번에 2학년이 되어서 전공을 결정해야 해요. 제가 들었던 교수님 수업이 정말로 재미있었고, 그리고 저는 교수님께서 훌륭하신 분이라고 생각했어요.

M: 그렇게 말해 주다니 고맙군요.

W: 그래서 전공으로 경제학을 선택하고 싶은데, 교수님께 제 경제학 지도 교수님이 되어 달라고 요청을 드리고 싶어요. 가능할까요?

M: 물론 가능하죠. 하지만 학생에게 질문을 하자면… 정말로 경제학을 전공하고 싶은가요?

W: 네, 교수님. 그래요. 실제로 이번 학기에 두 개의 경제학 수업을 들을 예정이에요. 첫 번째는 Monroe 교수님 수업이고 두 번째는, 음, Parkins 교수님 수업이죠.

M: 아, 좋은 수업일 거예요. 두 분 모두 매우 강의를 잘하시는 분들이시죠.

W: 네, 각각의 수업에서 많이 배우게 될 거예요. 그러면, 어, 제가 양식을 작성해

서 교수님 사인을 받아야 하죠, 맞나요?

M: 그렇기는 하지만 안타깝게도 제 사무실이 양식이 없는 것 같군요.

W: 걱정하지 마세요. 제가 가지고 왔어요. 교수님의 서명과 1학년 때의 제 지도 교수님의 서명만 받으면 되죠. 그분 서명은 교수님 사무실에서 나간 후에 바로 받을 생각이에요.

M: 이미 양식을 가지고 있다니 잘 되었군요. 볼펜을 좀 찾아볼게요.

📝 **Summary Note**

A

❶ her major

❷ a form

B

The student says that she took the professor's class last year and enjoyed it. Now, she wants to declare economics her major and have the professor be her academic advisor. The professor asks her if she is sure she wants to major in economics, and she says yes. So he agrees to be her advisor. The student is also taking two economics classes this semester. The professor needs to sign a form the student has already filled out. Then, she will get her freshman advisor's signature.

Exercise 3   1 Ⓐ   2 Ⓒ p.164

Script 🎧 06-10

M Student: Good afternoon. I'm looking for Juliet Harrison. Do you know where I can find her?

W Writing Center Employee: Hello. I'm Juliet. Is there something I can help you with?

M: I sure hope so. My name is Samuel Wallace. I spoke on the telephone with you earlier this morning.

W: Ah, right. You are here about a job as a writing tutor, right?

M: That's correct. I, uh, I have a letter of recommendation from Professor McMurray in the English Department. Here you are.

W: Thank you. Hold on and let me look at it really quickly, please . . .

M: Sure. Take your time.

W: Hmm . . . It looks like the professor thinks very highly of your writing skills. He also notes that you never make any grammar mistakes on your papers and that your writing is technically proficient.

M: He's very kind.

W: Well, we have a couple of jobs that are available for students like you. The first is to be a writing tutor. Basically, you would work one on one with various students to help them improve their writing.

M: What's the other position?

W: The other position is proofreader. You'd be responsible for proofreading students' essays and term papers. You would need to catch mistakes and also make suggestions on how to improve their papers. Personally, I think you'd be better off taking this job.

M: Why is that?

W: You can work from home since papers will be emailed to you. The pay is really good, and you'll have a chance to make a lot of money if you do a good job.

M: I guess I'll go with that position then. Thanks.

해석

M Student: 안녕하세요. Juliet Harrison 선생님을 찾고 있어요. 어디에서 그분을 찾을 수 있는지 아시나요?

W Writing Center Employee: 안녕하세요. 제가 Juliet이에요. 제가 도와 드릴 일이 있을까요?

M: 도와 주시면 좋겠어요. 제 이름은 Samuel Wallace예요. 오늘 아침 일직 신 선생님과 전화를 통화를 했죠.

W: 아, 맞아요. 글쓰기 교사의 일자리에 때문에 여기에 온 거죠, 그렇죠?

M: 맞아요. 저는, 어, 영문학과의 McMurray 교수님의 추천서를 가지고 있어요. 여기 있어요.

W: 고마워요. 잠시만 기다리시면 제가 정말로 빨리 살펴볼게요…

M: 그러세요. 천천히 보세요.

W: 흠… 교수님께서 학생의 글쓰기 실력을 매우 높게 생각하시는 것처럼 보이는군요. 또한 학생이 보고서에서 문법과 관련된 실수를 한 적이 없다는 점과 학생의 글이 기술적으로 우수하다는 점을 말씀하시네요.

M: 매우 친절하시죠.

W: 음, 학생과 같은 사람이 구할 수 있는 일자리는 두 개가 있어요. 첫 번째는 글쓰기 교사가 되는 것이에요. 기본적으로 학생은 다양한 학생들을 대상으로 그들의 글쓰기 실력을 향상시키기 위해 일대일로 교육을 하게 될 거예요.

M: 다른 자리는 어떤 건가요?

W: 다른 자리는 교정을 보는 것이에요. 학생들의 에세이와 기말 보고서를 교정보는 일을 맡게 될 거예요. 실수를 찾아내야 하고 또한 어떻게 보고서를 개선시킬 수 있는지에 관한 제안도 해야 하죠. 개인적으로는 이 일을 하는 것이 학생에게 더 좋을 것 같다고 생각해요.

M: 왜 그런가요?

W: 보고서들이 이메일로 학생에게 전송될 것이기 때문에 집에서 일을 할 수가 있어요. 급여도 정말 좋기 때문에 일을 잘 해내면 돈을 많이 벌 수 있는 기회도 갖게 될 것이고요.

M: 그럼 그 자리를 받아들여야 할 것 같군요. 감사합니다.

✏️ **Summary Note**

A

❶ a writing tutor
❷ letter of recommendation
❸ writing tutor

B

The student visits the writing center to talk about a job as a writing tutor. He has a letter of recommendation from a professor. The professor writes that the student never makes grammar mistakes and is a technically proficient writer. The woman describes the job of writing tutor and then says that a proofreading job is available as well. She recommends the proofreading job and then explains its benefits. The student decides to become a proofreader.

Exercise 4   1 Ⓐ   2 Ⓓ   p.166

Script 🎧 06-11

M Student: Hi, Professor Jones. May I speak with you for a few moments?

W Professor: Sure, Mark. How can I be of service to you today?

M: I heard you are in charge of the student exchange program for the International Studies Department.

W: That's right. Are you interested in studying abroad?

M: Well, I'd never thought about it before. But I've been reading my course book, and it recommends spending a semester abroad for students like me majoring in international law.

W: That's absolutely correct. For students in your major, it's recommended that you spend six months to a year abroad. It will prepare you for the type of work you'll be doing, and it will help you determine your country or region of focus. So where do you think you'd like to study?

M: Well, I've been thinking about a few places. I've always wanted to go to Sudan.

W: The Sudan? Isn't it in the middle of a civil war? Do you really want to go there?

M: I've been reading about it, and I think I could help save some lives or something.

W: Hmm, I don't think that's a very realistic place for you to get much studying done. Do you have a second or third choice?

M: Yeah, you're probably right. My parents are Hungarian. So I speak Hungarian fluently. It would be easy for me to study in Budapest since I speak the language.

W: Now that is a much more realistic idea. I actually know of a good law school located in Budapest. We have some of its students studying here now. Maybe I could introduce you to them, and you could make some connections.

M: That would be great. I'd love to make some friends if

I went there. It would be nice to know some people right away.

M Student: 안녕하세요, Jones 교수님. 잠깐 말씀을 나눌 수 있을까요?

W Professor: 물론이죠, Mark. 어떤 도움이 필요한가요?

M: 교수님께서 국제학부를 위한 교환 학생 프로그램을 담당하고 계신다고 들었습니다.

W: 맞아요. 유학에 관심이 있나요?

M: 음, 그에 대해서는 한 번도 생각해 본 적이 없어요. 하지만 책을 읽고 있는데, 책에서 저와 같은 국제법 전공 학생들에게 한 학기의 유학 생활을 추천하더군요.

W: 정말 맞는 얘기예요. 국제법 전공자들의 경우, 6개월에서 1년 동안 유학 생활을 하는 것이 권장되죠. 나중에 하게 될 일에 대한 준비도 되고, 초점을 맞출 국가나 지역을 결정하는데도 도움이 될 거에요. 그러면 어디에서 공부를 하고 싶은가요?

M: 음, 몇몇 지역을 생각 중이에요. 항상 수단에 가고 싶다는 생각은 했고요.

W: 수단이요? 지금 내전이 한창이지 않나요? 정말로 그곳에 가고 싶어요?

M: 그에 관한 글을 읽었는데, 제가 인명을 구하는 일 등에서 도움이 될 수 있을 것이라고 생각해요.

W: 흠, 그곳은 학생이 공부를 많이 할 수 있는 매우 현실적인 장소라고 생각되지 않는군요. 혹시 두 번째나 세 번째의 선택지가 있나요?

M: 그래요, 교수님 말씀이 맞는 것 같아요. 저희 부모님들께서는 헝가리 출신이세요. 그래서 제가 헝가리어에 능숙하죠. 헝가리어를 할 줄 알기 때문에 부다페스트에서 공부하면 수월할 것 같아요.

W: 훨씬 더 현실적인 생각이군요. 사실 저도 부다페스트에 있는 훌륭한 로스쿨에 대해 알고 있어요. 그곳 학생들 중 현재 이곳에서 공부를 하는 학생들도 있죠. 아마 제가 학생에게 그들을 소개시켜 주면 인맥을 쌓을 수도 있을 거에요.

M: 그러면 정말 좋겠어요. 만약 제가 그곳으로 가게 된다면 친구들을 사귀고 싶었거든요. 지금 당장 아는 사람이 생기면 좋을 것 같아요.

✏ Summary Note

A

❶ Sudan

❷ Good law school

B

The student is interested in studying abroad. He talks to the professor, who is in charge of the student exchange program. The professor asks the student where he would like to study. The student says he would like to study in the Sudan. The professor says it is an unrealistic idea because the country is in civil war. The student says his second choice is Budapest because he speaks Hungarian fluently. The professor thinks it is a good idea. He offers to introduce the student to some Hungarian exchange students at the school.

Exercises with Mid-Length Lectures

Exercise 1   1 ⓒ   2 ⓒ   p.168

Script 🎧 06-12

W Professor: Class, today I want to tell you about the process of pollination. Pollination is an important step in the reproduction of seed plants. This is the name for the transfer of pollen grains to the plant carpel. The carpel is the structure that contains the ovule. The pollen grains are the male gamete, and the ovule is the female gamete. The receptive part of the carpel is called a stigma in the flowers of angiosperms and a micropyle in gymnosperms.

The study of pollination brings together many disciplines, such as botany, horticulture, entomology, and ecology. Pollination is important in horticulture because most plant fruits will not develop if the ovules are not fertilized. The pollination process as an interaction between flower and vector was first addressed in the eighteenth century by Christian Konrad Sprengel.

The process of pollination requires pollinators as agents that carry or move the pollen grains from the anther to the receptive part of the carpel. The various flower traits that attract different pollinators are known as pollinator syndromes.

One method of pollination common with plants is entomophily, which is pollination by insects. Bees, wasps, butterflies, and flies are just a few of the insects that usually take part in this process. Another method is called zoophily. This denotes pollination by vertebrates, such as birds or bats. The hummingbird and the honeyeater are helpful with this process.

Yet another method of pollination is anemophily, which is by the wind. This is common with many types of grasses and deciduous trees. In the case of aquatic plants, pollination by water is called hydrophily. All of these pollination processes are covered by two categories, biotic and abiotic pollination. Biotic covers pollination by organisms, including entomophily and zoophily. This includes eighty percent of all pollination. Abiotic pollination covers all types not carried out by other organisms, including anemophily and hydrophily. Of the twenty percent this covers, ninety-eight percent is by wind and just two percent by water.

W Professor: 여러분, 오늘은 수분 과정에 대해 말씀을 드리고자 해요. 수분은 종자 식물의 번식에 있어서 중요한 단계입니다. 이는 화분립을 식물의 암술잎으로 옮기는 것을 말하죠. 암술잎은 식물의 밑씨를 포함하고 있는 구조입니다. 화분립은 수배우자이고 밑씨는 암배우자예요. 암술잎의 수용기 부분은, 피자 식물의 경우 암술머리라고 불리고, 나자 식물의 경우에는 주공이라고 불립니다.

수분 연구에는 다수의 학문 분야들, 예컨대 식물학, 원예학, 곤충학, 그리고 생태학이 관련되어 있어요. 밑씨가 수정되지 않는 경우 대부분의 식물들의 열매가 자라나지 않기 때문에 수분은 원예학에서 중요합니다. 꽃과 수분 매개자들 간의 상호 작용으로서 수분 과정이 처음 연구된 것은 18세기로, 이는 크리스티안 콘라트 스프렝겔에 의해 이루어졌어요.

수분 과정에는 또 다른 곳에서 나온 화분립을 암술잎의 수용기 부분으로 가지고 오거나 옮겨다 주는 수분 매개자들이 필요합니다. 각기 다른 수분 매개자들을 유인하는 다양한 꽃의 특성들은 수분 신드롬이라고 알려져 있죠.

식물의 흔한 수분 방법 중 하나는 충매로, 이는 곤충에 의한 수분을 뜻합니다. 꿀벌, 말벌, 나비, 그리고 파리들이 주로 이러한 과정에 참여하는 곤충들이에요. 또 다른 방법은 동물매입니다. 이는 새나 박쥐와 같은 척추 동물에 의한 수분을 가리키죠. 벌새와 꿀빨이새가 이러한 과정에 도움을 줍니다.

또 다른 수분 방법은 풍매로, 이는 바람에 의한 것이에요. 여러 종류의 풀과 낙엽수에 있어서 흔한 방식이죠. 수중 식물의 경우, 물에 의한 수분을 수매라고 부릅니다. 이러한 모든 수분 과정은 생물적 수분과 무생물적 수분이라는 두 가지 카테고리로 구분할 수 있어요. 생물적 수분에는 생물에 의한 수분이 해당되는데, 여기에는 충매와 동물매가 포함됩니다. 전체 수분의 80%가 여기에 속하죠. 무생물적 수분에는 기타 생물에 의해 이루어지지 않는 모든 유형의 수분이 해당되는데, 여기에는 풍매와 수매가 포함됩니다. 20% 중에서 98%는 풍매에, 그리고 2%는 수매에 해당됩니다.

📝 Summary Note

A

❶ ovule

❷ Abiotic

B

Pollination is important for the reproduction of seed plants. Many plants will not develop if their ovules are not fertilized. The process of pollination requires pollinators to act as agents and to carry pollen grains from the anther to the carpel. Pollination can either be carried out by biotic or abiotic means. Biotic refers to pollination by other living organisms. This often includes hummingbirds, bees, and bats. Abiotic refers to pollination by natural means, such as wind and water. Most pollination is biotic.

Exercise 2 1 Ⓓ 2 Ⓐ p.170

Script 🎧 06-13

M1 Professor: All right, class. Let's get started. I'd like to begin today's class with a simple activity. With your left hand, I want you to pat yourself on the head. With your right hand, I want you to rub your belly with a circular motion. Can you do it?

M2 Student: Hey, this is really difficult! I can't do it.

W Student: I've got it! It just takes a lot of attention. Check this out!

M1: Okay, everyone can stop now. I asked you to do this because I wanted you to notice how difficult it is for your brain and nervous system to coordinate two different actions at the same time. This is called splitting your attention. Attention is the cognitive process of selectively concentrating on one thing while ignoring other things. One example is listening carefully to what someone is saying while ignoring other conversations in the room. This is called the cocktail party effect. Attention can also be split, such as when a person drives a car and talks on a cellphone. Sometimes our attention shifts to matters unrelated to the external environment. This is referred to as mind wandering or spontaneous thought.

W: But I was able to pat my head and rub my belly at the same time. What does that mean about me?

M1: Well, that means that you are capable of splitting your attention. That reminds me of the most famous definition of attention by one of the first major psychologists, William James. He said, "Everyone knows what attention is. It is the taking possession by the mind in clear and vivid form, of one out of what seem to be several simultaneously possible objects or trains of thought. It implies withdrawal from some things in order to deal effectively with others."

W: Hmm, that sounds interesting. But how is the action of rubbing my belly and patting my head linked to focusing my mind?

M1: Good question. It is linked because your cerebral cortex controls your fine motor skills, which is what those motions require.

해석

M1 Professor: 좋습니다, 여러분. 시작하도록 하죠. 간단한 동작으로 오늘 수업을 시작하고자 해요. 왼손으로 머리를 가볍게 두드려 보시기 바랍니다. 오른손으로는 원 모양을 그리며 배를 문질러 보시고요. 하실 수 있나요?

M2 Student: 와, 이거 정말 어렵네요! 저는 못 하겠어요.

W Student: 저는 돼요! 신경을 많이 써야 하지만요. 보세요!

M1: 좋아요. 모두들 이제 그만하셔도 좋습니다. 제가 여러분께 그런 요청을 드린 것은 여러분 뇌와 신경계가 두 가지 서로 다른 동작을 동시에 해 내기가 얼마나 어려운지 여러분께서 아셨으면 했기 때문이에요. 이를 주의력 분산이라고 부릅니다. 주의는 한 가지에 선택적으로 집중하면서 다른 것은 무시하는 인지 과정이에요. 한 가지 예는 방 안에서 일어나는 다른 대화는 무시하면서 누군가가 하는 말에 주의를 기울여 듣는 것입니다. 이를 칵테일 파티 효과라고 불러요. 주의력은 또한, 예컨대 운전을 하면서 휴대 전화로 통화를 할 때와 같이, 분산될 수도 있습니다. 때때로 우리의 주의력은 외부 환경과 관계가 없는 문제로 옮겨 가기도 합니다. 이를 마음의 방황 또는 자발적 사고라고 부르죠.

W: 하지만 저는 머리를 두드리면서 동시에 배를 문지를 수 있었어요. 그건 무엇을 의미하나요?

M1: 음, 그러한 점은 학생이 주의력을 분산시킬 수 있다는 점을 의미해요. 그로 인해 최초의 중요한 심리학자 중 한 명이었던 윌리엄 제임스가 내린 주의력에 대한 가장 유명한 정의가 떠오르네요. 그는 "누구나 주의력이 무엇인지 안다. 주의력은 몇 가지 동시에 떠오르는 생각의 대상이나 일련의 생각 중에서 하나를 명료하고 생생한 형태로 마음에 담는 것이다. 이는 다른 일들을 효과적으로 처리하기 위해 몇 가지 일들을 제쳐 놓는다는 점을 암시한다."고 말을 했죠.

W: 흠, 흥미롭게 들리는군요. 하지만 어떻게 제 배를 문지르고 머리를 두드리는 것이 생각을 집중하는 것과 관련이 있나요?

M1: 좋은 질문이에요. 관련이 있는 이유는 그러한 동작에 필요한 미세한 운동 능력을 대뇌 피질이 제어하기 때문입니다.

Summary Note

A

❶ selectively concentrating

❷ two different actions

B

Coordinating the brain and the nervous system to do two different actions at the same time is called splitting attention. Attention is the cognitive process of selectively concentrating on one thing while ignoring other things. William James was one of the first major psychologists. He defined attention as "the taking possession by the mind, in clear and vivid form, of one out of what seem to be several simultaneous possible objects or trains of thought." The attention of one's mind is linked to the cerebral cortex, which controls fine motor skills.

Exercise 3 1 2   p.172

Script 🎧 06-14

M Professor: Right now, I'd like to tell you about the development of the American educational system. The first American schools opened during the Colonial Era. As the colonies began to develop, many of them instituted mandatory education schemes. In 1642, the Massachusetts Bay Colony made "proper" education compulsory. Similar statutes were accepted in other colonies in the 1640s and 1650s. Virtually all of the schools that opened as a result of this were private. Most of the universities which appeared between 1640 and 1750 form the contemporary Ivy League. They include Harvard, Yale, Columbia, Brown, and the University of Pennsylvania. After the revolution, an even heavier emphasis was put on education. This made the United States have one of the highest literacy rates of the time.

The school systems remained largely private and unorganized until the 1840s. Education reformers such as Horace Mann of Massachusetts began calling for public education systems for all. He helped create a statewide system of common schools, which referred to the belief that everyone was entitled to the same content in education. These early efforts focused primarily on elementary education.

The common-school movement began to catch on. By 1900, thirty-one states required children eight to fourteen years of age to attend school. In 1918, every state required students to complete elementary school. Lessons consisted of students reading aloud from their texts, such as the *McGuffery Readers*, and emphasis was placed on rote memorization. Teachers often used physical punishments, such as hitting students on the knuckles with birch switches for incorrect answers.

Secondary education progressed much more slowly, remaining the province of the affluent and the domain of private tutors. In 1870, only two percent of teens fourteen to seventeen years old graduated from high school. The introduction of strict child labor laws and the growing acceptance of higher education in general in the early twentieth century caused the number of high school graduates to skyrocket. Most states passed laws which increased the age for compulsory school attendance to sixteen.

해석

M Professor: 이제 미국 교육 시스템의 발달에 대해 말씀을 드리고자 합니다. 미국 최초의 학교는 식민지 시대에 문을 열었어요. 식민지들이 발전하기 시작하면서 다수의 식민지들이 의무 교육을 도입했죠. 1642년 매사추세츠 베이 식민지가 "정규" 교육을 의무화했습니다. 1640년대와 1650년대에는 다른 식민지들에서도 비슷한 법령이 통과되었어요. 이러한 결과로 문을 연 학교들은 거의 모두 사립이었습니다. 1640년과 1750년 사이에 생긴 대부분의 대학들이 현재의 아이비 리그를 이루고 있어요. 여기에는 하버드, 예일, 콜롬비아, 브라운, 그리고 펜실베이니아 대학이 포함되죠. 그러한 큰 변화가 있은 후 교육은 훨씬 더 강조되었어요. 이로 인해 당시 미국의 문자 해독률은 가장 높은 편에 속했습니다.

학교들은 1840년대까지 대부분 사립이었고 체계적이지 못했어요. 매사추세츠의 호레이스 맨과 같은 교육 개혁가들이 모든 이들을 위한 공립 교육 시스템을 요구하기 시작했습니다. 그는 주 전체의 공립 학교 시스템을 세우는데 도움을 주었는데, 이는 모두가 동일한 교육을 받을 자격이 있다는 믿음에 기반해 있었죠. 이러한 초기의 노력들은 주로 초등 교육에 집중되어 있었습니다.

공립 초등학교 운동은 인기를 얻기 시작했어요. 1900년경 31개의 주에서는 8세에서 14세까지의 아동들이 학교에 다녀야만 했습니다. 1918년에는 모든 주에서 학생들이 초등학교를 마쳐야만 했죠. 수업 시간에 학생들은 맥거퍼리 리더스와 같은 교재들을 큰 소리로 읽었으며, 기계적인 암기가 강조되었습니다. 종종 교사들은 오답을 말한 학생들의 손을 자작나무 회초리로 때리는 체벌을 가하기도 했어요.

중등 교육은 부유한 지방 및 개인 교사의 영역에 머물면서 훨씬 더 느리게 발전했습니다. 1870년에는 14세에서 17세 사이의 십대들 중 불과 2%만이 고등학교를 졸업했죠. 엄격한 아동 노동법이 도입되고 20세기 초반 고등 교육을 전반적으로 수용하는 경우가 많아지자 고등학교 졸업생 수가 급증하기 시작했어요. 대부분의 주들이 의무 교육 연령을 16세로 높이는 법안을 통과시켰습니다.

Summary Note

A

❶ compulsory

❷ Ivy League

❸ 16 years

B

The first American schools opened during the Colonial Era. After the revolution, a heavier emphasis was placed on education. School systems remained private until the 1840s. Then, educational reformers began calling for public education systems. They believed everyone was entitled to the same content in education. By 1900, thirty-one states required children eight to fourteen years of age to attend school. Secondary education progressed more slowly. In the early twentieth century, strict child labor laws and growing acceptance of higher education caused the number of high school graduates to skyrocket.

Exercise 4 1 ⓓ 2 ⓐ   p.174

Script 🎧 06-15

W1 Professor: That's enough about Venus. Let's move on to the fourth planet from the sun. It's named after Mars, the Roman god of war. Until the first flyby of Mars by *Mariner 4* in 1965, it was thought that there were channels of liquid water on the planet's surface. People called these Martian canals. Observations later showed that these channels do not exist. Still, of all the planets in our solar system after Earth, Mars is the most likely to harbor liquid water and possibly life.

M Student: What about time on Mars? I heard it takes longer to travel around the sun than Earth does.

W1: Very good. That's right. Mars has a similar axial tilt to that of Earth, so it has similar seasonal periods. But it's farther from the sun and takes longer to orbit. So a Martian year is 687 Earth days long. Interestingly enough, a solar day on Mars is almost the same as Earth, being twenty-four hours, thirty-nine minutes, and thirty-five seconds.

W2 Student: What about its atmosphere? Is it possible for humans to breathe on Mars?

W1: Well, Mars has an atmosphere. But since it contains only traces of oxygen, you wouldn't want to breathe it. The Martian atmosphere is ninety-five percent carbon dioxide, three percent nitrogen, and 1.6% argon. During the winter months, the atmosphere gets so cold that it condenses into thick slabs of dry ice.

M: But you just said that it's possible for life to exist there. What kind of life could live in that kind of atmosphere?

W1: That's an interesting question. Some evidence suggests that the planet was once significantly more habitable than it is today. But whether living organisms ever existed there is still an open question. The *Viking* probes of the mid-1970s carried experiments designed to detect microorganisms in Martian soil and had some positive results. But these were later disputed by many

scientists.

해석

W1 Professor: 금성에 대해서는 충분히 다룬 것 같군요. 오늘은 태양에서 네 번째 떨어져 있는 행성으로 넘어가 보죠. 로마의 전쟁의 신 이름을 딴 화성입니다. 1965년 *마리너 4*호의 첫 번째 근접 비행이 있기 전까지 이 행성의 표면에는 액체 상태의 물로 이루어진 수로가 있다고 생각되었어요. 사람들은 이를 화성 운하라고 불렀죠. 이후 관찰한 바에 따르면 이들 운하는 존재하지 않았어요. 하지만 태양계에 있는 행성 가운데 지구 다음으로 화성에 물과 생명체가 존재할 가능성이 가장 큽니다.

M Student: 화성에서의 시간은 어떤가요? 태양 주위를 도는데 지구보다 시간이 더 걸린다고 들었어요.

W1: 매우 훌륭하군요. 맞아요. 화성은 지구와 비슷한 기울기의 축을 가지고 있기 때문에 비슷한 계절이 나타납니다. 하지만 태양에서 더 멀리 떨어져 있고 공전 주기가 더 길어요. 그래서 화성에서의 1년은 지구 시간으로 계산하면 687일이 되죠. 흥미롭게도 화성에서의 태양일은 지구와 거의 같은 24시간 39분 35초입니다.

W2 Student: 대기는 어떤가요? 인간이 화성에서 숨을 쉴 수 있나요?

W1: 음, 화성에도 대기가 있죠. 하지만 대기에 포함된 산소가 매우 적기 때문에 숨을 쉬고 싶지는 않을 거예요. 화성의 대기는 95%가 이산화탄소, 3%가 질소, 그리고 1.6%가 아르곤으로 이루어져 있어요. 겨울에는 대기의 온도가 크게 내려가기 때문에 대기가 응결되어 두꺼운 얼음판이 됩니다.

M: 하지만 조금 전에 그곳에 생명체가 존재할 가능성이 있다고 말씀하셨잖아요. 어떤 종류의 생물이 그러한 대기에서 생존할 수 있을까요?

W1: 흥미로운 질문이네요. 일부 증거들은 이 행성이 한때 오늘날보다 훨씬 더 살기에 적합했다는 점을 암시합니다. 하지만 생명체가 존재한 적이 있었는지는 아직까지도 의문이에요. 1970년대 중반 *바이킹* 탐사선들이 화성의 토양에 있는 미생물을 탐지하기 위한 실험을 실시했는데, 몇 가지 긍정적 결과가 있었습니다. 하지만 이러한 결과들은 후에 많은 과학자들 사이에서 논쟁의 대상이 되었어요.

✏️ Summary Note

A

❶ liquid water
❷ Carbon dioxide

B

Mars is the fourth planet from the sun. Canals on the planet's surface that were once believed to exist do not. But Mars is still the most likely place in the solar system, besides Earth, to harbor liquid water and possibly life. Mars has seasonal periods similar to Earth's. But its year is almost twice as long. The Martian atmosphere contains only traces of oxygen. During the winter months, the atmosphere gets so cold that it condenses into dry ice. Whether living organisms exist on Mars is still an open question.

A

Script 🎧 06-16

> **M Professor:** Everyone, try to pat your heads with one hand and then rub your bellies with the other . . . It's difficult, right . . . ? This is an example of splitting your attention, which, uh, as you have learned, is extremely hard to do. Attention, by the way, is the cognitive process of selectively concentrating on one thing while ignoring other things. Now, uh, what about William James, who was one of the first major psychologists? James's definition of attention defines it as the mind taking possession of several simultaneous objects or trains of thought. As for the matter regarding how attention is linked to physical actions, a person's attention is linked to the cerebral cortex, which controls fine motor skills.

1 a. He asks them to pat their heads with one hand and to rub their bellies with their other.

  b. He tells them about patting their heads with one hand and rubbing their bellies with the other.

2 a. He says it is a cognitively selective process of concentrating and ignoring things.

  b. He explains that it is the cognitive process of selectively concentrating on one thing while ignoring other things.

3 a. It is linked by the cerebral cortex and fine motor skills.

  b. It is linked to the cerebral cortex, which controls fine motor skills.

B

Script 🎧 06-17

> **M Professor:** It's important for everyone to know that the first American schools opened during the Colonial Era. The Massachusetts Bay Colony was the first to make education compulsory. After the revolution, the U.S. put a heavier emphasis on education, which gave the country one of the highest literacy rates. Then, in the 1840s, education reformers began calling for public school systems. Horace Mann was a reformer who believed everyone was entitled to the same educational content. But many of the teaching methods were by rote memorization and punishment for incorrect answers. Secondary education did not become common until the twentieth century, when the number of high school graduates skyrocketed.

1 a. He begins by explaining that the first American schools opened during the Colonial Era.

  b. He begins with an explanation of the first American

schools and their opening during the Colonial Era.

2 a. A heavier emphasis was put on education by the United States after the revolution.

  b. The United States put a heavier emphasis on education after the revolution.

3 a. Many of the teaching methods were by rote memorization and punishment for incorrect answers.

  b. Many teaching methods were rote memorization and included punishment for incorrect answers.

Mini TOEFL iBT Practice Test
p.178

1 ⓓ	2 ⓒ	3 Ⓐ, ⓓ	4 Ⓑ	5 Ⓑ
6 ⓒ	7 Ⓐ	8 ⓓ	9 ⓓ	10 Ⓐ
11 Ⓐ				

[1-5]

Script 🎧 06-18

> **W Student:** Professor Watkins, I urgently need to speak with you.
>
> **M Professor:** Well, you're in luck, Katrina. I just finished my last class of the day, so I have a few minutes to speak with you. What's going on?
>
> **W:** I need to talk about the project I'm doing for your marketing class.
>
> **M:** Sure. How is it going?
>
> **W:** Well, that's what I need to speak to you about.
>
> **M:** There's a problem?
>
> **W:** Yes, there is. The problem is that my partner hasn't done anything at all on the project. In fact, I've only been able to meet her once, and that was on the first day you assigned partners to us.
>
> **M:** Hmm . . . Can you give me some more information, please?
>
> **W:** Sure. First, my partner's name is Karen Rochester. On the first day when we met, she seemed to be very interested in the project, and she had a few good ideas on what we could do.
>
> **M:** Go on.
>
> **W:** But after that, every time I called her and asked her to meet, she said that she was busy and didn't have time. I've also sent her a bunch of emails. She responded to the first one, but she hasn't answered any of the other ones that I've sent.
>
> **M:** That's strange.
>
> **W:** It is, isn't it? Anyway, I've been doing the project by

myself since she doesn't seem interested in it for some reason. But I thought you ought to know what's going on. Basically, I'm doing all of the work, and she has no input on this project.

M: Okay. I'm going to have to talk to Karen and get her side of the story, but it looks like you two have a big problem.

W: So what should I do?

M: Just work on the project by yourself. No matter what I find out, it appears as though you and Karen can't work together. I'm going to give her a call and ask her to visit me. I'll talk to her and then let you know what I find out.

W: Should I stay here in case she can come now?

M: No, that's not a good idea. I'd like to get her side of the story without you being around. I've got your email address somewhere, so I'll write you later and tell you what's going on.

W: Great. Thank you, sir.

M: And if you need any help on the project, please ask. Now, I need to make a phone call. I'll talk to you later.

해석

W Student: Watkins 교수님, 급하게 교수님께 말씀드릴 것이 있어서요.

M Professor: 음, 운이 좋군요, Katrina. 조금 전에 오늘의 마지막 수업을 끝냈기 때문에 몇 분 정도 학생과 이야기할 수 있는 시간이 있어요. 무슨 일인가요?

W: 교수님의 마케팅 수업에서 제가 하고 있는 프로젝트에 대해 말씀을 드리고 싶어요.

M: 그래요. 어떻게 되고 있나요?

W: 음, 그게 바로 제가 말씀드려야 할 내용이에요.

M: 문제가 있군요?

W: 네, 있어요. 문제는 제 파트너가 프로젝트에서 아무것도 하고 있지 않다는 점이에요. 실제로 저는 그녀를 단 한 차례 만날 수 있었는데, 그게 교수님께서 저희에게 파트너를 지정해 주신 첫 날이었어요.

M: 흠… 좀더 이야기를 해 줄 수 있나요?

W: 그럼요. 먼저, 제 파트너의 이름은 Karen Rochester예요. 우리가 처음 만난 날 그녀는 프로젝트에 매우 관심이 있는 것처럼 보였고, 우리가 무엇을 해야 하는지에 관해서도 몇 가지 아이디어를 가지고 있었죠.

M: 계속해 보세요.

W: 하지만 그 후 제가 그녀에게 전화를 해서 만나자고 할 때마다 그녀는 바빠서 시간이 없다고 대답했어요. 저는 그녀에게 여러 통의 이메일을 보내기도 했죠. 그녀는 첫 번째 이메일에만 답장을 하고 제가 보낸 나머지 이메일에는 전혀 답장을 하지 않았어요.

M: 이상하군요.

W: 이상하죠, 그렇죠? 어쨌든, 그녀가 어떤 이유로 프로젝트에 관심이 없어진 것 같아서 저는 혼자서 프로젝트를 수행하고 있어요. 하지만 무슨 일이 일어나고 있는지 교수님께서 반드시 아셔야 한다고 생각했어요. 기본적으로 제가 모든 일을 하고 있고, 그녀는 이번 프로젝트에 어떤 기여도 하고 있지 않아요.

M: 좋아요. 제가 Karen과 이야기를 해서 그녀의 입장을 들어봐야 할 것 같은데, 하지만 두 학생 모두에게 큰 문제가 있는 것 같아 보이네요.

W: 그러면 제가 어떻게 해야 할까요?

M: 혼자서 프로젝트를 수행하세요. 제가 무엇을 알아내던, 학생과 Karen은 함께 할 수 없는 것처럼 보이는군요. 제가 그녀에게 전화를 해서 저를 찾아오라고 할 거예요. 그녀와 이야기를 한 후 제가 알아낸 점을 학생에게 말해 줄게요.

W: 그럼 그녀가 올 경우에 대비해서 제가 여기에 있어야 하나요?

M: 아니요, 그건 좋은 생각이 아니에요. 학생이 없는 상태에서 그녀의 입장을 들어보고 싶어요. 어딘가에 학생의 이메일 주소가 있을 테니, 이후에 학생에게 이메일을 써서 무슨 일이 있는 것인지 알려 줄게요.

W: 잘 되었군요. 감사합니다, 교수님.

M: 그리고 프로젝트에 관해 도움이 필요하면 어떤 것이라도 얘기하세요. 자, 저는 전화를 걸어야 할 것 같군요. 나중에 이야기해요.

[6-11]

Script 🎧 06-19

M1 Professor: All right, today, we're going to be talking about something almost everybody here has used at one time or another: the bicycle. Who here rides a bike to class?

W Student: I just got a recumbent bicycle, but I didn't ride it to class today.

M1: It's funny that you would mention a recumbent bike because if you ask people in the International Union of Cycling, they don't consider it to be a true bicycle.

W: Seriously?

M1: It's true. I disagree with them, but they define the bicycle as a pedal-driven, human-powered vehicle with two wheels attached to the frame, one behind the other, with the seat positioned more or less above the pedals. Anyhow, I wonder if anybody can tell me why this child's toy is a significant invention in human history.

M2 Student: Maybe because it's popular in places where people don't have cars.

M1: Great! That was just the answer I was looking for. Bicycles were first introduced in Europe in the nineteenth century and now number more than one billion worldwide. They provide the principal means of transportation in many regions. They are also a popular form of recreation and have been adapted for use in many other fields of human activity, including children's toys, adult fitness, military and local police applications, courier services, and cycle sports.

M2: Wow, I never thought about bikes so seriously.

M1: Let's first consider how the shape and configuration of the bicycle's frame, wheels, pedals, saddle, and handlebars have changed. Since the first chain-driven model was developed around 1885, many important details have since been improved. On a modern bicycle, power is transmitted from the rider's legs to the rear wheel via the pedals, the crankset, the chain, and the rear hub. A cyclist's legs produce power optimally within a narrow pedaling speed range.

Now, let me go back to the earliest origins of the bicycle so we can see how much they've changed since then. The forebears of the bicycle were known as velocipedes. One of these was the dandy-horse. It was used in France in the 1790s. Historians believe that it was merely a seat with two wheels and no steering or pedal mechanisms.

In 1839, a Scottish blacksmith named Kirkpatrick MacMillan added a mechanical crank to the rear wheel of a pushbike, creating the first true bicycle. It was copied and improved upon by other Scottish builders.

해석

M1 Professor: 좋아요, 오늘은 여러분 거의 모두가 한두 번쯤 이용해 본 적이 있는 것에 대해 이야기를 하려고 해요. 바로 자전거입니다. 이 수업에 자전거를 타고 오는 사람이 있나요?

W Student: 저는 얼마 전에 리컴번트 자전거를 구입했지만, 오늘 수업에 타고 오지는 않았어요.

M1: 리컴번트 자전거를 언급하다니 재미있는데, 그 이유는 만약 국제 사이클 연맹의 사람들에게 물어본다면 그들은 그것을 진정한 자전거라고 생각하지 않을 것이기 때문이죠.

W: 정말인가요?

M1: 사실이에요. 저는 그들의 생각에 동의하지 않지만, 그들은 자전거를 페달에 의해 나아가고, 인간의 힘으로 작동하며, 프레임에 두 개의 바퀴가 앞뒤로 달려 있고, 페달 위쪽으로 안장이 위치해 있는 이동 수단으로 정의하고 있습니다. 그건 그렇고, 이러한 아이들을 위한 발명품이 인간 역사에서 중요한 이유를 아는 사람이 있는지 궁금하군요.

M2 Student: 아마도 차가 없는 사람들이 있는 곳에서 인기가 있기 때문일 것 같아요.

M1: 훌륭해요! 제가 기대했던 답이었어요. 자전거는 19세기 유럽에서 처음 등장해서 지금은 전 세계적으로 10억대 이상의 자전거가 존재합니다. 이들은 여러 지역에서 주요한 교통 수단이 되고 있어요. 또한 훌륭한 레크리에이션 형태이기도 하고, 다양한 분야의 인간 활동을 위해, 즉 아이들의 장난감, 성인용 운동 기구, 군 혹은 경찰 장비, 배달 수단, 그리고 사이클 스포츠 등의 용도에 따라 개조되어 왔습니다.

M2: 와, 저는 자전거에 대해 그렇게 진지하게 생각해 본 적이 없었어요.

M1: 우선 자전거의 프레임, 바퀴, 페달, 안장, 그리고 핸들바의 형태와 구조가 어떻게 변화했는지 살펴보도록 하죠. 1885년경 최초로 체인에 의해 나아가는 모델이 등장한 이래로 다수의 중요한 세부적인 사항들이 개선되었어요. 현대의 자전거에서는 동력이 라이더의 다리에서 페달, 크랭크셋, 체인, 그리고 러어 허브를 통해 뒷바퀴로 전달됩니다. 자전거를 타는 사람의 다리는 좁은 범위의 페달링 속도로 최적의 힘을 낼 수 있죠.

자, 자전거의 기원으로 돌아가서 그 이후로 얼마나 많은 변화들이 있었는지 살펴 봅시다. 자전거의 모태는 벨로시페드라고 알려져 있습니다. 이들 중의 하나가 댄디호스였죠. 이는 1790년대 프랑스에서 사용되었습니다. 역사가들은 이것이 단지 시트와 바퀴 두 개와 붙어 있는 것으로, 조종을 하거나 페달로 움직일 수 있는 것이 아니었다고 생각해요.

1839년 커크패트릭 맥밀란이라는 스코틀랜드의 대장장이가 푸시바이크 뒷바퀴에 크랭크 장치를 추가함으로써 최초의 진정한 자전거가 만들어졌어요. 이는 다른 스코틀랜드 제작자들에 의해 모방되고 개량되었습니다.

A   1 ⓒ   2 Ⓑ   3 Ⓚ   4 Ⓓ   5 Ⓜ
    6 Ⓛ   7 Ⓖ   8 Ⓙ   9 Ⓗ   10 Ⓐ
    11 Ⓘ   12 Ⓞ   13 Ⓝ   14 Ⓕ   15 Ⓔ

B   1 ⓒ   2 Ⓓ   3 Ⓑ   4 Ⓐ   5 Ⓔ

UNIT 07   Connecting Content

Basic Drill   p.186

Drill 1 Ⓐ

Script 🎧 07-02

M Student: Professor, here's the essay that's due tomorrow.

W Professor: Hmm . . . Hold on a minute there. Let me take a quick look at what you wrote.

M: I'm pretty sure I included all the details.

W: Actually, I don't think so.

M: Really?

W: Well, look at this. You have not explained the outcomes in any sort of detail at all.

M: What would you suggest I do?

W: By the looks of this, rewrite your introduction section so that you can make the cause-and-effect transition later in the essay. You also need to give me more supporting evidence on the causes so that you can easily describe the effects.

해석

M Student: 교수님, 내일 마감인 에세이 과제입니다.

W Professor: 흠... 잠깐만요. 어떻게 썼나 빨리 한 번 볼게요.

M: 분명 세부적인 것들을 모두 포함시켰어요.

W: 사실 그런 것 같지가 않네요.

M: 정말인가요?

W: 음, 이걸 봐요. 결과에 대해서는 전혀 자세하게 설명하지 않았잖아요.

M: 제가 어떻게 하면 될까요?

W: 이걸 보니 에세이 후반에 인과적인 전이 관계가 만들어질 수 있도록 도입부를 다시 쓰도록 하세요. 또한 결과를 쉽게 설명할 수 있도록 원인을 뒷받침해 주는 증거를 더 제시해야 해요.

Drill 2 Ⓐ

Script 🎧 07-03

M Student: Professor Sturgeon, I got your email. What do you want to talk about?

W Professor: You're planning to do a senior honors thesis during the next school year, right, Joe? I remember you said something about that.

M: That's correct, ma'am. Why do you ask?

W: I would like to suggest that you stay here this summer. You could find a job and start doing work on your thesis this summer. I could help you with your research.

M: Hmm . . . I was planning on going home, but I could change my plans if you think it's important.

W: I do. You'd be able to spend more time on the project, and that will let you produce better work.

해석

M Student: Sturgeon 교수님, 교수님의 이메일을 받았어요. 무엇에 대해 이야기하고 싶으신가요?

W Professor: 다음 학년에 졸업 논문을 쓸 계획이죠, 그렇죠, Joe? 학생이 그에 대해 이야기했던 것을 기억하고 있어요.

M: 맞아요, 교수님. 왜 물으시는 건가요?

W: 학생이 이번 여름에 이곳에서 지냈으면 좋겠어요. 이번 여름에 일자리를 찾고 논문 작업을 시작할 수 있을 거예요. 제가 연구를 도와 줄 수 있을 것 같아요.

M: 흠… 저는 집에 갈 계획이었는데, 교수님께서 그렇게 하는 것이 중요하다고 생각하신다면 제 계획을 바꿀 수 있어요.

W: 저는 그렇게 생각해요. 프로젝트에 대해 더 많은 시간을 쓸 수 있을 것이고, 그러면 더 좋은 논문을 작성할 수 있을 거예요.

Drill 3 Ⓒ

Script 🎧 07-04

W Student: Sir, may I have a word with you?

M Professor: Sure.

W: I can't decide which grad school I should go to.

M: Have you considered any overseas graduate programs?

W: Ah, well, not really. Are there any advantages to studying overseas?

M: Sure. I mean, not only would it give you a lot more choices of places where you can study, but, um, it would also broaden your chances at getting some practical experience in your major.

W: Well, I never thought of that.

M: You know, you really should consider it. Graduate students who study outside their home countries are much more serious with their grad school research.

해석

W Student: 교수님, 교수님과 이야기를 나눌 수 있을까요?

M Professor: 물론이죠.

W: 어떤 대학원에 다녀야 할지 결정을 내리지 못하겠어요.

M: 해외의 대학원 프로그램은 생각해 본 적이 있나요?

W: 아, 음, 아니에요. 해외 유학의 장점이 있나요?

M: 그럼요. 제 말은, 그러면 학생이 공부할 수 있는 장소에 대한 선택권이 더 많아지기도 하고, 음, 학생의 전공에 대한 실무적인 경험을 쌓을 수 있는 기회도 넓힐 수 있을 거예요.

W: 음, 그에 대해서는 한 번도 생각해 본 적이 없었어요.

M: 알겠지만, 꼭 고려해 보세요. 외국에서 공부를 하는 대학원생들은 자신의 연구에 훨씬 더 진지하게 임하죠.

Drill 4 Ⓑ

Script 🎧 07-05

M Professor: When Europeans first discovered the Magdalenian paintings of the Altamira Cave, Spain, in 1879, they were considered hoaxes by academics and ignored. Recent reappraisals and increasing numbers of discoveries, however, have illustrated their authenticity and have indicated high levels of artistry of Upper Paleolithic humans, who used only basic tools. The ages of the paintings at many sites remain a contentious issue since methods like radiocarbon dating can lead to faulty data by contaminating samples of older or newer material, and caves and rocky overhangs are typically littered with debris from many time periods.

해석

M Professor: 1879년 유럽인들이 스페인의 알타미라 동굴에서 막달레니안 벽화를 처음 발견했을 때 이 벽화들은 학계에 의해 조작된 것으로 간주되어 무시를 당했습니다. 하지만 최근에 재평가되고 점점 더 많은 발견이 이루어짐으로써 벽화의 진위가 확인되었고, 기본적인 도구만을 사용했던 후기 구석기인들의 뛰어난 예술성이 드러나게 되었습니다. 여러 장소에 있는 벽화의 연대에 대해서는 논란을 일으키는 문제가 여전히 존재하는데, 그 이유는 방사성 탄소 연대 측정법과 같은 방식들로 보다 오래된 혹은 보다 오래되지 않은 물질의 샘플들이 오염됨으로써 잘못된 데이터가 나올 수 있고, 동굴 및 돌출된 암석들이 보통 여러 시대에 걸쳐 만들어진 쓰레기들로 덮여 있기 때문입니다.

Drill 5 Ⓓ

Script 🎧 07-06

W Professor: Until a few decades ago, humans were thought to be quite different from other apes, so much so that many people still don't think of the term "apes" to include humans at all. However, it is not considered accurate by many biologists to think of apes in a biological sense without considering humans to be included. The terms "non-human apes" and "nonhuman great apes" are used with increasing frequency to show the relationship of humans to the other apes while still talking only about the nonhuman species.

W Professor: 수십 년 전까지 인간은 다른 유인원들과 크게 다르다고 생각되었기 때문에 아직까지 많은 사람들이 "유인원"이라는 용어에 결코 인간이 포함되지 않는다고 생각해요. 하지만 다수의 생물학자들에 따르면 포함되어야 하는 인간을 고려하지 않은 채 생물학적인 관점에서 유인원을 생각하는 것은 타당하지 않은 일입니다. "비인간 유인원" 및 "비인간 대형 유인원"과 같은 용어들이, 여전히 인간이 아닌 종들에 대해서만 이야기할 때 사용되기는 하지만, 인간과 다른 유인원들 간의 관계를 나타내기 위해 사용되는 경우가 점점 많아지고 있습니다.

Drill 6 Ⓐ

Script 🎧 07-07

W Professor: Dolphins are often regarded as one of the most intelligent animal species on the Earth, but it is difficult to say just how intelligent they are because of the complicated differences in sensory apparatus and response modes. They are social animals, living in pods of up to a dozen animals. In places with a high concentration of food, many pods can join temporarily, forming what is known as a super pod, and these groups may exceed 1,000 dolphins. These individuals communicate using a variety of clicks, whistles, and other vocalizations. Dolphins also use a type of echolocation by emitting calls. They listen to the echoes that return from various objects and then use these echoes to locate, range, and identify objects.

W Professor: 돌고래는 종종 지구에서 가장 똑똑한 동물 종 중 하나로 여겨지지만, 감각 기관과 반응 방식의 복잡한 차이 때문에 이들이 얼마나 똑똑한지 말하기는 어렵습니다. 이들은 사회적 동물로, 최대 12마리에 이르는 포드에서 살아갑니다. 먹이가 많이 모여 있는 곳에서는 여러 돌고래 떼들이 일시적으로 모여서 수퍼 포드라는 것을 형성하는데, 이러한 무리에는 1,000마리가 넘는 돌고래들이 있을 수도 있어요. 이들 각각의 돌고래들은 다양한 소리들을, 딸깍거리는 소리, 휘파람 소리, 그리고 기타 발성을 이용해 의사소통을 합니다. 돌고래들은 또한 소리를 냄으로써 일종의 반향 위치 추적을 합니다. 다양한 물체에서 되돌아오는 메아리를 들은 후에 이러한 메아리를 이용해서 물체의 위치, 범위, 그리고 정체를 알아내는 것이죠.

Exercises with Mid-Length Conversations

Exercise 1 1 Ⓐ 2 Ⓑ   p.188

Script 🎧 07-08

W Professor: Good afternoon, Hans. What are you

---

doing here?

M Student: I need to ask you for a big favor, Professor Voss.

W: Does this have to do with your presentation? Is your team not ready yet?

M: Yes, I am here about our presentation, but we are definitely ready. We finished all of the work a couple of days ago, and we're quite pleased with the results.

W: Then . . . what's going on?

M: As you know, there are four people in our group: Allison Watts, Martin Peterson, Sally Druthers, and myself. Unfortunately, it looks like Allison can't attend class on the day we're supposed to give our presentation.

W: Why not?

M: Apparently, she has a job interview scheduled for Friday. She tried to change it to another day, but the company told her she has to interview then. So she's going to miss class.

W: Can't you do the presentation without her?

M: Hmm . . . I guess we could, but she has an important speaking role. One of the other three of us would have to learn it quickly. We only have two days to do that.

W: I could ask another group in class today if they want to speak on Friday. But that's probably not going to happen. Most of the groups are not ready to speak yet.

M: Okay. Then what if we have to give our presentation on Friday?

W: Just learn Allison's role. I'll give you some leeway in case you make any mistakes. And I really need to talk to Allison. She's the one who should have come here. It shouldn't have been you.

M: Ah, okay. Thanks, ma'am.

W Professor: 좋은 오후예요, Hans. 여기에서 무엇을 하고 있나요?

M Student: 어려운 부탁을 드려야 할 것 같아서요, Voss 교수님.

W: 학생의 발표와 관련된 일인가요? 팀이 아직 준비가 되지 않았나요?

M: 네, 발표 때문에 오기는 했는데, 준비는 확실히 되어 있어요. 저희는 이틀 전에 모든 일을 끝냈고, 결과에 상당히 만족하고 있죠.

W: 그렇다면… 무슨 일인가요?

M: 아시다시피 저희 그룹에는 4명이 있어요. Allison Watts, Martin Peterson, Sally Druthers, 그리고 저예요. 안타깝게도, 저희가 발표를 하기로 예정된 날에 Allison이 수업에 들어오지 못할 것 같아요.

W: 왜 못 오나요?

M: 듣자 하니 금요일에 면접이 잡힌 것 같았어요. 그녀가 다른 날로 변경하려고 했지만, 회사에서 그때 면접을 보아야만 한다고 말을 해 주었죠. 그래서 그녀가 수업에 빠질 예정이에요.

W: 그녀가 없으면 발표를 할 수가 없나요?

M: 흠… 할 수는 있을 것 같은데, 그녀가 주로 말하는 역할을 맡고 있어서요. 우

리 중 한 명이 빨리 그 역할을 이어받아야 할 것 같아요. 그럴 수 있는 시간은 이틀뿐이고요.

W: 제가 수업의 다른 그룹에게 금요일에 발표를 하고 싶은지 물어볼 수는 있어요. 하지만 원하는 그룹이 없을 수도 있겠죠. 대부분의 그룹들이 아직 발표할 준비가 되어 있지 않을 거예요.

M: 그렇군요. 그러면 저희가 금요일에 꼭 발표를 해야 하는 경우에는 어떻게 하죠?

W: Allison의 역할을 이어받으세요. 실수를 하는 경우 상황을 감안해 줄게요. 그리고 저는 반드시 Allison과 이야기를 해야 해요. 여기에 와야 했던 사람은 바로 그녀이니까요. 학생이 아니고요.

M: 아, 그렇군요. 고맙습니다, 교수님.

✐ Summary Note

A

❶ job interview
❷ other groups

B

The student says that there is a problem with his group's upcoming presentation. One of the group members has a job interview on Friday, which is when the presentation is. The company will not change the date, so the student cannot attend the presentation. The professor says she will ask if any groups want to change times, but she doubts that will happen. She tells the student that his group might have to give their presentation on Friday, but she will give them some leeway since they have to learn the missing student's part.

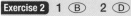

Exercise 2   1 ⓑ   2 ⓓ   p.190

Script 🎧 07-09

M Student: Hello. I'm here about the upcoming art exhibition the school gallery will be holding.

W Art Gallery Employee: Yes? What would you like to know about it?

M: It's going to take place in April, right?

W: That's correct. It will be held during the first two weeks of April like it always is.

M: That's great. So, uh . . . how can I get one of my works to be exhibited?

W: Hmm . . . Are you a student in the Art Department? Is that your major?

M: No, it's not. I'm just an amateur artist. I like to paint in my free time. I'm a chemistry major.

W: Well, the works that are exhibited here are normally selected by professors in the Art Department. They tend to choose students majoring in art since having a work displayed here is considered beneficial to the students.

M: I see. Well, uh, would you mind taking a look at my work really quickly? I have some pictures of my best paintings with me.

W: I don't mind doing that. Let me see them, please.

M: Here you are . . .

W: Well . . . Hmm . . . This is a very nice painting done in the Realist style . . . And this one is a great work that resembles the masters of the Italian Renaissance. Hmm . . . I must say I'm extremely impressed. Do you mind if I borrow your portfolio for a bit? I'm meeting some professors from the Art Department in ten minutes. I'd like to show them your work.

M: That would be wonderful. If it's okay with you, I'll just wait here and check out the artwork on display.

W: That's perfectly fine with me. I'll be back in around an hour.

해석

M Student: 안녕하세요. 곧 교내 박물관에서 개최될 예정인 미술전 때문에 왔는데요.

W Art Gallery Employee: 네? 그에 대해 무엇을 알고 싶으신가요?

M: 4월에 열릴 예정이죠, 맞나요?

W: 맞아요. 항상 그렇듯이 4월 첫째 주와 둘째 주에 개최될 예정이죠.

M: 잘 되었군요. 그러면, 어… 어떻게 하면 제 작품 중 하나를 전시할 수 있을까요?

W: 흠… 미대 학생인가요? 학생 전공이 미술이에요?

M: 아니요, 그렇지는 않아요. 저는 취미로 그림을 그리고 있어요. 여가 시간에 그림을 그리는 것을 좋아하죠. 화학 전공이고요.

W: 음, 이곳에 전시되는 작품들은 보통 미대 교수님들께서 선정하세요. 이곳에 작품을 전시하면 미대 학생들에게 도움이 되기 때문에 미술 전공 학생들을 선택하는 경향이 있으시죠.

M: 그렇군요. 음, 어, 잠깐만이라도 제 작품을 봐 주실 수 있으신가요? 제가 제일 잘 그린 그림 중 몇 개를 가지고 왔거든요.

W: 그렇게 하죠. 보여 주세요.

M: 여기 보시면…

W: 음… 흠… 이것은 사실주의 양식으로 그린 매우 멋진 작품이군요… 그리고 이것은 이탈리아 르네상스의 거장들의 작품과 비슷한 멋진 작품이네요. 흠… 제가 정말로 감명을 받았다고 말해야 할 것 같아요. 학생의 포트폴리오를 제가 잠시 빌려도 될까요? 10분 후에 미대 교수님 몇 분을 만날 예정이거든요. 그분들께 학생 작품을 보여 드리고 싶어요.

M: 그렇게 해 주시면 정말 좋겠어요. 괜찮으시면 저는 여기에서 기다리면서 전시된 미술 작품을 보고 있을게요.

W: 괜찮고 말고요. 한 시간 정도 후에 돌아올게요.

✐ Summary Note

A

❶ impressed with
❷ some art professors

B

The student asks the woman about getting a painting displayed at an upcoming exhibition. The woman asks if the student is an art major. He says that he is an amateur painter. The woman responds that most artwork chosen is by students in the Art Department. The student asks the woman if she would look at some pictures of his work. She agrees and is impressed with the work he has done. She wants to borrow his portfolio to show to some art professors she is meeting soon.

Exercise 3   1 Ⓐ   2 Ⓓ   p.192

Script 🎧 07-10

W Student: Professor Alvarez, I have something of a problem concerning my recent lab.

M Professor: What happened? Did you break some equipment?

W: Uh, no. I didn't do that. It's just that the results I got are incredibly different than what everyone else got.

M: That happens sometimes.

W: Yeah, but . . . what am I supposed to do?

M: Just write your lab report with your partner and turn it in.

W: It doesn't matter if the results I got were wrong?

M: How do you know that your results are wrong and that everyone else's results are right? Just because everyone else got different answers doesn't necessarily make them correct.

W: I, uh . . . I never thought of it like that.

M: Let me tell you something. The lab you just did is one of the trickiest of the semester. Every year, more than eighty percent of the class does this lab improperly and gets incorrect results.

W: Why do you give such a hard assignment?

M: It's not actually hard. It's basically a test to see if the students can follow the directions precisely. Most of the students don't pay close attention, so they make a mistake or two. That leads to wrong results. So . . . it's entirely possible that you're right while everyone else isn't.

W: I see. Okay. Thanks for letting me know, sir.

M: Good luck. See you in class tomorrow.

해석

W Student: Alvarez 교수님, 최근 실험과 관련해서 한 가지 문제가 생겼어요.

M Professor: 무슨 일이 있었나요? 장비를 파손시켰나요?

W: 어, 아니에요. 그렇지는 않아요. 제가 얻은 결과와 다른 모든 사람들이 얻은 결과가 엄청나게 달라서요.

M: 그런 일은 때때로 일어나요.

W: 그렇지는 하지만… 제가 어떻게 해야 할까요?

M: 파트너와 함께 실험 보고서를 작성해서 제출하도록 하세요.

W: 제가 얻은 결과가 잘못된 것은 상관이 없나요?

M: 학생의 결과가 잘못되었다는 것과 다른 모든 사람들의 결과가 옳다는 것을 어떻게 아나요? 다른 모든 사람들이 다른 결과를 얻었다는 점 때문에 그들이 반드시 옳다고 할 수는 없어요.

W: 저는, 어… 그렇게 생각해 본 적이 한 번도 없어요.

M: 제가 알려 드리죠. 학생이 한 실험은 이번 학기 동안 가장 까다로운 실험 중 하나예요. 매년 수업의 80% 이상이 실험을 잘못해서 올바르지 않은 결과를 얻게 되죠.

W: 왜 그처럼 어려운 과제를 내 주시는 건가요?

M: 사실 어려운 것이 아니에요. 기본적으로 학생들이 지침을 정확하게 따를 수 있는지를 보기 위한 하나의 테스트이죠. 대부분의 학생들이 주의를 잘 기울이지 않기 때문에 한두 개의 실수를 해요. 그래서 잘못된 결과를 얻게 되는 것이고요. 그래서… 학생이 맞고 다른 모든 사람들이 틀렸을 가능성도 커요.

W: 그렇군요. 알겠습니다. 알려 주셔서 감사해요, 교수님.

M: 행운을 빌게요. 내일 수업에서 봐요.

📝 **Summary Note**

A

❶ lab results
❷ pay attention

B

The student says she has a problem with her lab results because they are different than those of other students in the class. The professor tells her to write her lab report and to turn it in. He says that the other students may be wrong while she may be right. He then adds that the lab is tricky and that many students do it improperly because they do not pay attention.

Exercise 4   1 Ⓒ   2 Ⓓ   p.194

Script 🎧 07-11

M Student: Hello. I wonder if you can give me some assistance.

W Student Housing Office Employee: If it has to do with your dorm room, I'll give it my best shot.

M: Thanks a lot. I have a single in Robertson Hall, but I'm thinking of transferring to another dorm.

W: Huh? You want to transfer out of a single? You know that most of the rooms currently available are either doubles or triples, right? You don't look like a freshman to me.

M: No, I'm a senior.

W: Then why do you want to move?

M: Basically, the students on my floor are incredibly loud and make way too much noise at all hours of the day. I'm taking a full load of courses, including two seminars, I have a part-time job, and I'm busy applying to graduate schools. I can't deal with the constant interruptions. I need to get out of there.

W: Ah, sure. I completely understand that. Where are you thinking of going?

M: I heard that the new dorm that just opened has a couple of quiet floors. Is that correct?

W: Yes, it is. The fourth and fifth floors of Stanley Hall are designated as quiet zones, so students living there have to be quiet twenty-four hours a day.

M: It sounds like heaven. Are there any rooms open there?

W: Let me check . . . Hmm . . . That's incredible. Do you know what? Today is your lucky day.

M: How so?

W: A single on the fifth floor of Stanley Hall just became available about thirty minutes ago. Are you interested?

M: Sign me up, please!

해석

M Student: 안녕하세요. 제게 도움을 주실 수 있는지 궁금해서요.

W Student Housing Office Employee: 기숙사 방과 관련된 문제라면 최선을 다해 도와 드리죠.

M: 정말 고맙습니다. 저는 Robertson 홀 1인실에서 살고 있는데, 다른 기숙사로 방을 옮기는 것에 대해 생각 중이에요.

W: 그래요? 1인실에서 옮기고 싶다고요? 현재 구할 수 있는 대부분의 방들은 2인실이나 3인실이라는 건 알고 있죠, 그렇죠? 학생이 신입생처럼 보이지는 않는데요.

M: 네, 저는 4학년이에요.

W: 그런데 왜 방을 옮기고자 하나요?

M: 기본적으로 제 층에 사는 학생들이 너무 시끄럽고 하루 종일 너무나 소란스럽게 굴어요. 저는 2개의 세미나 수업을 포함해서 수업을 최대한으로 듣고 있고, 아르바이트를 하고 있는데다가, 대학원에 지원하느라 바쁘게 지내고 있어요. 저는 계속되는 방해를 견딜 수가 없어요. 저는 그곳에서 나가야 해요.

W: 아, 그래요. 완전히 이해가 가는군요. 어디로 갈 생각인가요?

M: 얼마 전에 문을 연 신설 기숙사에 조용한 층이 두 군데 있다고 들었어요. 맞나요?

W: 네, 그래요. Stanley 홀의 4층과 5층이 정숙 구역으로 지정되어서 그곳에 사는 학생들은 하루 24시간 동안 조용히 지내야 하죠.

M: 천국처럼 들리는군요. 그곳에 빈 방이 있나요?

W: 확인해 볼게요… 흠… 믿을 수가 없네요. 그거 알아요? 오늘은 학생에게 운이 좋은 날이군요.

M: 어째서요?

W: Stanley 홀 5층의 1인실 하나가 30분 전에 나갔어요. 관심이 있나요?

M: 등록해 주세요!

Summary Note

A

❶ too loud

❷ quiet floors

B

The student says that he wants to transfer from his single room, and the woman is surprised. She says that most available rooms are double or triple rooms. The student says that the students in his current dorm are very noisy. He needs to study and does not want constant interruptions. He asks about the new dorm with quiet floors. The woman checks for him and learns that there is a single room available on a quiet floor. The student wants to take it.

Exercises with Mid-Length Lectures

Exercise 1 1 Ⓓ   2 Gorillas: ②, ③, ④   p.196
Chimpanzees: ①

Script 🎧 07-12

M Professor: Let's talk about the similarities of the cognitive skills between apes and humans. As you all know, humans and apes share many similarities, including the ability to use tools properly and to imitate others.

W Student: Sir, can you explain how apes learn such skills?

M: Well, various studies have shown that baby chimps learn from experience while baby humans just imitate what they are shown. These studies have given scientists some key information in understanding the cultural aspects of ape life and the evolutionary similarities between humans and apes.

W: Can you give us any specific examples showing how, um, humans and apes are so similar?

M: Sure. Let's take the gorilla. With ninety-two to ninety-eight percent of its DNA being identical to that of a human, it is the next closest living relative to humans after the chimpanzee. A few individuals in captivity, such as, ah, Koko, have even been taught a subset of sign language.

W: But isn't Koko an isolated case? I mean, I haven't heard of any other situations where gorillas have shown any kind of cognitive process.

M: Actually, there's much more evidence available to support this fact. For example, a team of scientists observed gorillas using tools in the wild. A female gorilla, um, was recorded using a stick to gauge the depth of water while crossing a swamp. A second female was seen using a tree stump as a bridge and also as a support while fishing in a swamp. While this was the first such observation for a gorilla, um, for over forty years, chimpanzees had been seen using tools in the wild such as when hunting for termites.

W: Are you serious? You can count those examples on one hand. Surely, more observations are needed to infer that apes and humans have similar cognitive skills.

M: That's true, and I agree that there have not been enough observations to make any valid conclusions, and that's why several field studies are currently underway. But let's not forget about the studies we have discussed here. We should also be realistic, um, with the numbers of studies available since it's not easy to study apes in the wild.

해석

M Professor: 유인원과 인간 사이의 인지 능력의 유사성에 대해 이야기해 보죠. 여러분 모두가 아시는 것처럼, 인간과 유인원은 도구를 적절히 사용하는 능력과 다른 이들을 흉내내는 능력을 포함하여 많은 유사성을 공유하고 있죠.

W Student: 교수님, 유인원이 어떻게 그런 능력을 익히는지 설명해 주실 수 있나요?

M: 음, 여러 연구에 따르면 인간의 아기는 단지 보이는 것을 따라 하는 반면에 침팬지 새끼들은 경험에서 배우는 것으로 알려져 있어요. 이러한 연구들로 인해 과학자들은 유인원의 문화적 측면 및 인간과 유인원 간의 진화적 유사성에 대해 중요한 사실들을 알게 되었습니다.

W: 인간과 유인원이 어떻게 해서 그렇게 비슷한지, 음, 구체적인 예를 들어 주실 수 있나요?

M: 물론이죠. 고릴라를 예로 들어 볼게요. DNA의 92%에서 98%가 인간의 DNA와 동일한 고릴라는 침팬지 다음으로 인간과 가까운 동물입니다. 예컨대, 어, 코코와 같은 포획 상태의 몇몇 고릴라들은 약간의 수화를 배우기도 했어요.

W: 하지만 코코는 고립된 상태의 고릴라이지 않았나요? 제 말은, 기타 다른 상황에서 고릴라가 인지 과정을 보여 주었다는 이야기는 들어본 적이 없어요.

M: 사실 이러한 사실을 입증해 줄 증거는 훨씬 더 많아요. 예를 들어 한 과학자 팀은 고릴라가 야생 상태에서 도구를 사용하는 모습을 목격했습니다. 한 암컷 고릴라가, 음, 늪을 건널 때 막대기를 이용해 깊이를 측정하는 모습이 기록되었죠. 두 번째 암컷은 나무의 그루터기를 다리로 사용하는 모습이 목격되었고, 또한 늪에서 물고기를 잡을 때 나무의 그루터기를 지지대로 사용하는 모습도 관찰되었죠. 고릴라의 경우 이것이 첫 목격 사례였지만, 음, 야생 상태의 침팬지가 흰개미를 사냥할 때 도구를 사용하는 모습은 40년 넘게 관찰되었어요.

W: 사실인가요? 한편으로는 그러한 예들을 신뢰할 수 있을 거예요. 분명, 인간과 유인원 사이에 유사한 인지 능력이 존재한다는 점을 추론하기 위해서는 보다 많은 관찰이 필요할 것이고요.

M: 맞아요, 그리고 저도 타당한 결론을 도출할 수 있을 정도로 증거가 충분하지 않다는 점은 동의하고, 그러한 이유 때문에 몇몇 분야에서 연구가 현재 진행 중이죠. 하지만 여기에서 우리가 논의했던 연구에 관해서는 잊지 맙시다. 또한 야생 상태의 유인원을 연구하는 일은 쉽지가 않기 때문에, 음, 참고할 수 있는 연구의 수에 관해서도 현실적으로 생각해야 합니다.

Summary Note

A

❶ sign language
❷ tools in the wild

B

Not long ago, humans were thought to be distinctly set apart from apes. Recent research has shown that this is not the case. For example, the DNA content of apes and humans is very similar in addition to the fact that some studies of apes in the wild have shown conclusive evidence of apes being capable of learning. It is known that certain species of apes are able to use tools. What is not known is the extent of apes' learning capabilities as well as the limit to what they can actually learn. Further studies are needed to answer these questions although this could be quite difficult to do.

Exercise 2 1 Ⓐ 2 Ⓒ   p.198

Script 🎧 07-13

M Professor: All right, are we ready to begin? Good. In the last class, we left off with, um, an introduction concerning the dolphin's ability to communicate with others of its species. As you know, dolphins are regarded as one of the most intelligent animal species on the Earth, but it is hard to say just how intelligent they are. The reason is due to this mammal's ability to communicate by using a variety of clicks, whistles, and other vocalizations. Now, let me talk about the different ways dolphins communicate.

Okay, the first of these communication methods includes a form of echolocation, in which dolphins locate an object by producing sounds and then listening for the echo. It works like this . . . Broadband clicking sounds are emitted in a focused beam toward the front of a target. As the object of interest is approached, the echo grows, um, louder; and the dolphins adjust by decreasing the inter-click interval and the intensity of their emitted sounds. We know dolphins use different rates of click production in a, um, click train, which gives rise to the familiar barks, squeals, and growls they use. A click train with a repetition rate of more than 600 per second is called a burst pulse. Because of this process, it has been accepted by researchers that dolphins are able to form an echoic image of their targets. I guess you could say it's a lot like a submarine's sonar system.

Dolphins also communicate with body movements and vocal bursts. These vocal bursts are produced by using six air sacs near their blowhole since dolphins lack vocal cords. What these vocal bursts represent is not really understood. Yet each animal does have a characteristic frequency-modulated, narrow-band signature whistle, which is uniquely identifying. In this mode of communication, um, dolphins do use about thirty distinguishable sounds. However, many researchers scoff at the idea that this is a form of dolphin language.

해석

M Professor: 좋아요, 시작할 준비가 되셨나요? 좋습니다. 지난 번에는, 음, 같은 종끼리 서로 커뮤니케이션을 하는 돌고래의 능력을 소개하다가 수업이 끝났어요. 여러분도 알고 있는 것처럼, 돌고래들은 지구에 존재하는 동물 가운데 가장 똑똑한 동물 중 하나로 생각되지만, 얼마나 똑똑한지 이야기하는 일은 쉽지가 않습니다. 그 이유는 이 포유 동물이 클릭음, 휘슬음, 그리고 기타 발성을 이용해 커뮤니케이션을 하는 능력 때문이에요. 자, 돌고래들이 커뮤니케이션을 하는 다양한 방식에 대해 이야기를 해 보죠.

좋아요, 그러한 커뮤니케이션 방법 중 첫 번째에는 반향 위치 측정이 포함되는데, 이때 돌고래들은 소리를 내서 돌아오는 메아리를 듣고 물체의 위치를 파악합니다. 이런 식이에요… 광대역의 클릭음을 집속 광선 형태로 대상의 정면을 향해 보냅니다. 관심의 대상이 되는 물체가 접근을 하면 메아리가, 음, 점점 커지죠. 그러면 돌고래는 클릭음의 간격 및 내보내는 소리의 강도를 낮추면서 클릭음을 조절합니다. 우리는 또한 돌고래가 다양한 형태로 클릭음을, 음, 클릭 트레인 형태로 냄으로써, 이들이 짖는 소리, 비명 소리, 그리고 으르렁대는 소리와 같은 친숙한 소리를 만들어 낸다는 점을 알고 있어요. 초당 600번 이상 반복되는 클릭 트레인은 버스트 펄스라고 불립니다. 이러한 과정 때문에 연구자들은 돌고래가 메아리를 통해 대상을 이미지화할 수 있다는 점을 인정하게 되었어요. 잠수함의 수중 음파 탐지 장치와 매우 비슷한 것이라고 말할 수도 있겠군요.

돌고래는 또한 신체의 움직임이나 갑작스러운 소리를 통해서도 커뮤니케이션을 해요. 이러한 갑작스러운 소리는 분수공 근처의 여섯 개의 기능을 이용해 냅니다. 이 갑작스러운 소리가 정확히 무엇을 나타내는지는 아직 밝혀지지 않았어요. 하지만 각각의 돌고래들은 특징적인 주파수 변조 형태를 띠는 협대역의 고유 휘슬음을 가지고 있으며, 이들은 각각 서로 다른 특징을 나타냅니다. 이러한 방식의 커뮤니케이션으로, 음, 돌고래들은 약 30가지의 구별 가능한 소리를 사용할 수 있어요. 하지만 이것이 일종의 돌고래 언어라는 아이디어에 대해서는 많은 연구자들이 코웃음을 치고 있습니다.

✏️ Summary Note

A

❶ louder

❷ echo image

B

Dolphins are considered one of the most intelligent animal species on the Earth. This is due to their ability to communicate by using a variety of clicks, whistles, and other vocalizations. For example, the most effective method of communication they use is a form of echolocation, in which they emit a series of clicking sounds to locate a target. This is done much like a submarine's sonar system. They also use whistles, which are unique to each individual. The use of body movements and vocal bursts is still not fully understood.

Exercise 3 1 ⓒ 2 Sam Spade: 4 Philip Marlow: 2 Mike Hammer: 1, 3 p.200

Script 🎧 07-14

W Professor: I'd like to explore some of the greatest American detective novels written by three of the best novelists of the twentieth century. My personal favorite is *The Maltese Falcon*, written by American author Samuel Dashiell Hammett. His most famous character, of course, is Sam Spade, a man who sees the, um, wretched and corrupt side of life but still retains his tarnished idealism. Even though Spade is a tough guy, he is also a sentimentalist at heart, which makes him one of the most enduring detective characters ever created.

Next is American author Raymond Chandler, who based his main character, detective Philip Marlowe, initially on Hammett's Sam Spade. Marlowe first appears in the novel *The Big Sleep*, published in 1939. Underneath the wisecracking tough guy public image, Marlowe is quietly philosophical and enjoys chess and poetry. While he is not afraid to risk physical harm, he, hmm, never becomes violent merely to settle scores. Chandler's treatment of the detective novel exhibits a continuing effort to develop the art form. His first full-length book, *The Big Sleep*, was published when Chandler was fifty-one years old while his last, *Playback*, came out when he was seventy. Incidentally, all seven of his novels were produced in the last two decades of his life. I can say that all of these novels maintain the integrity of Philip Marlowe's character, but each novel has unique qualities of narrative tone, depth, and focus that set it apart from the others.

Finally, I just love reading the last writer's work. I'm talking about Mickey Spillane, who created fictional detective Mike Hammer in the book *I, the Jury*. Hammer is in many ways the prototypical tough guy detective since he is brutally violent and fueled by a, um, genuine rage that never afflicts Chandler's and Hammett's heroes. While other detective heroes kind of bend the law, Hammer holds it in total contempt, seeing it as nothing more than a means to an end. And, well, this is contrary to Chandler's and Hammett's characters.

해석

W Professor: 20세기 최고의 소설가 중 세 명이 쓴 미국 최고의 추리 소설 몇 편에 대해 살펴보고자 합니다. 제가 개인적으로 가장 좋아하는 작품은 미국인 작가 사무엘 대실 해밋이 쓴 몰타의 매예요. 그의 가장 유명한 캐릭터는 물론 샘 스페이드로, 그는, 음, 삶의 비참하고 타락한 측면을 목격하면서도 퇴색한 이상주의를 믿고 있는 인물이죠. 스페이드는 터프 가이지만 속으로는 감상주의자인데, 이러한 점 때문에 스페이드는 불후의 탐정 소설 캐릭터 중 한 명이 되었습니다.

다음은 미국 작가인 레이먼드 챈들러로, 그의 주인공인 필립 말로 탐정은 원래 해밋의 샘 스페이드를 기반으로 만들어진 인물이었습니다. 말로는 1939년에 출간된 소설 *빅 슬립*에서 처음 등장해요. 재치 있는 터프 가이라는 대중적인 이미지에도 불구하고, 말로는 은근히 철학적이며 체스와 시를 좋아하죠. 몸을 사리는 편은 아니지만, 흠, 결코 원한을 풀기 위해 폭력을 행사하지는 않습니다. 챈들러는 추리 소설을 하나의 예술 형태로 발전시키기 위해 끊임없이 노력했어요. 그의 첫 장편 소설인 *빅 슬립*은 그가 51세 때 출간되었고, 그의 마지막 장편 소설인 *플레이백*은 그가 70세일 때 출시되었죠. 우연히도 그가 쓴 7권의 소설 모두 그가 죽기 전 20년 이내에 쓰여졌어요. 이 모든 소설에는 필립 말로가 등장하지만, 각 소설들은 고유한 방식의 서술 어조, 깊이, 그리고 초점을 가지고 있기 때문에 서로 구분이 됩니다.

마지막으로, 저는 마지막 작가의 작품을 읽는 것을 정말 좋아해요. 미키 스필레인을 말씀드리는 것인데, 그는 *내가 심판한다*라는 책에서 마이크 해머 탐정이라는 가상의 인물을 만들어 냈습니다. 해머는 대단히 폭력적이고, 음, 챈들러와 해밋의 히어로들에게는 결코 영향을 끼치지 않았던 진정한 분노에 휩싸이기 때문에 여러 가지 면에서 전형적인 터프 가이 탐정이에요. 다른 탐정 히어로들은 어느 정도 법을 지키려 하지만, 해머는 법을 완전히 경멸해서 법을 목적을 이루기 위한 수단으로만 보았어요. 그리고, 음, 이러한 점이 챈들러나 해밋의 캐릭터들과 대조되는 부분이죠.

📝 Summary Note

A

❶ *The Big Sleep*
❷ brutally violent

B

Some of the greatest American detective novels written were created by three authors: Samuel Dashiell Hammett, Raymond Chandler, and Mickey Spillane. Each of these authors created at least one memorable detective character that has endeared readers for over fifty years. Characters like Sam Spade, Mike Hammer, and Philip Marlowe have many similar attributes, yet each character has at least one major characteristic which sets him apart from the others. All three of these detective characters are characterized as tough guys, which probably makes them so memorable.

Exercise 4 1 ⓒ 2 Europe: [2], [3] Other p.202
Places: [1], [4]

Script 🎧 07-15

M Professor: Why don't we move on to cave paintings now? As we discussed previously, cave paintings were an important communication tool used by our ancestors for thousands of years. Cave paintings were relatively unknown until Europeans first encountered the Magdalenian paintings of the Altamira Cave, in Spain, um, in 1879.

W Student: Professor, could you tell us which cave has the oldest drawings?

M: The place with the oldest cave art is the Chauvet Cave in southern France. It has been measured through radiocarbon dating back to 32,000 years. The cave was named after Jean-Marie Chauvet, who discovered it on December 18, 1994.

W: What's so special about the Chauvet Cave?

M: Well, it is uncharacteristically large, and the quality and, hmm, quantity of paintings found in it, makes it, well, unsurpassed compared to other caves that have been found with similar paintings. The walls of the Chauvet Cave are covered with predatory animals like lions, panthers, bears, owls, rhinos, and hyenas. Um, as is typical of most cave art, there are no paintings of complete human figures. Researchers have found that the cave had been untouched for 20,000 to 30,000 years.

W: Are there any other caves that have been discovered with similar paintings in other parts of the world?

M: Oh, sure. For example, in South Africa, there are caves in which the paintings are thought to have been done by the San people, who settled in the area 8,000 years ago. The paintings depict animals and humans and are thought to represent religious beliefs.

W: Are there any other examples?

M: There are also rock paintings in caves in Malaysia and Indonesia. In Thailand, in the nineteenth century, some caves were found along the Thai-Burmese border as well as other caves overlooking the Mekong River in Nakhon Sawan Province. They all contain galleries of rock paintings thought to be about 6,000 years old.

해석

M Professor: 이제 동굴 벽화로 넘어가 볼까요? 전에 논의했던 것처럼 동굴 벽화는 수천 년간 우리 조상들이 사용했던 중요한 커뮤니케이션 수단이었어요. 1879년 유럽인들이 스페인 알타미라 동굴의 막달레니안 벽화를 처음 발견하기 전까지 벽화는 비교적 잘 알려져 있지 않았습니다.

W Student: 교수님, 가장 오래된 벽화가 있는 동굴은 어디인지 말씀해 주실 수 있나요?

M: 가장 오래된 벽화는 프랑스 남부의 쇼베 동굴에 있습니다. 방사성 탄소 연대 측정법을 통해 약 32,000년 전의 것으로 측정이 되었죠. 1994년 12월 18일에 동굴을 발견했던 마리 쇼베의 이름을 따서 쇼베 동굴이라는 이름이 지었습니다.

W: 쇼베 동굴이 특별한 것은 무엇 때문인가요?

M: 음, 엄청나게 크고, 흠, 동굴 안에서 발견된 벽화의 수준이, 그러니까, 이전에 발견된 동굴에 들어 있던 비슷한 벽화들과 비교가 되지 않아요. 쇼베 동굴의 벽은 사자, 흑표범, 곰, 부엉이, 코뿔소, 그리고 하이에나와 같은 포식 동물들로 뒤덮여 있어요. 음, 대부분의 동굴 미술에서 그런 것처럼, 완전한 인간의 형상을 그린 그림은 없고요. 연구자들은 이 동굴에 약 2만에서 3만 년 정도 인간의 손길이 닿지 않았다는 점을 알아 냈어요.

W: 전 세계 다른 곳에서도 비슷한 벽화가 발견된 동굴이 있나요?

M: 오, 그럼요. 예를 들어 남아프리카에는 약 8,000년 전 그 지역에 살았던 산족이 남긴 것으로 추정되는 동굴 벽화가 있어요. 이들 벽화는 동물과 인간을 묘사하며 종교적인 신념을 나타내는 것으로 생각되고 있죠.

W: 다른 사례도 있나요?

M: 말레이시아와 인도네시아에도 암각화가 있습니다. 태국에서는 19세기에 태국과 버마의 국경 지대에서 몇개의 동굴들이 발견되었고, 또한 나콘 사완 지방에서도 메콩강을 내려다보는 동굴들이 발견되었죠. 이들 동굴 모두에 약 6,000년 전의 것으로 생각되는 암각화들이 그려져 있습니다.

✏️ Summary Note

A

❶ Chauvet Cave
❷ South Africa

B

Cave paintings were an important communication tool used by humans' ancestors for thousands of years. Cave paintings were unknown to modern man until Europeans first encountered them in 1879. The best example is the Chauvet Cave, which is uncharacteristically large and has the best quality and quantity of cave art discovered so far. For example, the walls of the Chauvet Cave are covered with predatory animals such as lions, panthers, bears, owls, rhinos, and hyenas. As is typical of most cave art, there are no paintings of complete human figures.

Integrated Listening & Speaking p.204

A

Script 🎧 07-16

> **M Professor:** As you know, dolphins are considered one of the most intelligent animal species on the Earth. This is due to their ability to communicate by using a variety of clicks, whistles, and other vocalizations. The most effective method they use is a form of echolocation. It's a lot like a submarine's sonar system. It works like this: First, broadband clicking sounds are emitted in a focused beam toward the front of the animal. Then, as the object is approached, the echo grows louder. Dolphins adjust by decreasing their emitted sounds and the intensity of the inter-click intervals. It has now been accepted that dolphins are able to form an echo image of their targets.

1 a. The most effective method of communication for dolphins is echolocation.
   b. An effective method of communication used by dolphins is echolocation.

2 a. Dolphins can form an echo image of their targets.
   b. Dolphins are able to create an echo image of their targets.

3 a. Dolphin intelligence can be accounted for in its vocalizations, such as whistles.
   b. In a display of high intelligence, dolphins use

vocalizations, such as whistles.

B

Script 🎧 07-17

> **W Professor:** As I've mentioned before, some of the greatest American detective novels written were created by three authors: Samuel Dashiell Hammett, Raymond Chandler, and Mickey Spillane. Each of these authors created at least one memorable detective character that has endeared readers for over fifty years. Characters like Sam Spade, Mike Hammer, and Philip Marlowe have many similar attributes, yet each character has at least one major characteristic which sets him apart from the other two. All three of these detective characters are characterized as tough guys, which probably makes them so memorable.

1 a. Each author created at least one memorable character.
   b. At least one memorable character was created by each author.

2 a. Each detective's tough guy image is similar.
   b. Similarly, each detective has a tough guy image.

3 a. There are three authors mentioned in the passage.
   b. In the passage, three authors are mentioned.

Mini TOEFL iBT Practice Test p.206

1 Ⓒ   2 Ⓑ   3 Ⓑ,Ⓒ   4 Ⓐ   5 Ⓐ
6 Ⓓ   7 Ⓑ   8 Ⓓ   9 Ⓐ,Ⓓ   10 Ⓒ
11 Ⓑ

[1-5]

Script 🎧 07-18

> **W Student:** Good morning, sir. Thanks for seeing me on such short notice.
>
> **M Professor:** No problem. How can I help you?
>
> **W:** I'm here to see you about how I go about becoming a teaching assistant in the department next semester.
>
> **M:** Oh, good. We can always use some bright grad students to take care of all those lengthy required course assignments that most professors just don't have the time to deal with.
>
> **W:** Well, I understand, and that's why I'm here. I think I'm a very capable student and feel I would do well as a teaching assistant. Do you have any advice on how I might make myself look like a reasonable candidate for the department's selection committee?

M: Sure, no problem. First, you need to post your name on the department's teaching assistant candidate list. But before you do that, let me take a look at your up-to-date transcripts. Do you have a copy with you?

W: Yes, sir, right here. Take a look.

M: Hmm, all right, high grade average across the board. Very good. Next, you have to submit a paragraph summarizing your current graduate studies research. You wouldn't have that with you, would you?

W: Yes, sir. Ah, here it is. I . . .

M: Great! Now, let me take a look at that. Hmm . . . Let me give you the rundown. As you know, a teaching assistantship is a contractual agreement between the university and the student for a specified number of teaching hours. A teaching assistantship provides teaching support to undergraduate courses and is a good way to make extra money for a considerable number of graduate students. I'm sure you already know this.

W: Yes, sir.

M: Good. Moving on then, a TA serves under the supervision of a course supervisor in one or more of the following capacities: as a grader, a laboratory demonstrator, a tutorial leader, or another supporting role in the delivery or preparation of degree-credit courses.

W: Understood.

M: Okay, well, to wrap this up, a TA has a duty to acquire and maintain general knowledge of the content of the course as well as a thorough understanding of the components of the course for which he or she is directly responsible. Do you have any questions?

W: No, sir. It sounds fairly simple. I think I will sign up right now. Thanks for your help.

해석

W Student: 안녕하세요, 교수님. 갑자기 뵙자고 말씀을 드렸는데 만나 주셔서 감사합니다.

M Professor: 괜찮아요. 어떻게 도와 드릴까요?

W: 다음 학기에 제가 수업 조교가 되는 것에 대해 어떻게 생각하시는지 여쭤 보려고 왔어요.

M: 오, 좋죠. 항상 똑똑한 대학원생들을 고용해서 대부분의 교수들이 시간상 살펴보지 못하는 필수 과목의 많은 과제들을 처리할 수가 있죠.

W: 음, 그건 저도 알고 있는데, 제가 여기에 온 이유도 그것 때문이에요. 저는 제 자신이 매우 유능하며 수업 조교 역할을 잘 해낼 것이라고 생각해요. 제가 어떻게 하면 학과 선출 위원회에 적절한 후보로 비춰질 수 있는지 제게 해 주실 조언이 있을까요?

M: 그럼요, 물론이죠. 먼저, 학과의 수업 조교 후보 목록에 학생의 이름을 올려야 해요. 하지만 그에 앞서 학생의 최근 성적표를 한번 보죠. 사본을 가지고 왔나요?

W: 네, 교수님. 여기요. 보세요.

M: 흠, 좋아요. 전체적으로 평점이 높군요. 아주 좋아요. 다음으로 현재 하고 있는 대학원 연구에 대한 요약문을 제출해야 해요. 그건 가지고 있지 않죠, 아닌가요?

W: 가지고 왔어요, 교수님. 아, 여기에 있어요…

M: 잘 됐군요! 자, 한번 봅시다. 흠… 짧게 설명해 줄게요. 학생도 알겠지만, 수업 조교는 정해진 수업 시간 동안 대학과 학생 간에 이루어지는 계약에 따른 것이에요. 수업 조교는 학부 수업에 수업과 관련된 도움을 제공해 주고, 상당수의 대학원생들에게 여윳돈을 벌 수 있게 해 주는 좋은 방법이죠. 이러한 점은 이미 알고 있으리라 생각해요.

W: 네, 교수님.

M: 좋아요. 그럼 다음으로 넘어가서 수업 조교는 다음과 같은 하나 혹은 그 이상의 영역에서, 즉 채점자, 실험실 조교, 개별 지도 교사, 혹은 학점이 부여되는 수업의 진행이나 준비에 관한 다른 보조 역할을 하면서 수업 감독관의 감독을 받으며 일을 하게 돼요.

W: 잘 알겠습니다.

M: 좋아요, 음, 정리하면, 수업 조교는 담당 수업에 대한 전반적인 지식을 습득해서 가지고 있어야 하고, 아울러 자신이 직접 책임지는 수업에 관한 내용들을 완전히 이해하고 있어야 해요. 질문이 있나요?

W: 없어요, 교수님. 상당히 간단한 것처럼 들리는군요. 지금 당장 신청을 해야겠어요. 도와 주셔서 감사합니다.

[6-11]

Script 🎧 07-19

W Professor: Today's lecture will focus on the polar bear's ability to survive in the Arctic. As you know, polar bears are at the top of the food chain in the Arctic, and they are well adapted to their habitat with their, um, thick blubber and fur, which insulates them against the cold. A polar bear's coat is about one or two inches thick, and its white-colored fur also camouflages it from its prey. Um, camouflage means that the bear is hard to see and nearly invisible. Its fur has a dense, wooly, insulating layer of under-hair which is covered by a relatively thin layer of guard hairs, which are about six inches long.

Now, these guard hairs are very stiff, shiny, and erect, and they stop the undercoat from matting when wet. This is good for the bear because water can then be easily shaken off before it can freeze. This excellent insulation keeps a polar bear warm even when air temperatures drop to thirty-four degrees below zero Fahrenheit. These stiff hairs grow on the soles of its paws, and these hairs insulate and provide traction on ice.

Amazingly, and I'm sure you all know this, polar bears are so well insulated that they tend to overheat, so they move slowly and often rest to avoid this. Their thick undercoat does however, ah, insulate the bears to the point where they can overheat at temperatures above fifty degrees Fahrenheit. Any excess heat is released at the muzzle, the nose, the ears, the footpads, the inner thighs, and the shoulders. As we all know, polar bears also swim, and they do this to cool down on warm days or after physical activity.

Now this point is crucial. Contrary to popular belief, polar bears don't enter deep hibernation but enter a state of carnivore lethargy, um, which is another way of saying they can still hunt while they are almost asleep. Ah, only pregnant female polar bears hibernate. Hibernating females sleep soundly, but they're easily and quickly aroused. Incredibly, unlike most other hibernators, female polar bears give birth while hibernating. A high body temperature is needed to meet the demands of pregnancy, birth, and nursing. Finally, during the nursing period, mother bears do not emerge from their caves while their cubs are very young. In this situation, the mother will not have eaten for an astounding nine months, and she relies on stored body fat for both her own nutrition and that of the cubs. Okay, are there any questions?

해석

W Professor: 오늘은 북극에서 생존할 수 있는 북극곰의 능력에 대해 초점을 맞춰보도록 하죠. 여러분도 아시는 것처럼, 북극곰은 북극의 먹이 사슬 중 맨 위에 존재하며, 음, 추위를 차단시키는 두꺼운 지방과 털을 지니고 있기 때문에 서식지에 잘 적응하고 있습니다. 북극곰의 외피는 두께가 1인치에서 2인치 정도이며, 또한 흰색의 털 때문에 위장이 되어 있어서 먹이의 눈에 잘 띄지 않습니다. 음, 위장은 곰이 잘 보이지 않고 거의 눈에 띄지 않는다는 점을 의미하죠. 북극곰의 털에는 촘촘하고 복슬복슬하며 열을 차단시키는 속털로 이루어진 층이 있는데, 이는 길이가 약 6인치에 이르는 상대적으로 가는 겉털로 이루어진 층으로 덮여 있어요.

자, 이 겉털은 상당히 뻣뻣하고, 광택이 나고, 그리고 곧게 서 있으며, 물에 젖는 경우 속털이 엉키지 않도록 해 줍니다. 이러한 점은 북극곰에게 도움이 되는데, 그 이유는 물이 얼어 버리기 전에 물을 쉽게 털어낼 수 있기 때문입니다. 이처럼 훌륭한 단열 장치 덕분에 기온이 화씨 영하 34도까지 떨어질 때조차 북극곰은 따뜻한 상태를 유지할 수 있어요. 이러한 뻣뻣한 털은 발바닥에서도 자라서 단열 기능도 해 주고, 얼음 위에서는 마찰력을 제공해 주기도 하죠.

놀랍게도, 그리고 여러분 모두들 알고 있으리라 확신하는데, 북극곰은 단열 능력이 너무 뛰어나서 체온이 과도하게 올라가는 경우도 있는데, 이를 방지하기 위해 북극곰들은 천천히 이동을 하고 종종 휴식을 취합니다. 하지만, 아, 두꺼운 속털로 이루어진 층의 단열 기능 때문에 북극곰의 체온이 화씨 50도 이상 과도하게 오를 수도 있어요. 과도한 열은 주둥이, 코, 귀, 발바닥, 허벅지 안쪽, 그리고 어깨 등을 통해 발산됩니다. 우리 모두가 아는 것처럼 북극곰은 헤엄을 치기도 하는데, 그렇게 하는 이유는 따뜻한 날이거나 신체 활동을 한 후 체온을 내리기 위해서입니다.

자, 다음과 같은 점이 중요해요. 일반적으로 알려진 것과는 달리, 북극곰은 깊은 동면에 빠지지 않고 오히려 육식성 무기력 상태로 들어가는데, 이때에도 북극곰은 거의 잠든 상태로 사냥을 계속할 수가 있습니다. 아, 임신을 한 암컷만 동면을 해요. 동면을 하는 암컷은 곤히 잠을 자지만, 쉽게 그리고 빠르게 잠에서 깨어납니다. 놀랍게도 다른 동면 동물들과 달리 북극곰의 암컷은 동면을 하는 동안 새끼를 출산해요. 임신, 출산, 그리고 양육을 위해서는 체온이 높아야 합니다. 마지막으로, 양육 기간 중 새끼가 아주 어릴 때에는 어미 북극곰이 동굴 밖으로 나오지 않습니다. 이러한 상황에서는 놀랍게도 어미가 9개월 동안 아무것도 먹지 않고 자신과 새끼를 위해 비축해 둔 지방에만 의존합니다. 좋아요. 혹시 질문이 있나요?

Vocabulary Check-Up

p.211

A 1 Ⓗ 2 Ⓖ 3 Ⓒ 4 Ⓛ 5 Ⓓ
6 Ⓙ 7 Ⓝ 8 Ⓐ 9 Ⓘ 10 Ⓕ
11 Ⓑ 12 Ⓔ 13 Ⓞ 14 Ⓚ 15 Ⓜ

B 1 Ⓓ 2 Ⓑ 3 Ⓒ 4 Ⓐ 5 Ⓓ

UNIT 08 Making Inferences

Basic Drill

p.214

Drill 1 Ⓐ

Script 08-02

W Student: Professor Nelson, I want to thank you for writing that wonderful reference letter for my scholarship application. I just found out this morning that I won the scholarship.

M Professor: That's great news, Angela. There was no doubt in my mind that you wouldn't. You deserve it.

W: Oh, you're so kind. By the way, may I ask what exactly you wrote about me?

M: Well, I basically wrote that you are a joy to have in my seminar. You are insightful and quite intelligent. I also mentioned that you are one of the best writers that I have ever seen come through our department in many, many years.

W: Wow, I just don't know how to thank you.

해석

W Student: Nelson 교수님, 장학금 신청에 그처럼 훌륭한 추천서를 써 주셔서 정말 감사 드려요. 오늘 아침에 제가 장학금을 받게 되었다는 점을 알게 되었어요.

M Professor: 좋은 소식이군요, Angela. 제 생각으로는 분명 학생이 받을 줄 알았어요. 자격이 충분하니까요.

W: 오, 정말 친절하시군요. 그건 그렇고, 저에 대해서 정확히 어떤 내용을 쓰셨는지 여쭤 봐도 될까요?

M: 음, 기본적으로 학생이 제 세미나 수업을 듣는다 점을 기쁘게 생각한다고 썼어요. 통찰력도 우수하고 매우 똑똑하잖아요. 또한 여러 해 동안 우리 학과에서 제가 본 학생 중에 가장 글쓰기 실력이 뛰어난 학생 중 한 명이라는 점도 언급을 했죠.

W: 와, 어떻게 감사를 드려야 할지 모르겠군요.

Script 🎧 08-03

> **M Student:** Excuse me, but I received this letter that I haven't paid my tuition and that all of my classes would be canceled if it isn't paid by tomorrow. Can I get an extension?
>
> **W Bursar's Office Employee:** I think I can arrange that. May I ask why you haven't been able to pay yet?
>
> **M:** I'm waiting for my financial aid check to get here.
>
> **W:** Oh, financial aid. Why didn't you just tell me that in the first place? In your situation, we can defer your tuition payment indefinitely.
>
> **M:** Really? That's a relief.

해석

M Student: 실례지만, 제가 등록금을 내지 않아서 만약 내일까지도 내지 않으면 수업이 전부 취소될 것이라는 이 편지를 받았어요. 납부 기간을 연장할 수 있을까요?

W Bursar's Office Employee: 제가 처리해 드릴 수 있을 것 같군요. 그런데 왜 납부를 하지 않았는지 물어봐도 될까요?

M: 학자금 지원 수표가 오기를 기다리고 있는 중이에요.

W: 오, 학자금 지원을 신청했군요. 왜 제일 먼저 이야기를 하지 않았나요? 학생과 같은 상황이라면 등록금 납부를 무기한으로 연기해 줄 수 있어요.

M: 정말인가요? 다행이네요.

Script 🎧 08-04

> **M Student:** I'm sorry I haven't been more active in your class, Professor Clementine.
>
> **W Professor:** Is everything okay? Last semester, you were much more talkative. You know that class participation is a major part of your final grade, right? You must contribute more to the discussions.
>
> **M:** I know. I know. I just feel really intimidated with all of the upperclassmen in the class. Their views are so profound.
>
> **W:** Oh, don't worry about that. They just have a bit more experience than you. Last semester, you always had something intelligent to say, so I know you've got it in you. You just need to build up your confidence some.
>
> **M:** All right. I'll try my best.

해석

M Student: 수업 시간에 더 적극적으로 참여하지 못해서 죄송해요, Clementine 교수님.

W Professor: 다 괜찮은 건가요? 지난 학기에는 훨씬 더 많이 말을 했잖아요. 수업 참여가 기말 고사 성적에 중요하다는 점은 알고 있죠? 토론에 보다 적극적

으로 참여해야 해요.

M: 알아요. 알고 있어요. 다만 수업을 듣는 상급생들 때문에 정말로 기가 죽어서 그래요. 통찰력들이 너무 뛰어나니까요.

W: 오, 그런 걱정은 하지 마세요. 학생보다 경험이 약간 더 많을 뿐이에요. 지난 학기에 학생이 항상 수준 높은 발언을 했기 때문에 학생에게 능력이 있다는 점은 제가 알고 있어요. 단지 자신감을 조금 더 키우도록 하세요.

M: 알겠습니다, 최선을 다할게요.

Script 🎧 08-05

> **M Professor:** In animals, the brain is the control center of the central nervous system. In most animals, the brain is located in the head, is protected by the skull, and is close to the primary sensory apparatus of vision, hearing, taste, and olfaction. In humans, it is an organ of thought. While all vertebrates have a brain, invertebrates have either a centralized brain or collections of individual ganglia. Brains can be extremely complex. The human brain also has a massive number of synaptic connections, allowing for a great deal of parallel processing. For example, the human brain contains more than one hundred billion neurons, each linked to as many as 10,000 others.

해석

M Professor: 동물의 경우, 뇌는 중추 신경계의 제어 센터입니다. 대부분의 동물에 있어서 뇌는 머리에 위치하며, 두개골의 보호를 받고, 그리고 시각, 청각, 미각 및 후각을 느끼는 일차 감각 기관 가까이에 있습니다. 인간의 경우, 뇌는 사고의 기관이에요. 모든 척추 동물들은 뇌를 가지고 있는 반면에 무척추 동물들은 집중되어 있는 뇌나 개별적인 신경절의 집합체 중 하나를 가지고 있죠. 뇌는 극도로 복잡할 수 있습니다. 인간의 뇌 역시 수많은 시냅스로 연결되어 있기 때문에 대량의 병렬 처리가 가능합니다. 예를 들어 인간의 뇌에는 1천억개 이상의 뉴런이 포함되어 있는데, 이들 각각은 1만 개의 다른 뉴런들과 연결되어 있죠.

Script 🎧 08-06

> **W Professor:** Linguistic theories hold that children learn through their natural ability to organize the laws of language but cannot fully utilize this talent without the presence of other humans. This does not mean, however, that the child requires formal teaching of any sort. Nativist theorist Noam Chomsky claims that children are born with a language acquisition device in their brains. They are born with the major principles of language in place but with many parameters to set, such as whether sentences in the language they are to acquire must have explicit subjects. According to Chomsky, when a young child is exposed to a language, the language acquisition device makes it possible for the child to set

the parameters and to deduce the grammatical principles because the principles are innate.

해석

W Professor: 언어학 이론들에 따르면 아이들은 언어의 법칙을 조직화하는 선천적 능력을 통해 언어를 배우지만, 다른 사람들이 없는 상태에서는 이러한 재능을 완전히 이용하지 못한다고 해요. 하지만 이러한 점이 아동들에게 정식 교육이 필요하다는 점을 의미하는 것은 아닙니다. 생득적 이론가인 노암 촘스키는 아이들이 뇌 속에 언어 습득 장치를 가지고 태어난다고 주장했어요. 아이들은 주요한 언어 원칙들을 아는 상태로 태어나지만, 여러 가지 지켜야 할 조건들이, 예컨대 그들이 습득해야 할 언어로 된 문장에 반드시 명백한 주어가 있어야 하는지와 같은 조건들이 존재합니다. 촘스키에 따르면 어린 아이가 어떤 언어에 노출되면 언어 습득 장치로 인해 이 아동은 조건을 설정할 수 있고 문법의 원칙들을 이끌어 낼 수가 있는데, 그 이유는 이러한 원칙들이 생득적인 것이기 때문입니다.

Drill 6

Script 🎧 08-07

M Professor: The environmental movement is a diverse scientific, social, and political movement. In general terms, environmentalists advocate the sustainable management of resources and stewardship of the natural environment through changes in public policy and individual behavior. In its recognition of humanity as a participant in, not enemy of, ecosystems, the movement is centered around ecology, health, and human rights. The environmental movement is represented by a range of organizations from the large to the grassroots. Due to its large membership, varying and strong beliefs, and occasionally speculative nature, the environmental movement is not always united in its goals. At its broadest, the movement includes private citizens, professionals, religious devotees, politicians, and extremists.

해석

M Professor: 환경 운동은 다양한 과학적, 사회적, 그리고 정치적인 운동입니다. 일반적인 의미에서 환경보호주의자들은 공공 정책 및 개인 행동의 변화를 통해 자원의 지속 가능한 관리와 자연에 대한 책무를 주장하죠. 이 운동은, 인간을 생태계의 적이 아닌 생태계의 참가자로 본다는 점에서 생태학, 건강, 그리고 인권에 초점을 두고 있어요. 환경 운동에는 거대한 조직에서 풀뿌리 조직까지 다양한 단체들이 참여하고 있습니다. 대규모의 참여 인원, 다양하고 굳건한 신념, 그리고 때로는 투기적인 성향 탓에 환경 운동의 목표는 보통 단일화되어 있지 않아요. 범위를 가장 넓게 잡는 경우, 이 운동에는 시민 개개인, 전문가, 종교 신자, 정치인, 그리고 극단주의자들이 참여하고 있습니다.

Exercises with Mid-Length Conversations

Exercise 1　1 Ⓐ　2 Ⓑ　　　　　　　　p.216

Script 🎧 08-08

M Student: Good afternoon. I saw the ad that was in the paper about your need for workers here.

W Student Newspaper Employee: That's great. What kind of work are you interested in doing at the paper?

M: I'd really love to be a photographer.

W: Huh, most people say that they want to write opinion pieces. It's nice to hear something different for a change.

M: Photography is my hobby. I've been doing it for several years. I'm, uh, I'm not really much of a writer, so I don't think I could help you out very much there.

W: That's not a problem. We have several writers on staff, and most of them are underclassmen, so they'll be here for at least another year or two after this one finishes.

M: That's great to hear. So . . . do you happen to need a photographer?

W: We have one, but she's pretty busy these days and doesn't always have time to take pictures. So, yes, we could use your help.

M: I'm happy to hear that.

W: Do you happen to have any examples of your work with you?

M: Yes, I do. I brought a few examples with me. You can take a look at them.

W: Hmm . . . These are all pretty good. It's nice to see that you don't just take landscape photos like many people do. These pictures of people doing various activities are well done.

M: Thanks for saying that. I've got a really nice camera that lets me take good photos.

W: Cool. So how much time do you think you can dedicate to the paper each week, and when are you typically available?

해석

M Student: 안녕하세요. 이곳에서 일할 사람을 구한다는 신문 광고를 봤는데요.

W Student Newspaper Employee: 잘 되었군요. 신문사의 어떤 일에 관심이 있으신가요?

M: 저는 꼭 사진 기자가 되고 싶어요.

W: 허, 대부분의 사람들은 사설을 쓰고 싶다고 말을 하거든요. 변화를 줄 수 있는 무언가 다른 말을 듣게 되다니 반갑네요.

M: 사진이 제 취미이죠. 몇 년 동안 사진을 찍고 있어요. 저는, 어, 저는 그다지 글을 잘 쓰는 편은 아니기 때문에 그 부분에 있어서는 큰 도움이 되지 못할 것 같아요.

W: 괜찮아요. 글을 쓰는 직원은 몇 명 있는데다가 그들 대부분이 하급생이라서 이번 학년이 끝난 후에도 최소한 1년이나 2년 동안은 여기에 있을 거예요.

M: 그런 이야기를 들으니 다행이군요. 그러면… 혹시 사진 기자가 필요한가요?

W: 한 명 있기는 하지만, 그녀가 요즘 꽤 바빠서 사진을 찍을 수 있는 시간을 항

상 낼 수가 없어요. 그래서, 네, 도움을 주시면 좋겠어요.

M: 그런 말을 들으니 기쁘군요.

W: 혹시 사진 샘플을 가지고 왔나요?

M: 네, 그래요. 몇 장 가지고 왔죠. 한 번 보세요.

W: 흠… 전부 좋군요. 많은 사람이 하는 식으로 사진을 찍지 않은 것 같아서 좋네요. 다양한 활동을 하고 있는 사람들을 찍은 이 사진들도 잘 찍었어요.

M: 그렇게 말씀해 주셔서 고마워요. 정말 좋은 카메라를 가지고 있기 때문에 좋은 사진을 찍을 수가 있죠.

W: 잘 되었군요. 그러면 매주 신문사 일에 어느 정도의 시간을 할애할 수 있는지, 그리고 보통 언제 시간이 되시는지 알려 주실래요?

✏ Summary Note

A

❶ photographer

❷ nice camera

B

The student responds to an ad about the need for workers at the student newspaper. He says that he wants to be a photographer. The woman is surprised because most people want to write opinion pieces. The newspaper has a photographer, but she is busy, so the student can work at the paper. The student shows the woman some of his pictures, and she thinks they are good. The student says that he has a nice camera that lets him take good pictures. The woman then asks him how much time he can spend working each week.

Exercise 2   1 Ⓐ   2 Ⓓ   p.218

Script 🎧 08-09

W Professor: Russ, I've finished checking out your paper proposal. Do you have a couple of moments to look at it with me now?

M Student: Sure, Professor Bascomb. I'm all done with my classes for the day.

W: Wonderful. Why don't you have a seat there, please?

M: Thanks a lot.

W: Okay, uh, here is the proposal that you wrote.

M: Um . . . **There's a lot of red ink on the paper.**

W: Yes, I had quite a few comments about it.

M: I guess you didn't like it, did you?

W: Well, let's just say that I found some ways to make it better. You see, uh, Russ, the paper that you proposed is simply too general. You want to write about economic recessions. That's a fine topic, but you didn't provide any details.

M: What do you mean?

W: Well, according to your proposal, all you're planning to do is describe what recessions are. That's too general. You need to go into the topic in depth.

M: How can I do that?

W: Well, mostly, you need to focus on a couple of recessions that happened in the past. Research them and write about what caused them as well as what their effects were. You could try choosing two historical recessions and then comparing and contrasting their causes and effects. If you read my comments, you'll see that I suggested a couple of recessions from the 1900s.

M: Wow. Thanks a lot, Professor. I really appreciate your making an effort to help me. I think I understand what you want a lot better now.

해석

W Professor: Russ, 학생의 보고서에 관한 제안서를 조금 전에 확인했어요. 지금 저와 함께 잠깐 살펴볼 시간이 있나요?

M Student: 물론이죠, Bascomb 교수님. 오늘 수업은 모두 끝났거든요.

W: 잘 되었네요. 그곳에 앉겠어요?

M: 감사합니다.

W: 좋아요, 어, 학생이 쓴 제안서가 여기에 있어요.

M: 음… 문서에 빨간색 잉크로 표시된 부분이 많네요.

W: 네, 제가 몇 가지 평을 달았어요.

M: 마음에 들지 않으셨군요, 그렇죠?

W: 음, 개선시킬 수 있는 몇 가지 방법을 찾았다고 말하도록 하죠. 알겠지만, 어, Russ, 학생이 제안한 보고서는 너무 일반적이에요. 학생은 경기 침체에 대한 글을 쓰고 싶어하죠. 좋은 주제이기는 하지만, 세부적인 내용은 어떤 것도 제시하지 않았어요.

M: 무슨 말씀이신가요?

W: 음, 학생의 제안서에 따르면, 학생이 계획하고 있는 것은 경기 침체가 무엇인지 설명하는 것이 전부예요. 너무 일반적이죠. 주제를 보다 상세하게 기술해야 해요.

M: 제가 어떻게 하면 될까요?

W: 음, 주로 과거에 일어났던 두어 번의 경기 침체에 초점을 맞추도록 해요. 그에 대해 조사해서 무엇이 경기 침체를 일으켰는지, 그리고 그 영향은 어떠했는지에 대해 쓰세요. 두 차례의 역사적인 경기 침체를 선택한 후 그들의 원인과 결과를 비교 및 대조할 수도 있을 거예요. 제 평을 읽으면 제가 1900년대에 있었던 두 차례의 경기 침체를 제안했다는 점을 알게 될 거예요.

M: 와, 정말 고맙습니다, 교수님. 저를 도우시려고 노력해 주신 점에 대해 정말로 감사를 드려요. 이제 교수님께서 원하시는 바를 훨씬 더 잘 알게 된 것 같아요.

✏ Summary Note

A

❶ go into depth

❷ two recessions

B

The professor wants to talk to the student about a paper

proposal that he submitted. The student sees a lot of red ink and thinks the professor disliked it. The professor says that his proposal is too general. He should not just describe what recessions are. Instead, she wants him to choose two recessions from the 1900s. Then, he can compare and contrast them in his paper. The student appreciates the help that the professor gives him.

Exercise 3 1 Ⓑ   2 Ⓓ   p.220

Script 🎧 08-10

M Student: Excuse me, Professor Adams. Do you have a minute?

W Professor: Sure. What would you like to talk about?

M: It's about the test we had last week. I didn't do very well, and I was hoping I could take it again.

W: A retest? You know, I don't usually allow students to take tests over unless they have a very, very good reason. Explain to me why I should make an exception in your case.

M: Well, um, I'm afraid that if I get lower than a C in this class, I could lose my scholarship. My academic scholarship states that I must maintain an A average in all of my classes, and in your education class, my grade is slipping a bit.

W: Hmm, let me see. Uh, yes, it looks like you got a C+ on the test last week, which has brought your overall average down to a B right now. Why do you think your grade has been slipping in my class? Is the workload too much?

M: Honestly, ma'am, I haven't really had enough time to study because of my part-time job. I've been working the night shift as a security guard to earn some extra money, but it has really been disrupting my academics, so I quit yesterday.

W: Well, I respect your decision. I know how hard it can be to support yourself while attending school full time. I'm not going to allow you to retake the test, but I am going to assign you an extra credit essay. If you complete the essay to my satisfaction, I'll bump your score up on the test to a B+. This way, you'll be able to get an A- or possibly even an A in the class, depending on how you do on the final. How does that sound to you?

M: That sounds great! Thank you, ma'am, for being so understanding and for giving me the opportunity to make up the extra points. I won't let you down.

해석

M Student: 실례합니다, Adams 교수님. 잠깐 시간이 되시나요?

W Professor: 그럼요. 무엇에 대해 이야기하고 싶은가요?

M: 지난 주에 봤던 시험에 관해서요. 제가 시험을 잘 보지 못해서 재시험을 볼 수 있으면 좋을 것 같아요.

W: 재시험이요? 알겠지만, 보통은 매우, 매우 합당한 이유가 있지 않은 이상 학생이 시험을 다시 보는 것은 허용되지 않아요. 학생의 경우에 제가 왜 예외를 두어야 하는지 설명해 보세요.

M: 그러니까, 음, 안타깝게도 이번 수업에서 제가 C보다 낮은 점수를 받게 되면 더 이상 장학금을 못 받게 되어요. 제 성적 장학금은 모든 과목에서 평균 A-이상의 성적을 받아야 유지되는데, 교수님의 교육학 수업에서 제 성적이 약간 떨어지고 있어요.

W: 흠, 한번 볼게요. 어, 그래요, 지난 주 시험에서 C+을 받은 것 같은데, 그로 인해 지금은 전체 평균 학점이 B로 내려갔군요. 제 수업에서 학생 성적이 왜 떨어지고 있다고 생각하나요? 해야 할 공부가 너무 많은가요?

M: 교수님, 솔직하게 말씀을 드리면, 아르바이트 때문에 정말로 공부할 시간을 낼 수가 없었어요. 돈을 벌기 위해 경비원으로 야간 근무를 하는 중이었는데, 학업에 너무 방해가 되어서 어제 일을 그만두었죠.

W: 음, 학생의 결정을 존중해요. 스스로 학비를 벌면서 풀타임으로 학교에 다니는 것이 얼마나 힘든 일인지 알아요. 시험을 다시 보는 것은 허락하지 않겠지만, 추가 점수를 받을 수 있는 에세이 과제를 하나 내 줄게요. 이렇게 하면, 기말고사에서 어떻게 하느냐에 달렸지만, 수업에서 A-나 심지어 A도 받을 수 있을 거예요. 어떻게 들리나요?

M: 좋아요! 이해해 주시고 제게 점수를 만회할 수 있는 기회를 주셔서 감사합니다. 실망시켜 드리지 않을게요.

✏️ **Summary Note**

A

❶ scholarship

❷ extra essay

B

A student is discussing a test he took in the professor's class the previous week. The student is not satisfied with his performance and is afraid he will lose his scholarship. He asks the professor if he can take it again. The professor asks the student why he believes he did so poorly. The student explains that he was too busy with his part-time job that he recently quit. Because of his honesty, the professor decides not to allow him to retake the exam but to do some extra credit work instead.

Exercise 4 1 Ⓓ   2 Ⓒ   p.222

Script 🎧 08-11

W Student: Hello, Mr. Carmichael. My name is Kathy Scriber. I spoke with you on the phone yesterday.

M Theater Manager: Hello. Uh, I'm really sorry, but I've had a busy week and don't remember your call. Could you let me know what we discussed?

W: Of course. I'm the president of the drama club, and we're putting on a performance this spring.

M: Ah, right. I remember now. You need to schedule a time to use the theater so that you can rehearse. That's what we talked about, isn't it?

W: That's correct.

M: So when would you like to reserve the theater for rehearsals?

W: Well, we'd like to rehearse twice a week on Monday and Thursday. We're thinking that six to seven thirty would be ideal. Does that work for you?

M: Let me take a look in my reservation book here . . . Hmm . . . Monday from six to seven thirty is not a problem at all. However, the Drama Department has booked Thursday evenings from five to seven.

W: Is anyone using the theater after seven?

M: Oh, yeah. It looks like the school choir is going to be practicing at that time. I'd say that Thursday is not going to happen for your group.

W: What about Wednesday?

M: Unless you only want to practice once a week, you're going to have to reserve a time on Friday evening.

W: That's not what we were hoping for, but if we have no choice, then we'll do it. How about five thirty to seven on Friday? Is that available?

M: I'll write you down for that time.

해석

W Student: 안녕하세요, Carmichael 선생님. 제 이름은 Kathy Scriber예요. 어제 전화로 선생님과 이야기를 나누었죠.

M Theater Manager: 안녕하세요. 어, 정말로 죄송하지만 이번 주에 바빠서 학생과의 전화 통화가 기억나지 않네요. 우리가 무엇에 대해 이야기했는지 알려 줄 수 있나요?

W: 물론이죠. 저는 연극 동아리의 회장이고, 저희는 이번 봄에 공연을 할 예정이에요.

M: 아, 맞아요. 이제 기억이 나는군요. 리허설을 할 수 있도록 극장을 예약해야 하죠. 그것이 우리가 나누었던 이야기에요, 그렇지 않나요?

W: 맞아요.

M: 그러면 리허설을 위해 언제 극장을 예약하고자 하나요?

W: 음, 일주일에 두 번, 월요일과 목요일에 리허설을 했으면 해요. 6시에서 7시 30분까지가 이상적일 것 같고요. 가능할까요?

M: 여기 예약 기록을 한번 볼게요… 흠… 월요일 6시부터 7시 30분까지는 전혀 문제가 되지 않아요. 하지만 목요일 저녁 5시부터 7시까지는 연극학과가 예약을 해 두었어요.

W: 7시 이후에 극장을 사용하는 사람이 있나요?

M: 오, 그래요. 교내 합창단이 그 시간에 연습을 할 예정인 것 같아요. 목요일은 학생 동아리에 맞지 않는다고 말씀드리고 싶네요.

W: 수요일은요?

M: 일주일에 한 번만 연습하고자 하는 경우가 아니라면 금요일 저녁 시간을 예약해야 할 거예요.

W: 그건 저희가 원하는 것이 아니지만 선택권이 없는 경우라면 그렇게 해야 할 것 같군요. 금요일 5시 30분부터 7시까지는 어떤가요?

M: 그 시간에 이름을 적어 놓을게요.

✎ **Summary Note**

A

❶ rehearse in theater
❷ Wednesdays and Thursdays

B

The student visits the theater manager to discuss scheduling a time to use the theater. She is the president of the school drama club, so the members need to practice for their performance. The student suggests reserving times on Monday and Thursday. The man says that there is time on Monday but no time on Thursday. Likewise, there are no time slots available on Wednesday. She decides to reserve a time on Friday evening so that the members can practice twice a week.

Exercises with Mid-Length Lectures

Exercise 1 1 ⓒ 2 ⓑ   p.224

Script 🎧 08-12

M Professor: Warm-blooded animals maintain thermal homeostasis. What I mean is they keep their body core temperature at a nearly constant level regardless of the temperature of the surrounding environment, which is the outside climate. What we call this is endothermy.

Endothermy is the ability of some creatures to control their body temperatures through internal means such as shivering, fat burning, panting, and sweating. You all know what I'm talking about, right? When you shiver because it's so cold in the winter or when you are sweating buckets in the summer, all your body is trying to do is maintain a constant internal temperature of 98.6 degrees.

Now, um, there are some advantages and disadvantages to all of these. The advantages are increased enzyme activity and a constant body temperature, which allows warm-blooded animals to be active in cold temperatures. A big disadvantage is the, uh, need to maintain thermoregulation or, in other words, heat production, even during inactivity; otherwise, the organism will die. That's right. It could mean life or death.

Heat regulation is one of the most important survival strategies in a warm-blooded organism. For example, in the winter, there may not be enough food to enable an endotherm such as a hungry grizzly bear to keep its metabolic rate stable all day. Um, so some animals, like the grizzly bear, go into a controlled state of hypothermia called hibernation, or torpor. This deliberately lowers the body temperature to conserve energy. Is everyone still with me? Good. Now, in hot weather, like when you were at the beach last weekend soaking up all those dangerous ultraviolet rays to make yourself look tan and pretty, endotherms expend considerable energy to avoid overheating. They may pant, sweat, lick, or seek shelter or water.

해석

M Professor: 온혈 동물은 열 항상성을 유지합니다. 다시 말해 외부 날씨에 해당되는 주변 환경의 온도와 상관없이 몸의 중심부 온도를 거의 일정한 수준으로 유지를 하죠. 이를 내온성이라고 부릅니다.

내온성은 어떤 동물이 몸을 떨고, 지방을 연소시키고, 숨을 헐떡거리고, 그리고 땀을 흘리는 것과 같은 신체 내부의 활동을 통해 체온을 조절하는 능력이에요. 모두들 무슨 말인지 아시죠, 그렇죠? 겨울에 너무 추워서 몸을 떨거나 여름에 비 오듯 땀을 흘리는 경우, 여러분의 신체는 체내 온도를 98.6도로 일정하게 유지하려는 중입니다.

자, 음, 이 모든 것에는 몇 가지 장점과 단점이 있어요. 장점은 효소 활동이 활발해지고 체온이 일정하게 유지된다는 점으로, 이 때문에 온혈 동물들은 추운 날씨에서도 활동을 할 수가 있습니다. 한 가지 커다란 단점은 활동을 하지 않는 경우에도, 어, 체온 조절을 해야 한다는 점인데, 이는 다른 말로 열을 생산해야 한다는 뜻이에요. 그렇지 않으면 그 생물은 죽게 될 테니까요. 맞아요. 생사의 문제가 될 수 있는 것이죠.

체온 조절은 온혈 동물의 가장 중요한 생존 전략 중 하나입니다. 예를 들어 겨울에는, 예컨대 굶주린 회색곰과 같은 온혈 동물이 하루 종일 대사율을 일정하게 유지할 수 있을 정도의 먹이가 없을 수도 있어요. 음, 그래서 회색곰과 같은 몇몇 동물들은 동면 또는 휴면이라는 저체온 유지 상태에 들어가게 되죠. 의도적으로 체온을 낮춤으로써 에너지를 보존하는 것이에요. 다들 이해가 되시죠? 좋아요. 자, 더운 날씨에는, 지난 주말 해변에서 여러분이 그 위험한 자외선을 모두 받으면서 선탠을 하고 예쁘게 보이려고 했던 때와 같은 날씨의 경우, 온혈 동물들은 막대한 에너지를 소비해서 몸이 과열되는 것을 막습니다. 숨을 헐떡거리거나, 땀을 흘리거나, 몸을 핥거나, 혹은 숨을 곳이나 물을 찾을 수도 있어요.

✏ Summary Note

A

❶ constant temperature body
❷ Control body temperature
❸ die

B

Warm-blooded animals are able to keep their body temperatures at a constant level. They use means such as shivering and sweating to do this. Another term for this temperature control is endothermy. Endotherms spend a great amount of energy to maintain body temperature. If they do not do this, they could perish. Advantages of this regulation are increased enzyme activity and increased activity in cold-weather situations.

Exercise 2   1 Ⓐ   2 Ⓓ   p.226

Script 🎧 08-13

W Professor: Okay, everyone. Calm down. I know you are all really excited about being able to read a bit of Old English. I congratulate you. Job well done, but we've got a ways yet to go. Now, it is time for us to take a look at the history of English. Who can tell me where English originated?

M Student: That's easy. England, of course. Everyone knows that the language is named after the country.

W: Uh, that's partly correct. English is a West Germanic language. It came from the Anglo-Frisian dialects brought to Britain by settlers from parts of what is now northwest Germany and the northern Netherlands. At first, Old English was a group of dialects reflecting the different origins of the Anglo-Saxon kingdoms of England. The original Old English language was then influenced by two waves of invasion. The first was by language speakers of the Scandinavian branch of the Germanic family. They conquered and colonized parts of Britain in the eighth and ninth centuries. The second was the Normans in the eleventh century. They spoke a variety of French. These two invasions caused English to become mixed to some degree. What kind of effect do you guys think this mixing had on English?

M: Wouldn't that have made English pretty diverse?

W: I see somebody is paying attention. Exactly. English became a very rich, elaborate layer of words. And later, English developed into a borrowing language of great flexibility with a huge vocabulary. So what about modern English? Who can give us an idea of when it began?

M: I believe it was around the, um, fifteenth century, wasn't it?

W: Yes, it was. Modern English is basically dated from the Great Vowel Shift, which took place mainly during the fifteenth century. English was also influenced by the spread of a standardized London-based dialect in government and administration and by the standardizing effect of printing. By the time of William Shakespeare, around the, uh, middle to late sixteenth century, the language had become clearly recognizable as modern English.

해석

W Professor: 좋아요, 여러분. 조용히 해 주세요. 여러분 모두 고대 영어를 읽을 수 있게 되었다는 생각에 크게 들떠 있다는 점은 저도 알고 있어요. 축하해요. 잘들 하셨지만, 갈 길이 멉니다. 자, 이제 영어의 역사를 살펴볼 시간이에요. 영어가 어디에서 시작되었는지 말해 볼 사람이 있나요?

M Student: 그건 쉽네요. 물론 영국입니다. 영어라는 이름이 영국에서 나왔다는 점은 모두가 알고 있죠.

W: 어, 부분적으로는 맞아요. 영어는 서게르만계 언어예요. 현재의 독일 북서부와 네덜란드 북부의 일부 지방 출신의 정착민들이 영국으로 가져온 앵글로-프리지아 방언에서 비롯되었죠. 원래의 고대 영어는 방언들이 섞여 있는 것으로서 영국의 앵글로 색슨계 왕국들의 기원이 서로 다르다는 점을 반영해 주었어요. 최초의 고대 영어는 두 차례의 침입에 의한 영향을 받았습니다. 첫 번째는 게르만족의 스칸디나비아계 언어 사용자들에 의한 것이었어요. 이들은 8세기와 9세기에 영국의 일부 지역을 정복하고 식민지화 했죠. 두 번째는 11세기 노르만족에 의한 것이었습니다. 이들은 다양한 불어를 구사했어요. 이러한 두 차례의 침입으로 영어는 어느 정도 섞이게 되었습니다. 이처럼 섞임으로써 영어가 어떤 영향을 받았을 것이라고 생각하나요?

M: 그래서 영어가 상당히 다양해지지 않았을까요?

W: 주의를 기울이고 있는 사람이 있군요. 정확해요. 영어는 매우 풍부하고 정교한 언어가 되었어요. 그리고 이후에는 어마어마한 어휘를 보유하고 대단히 유연한 차용어로 발전했죠. 그러면 현대 영어는 어떨까요? 현대 영어가 언제 시작되었는지 말해 볼 사람이 있나요?

M: 대략, 음, 15세기경이라고 알고 있습니다, 아닌가요?

W: 네, 맞아요. 현대 영어는 기본적으로 15세기에 일어났던 대모음 추이에서 비롯되었어요. 영어는 또한 정부 및 행정부에서 런던 방언에 기반한 영국 표준어의 사용이 확대되고 인쇄술이 표준화되면서 그에 따른 영향을 받았습니다. 셰익스피어 시대에, 어, 16세기 중후반 무렵, 이때의 언어가 현대 영어로서 명확하게 인식되기 시작했어요.

✏️ Summary Note

A

❶ Normans
❷ 15th century

B

English is a West-Germanic language that originated in German and the Netherlands and was brought to England by settlers. Two later invasions by the Scandinavians and Normans heavily influenced the language by making it more diverse and elaborate. Modern English began around the fifteenth century. It was affected by the standardized dialect of the government. By the time of Shakespeare, modern English was a clearly recognized language which stood on its own.

Exercise 3   1 ⑧   2 ⓒ   p.228

Script 🎧 08-14

W Professor: The Amazon River pulsates, surging once a year. From November through May, the volume of the, uh, main stream swells. For example, as stated in your text, on June 1, 1989, the level of the river at Manaus, 900 miles from the ocean, was forty-five feet above low water, nearly reaching the 1953 all-time high-water mark on the flood gauge. Now, the Amazon's volume in that month far exceeded the combined flow of the next eight largest rivers on the Earth, a pretty extraordinary stat if you think about it. It does this by the end of every May, even in years of normal flow. During the second half of the year, this, um, regular flow diminishes. All right, uh, yes, here it is in your text on page 372. In November of 1990, also around Manaus, stretches of white beaches and sandbars were exposed to the sun for the first time in living memory. The river had fallen fifty feet to its lowest level on record this century. The only official studies of the main stream flow were done in 1963 and 1964, which, uh, were years estimated as, uh, having less than average rainfall by the U.S. Geological Survey. Measurements were made at Obidos, 600 miles inland, where the Amazon squeezes through a single channel—very narrow in comparison—a little more than a mile wide. Findings gave the average minimum discharge at three million cubic feet per second while the average maximum reached 8.5 million.

For comparison, our own Mississippi River at Vicksburg averages 620,000 cubic feet per second. It has been suggested that the Amazon's average annual discharge equals twenty percent of the total continental runoff of all rivers on the Earth. Note that this does not mean that the Amazon system holds one-fifth of the entire world's fresh water, as some books have interpreted this data. In fact, all the Amazon's waterways hold less than one ten-thousandth of the world's fresh water, most of which, by the way, is locked up in polar ice.

해석

W Professor: 아마존강은 1년에 한 번씩 강물이 불어나면서 넘칩니다. 11월에서 5월까지, 어, 본류의 강물이 불어나죠. 예를 들어 교재에 나와 있는 대로 1989년 6월 1일에 바다에서 900마일 떨어진 마나우스에서의 강 수위가 저수위로부터 45피트였는데, 이는 강 수위 측정 수치상 1953년의 최고 수위에 근접한 것이었어요. 자, 그 달의 아마존강 수량은 지구에서 그 다음으로 큰 여덟 개 강의 수량을 모두 합친 것보다 훨씬 컸는데, 이는 생각해 보면 상당히 이례적인 수치입니다. 심지어 강물의 흐름이 정상적인 해에도 매년 5월말이면 이런 현상이 나타나죠. 매년 하반기에는, 음, 정상적으로 흐르는 강물의 양이 감소해요. 좋아요, 어, 교재 372 페이지에 나와 있군요. 1990년 11월 역시 마나우스 인근에 펼쳐져 있는 백사장 및 하구의 모래톱이 처음으로 햇빛에 노출되었던 것으로 알려져 있습니다. 이번 세기에 강 수위가 50피트나 떨어져 최저치를 기록했어요. 본류 흐름에 대한 유일한 공식적인 연구는 1963년과 1964년에 이루어졌는데, 어, 미국 지질 조사국의 추산에 따르면 이때의 강수량은 평균 강수량보다 적었습니다. 측정은 내륙 쪽으로 600마일 지점에 있는 오비도스에서 이루어졌는데, 이곳에서 아마존강은, 비교적 매우 폭이 좁은 편인, 폭이 1마일이 약간 넘는 하나의 해협을 통과합니다. 조사 결과에 따르면 평균 최저 유량은 3백만 입방 피트였고 평균 최대 유량은 초당 850만 입방 피트였어요.

비교를 해 보면, 미시시피강의 경우 빅스버그에서의 평균 유량은 초당 62만 입방 피트입니다. 아마존강의 연간 평균 유량이 지구에 존재하는 모든 강의 전체 유거수 중 20%에 해당된다는 주장이 있어요. 그렇다고 해서 다른 책에서 이러한 자료를 해석한 것처럼 아마존강에 지구 전체의 담수 중 1/5이 포함되어 있다는 의미는 아니에요. 실제로 아마존강의 수로에는 지구 전체 담수의 1000분의 10 미만이 포함되어 있을 뿐인데, 참고로 말씀을 드리면, 담수의 대부분은 얼음 형태로서 극지방에 존재합니다.

✏️ Summary Note

A

❶ 20 percent

❷ 45 feet

❸ 50 feet

B

The Amazon River experiences a large surge about once a year. This occurs between the months of November and May. Some areas reported increases in the waterline by as much as forty to fifty feet in the late 1980s. During the other half of the year, the water recedes, exposing sandbars and beach-like white sand. The average discharge of the river is between three and 8.5 million cubic feet per second. Finally, contrary to some published accounts, the Amazon holds less than one ten-thousandth of all the world's fresh water.

Exercise 4 1 Ⓐ 2 Ⓑ   p.230

Script 08-15

M Professor: Could you close the door, please? Great. Thanks. Today, we're going to discuss dirty water. That's right; dirty water, or more importantly, how to purify it yourselves so that you can drink it and not get sick. Sure, you can go out and buy portable drinking water systems or expensive designer mineral water, but there are other methods you can use if you don't have this stuff available. Who can name one?

W Student: Whenever my dad takes us all camping, he just boils it, and no one in my family has ever gotten sick.

M: Sure. Boiling water on a portable stove or fire will kill most bacteria and viruses. At higher elevations, though, the boiling point of water drops, so several minutes of continuous boiling are required. Another option is just to be sure you carry a portable pump filter. Some of these, um, like the charcoal filter ones, don't remove viruses. In this case, you have to disinfect the water with a third method. Who can tell me what a third might be?

W: How about electricity?

M: Not quite. No, actually, I was thinking of a couple of chemicals. One is iodine, which kills many, but not all, of the most common, uh, pathogens in natural fresh water sources. Second, to be used only in emergency situations, is chlorine-based bleach. Just add two drops of five-percent bleach per quart of clear water and let it stand, uh, covered, for about an hour. All right, now that is three so far. Would anyone like to take a stab at the last option?

W: Uh, sunshine?

M: Very well done. Yes, sunlight is another valid option.

We call it solar purification. Water is placed in a transparent plastic bottle, which is oxygenated by shaking. It is placed in full sun for six hours, which raises the temperature and gives an extended dose of solar radiation, killing any microbes that may be present.

해석

M Professor: 문 좀 닫아 줄래요? 좋아요. 고마워요. 오늘은 오수에 대해 논의할 예정입니다. 맞아요. 오수인데, 보다 중요하기는, 그 물을 마시고 아프지 않기 위해 어떻게 정화를 하는지에 대해서입니다. 물론 밖에 나가서 휴대용 정수기나 값비싼 생수를 살 수도 있겠지만, 이런 것을 구할 수 없는 경우 이용할 수 있는 다른 방법들이 있어요. 누가 말해 볼까요?

W Student: 아버지께서 저희를 데리고 캠핑을 가실 때마다 물을 끓여 주시는데, 저희 가족 중 아팠던 사람은 없었어요.

M: 그렇죠. 휴대용 스토브나 불로 물을 끓이면 대부분의 박테리아 및 바이러스가 죽게 되죠. 하지만 보다 고도가 높은 곳에서는 물의 끓는 점이 낮아지기 때문에 몇 분 동안 계속해서 물을 끓여야 해요. 또 다른 방법은 휴대용 펌프 필터를 가지고 다니는 것이에요. 이들 중 일부는, 음, 숯 필터와 같은 것들은 바이러스를 제거하지 못합니다. 이러한 경우, 세 번째 방법으로 물을 소독해야 하죠. 세 번째 방법이 무엇인지 누가 말해 볼까요?

W: 전기와 관련된 것인가요?

M: 아니에요. 그건 아니고, 저는 사실 두 가지 화학 물질을 생각하고 있었어요. 하나는 요오드로, 어, 요오드는 자연 상태의 민물에 들어 있는 병원균을, 전부는 아니지만, 다수 제거합니다. 두 번째는, 위급 상황에서만 사용해야 하는데, 염소계 표백제입니다. 깨끗한 물 1쿼터당 5퍼센트의 표백제를 두 방울 떨어뜨린 후, 어, 약 한 시간 동안 뚜껑을 덮어두기만 하면 되죠. 좋아요, 지금까지 세 가지를 살펴 봤네요. 마지막 방법을 맞춰볼 사람이 있을까요?

W: 어, 햇빛인가요?

M: 아주 훌륭해요. 네, 햇빛이 사용 가능한 또 다른 방법입니다. 이를 태양열 정화라고 부르죠. 물을 투명한 플라스틱 병에 담은 후 흔들어서 산화를 시킵니다. 이를 햇빛이 잘 비치는 곳에 여섯 시간 동안 두면 온도가 상승하고 태양 복사량이 증가하여 있을 수도 있는 미생물들이 모두 제거됩니다.

✏️ Summary Note

A

❶ Boiling water

❷ Solar purification

B

Water purification is important when camping or doing other outdoor activities. If it is not done, dirty or polluted water can be harmful to human beings. There are four main methods of purifying water in the outdoors: boiling, filtering, using chemicals, and using sunlight. Boiling is the easiest and most complete while filtering might not kill all of the viruses. Iodine is a chemical used to kill most pathogens in water, and sunlight, though time consuming, is another valid option.

Script 08-16

> **W Professor:** The Amazon River is a river in great flux most of the year. It experiences a great increase in water level each year, typically between the months of November and May. In June, 1989, the water level rose to forty-five feet above the low-level line, which nearly made it a record reading. That same month, the volume of the Amazon was greater than the combined flow of the next eight largest rivers in the world. The only official studies of the river capacity were done in the mid-1960s. In comparison to the Mississippi River in the U.S., the Amazon is a monster even during low rainfall seasons. The average discharge of the Amazon can reach seven to eight million cubic feet per second while the Mississippi averages 600,000.

1 a. The Amazon is in constant change throughout the year.

   b. Throughout the year, the Amazon is in constant change.

2 a. The water level reached forty-five feet above the low-level line.

   b. The water level rose to forty-five feet above the low-level line.

3 a. Compared to the Mississippi, the Amazon's average discharge is over ten times greater.

   b. The Amazon's average discharge is over ten times greater than the Mississippi's.

Script 08-17

> **M Professor:** Purifying water is very important for individuals who spend time camping and doing other outdoor activities. If people don't purify water from lakes, rivers, and other sources, they could become ill and possibly even die. Boiling water is one of the easiest and best methods of cleaning water. Another method is a water filter, though it does not always kill all the bad organisms in the water. A third method is using chemicals such as iodine or chlorine. Chlorine should only be used in emergency situations. Finally, people can use sunlight to sanitize their drinking water. Yet solar purification takes a great amount of time—usually about six hours.

1 a. The best method of water purification is boiling.

   b. Boiling is the best method of water purification.

2 a. Solar purification takes about six hours.

   b. At six hours, solar purification takes a long time.

3 a. The lecture focuses on methods of water purification.

   b. In the lecture, methods of water purification are focused on.

Mini TOEFL iBT Practice Test   p.234

1 Ⓐ	2 Ⓒ	3 Ⓑ, Ⓓ	4 Ⓒ	5 Ⓑ
6 Ⓐ	7 Ⓐ, Ⓓ	8 Ⓒ	9 Ⓐ	10 Ⓓ
11 Ⓓ				

[1-5]

Script 08-18

> **W Student:** Good afternoon. I'm looking for a part-time job and wonder if you have any openings at the moment.
>
> **M Dining Services Office Employee:** Well, actually, we do have a couple of openings. Because it is the beginning of the semester, we're really swamped right now and are understaffed. When are you available?
>
> **W:** I'd really prefer to work during lunch if that's possible. I have a really heavy load of classes this term, so my mornings are completely booked. I'm also in a jazz band, and we usually have our practice sessions in the evening, so that wouldn't be a good time for me either. Would a lunch schedule be possible?
>
> **M:** Let me see. Um, we have a cashier's position available. Hold on a second so that I can check the schedule really quickly . . . Uh, here it is. Yes, the hours would be Monday through Friday from eleven in the morning to two in the afternoon. Do you have any experience using a computerized register and handling money? If you don't, don't worry about it. We can train you, and it is very easy to pick up.
>
> **W:** Sure! I worked at a bookstore for a few months last summer and used one of those kinds of registers. It was a really busy store right next to campus. I got good at handling all the money and making change. It was a little stressful at first, but I think I, uh, adapted pretty well. By the end of the first month, my manager was asking me to train new employees.
>
> **M:** Good! And the hours? Would that be a workable schedule with you? You sound like a very busy person. **I don't want you to get in over your head.**
>
> **W:** The hours are perfect. My morning classes finish by ten, and I've only got one afternoon seminar each day, and that doesn't start until three. Um, I want to ask you about weekends. Would that be a possibility, too? I could really use the extra money.

M: Of course. That isn't a problem, and it would basically be up to you. I think you would be an excellent addition to our staff. You have good experience and a great personality. I'll start you off at twelve dollars an hour. Why don't you just come in next Monday at 10:30 so that you can get started?

W: Great. You just made my day.

해석

W Student: 안녕하세요. 아르바이트를 구하는 중인데, 지금 빈 자리가 있는지 궁금해서요.

M Dinning Services Office Employee: 음, 사실 빈 자리가 두 개 있어요. 학기가 시작되는 시기라서 지금 정신없이 바쁜데 일손은 부족하죠. 언제 일할 수 있나요?

W: 가능하면 점심 시간에 일을 하고 싶어요. 이번 학기에 듣는 수업이 정말 많아서 아침 시간은 꽉 차 있죠. 그리고 제가 재즈 밴드부 소속이라 저녁에는 보통 연습을 하기 때문에 그 시간 역시 힘들 것 같아요. 점심 시간 근무가 가능할까요?

M: 어디 봅시다. 음, 계산원 자리가 비어 있군요. 잠깐 기다리시면 시간표를 빨리 확인해 볼게요… 어, 여기 있네요. 네, 월요일부터 금요일까지 오전 11시에서 오후 2시 사이에 근무가 가능해요. 전자 금전 등록기를 사용해서 돈 계산을 해 본 적이 있나요? 없다고 해도 걱정하지 마세요. 저희가 교육을 시켜 주는데, 매우 쉽게 익힐 수 있어요.

W: 물론 있어요! 저는 지난 여름 몇 달 동안 서점에서 일을 했고 전자 금전 등록기도 사용해 봤죠. 학교 바로 옆에 있는 정말 붐비는 서점이었어요. 계산을 하고 잔돈을 주는 일에 익숙해졌죠. 처음에는 스트레스를 좀 받았지만, 어, 꽤 잘 적응을 했다고 생각해요. 첫 번째이 끝날 무렵에는 매니저가 제게 신입 직원들을 교육시켜 달라는 요청을 하기도 했고요.

M: 잘 되었군요! 그러면 시간은요? 그 시간이 가능한 시간인가요? 학생이 굉장히 바쁜 사람처럼 보여서요. 학생에게 너무 무리가 가지는 않았으면 좋겠어요.

W: 시간은 딱 좋아요. 오전 수업은 10시에 끝나고 매일 오후에는 세미나 수업만 하나 있는데, 이 수업은 3시 이후에 시작하죠. 음, 주말에 대해서도 여쭙고 싶군요. 주말도 가능한가요? 여윳돈이 있었으면 좋을 것 같아서요.

M: 물론이죠. 문제 없고, 기본적으로 학생에게 달려 있는 일이에요. 우수한 직원이 될 것 같네요. 경험도 많고 성격도 좋으니까요. 시간당 12달러로 시작하죠. 다음 주 월요일 10시 30분에 와서 일을 시작하는 것이 어떨까요?

W: 좋아요. 덕분에 좋은 하루가 되었어요.

[6-11]

Script 🎧 08-19

M Professor: Good morning, all. Everyone, please take a seat so that we can get started. Thanks. Now, today's topic is neurons, a major class of cells in the nervous system. And the main role of these neurons is to process and transmit information. In vertebrates, um . . . You all remember what a vertebrate is, right? Good. Now, in vertebrates, neurons are found in the brain, the spinal cord, and the nerves and the ganglia of the peripheral nervous system. In the most basic of terms, the neuron is composed of a cell body, a dendritic tree, and an axon. In the classical view of the neuron, the cell body and the dendritic tree receive input from other neurons, and the axon transmits output signals.

Is everyone following me? Excellent. So the way neurons are able to do this is that they have the ability to generate electrical impulses. They zap specific information through connectors to other neurons in what we scientists like to call a synaptic transmission. That's right. Neurons communicate with each other via synapses, where the axon of one cell touches the dendrite of another. Synapses can be excitatory or inhibitory. That is, they produce or stop signals and will either increase or decrease activity in the target neuron.

Now, some neurons in your cerebellum—the large part of your brain which controls many of your movements—can have over 1,000 dendrite branches which connect with thousands of other cells. And, um, on the other hand, certain neurons might have only one or two dendrites, each of which receives thousands of synapses. Furthermore, the human brain has a huge number of neurons and an even huger number of synapses. Now listen closely to this. Each of one hundred billion neurons has on average 7,000 synaptic connections to other neurons. Most authorities estimate that the brain of a three-year-old child has about one thousand trillion synapses. Of course, uh, this number declines with age and stabilizes when you are older—say, in your early twenties—when the number of synapses ranges from one to five hundred trillion synapses in most adults.

해석

M Professor: 안녕하세요, 여러분. 시작을 할 테니 모두 자리에 앉아 주시기 바랍니다. 고마워요. 자, 오늘의 주제는 뉴런, 즉 신경계에 모여 있는 세포들입니다. 그리고 이러한 뉴런들의 주된 역할은 정보를 처리하고 전달하는 것이에요. 척추 동물의 경우, 음… 여러분 모두 척추 동물이 무엇인지 기억하고 있죠, 그렇죠? 좋습니다. 자, 척추 동물에서 뉴런은 뇌와 척수에서 찾아볼 수 있으며, 말초 신경계의 신경 및 신경절에서도 찾아볼 수 있습니다. 가장 기본적인 측면에서 뉴런은 신경세포체, 수상돌기, 그리고 축삭으로 이루어져 있어요. 뉴런에 대한 전통적인 견해에서는 신경세포체와 수상돌기가 다른 뉴런으로부터 입력 신호를 전달받고 축삭이 출력 신호를 전송하죠.

모두들 이해가 되나요? 훌륭하군요. 그러면 뉴런이 그러한 일을 할 수 있는 이유는 이들이 전기적인 충격을 발생시키는 능력을 가지고 있기 때문이에요. 이들은 우리 과학자들이 시냅스 전달이라고 부르는 방식으로 연결 장치를 통해 다른 뉴런에게 특정 정보를 빠르게 보냅니다. 맞아요. 뉴런은 시냅스를 통해 서로 커뮤니케이션을 하는데, 이곳에서 한 세포의 축삭이 다른 세포의 수상돌기와 접해 있습니다. 시냅스는 흥분성을 띨 수도 있고 억제성을 띨 수도 있어요. 다시 말해 신호를 만들거나 중단시킬 수 있다는 뜻인데, 이로써 대상이 되는 뉴런의 활동이 증가하거나 감소하게 되죠.

자, 뇌에서 많은 부분을 차지하고 다수의 움직임을 제어하는 소뇌에 들어 있는 뉴런들은 수천 개의 다른 세포와 연결된 1,000개 이상의 수상돌기를 가지고 있을 수도 있어요. 그리고, 음, 반면에 어떤 뉴런은 한두 개의 수상돌기만을 가지고 있을 수도 있는데, 이들 각각이 수천 개의 시냅스로부터 신호를 받습니다. 더 나아가 인간의 뇌에는 엄청난 수의 뉴런과 그 보다 훨씬 많은 시냅스가 들어 있어요. 이제 잘 들으시기 바랍니다. 1천억 개의 뉴런은 각각 평균적으로 7천개의 시냅스를 통해 다른 뉴런들과 연결되어 있어요. 대부분의 전문가들은 세 살짜리 아이의 뇌에 약 1천조 개의 시냅스가 들어 있다고 추정합니다. 물론, 어, 이러한 숫자는 나이가 들면서 감소하고, 예컨대 20대 초반 정도의 나이가 되면 안정화 되는데, 대부분의 성인의 경우에는 시냅스의 수가 100조에서 500조 개 사이에 머물게 되죠.

Vocabulary Check-Up

A
1 ⓛ 2 Ⓕ 3 Ⓗ 4 Ⓚ 5 Ⓓ
6 Ⓑ 7 Ⓒ 8 Ⓜ 9 Ⓘ 10. Ⓔ
11 Ⓐ 12 Ⓝ 13 Ⓞ 14 Ⓖ 15 Ⓙ

B
1 Ⓒ 2 Ⓑ 3 Ⓔ 4 Ⓐ 5 Ⓓ

Actual Test

Actual Test

PART 1
1 Ⓒ 2 Ⓓ 3 Ⓐ 4 Ⓐ 5 Ⓓ
6 Ⓓ 7 Ⓐ 8 Ⓑ 9 Ⓑ 10 Ⓒ
11 Ⓐ

PART 2
1 Ⓓ 2 Ⓑ 3 Ⓒ 4 Ⓐ, Ⓓ 5 Ⓐ
6 Ⓓ 7 Ⓑ 8 Ⓒ 9 Ⓑ 10 Ⓑ
11 Ⓓ
12 Ⓒ 13 Ⓐ 14 Ⓒ 15 Ⓓ 16 Ⓓ
17 Ⓒ

PART 1

[1-5]

Script 🎧 09-03

> **W Student:** Hello, Marcus. Alana said that you are looking for me. What can I do for you?
>
> **M Residential Assistant:** Hi, Teresa. I heard from another student that you have a refrigerator in your room. Is that true?
>
> **W:** Yeah, sure. I keep cold drinks and snacks in it. It's great.
>
> **M:** Um . . . I'm not sure if you're aware of this or not, but students aren't allowed to have refrigerators in their dorm rooms here. The only large electronic devices permitted are televisions and computers.
>
> **W:** Huh? Is that a new rule? I've never heard anything like that.
>
> **M:** It's a rule here.
>
> **W:** But . . . But I have friends in other dorms, and all of them have refrigerators in their rooms. Why can't I have one?
>
> **M:** Mastodon Hall is the oldest dorm on campus. It was built several decades ago, and the wiring is a bit outdated. Refrigerators are big electricity hogs, so if every student here were to have one, the power would cut out constantly.
>
> **W:** I see . . .
>
> **M:** So what I need you to do is to get rid of your refrigerator by this Friday.
>
> **W:** That's just two days from now.
>
> **M:** I'm being generous. I could just tell you to get rid of it

right now, and you'd have to do it.

W: What happens if I don't comply?

M: The first time you don't, you'll be fined. I think the amount is one hundred dollars.

W: And the second time?

M: You'll be kicked out of the dormitory and won't be permitted access to university housing until a full calendar year has passed. You really don't want that to happen because off-campus housing in this area is not only hard to get but also extremely expensive.

W: Okay. You win.

M: Thanks, Teresa. Look, uh, I'm really sorry about this. I wish I could have a fridge in my room as well. But the rules are the rules, and everyone needs to follow them.

W: Well, why didn't the school let us know about this rule when we were choosing our housing assignments last semester? I love the location of this dorm since it's close to my classes, but I would have never decided to live here if I knew I couldn't have a fridge in my room.

M: That's a really good question. You'll probably need to ask someone in the administration about that. You might want to try the student housing office as well.

W: I'm going to do that in just a few moments. I'm going to go there and see if I can change dorms now. There might be some rooms available in other dorms on campus. Oh . . . what am I supposed to do with the fridge? I don't have a storage area.

M: Just keep it unplugged for now. If you change dorms, you'll be able to take it with you and use it in your new room. Good luck. I hope you get what you want.

해석

W Student: 안녕하세요, Marcus. 저를 찾고 있다고 Alana가 말하더군요. 어떻게 도와 드릴까요?

M Residential Assistant: 안녕하세요, Teresa. 또 다른 학생으로부터 학생 방에 냉장고가 있다는 이야기를 들었어요. 사실인가요?

W: 네, 그래요. 그 안에 차가운 음료와 간식들을 보관하고 있죠. 잘 된 일이에요.

M: 음… 이러한 점은 모르고 있는 것 같은데, 학생들이 이곳 기숙사 방에 냉장고를 두는 것은 허용되지 않아요. 허용되는 대형 전자 제품은 텔레비전과 컴퓨터뿐이에요.

W: 네? 새로운 규정인가요? 그와 같은 이야기는 들어본 적이 없어서요.

M: 이곳 규정이에요.

W: 하지만… 하지만 다른 기숙사에 친구들이 있는데, 그들 모두 방에 냉장고를 두고 있어요. 왜 저는 두면 안되나요?

M: Mastodon 홀은 교내에서 가장 오래된 기숙사예요. 수십 년 전에 지어졌고 전기 배선 방식이 약간 구식이죠. 냉장고는 전기를 많이 잡아 먹기 때문에 이곳 모든 학생들이 냉장고를 가지고 있다면 전기가 항상 끊길 거예요.

W: 그렇군요…

M: 그러면 학생이 해야 할 일은 이번 주 금요일까지 냉장고를 처분하는 것이에요.

W: 지금부터 이틀 밖에 남지 않았군요.

M: 봐 주는 거예요. 지금 당장 처분하라고 말할 수도 있는데, 그러면 따라야만 할 거예요.

W: 제가 따르지 않는다면 어떻게 되나요?

M: 처음 따르지 않는 경우에는 벌금을 물게 될 거예요. 금액이 100달러라고 알고 있어요.

W: 그러면 두 번째 경우에는요?

M: 기숙사에서 퇴실을 하게 될 것이고, 꼬박 1년이 지나기 전까지는 교내 주거 시설을 이용하는 것이 허용되지 않을 거예요. 이곳 캠퍼스 밖에서 방을 얻는 일은 힘들 뿐만 아니라 엄청난 비용이 들기 때문에 그러한 일이 일어나는 것은 정말로 원치 않을 거예요.

W: 좋아요. 이기셨네요.

M: 고마워요, Teresa. 보세요, 어, 이번 일은 정말 유감이에요. 저 또한 제 방에 냉장고를 두면 좋을 것 같아요. 하지만 규칙은 규칙이고, 모두가 규칙을 따라야만 하죠.

W: 음, 지난 학기에 우리가 숙소를 선택할 때 왜 학교에서 이러한 규칙을 알려 주지 않았을까요? 수업 장소와 가깝기 때문에 이곳 기숙사의 위치가 정말 마음에 들지만, 방에 냉장고를 둘 수 없다는 점을 알았더라면 결코 이곳에 사는 것을 선택하지 않았을 거예요.

M: 정말 좋은 질문이군요. 그에 대해서는 아마도 행정부서의 누군가에게 이야기를 해야 할 거예요. 또한 기숙사 사무실을 방문하고 싶어할 수도 있겠네요.

W: 잠시 후에 그렇게 하려고요. 그곳에 가서 기숙사를 바꿀 수 있는지 알아볼 거예요. 교내의 다른 기숙사에 구할 수 있는 방이 남아 있을 수도 있겠죠. 오… 냉장고는 어떻게 해야 하나요? 보관할 수 있는 곳이 없거든요.

M: 지금으로서는 플러그만 뽑아 두세요. 기숙사를 바꾸게 되면 새로운 방으로 냉장고를 가지고 가서 사용할 수도 있으니까요. 행운을 빌게요. 학생이 원하는 바를 이루면 좋겠어요.

[6-11]

Script 🎧 09-04

M Professor: Let's carry on with some more American music history, shall we? For this lecture, I will discuss the effect that ragtime music had on the way the piano was played after, um, ragtime's inception. From a historic point of view, um, ragtime is an American musical genre enjoying its peak popularity from 1899 to 1918. Ragtime was the first truly American musical genre, preceding jazz. It originated in African-American musical communities and was descended from the jigs and the marches played by all-black bands common in northern cities with black populations.

Ragtime began as dance music years before being published as popular sheet music for piano. Scott Joplin, the composer and pianist who was known as the "King of Ragtime" called the effect "weird and intoxicating." By 1897, several important early rags were published, and in 1899, Joplin's *Maple Leaf Rag* was published. Now, some authorities consider ragtime to be a form of classical music. Additionally, the name swing later came to be applied to an early genre of jazz that developed from ragtime. So we can see that ragtime had a great influence on music in general at that time.

Okay. Now, let's get to its influence on the piano. To start, the heyday of ragtime was before the widespread availability of sound recording. Like classical music, and unlike jazz, classical ragtime was a written tradition, being distributed in sheet music rather than through recordings or by imitation of live performances. Ragtime music was also distributed via piano rolls for player pianos.

Let's talk about the piano roll. By definition, um, a piano roll is the medium used to operate the player piano, band and fairground organs, calliopes, and hand-cranked organs and pipe organs. Basically, a piano roll is a roll of paper with holes punched in it. The positions and the lengths of the perforations determined the notes played on the piano. The piano roll moves over a device known as the tracker bar, which had eighty-eight holes, um, or one for each piano key. When a perforation passed over the hole, a note sounded. Believe it or not, piano rolls have been in continuous mass production since around 1897. So even though a piano roll was used to make a piano play without an actual person playing, we must remember that pianists created the music for the piano rolls. Confused? I hope not. Let's move on then.

Another change was called the novelty piano, which can be considered a pianistic cousin of jazz. This appeared around the same time as the piano roll. Its originators were mostly piano roll artists from the Chicago area. Actually, the novelty piano was developed as a vehicle to showcase the talents of these professionals and was more often sold in the form of recordings and piano rolls than as sheet music.

Anyways, novelty piano slowly fell out of favor, or was absorbed into the new orchestral styles as the piano moved off center stage and took a support role. By, um, 1920, though, two new technologies had appeared which allowed the general public to hear music as performed by skilled musicians: the hand-played piano roll and the phonograph record.

Now, the most important new form of actually playing the piano in a live performance was called, ah, stride piano, and it was used primarily in jazz. The distinctive technique originated in Harlem in or about 1919. It was partially influenced by ragtime, which features improvisation, blue notes, and swing rhythms. The over simplistic name "stride" comes from the "striding" left-hand movement. In addition, the pedal technique further varied the left-hand sound. Quite frankly, stride piano is one of the most difficult styles of jazz piano playing because it takes years to master and is often confused with other jazz piano where the left hand alternates.

Okay, on a final note, a significant ragtime revival occurred in the 1950s. Ragtime styles of the past were made available on records, and new rags were composed, published, and recorded. A number of popular recordings featured, um, prepared pianos, simulating the sound of a piano in an old honky-tonk. So as you can see, we still have portions of piano ragtime music incorporated into the music we hear today.

해석

M Professor: 미국 음악의 역사에 대해 좀 더 살펴보기로 할게요, 괜찮죠? 이번 강의에서는 래그타임 음악이, 음, 래그타임이 시작된 이래로 피아노 연주법에 미친 영향에 대해 논의하려고 합니다. 역사적인 관점에서 볼 때, 음, 래그타임은 1899년에서 1918년 사이에 전성기를 구가했던 미국의 음악 장르예요. 래그타임은 재즈에 앞서 진정한 의미의 미국 음악 장르였죠. 이는 미 흑인들의 음악 커뮤니티에서 탄생했으며, 흑인들이 사는 북부 도시에서 일반적이었던, 흑인으로만 구성된 밴드가 연주하는 행진곡 및 지그 음악에서 비롯되었습니다.

래그타임은 댄스 음악으로 시작되었고, 몇 년 후 악보로 발행되는 음악으로서 인기를 얻게 되었어요. "래그타임의 왕"이라고 알려진 작곡가이자 피아니스트였던 스콧 조플린은 이러한 현상을 "이상하고 중독적인 것"이라고 했죠. 1897년경 래그타임의 중요한 초기 곡들이 발표되었고, 1899년에는 스콧 조플린의 *단풍잎 래그*가 발표되었습니다. 현재 몇몇 전문가들은 래그타임을 일종의 클래식 음악으로 간주하기도 하죠. 또한 스윙이라는 이름이, 나중에 래그타임에서 발전된 초기의 재즈 장르에 적용되기 시작했어요. 따라서 래그타임이 당시의 전반적인 음악에 커다란 영향을 미쳤다는 점을 알 수가 있습니다.

좋아요. 이제 피아노에 끼친 영향을 살펴보죠. 우선, 래그타임의 전성기는 녹음이 보편화되기 전이었어요. 클래식 음악과 마찬가지로, 하지만 재즈와는 달리, 클래식 래그타임은 활자화된 형태였는데, 녹음에 의하거나 라이브 공연을 모방하는 방식이 아닌, 악보로 발행되는 음악으로서 퍼졌습니다. 래그타임 음악은 또한 자동 피아노를 위한 피아노 롤을 통해 확산되기도 했어요.

피아노 롤에 대해 이야기해 보죠. 피아노 롤은, 음, 정의상으로는 자동 피아노, 밴드 오르간 및 페어그라운드 오르간, 증기 오르간, 그리고 핸드-크랭크트 오르간 및 파이프 오르간을 작동시키는데 사용되는 매체입니다. 기본적으로 피아노 롤은 구멍이 나 있는 두루마리 종이에요. 천공의 위치와 길이에 따라 피아노에서 연주되는 음이 결정되죠. 피아노 롤은 88개의 구멍, 음, 하나의 피아노 건반당 하나의 구멍이 있는 트래커 바라는 장치 위에서 움직입니다. 천공이 구멍 위를 통과할 때 음이 들리죠. 믿거나 말거나 간에, 피아노 롤은 약 1897년 이후로 계속해서 대량 생산되어 왔어요. 실제로 연주하는 사람 없이 피아노가 연주되도록 하기 위해 피아노 롤이 사용되었음에도 불구하고, 피아니스트들은 피아노 롤을 위한 음악을 만들었다는 점을 기억해야 합니다. 당황스럽나요? 아니길 바랍니다. 그럼 다음으로 넘어가 보죠.

또 다른 변화는 노벌티 피아노라고 불리는 것으로, 이는 재즈 피아노의 사촌으로 생각될 수 있어요. 이 스타일은 피아노 롤과 거의 동일한 시기에 등장했습니다. 이를 처음 만든 사람들은 대부분 시카고 지역 출신의 연주자들이었어요. 사실 노벌티 피아노는 이러한 전문 연주자들의 재능을 보여 주기 위한 수단으로 만들어졌는데, 악보보다는 레코드 및 피아노 롤의 형태로 음악이 더 많이 판매되었어요.

어쨌든, 피아노가 무대 중앙에서 빠지고 보조적인 역할을 맡게 되면서 노벌티 피아노는 서서히 밀려나거나 새로운 오케스트라 스타일에 흡수되었어요. 하지만, 음, 1920년경 새로운 두 가지 기술이 등장함으로써 일반 대중들도 뛰어난 연주자들이 연주하는 음악을 들을 수 있게 되었습니다. 바로 수동 피아노 롤과 축음기 음반이죠.

자, 라이브 공연에서 실제로 피아노를 연주했던 가장 중요하고 새로운 형식은, 어, 스트라이드 피아노라고 불렸는데, 이는 주로 재즈 공연에서 사용되었습니다. 이 독특한 기술은 1919년, 혹은 그 무렵에 할렘에서 탄생했어요. 즉흥 연주, 블루 노트, 그리고 스윙 리듬이 특징인 래그타임의 영향을 부분적으로 받은 것이었죠. 지나치게 단순한 이름인 "스트라이드"는 "크게" 움직이는 왼손의 움직임에서 따온 것입니다. 게다가 페달 기술이 왼손의 소리를 더욱 다양하게 만들었어요. 솔직히 말씀을 드리면, 스트라이드 피아노는 가장 어려운 재즈 피아노 연주 스타일 중 하나인데, 그 이유는 이를 익히기까지 여러 해가 걸리며 왼손을 번갈아 가면서 사용하는 다른 재즈 피아노 스타일과 종종 혼동되기 때문입니다.

좋아요, 마지막으로, 1950년대에 래그타임이 크게 부활을 했어요. 과거의 래그타임 스타일을 레코드로 들을 수 있게 되었고, 새로운 래그타임 곡들이 작곡되고, 발표되고, 그리고 녹음되었습니다. 다수의 인기 음반에, 음, 올드 홍키통크 스타일의 피아노 소리를 흉내 낸 프리페어드 피아노 연주가 들어가 있었어요. 그래서 여러분도 아는 것처럼, 오늘날 우리가 듣는 음악에 여전히 래그타임 스타일의 피아노 연주가 포함되어 있습니다.

PART 2

[1-5]

Script 🎧 09-06

W Student: Professor Roberts, I have something urgent that I need to discuss with you. Please tell me that you are available to chat for a bit.

M Professor: Sure, Stephanie. I can speak with you for a bit. What has you so upset this morning?

W: You know that topic you assigned me for my astronomy paper? I've spent the past couple of days in the library, and I just can't find enough information about it. I'm not really sure what to do.

M: Please remind me . . . What is the topic of your report?

W: I'm supposed to write about the star Canopus.

M: You haven't found anything on it?

W: Well, I wouldn't say that. I've learned that it's extremely bright and how far away from the solar system it is. I've also learned that it was a fairly important star to the ancient Egyptians and Greeks. I could write a lot about that, but, uh, I'm not really sure what that would have to do with astronomy.

M: That was a wise decision. You know, uh, I'm kind of surprised that you can't find that much about it. I would have thought there was plenty of information about it.

W: I just haven't had any luck. So . . . can I change topics?

M: I guess you're going to have to do that. Do you have any suggestions? Is there something that you would like to write about?

W: I really loved your lecture on Venus, and I'd love to do some research on its atmosphere. I think that would be a pretty cool topic.

M: It is pretty cool, as you say, but I've already assigned that topic to another student. I'm afraid I can't let you do that as I don't permit two students to cover the same

topic.

W: Hmm . . . How about the Andromeda Galaxy?

M: Same issue as Venus. Someone in your class is already doing it.

W: I'm not really sure what I should do then. It seems like all of my ideas are those you have already assigned.

M: I've got a thought. How about writing about one of the dwarf planets in the Kuiper Belt? You should be able to get enough information about them.

W: Okay. I can do that.

M: Now don't forget that you need to write between ten and twelve pages.

W: I remember. I'll also be sure to include a bibliography featuring at least four different sources.

M: Outstanding. I always like to know where my students get their information from. Oh, and do remember that you need to write a clear, concise thesis statement in your introduction.

W: Yes, I will do that. Thanks for all of the advice, sir.

M: Anytime. Good luck with the paper. I'm looking forward to reading it.

해석

W Student: Roberts 교수님, 교수님과 긴급하게 이야기할 것이 있어요. 잠깐 이야기를 나눌 시간이 있다고 말씀해 주세요.

M Professor: 그래요, Stephanie. 잠시 학생과 이야기할 수 있어요. 무엇 때문에 오늘 아침부터 그처럼 격양되어 있나요?

W: 교수님께서 정해 주신 제 천문학 보고서의 주제를 알고 계시죠? 지난 이틀을 도서관에서 보냈는데, 그에 관한 충분한 정보를 찾을 수가 없더군요. 제가 어떻게 해야 할지 정말로 모르겠어요.

M: 생각해 볼게요… 보고서 주제가 무엇이었죠?

W: 카노푸스 항성에 대해 쓰기로 되어 있어요.

M: 그에 대해 아무것도 찾지 못했다고요?

W: 음, 정확히 그런 것은 아니에요. 저는 그 항성이 엄청나게 밝다는 점과 태양계에서 얼마나 떨어져 있는지 배웠어요. 또한 고대 이집트인들 및 그리스인들에게 그것이 상당히 중요한 항성이었다는 점도 배웠죠. 그에 대해서는 많은 것을 쓸 수 있을 것 같은데, 하지만, 어, 그러함 점이 천문학과 어떤 관련이 있는지는 정말로 모르겠어요.

M: 현명한 결정이었군요. 알다시피, 어, 저는 학생이 그에 대해 많은 것을 찾을 수 없다는 점에 약간 놀랐어요. 그에 관한 정보가 많다고 생각했거든요.

W: 제가 운이 없는 편이죠. 그러면… 제가 주제를 변경해도 될까요?

M: 그래야 할 것 같네요. 제안할 것이 있나요? 쓰고 싶은 주제라도 있나요?

W: 저는 화성에 대한 교수님 강의가 정말로 마음에 들어서, 화성의 대기에 대해 조사를 해 보고 싶어요. 상당히 좋은 주제가 될 것 같아요.

M: 학생 말대로 상당히 좋은 주제이기는 하지만 그 주제는 이미 다른 학생에게 맡겼어요. 두 명의 학생이 동일한 주제를 다루는 것은 허용되지 않은 일이라서 안타깝지만 학생이 그렇게 하도록 할 수는 없어요.

W: 흠… 안드로메다 성운은 어떨까요?

M: 화성의 경우와 마찬가지에요. 수업을 듣는 다른 사람이 이미 하고 있죠.

W: 그러면 제가 어떻게 해야 할지 정말 모르겠군요. 제 아이디어를 모두 교수님께서 이미 배정해 주신 것 같아요.

M: 제게 생각이 있어요. 카이퍼 벨트의 왜성 중 하나에 대한 글을 써 보면 어떨까요? 그에 대해서는 충분한 정보를 구할 수 있을 거예요.

W: 좋습니다. 그렇게 할게요.

M: 그럼 10페이지에서 12페이지 사이의 글을 써야 한다는 점을 잊지 마세요.

W: 기억하고 있어요. 그리고 최소 4개의 서로 다른 출처가 포함되어 있는 참고 문헌 목록도 반드시 포함시키도록 할게요.

M: 훌륭하군요. 저는 학생들이 어디에서 정보를 얻었는지 항상 알고 싶어하거든요. 오, 그리고 서론에서 명확하고 간결한 주제 문장을 써야 한다는 점도 잊지 마세요.

W: 네, 그럴게요. 조언에 감사를 드립니다. 교수님.

M: 천만에요. 보고서에 행운이 있기를 바라요. 기대하고 있을게요.

[6-11]

W Professor: Today, I will lecture on some pretty strange plants. As a matter of fact, the plants we will discuss are from the Rafflesia, a parasitic plant. So without further delay, let me begin. The Rafflesia is a genus of parasitic flowering plants. It contains, um . . . at least fifteen species, all found in southeastern Asia. It's found on the Malay Peninsula and in Borneo, Sumatra, West Malaysia, and the Philippines. The flowers have no leaves and hardly any stem. It's mostly just a huge, speckled, five-petal flower with a diameter up to 106 centimeters, and it weighs up to ten kilograms. Even the smallest species, um, *R. manillana*, has fifteen-inch-diameter flowers. The flowers smell like rotting meat, so we get certain local names for these plants which translate to, um, "corpse flower" or "meat flower." The vile smell that the flower gives off can sometimes attract flies, which these plants use as a food source. Additionally, it is parasitic on vines in the genus Vitaceae, spreading its roots inside the vine.

Now, let's talk about specific varieties of rafflesia. I'll begin with the *Nepenthes rafflesiana*, a species of pitcher plant named after Stamford Raffles, the founder of Singapore. This plant has a very wide distribution covering, um, Borneo, Sumatra, Malaysia, and Singapore. *N. rafflesiana* is extremely variable with numerous forms and varieties. For example, in Borneo alone, there are at least four distinct varieties. The most impressive form, known as *N. rafflesiana gigantea*, produces enormous pitchers. These pitchers, which are heavily modified leaves, are used to capture and kill insect prey for nutrients.

Well, like it or not, all nepenthes are, um, passive carnivores. They are classified as passive because they have no moving parts, unlike their distant cousins the Venus flytrap, an active carnivore. Okay . . . So the *N. rafflesiana* kills by luring its prey into its, ah, pitchers,

whose peristomes secrete sweet-tasting nectar. Once the insect is inside, it quickly finds the walls of the pitcher too slippery to scale and, as you may expect, drowns. Digestive enzymes released by the plant into the liquid break down the prey and make soluble nutrients, which are absorbed by the plant through the walls of the pitcher. The carnivorous nature of nepenthes is supposedly a consequence of, um, living in nutrient-poor soils since the main method of nutrient absorption in most plants, the root, is insufficient in these soils, so the plants have evolved other ways to gain nutrients. Finally, *N. rafflesiana* enjoys hot, humid conditions most of the time as it is found in tropical jungle lowlands.

Okay, so far, so good. The next plant I will discuss is the *Rafflesia arnoldii*, another member of the genus Rafflesia. Not only is it the world's largest flower, but it is also one of the most bizarre and improbable organisms on the planet. There are some plants with larger flowering organs, for example, the titan arum and the talipot, but these are technically clusters of many flowers. *Rafflesia arnoldii* is the largest, and you can take this to the bank because its flower attains a diameter of nearly one meter and can weigh up to eleven kilograms.

It lives as a parasite on the tetrastigma vine, as its host, which grows only in undisturbed rainforests. While many parasites appear like normal plants, um, the rafflesia lacks any observable leaves, roots, and even stems, and this is what makes it so strange. A lot like fungi, individual rafflesias grow as thread-like strands of tissue completely embedded within and in intimate contact with surrounding host cells from which, um, nutrients and water are obtained. The only part of the rafflesia that is identifiable as distinctly plant-like is the, ah, flowers although even these are bizarre because they attain a massive size and are usually reddish-brown and stink of rotting flesh. The flower is pollinated by flies . . . which are attracted by its scent. *Rafflesia arnoldii* is very rare and fairly hard to locate. It is especially difficult to see in flower because the buds take many months to develop, and the flowers last for just a few days.

해석

W Professor: 오늘은 꽤 이상한 식물에 대해 강의할 예정입니다. 실제로 우리가 논의할 식물은 기생 식물인 라플레시아예요. 그러면 바로 시작해 보죠. 라플레시아는 기생 현화 식물의 한 속이에요. 여기에는 음… 최소 15개의 종이 포함되는데, 이들 모두 동남아시아에서 찾아볼 수 있습니다. 말레이반도와 보르네오, 수마트라, 서말레이시아, 그리고 필리핀에서 찾아볼 수 있죠. 이 꽃에는 잎이 없고 줄기도 거의 없습니다. 대부분 크고, 반점이 있고, 직경이 최대 106센티미터에 이르는 5개의 꽃잎을 가지고 있으며, 꽃의 무게는 10킬로그램까지 나갑니다. 가장 작은 종인, 음, *R. 마닐라나*의 꽃도 직경이 15인치 정도죠. 이 꽃에서는 고기 썩는 냄새가 나기 때문에 일부 지역에는 이들을 따로 부르는 말이 있는데, 이러한 이름은 "시체 꽃" 또는 "고기 꽃"이라고 의미를 나타냅니다. 꽃에서 나는 고약한 냄새가 이들 식물이 먹이로 삼는 파리를 때때로 유인하기도 하죠. 또한 포

도속 식물의 덩굴에 기생해 살면서 덩굴 안으로 뿌리를 내리기도 합니다.

자, 라플레시아에 속하는 특정 식물들에 대해 이야기해 보죠. *네펜시스 라플레시아나*로 시작할 텐데, 이는 싱가포르의 건국자인 스탬포드 라플즈의 이름을 딴 낭상엽 식물의 종입니다. 이 식물은, 음, 보르네오, 수마트라, 말레이시아, 그리고 싱가포르에 이르는 광범위한 지역에서 분포해요. *N. 라플레시아나*는 대단히 다양해서 수많은 형태와 종류가 존재합니다. 예를 들어 보르네오에서만 최소 네 종류 이상이 존재하죠. *N. 라플레시아 자이겐샤*라고 알려진 가장 인상적인 형태는 어마어마한 크기의 낭상엽을 가지고 있어요. 이 낭상엽, 즉 크게 변형된 형태의 잎은 영양분을 얻기 위해 곤충을 잡아먹는 용도로 사용됩니다.

음, 마음에 들던 들지 않건 간에, 모든 네펜시스 식물은, 음, 수동성 식충 식물이에요. 전혀 움직이는 부분이 없기 때문에 이들은 수동성으로 분류되지만, 먼 사촌뻘인 파리지옥은 능동성 식충 식물입니다. 좋아요… 그래서 *N. 라플레시아*는 먹이를, 아, 낭상엽으로 유인해 잡아먹는데, 낭상엽의 입구에서는 단맛을 내는 꿀이 분비됩니다. 일단 안으로 들어오면 곤충은 곧 낭상엽 벽이 너무 미끄러워 빠져나갈 수 없다는 점을 알게 되고, 짐작하실 수 있듯이, 죽게 되죠. 식물에 의해 액체 안으로 분비된 소화 효소들이 먹이를 분해시켜 녹일 수 있는 영양분을 만들어 내는데, 이는 낭상엽의 벽을 통해 식물에게 흡수됩니다. 네펜시스의 식충성은 아마도, 음, 영양분이 부족한 토양에서 살기 때문에 생긴 것으로, 대다수의 식물들이 영양분을 얻는 수단인 뿌리가 그러한 토양에서는 충분한 역할을 하지 못하기 때문에 이 식물들은 다른 방법을 발전시켜 영양분을 얻는 것이죠. 마지막으로 *N. 라플레시아*는 대체로 고온 다습한 기후를 좋아해서 열대 정글의 저지대에서 찾아볼 수 있습니다.

좋아요, 지금까지는 괜찮군요. 다음으로 논의할 식물은 라플레시아속에 속하는 또 다른 식물인 *라플레시아 아르놀디*예요. 이는 세상에서 가장 큰 꽃일 뿐만 아니라 지구에서 가장 이상하고 기이한 생물 중 하나입니다. 예를 들어 시체꽃이나 탈리풋야자처럼 더 큰 꽃을 지니고 있는 식물들도 있지만, 이들은 엄밀히 말해서 여러 개의 꽃이 모여 있는 다발 형태예요. *라플레시아 아르놀디*가 가장 큰데, 이 말을 전적으로 믿을 수 있는 이유는 이 식물의 꽃의 직경이 거의 1미터에 이르고 그 무게가 11킬로그램까지 나갈 수 있기 때문이죠.

이 식물은 깊은 열대 우림에서만 자라는 테트라스티그마를 숙주로 삼아 그 덩굴에서 기생해 살아갑니다. 많은 기생 식물들이 정상적인 식물처럼 보이지만, 음, 라플레시아는 눈에 띄는 잎, 뿌리, 그리고 심지어 줄기도 가지고 있지 않다는 점에서 상당히 특이해요. 균류와 상당히 비슷하게, 라플레시아의 실과 같은 조직 세포는 주변 숙주 세포 안에 들어간 상태로, 그리고 숙주 세포와 접촉한 상태로 자라며, 음, 이러한 숙주 세포로부터 양분과 수분을 얻습니다. 라플레시아가 확실히 식물이라는 점을 알 수 있는 유일한 부분은 꽃인데, 어, 이 조차도 크기가 거대하고 보통 적갈색을 띠며 썩는 고기 냄새를 내뿜기 때문에 특이한 편이에요. 꽃은 파리에 의해 수분이 되며… 파리들은 냄새로 유인이 됩니다. *라플레시아 아르놀디*는 매우 희귀한 편이라서 찾아보기가 매우 힘들어요. 봉오리가 맺히기까지 수 개월이 걸리고 꽃도 불과 며칠 동안만 피기 때문에 꽃을 피운 모습은 특히 보기가 어렵습니다.

[12-17]

Script 🎧 09-08

W1 Professor: Let's move on to discuss the modern printing process. I will begin with the changes in the printing process introduced in the nineteenth century. First of all, does anyone know the first step a nineteenth-century printer had to do in order to print something?

W2 Student: I haven't a clue.

W1: Well, make sure you take good notes then. Okay, the first step in the printing process was to create the typeset. Let me explain. By the nineteenth century, printers began using what we now call the hot metal typeset. Hot metal typesetting is a method of creating a relief printing surface by injecting a molten metal alloy into a matrix.

M Student: Ma'am, I don't want to sound uninformed, but, uh, what's an alloy?

W1: Hmm. An alloy is simply a mixture of two or more metals in order to create a new metal. Anyway, this alloy was typically made of lead, tin, and a small amount of antimony. The resulting lines of type could range in size from six to twenty-four points. It was pioneered by the companies Monotype and Linotype in the late nineteenth century, and their typesetting machines dominated the industry for the next century.

W2: Do you mean they were using this in the twentieth century?

W1: Sure. Remember that computers weren't commonplace in the printing industry until the 1980s. Now, uh, moving along, the Linotype machine uses a ninety-character keyboard to create an entire line of metal type at once. This allows much faster printing than with the Gutenberg-style system, um, in which operators placed down one letter at a time. The machine revolutionized newspaper publishing, making it possible for a relatively small number of operators to set type for many pages on a daily basis.

M: So this was the first new printing process since Gutenberg?

W1: Correct. Let me explain how it works. This new process was produced by Ottmar Mergenthaler in 1886. His Linotype machine was 2.1 meters high. First of all, a typesetter would put the letter molds to be used to form a line on a page. Once an entire line of molds was assembled, the machine poured molten type metal, which is an alloy of lead, tin, and antimony, into the stacked-up molds. This produced a complete line of type in reverse, so it would read properly when used to transfer ink onto paper. The lines of type were then assembled by hand onto a page. Are we good so far?

M: So this was all done by hand?

W1: Naturally. But the most difficult process was punch cutting. The cutting of letter punches was a highly skilled craft requiring much patience and practice. The punch-cutter began by, um, transferring the outline of a letter design to one end of a metal bar. Next, the outer shape of the letter punch could be cut directly, but the internal curves of a small punch were particularly difficult, as it was necessary to cut deep enough and straight into the metal. This was almost never done with cutting tools, so they used what is called a counterpunch, which is a type of punch used in the cutting of other punches.

W2: This means that they used a counterpunch to cut into the letter punch?

W1: Exactly. Of course, the counterpunch had to be harder than the letter punch itself. This was accomplished by heat-tempering the counterpunch and by softening the type punch. Once the punches were read, um, a mold could then be created from the punch by using the punch on a softer metal, like copper, to create a matrix. Then, the type metal, that alloy of lead, tin, and antimony, flowed into the matrix to produce a single piece of type ready for typesetting. One characteristic of type metal that makes it valuable for this use is that it expands as it cools, filling in any gaps present in the thinner portions of letters. I hope I didn't confuse anyone.

해석

W1 Professor: 넘어가서 현대의 인쇄술에 대해 논의하도록 하죠. 19세기에 도입된 인쇄 기술의 변화에 대한 이야기로 시작해 보겠습니다. 먼저, 무언가를 인쇄하기 위해 19세기 인쇄공들이 제일 먼저 해야 했던 일을 아는 사람이 있나요?

W2 Student: 전혀 모르겠어요.

W1: 음, 그렇다면 필기를 잘 해 두세요. 좋아요, 인쇄의 첫 번째 단계는 판을 짜는 것이었어요. 설명해 드리죠. 19세기경 인쇄공들은 현재 뜨거운 조판이라고 불리는 방법을 사용하기 시작했어요. 뜨거운 조판은 녹아 있는 합금을 모형에 주입함으로써 양각 형태의 인쇄 면을 만드는 방식이었습니다.

M Student: 교수님, 무식한 소리로 들리지는 않았으면 좋겠는데, 어, 합금이 무엇인가요?

W1: 흠. 합금은 새로운 금속을 만들기 위해 두개 이상의 금속을 섞은 것이에요. 어쨌든 이러한 합금은 보통 납, 주석, 그리고 소량의 안티몬으로 이루어져 있었죠. 그 결과로 생기는 활자의 라인은 크기가 6포인트에서 24포인트까지 다양할 수 있었어요. 이는 19세기 후반 모노타이프와 라이노타이프라는 회사에 의해 처음 개발되었는데, 이들의 조판기들이 그 다음 세기의 인쇄업계를 지배했습니다.

W2: 20세기에 그러한 방법을 사용하고 있었다는 말씀이신가요?

W1: 그래요. 컴퓨터는 1980년대가 되어서야 인쇄업계에서 보편적으로 사용되기 시작했다는 점을 기억해 두세요. 자, 어, 계속해서, 라이노타이프 기계는 90개의 자판을 이용해서 한 번에 금속 활자들을 한 줄에 채워 넣습니다. 이로써 식자공이 한 번에 하나의 글자를 심는 방식이었던, 음, 구텐베르크 방식의 시스템으로 인쇄하는 것보다 훨씬 더 빠른 인쇄가 가능해지죠. 이 기계는 신문 발행에 혁명을 가져다 주었고, 이로써 비교적 소수의 식자공들이 매일 다량의 페이지를 조판하는 것이 가능해졌어요.

M: 그러면 그것이 구텐베르크 이후로 첫 번째 새로운 인쇄술이었나요?

W1: 맞아요. 작동 원리를 설명해 드릴게요. 이 새로운 기술은 1886년 오트마 메르겐탈러에 의해 소개되었습니다. 그의 라이노타이프 기계는 높이가 2.1미터였어요. 우선 식자공이 한 페이지에 한 줄을 넣기 위해 사용할 활자 주형을 놓습니다. 한 줄 전체에 대한 주형이 마련되면 기계가, 납, 주석, 그리고 안티몬 합금인, 녹아 있는 활자 금속을 쌓아 둔 주형에 붓습니다. 이렇게 하면 한 줄이 거꾸로 된 상태로 완성되기 때문에 종이에 잉크를 바르면 제대로 읽히게 되죠. 그런 다음 활자의 라인들을 손으로 조합해서 하나의 페이지를 만들었습니다. 여기까지 이해가 가나요?

M: 그 모든 과정이 손으로 이루어졌나요?

W1: 당연하죠. 하지만 가장 어려운 과정은 펀치 커팅이었어요. 문자 펀치 커팅

은 상당한 인내와 연습을 필요로 하는 고도의 기술이었습니다. 펀치 커터들은 글자 디자인의 외곽선을 금속대의 한쪽 끝으로 옮기는 것으로 일을 시작했어요. 그 다음, 문자 펀치의 바깥쪽 형태는 직접 커팅이 가능했지만, 작은 펀치의 안쪽 곡선을 커팅하는 것은 특히 어려운 일이었는데, 그 이유는 금속을 충분히 깊고 똑바르게 커팅해야 했기 때문이었죠. 이는 커팅 도구로는 거의 할 수 없는 일이었기 때문에 소위 카운터펀치라고 불리는 도구, 즉 다른 펀치들을 커팅하는데 사용하는 일종의 펀치가 사용되었어요.

W2: 카운터펀치를 사용해 문자 펀치를 커팅했다는 뜻인가요?

W1: 정확해요. 물론, 카운터펀치는 문자 펀치보다 더 단단해야 했어요. 카운터펀치는 열처리를 하고 활자 펀치는 연화시킴으로써 그렇게 할 수 있었습니다. 일단 펀치들이 읽히면, 음, 구리와 같은 보다 부드러운 금속에 펀치를 눌러 모형을 만듦으로써 펀치로부터 주형을 만들 수 있었어요. 그런 다음에는 납, 주석, 그리고 안티모니의 합금인 활자 금속을 모형에 부어 조판에 사용될 하나의 활자를 만들었습니다. 이러한 용도에 알맞는 활자 금속의 한 가지 특징은 활자 금속이 식으면서 팽창한다는 점인데, 이로써 문자의 보다 얇은 부분에 존재하는 틈들이 메워지죠. 제 말에 당황하는 분이 없기를 바랍니다.